From the Boer War to the Cold War

A. J. P. TAYLOR

From the Boer War to the Cold War
Essays on Twentieth-Century Europe

* * *

EDITED WITH AN INTRODUCTION
BY CHRIS WRIGLEY

HAMISH HAMILTON · LONDON

HAMISH HAMILTON LTD

Published by the Penguin Group
Penguin Books Ltd, 27 Wrights Lane, London w8 5tz, England
Penguin Books USA Inc., 375 Hudson Street, New York, New York 10014, USA
Penguin Books Australia Ltd, Ringwood, Victoria, Australia
Penguin Books Canada Ltd, 10 Alcorn Avenue, Toronto, Ontario, Canada m4v 3b2
Penguin Books (NZ) Ltd, 182–190 Wairau Road, Auckland 10, New Zealand

Penguin Books Ltd, Registered Offices: Harmondsworth, Middlesex, England

This collection first published 1995
1 3 5 7 9 10 8 6 4 2

Filmset by Datix International Limited, Bungay, Suffolk
Printed in England by Clays Ltd, St Ives plc
Set in 11/13 pt Monophoto Baskerville

A CIP catalogue for this book is available from the British library
ISBN 0-241-13445-5

Contents

Introduction

For some forty years before his death on 7 September 1990 Alan Taylor was one of the best-known historians in Britain. Probably for a good part of that time he was *the* best-known. He appealed to a wide public audience. He also held the respect of most academic historians and was greatly admired by many of them. His work was readily recognized not only for its characteristic style but also because it was stamped with his assertive, irascible and markedly irreverent public persona.

Alan Taylor's renown owed much to his being an early radio and television personality. He had been in the right place at the right time with the right experience during the Second World War. He was based in Oxford University giving successful extra-mural lectures on the course of the war at a time when so many others were away on war work. He had already gained a taste for publicly expressing his opinions in the *Manchester Guardian*, a connection which had come about initially through writing books while a lecturer at Manchester University (1930–38). Alan Taylor's wartime radio career had begun in 1942 with broadcasts on the course of the war but he had later moved into discussion programmes, including taking part in January 1945 in that most notable forum of the opinionated, *The Brains Trust*. In the first few years after the war he was a frequent contributor to current-affairs programmes, especially those with an international dimension.

However, it was television which made him into a household name. He became a star of *In The News*, a forerunner of *Question Time*. However, unlike the latter with its continually changing panel of commentators, *In The News* soon came to have a regular team. They were mavericks, not safe party people. Two were on the left: Michael Foot and Alan Taylor; two were on the right: Bob Boothby and W J Brown. Between 25 August 1950 and 10 December 1954 Alan Taylor appeared forty-nine times. *In The News* had been designed 'to stimulate discussion . . . rather than elucidate and to inform', and was attempting to emulate the success of similar programmes in the United States. Alan Taylor fitted the bill very well, delighting in controversy. When he left the programme, the BBC Research Panel's index of viewer appreciation dropped by five points. However, the period of frequent programmes featuring the Big Four was short, as the BBC responded to political calls for more representative speakers. When ITV began, Taylor, along with Boothby, Brown and Foot, transferred to an ITV discussion programme, the pointedly entitled *Free Speech*. The fame, or even notoriety, that his television appearances gave him provided an entry into popular journalism. From January 1951 he wrote regular columns successively for the *Sunday Pictorial*, *Daily Herald* and *Sunday Express*.

Yet if Taylor's standing as a popular historian owed much to his activities in the national media, it nevertheless rested on the lucidity and the originality in interpretation of his writing. His work is marked by brevity, pungency, humanity and wit. He took great pains in his presentation of history, be it public lecture or printed word. He took the view that any subject worthy of research time and effort deserved equally meticulous consideration of its presentation. Though he often later denied any substantial intellectual debt to Sir Lewis Namier, he did learn some lessons about style from him; notably the merits of providing an essay with a good anecdote or some other attention-grabbing opening. He also learned from his early *Manchester Guardian* journalism: A P Wadsworth, the newspaper's editor from 1944 to 1956 and a distinguished economic historian, impressed on the young Taylor that writing must be clear and that the author should have at the front of his mind the question: 'What is the reader going to make of this?'

Over the years Alan Taylor crafted a very distinctive style. He would say that his style was a reflection of himself: 'sharp, clear and impatient of long-winded explanations'. He also liked his writing to include jokes where appropriate: 'Jokes are a good thing, as in life.' From the time of his *The Course of German History* (London, Hamish Hamilton, 1945) onwards, his writing was notable for its many epigrams. He had always liked using these, deriving his taste in part from one of his literary heroes, Dr Samuel Johnson. He ascribed his heavier use of epigrams and other improvements in his style at the time of the Second World War to the influence of the writings of Albert Sorel (1842–1906) and to *The Thirties* (London, Hamish Hamilton, 1940) by Malcolm Muggeridge. Taylor later reflected, 'Epigrams are very hard to use. They are the culmination of everything that has gone before.' Difficult to use or not, they became a major feature of his work. As he put it on one occasion:

My own taste in history is for the book that simplifies and sharpens. I want to see the skeleton of the past and am not much interested in its flesh. One good epigram counts for more with me than pages of luscious description.

Alan Taylor's appeal also owed much to the freshness of his interpretations. He delighted in overturning what had hitherto appeared safe orthodoxies. In his writing he twisted this way and that, probing alternative explanations and usually coming up with surprising conclusions. He argued over past politics in his writings much as he argued over current politics on radio and television or on public platforms: pugnaciously, firm in the rightness of his views and with no signs of philosophic doubt. When he published his contribution to the Oxford History of England, *English History 1914–1945* (Oxford, Oxford University Press, 1965) he thanked his colleague Kenneth Tite for having 'tempered the dogmatism of my style. He must take part of the blame if the word "probably" occurs too often.' Generally, though, Taylor's style and his disposition allowed room for few 'ifs' and 'buts'.

In his writing he relied much on his intuition, on what he liked to refer to as his historian's equivalent of the gardener's 'green fingers'. Often his understanding of the people of the past's characters and their likely actions in certain circumstances enabled him to guess brilliantly what had occurred, guesses later confirmed when archives were opened. Yet at other times his surmises could be markedly wrong. He was aware of the risks, later commenting: 'Intuition gives you warnings. It may warn you against guessing.' He felt that he had developed his intuition throughout his career; it was something which had come with experience and greater knowledge.

Alan Taylor always consciously wished to write for a large public audience. From early on in his career he aspired to have as great an appeal as Edward Gibbon (1737–94) and Thomas Babington Macaulay (1800–1859) had in their days. He often pondered what constituted great history. On one occasion he observed: 'The highest history combines scholarship and art.' On another he commented:

history is more than scholarship, more even than a method of research. It is above all a form of understanding; and the general reader will not put a historian in the highest rank unless he has supplied a new version and a new vision.

Taylor succeeded in providing new versions and new visions of history, and in attracting public interest to modern history in a way somewhat similar to Sir Mortimer Wheeler's impact in the popularizing of archaeology.

*   *   *

Alan John Percivale Taylor was born on 25 March 1906 at Birkdale, Southport, in Lancashire. He grew up in a wealthy middle-class household with servants. His father, Percy Lees Taylor, was senior partner in the family firm, James Taylor and Sons. The firm was part of Manchester's cotton cloth trade with India and China.

Alan Taylor was a much looked-after only child. He had an elder sister, Miriam, but she died of tuberculosis at the age of three, when Alan was eighteen months old. Not surprisingly his parents were anxious about his health as he was small and far from robust. His mother took him to a homeopath, the resulting treatment being deemed to have been very effective. His father doted on him, delighting to be in his company.

Alan Taylor was brought up in a household where ideas, radical ideas, were important and vigorous discussion a norm. Before the First World War his parents had been political Liberals. The war saw them move to the left, both joining the Independent Labour Party. His father sold his share of the family business for £100,000 in 1920, at the height of the post-war boom, and thereafter lived in semi-retirement (maintaining some business interests). He spent much of his time in local Labour politics as a Labour councillor and a member of the Preston Trades Council.

Alan Taylor's mother, Constance Sumner Thompson, moved further to the left than her husband. Her revolt from Liberalism was much affected by the experiences of her brother Harry as a conscientious objector during the war. He was an 'absolutist', one who refused to undertake any work at all for the war effort. This he did out of a radical belief in individual liberty, not from religious or Marxist ideals. She vigorously supported him in his stand. Her hatred of militarism ensured that Alan was not sent to Rugby as had been intended, for pupils there were expected to be members of the Officers' Training Corps. Instead in 1917 he went to a Quaker public school, The Downs, near Malvern. After the end of the war Connie Taylor began a long and close friendship with one of Harry's fellow conscientious objectors, Henry Sara (1886–1953). Sara had also been an 'absolutist', but in his case he opposed the war on Marxist grounds and later was to claim that he had despised non-revolutionary pacifism. He brought to the Taylor household a grasp of Marxist, anarchist and syndicalist thinking as well as strong connections with international socialism. Sara was a founder member of the Communist Party of Great Britain and later a member of the Balham Group, the starting point of British Trotskyism.

Those who knew Connie and Harry's generation of the Thompson family remembered them as 'great arguers'. The young Alan Taylor soon learned to put forward his views with vigour and clarity. Before the First World War, when the family had lived in Birkdale, he had often been present when his parents had discussed politics, sometimes with visiting radical politicians, at the house of their fellow Congregationalists, the Blackwells. After the First World War, when the family lived in Preston, he had become accustomed to discussing Labour politics at the top level, as men such as Arthur Henderson, George Lansbury and Harry Pollitt stayed at the Taylors' house if speaking in the area. Alan Taylor loved and enjoyed the company of his father. He craved the approval of his mother, and sought to win it by intellectual prowess. He liked Henry Sara and was much influenced by him before his mid-twenties.

The imprint of his Nonconformist background always remained on him, even though he lost any formal Christian faith that he may have had. He had been brought up in Congregationalist surroundings and educated at Quaker schools. He owed many intellectual debts to his background. His favourite reading included John Bunyan's *Pilgrim's Progress*. At Bootham, the Quaker public school he attended between 1919 and 1924, he had heard many times several of John Bright's speeches against the Crimean War declaimed for an annual prize. His own rather individualist radicalism owed much to the old-style northern radicalism of Cobden and Bright as well as to the Independent Labour Party socialism of his parents, and something to the international Marxism of Sara. For all his contradictions Alan Taylor was always essentially a man of the Left; but, as with his history, over the years he moulded his own distinctive radical outlook.

Alan Taylor's radicalism had something of the 'Free-Born Englishman' about it. He was more than happy to cock a snook at the great and the good. He often commented, with a pugnacious pride: 'I am no better than anyone else, and no one is better than me.' Those who had helped bring about such egalitarianism were his heroes. His great tradition was one running through such figures as John Wilkes, Charles James Fox, William Cobbett, Richard Cobden and John Bright to twentieth-century figures such as E D Morel and Taylor's friend Michael Foot. Alan Taylor's style of radicalism also had more than a touch of John Bull about it. The central European liberals and radicals had failed to follow the path of British 'Friends of Liberty' and secure a 1688-style Whig Revolution or Reform (as in 1832 or 1867 in Britain). Thus he wrote of 1848 in *The Course of German History*:

For the first time since 1521, the German people stepped on to the centre of the German stage only to miss their cues once more. German history reached its turning-point and failed to turn. This was the fateful essence of 1848.

He was as proud of his Englishness as Sir Arthur Bryant or Winston Churchill were in their historical writings. His was of a different tradition, a northern nonconforming radical strain. When he wrote the 1914–45 volume in the Oxford History of England he was characteristically vigorous in his defence of his remit being 'England' rather than Britain. He wrote to the series editor that he would take this limitation literally and commented: 'We shall have trouble with the Scotch (Scots? Scottish?) who claim that England ceased to exist in 1707. I shall speak for England in the preface.' Later, in 1981, he reflected on television: 'I am English, very much English. We have shameful things in our record, but also some good things. If others model themselves on us they would gain some benefit.'

*   *   *

Alan Taylor liked to suggest that he drifted into being a historian by chance. There is something in this, but perhaps only something. He also suggested in his intellectual autobiography that he was surprised that he gained first-class honours as an undergraduate at Oxford: 'I had thought that perhaps I was clever-clever, but certainly not that I was history-clever.' He may have been surprised but others probably felt that it was not unexpected. Moreover, as he always tended to be competitive in academic matters, it is probably safe to assume that it would have been a substantial setback for his self-esteem had he been awarded less.

He was short, slight and bookish. He had been able to read and write at a prodigiously early age. As a boy he read the classics of English literature and developed a taste for historical novels, ranging from those of Sir Walter Scott to G A Henty (the subject of one of the essays in this collection). Throughout his schooldays he was well in advance of most of his contemporaries. He even avoided bullying at Bootham by trading on his abilities. He later recalled, 'I . . . learnt how to exploit my cleverness, doing the prep of the bigger boys and winning protection in return.' At Oxford, apart from revelling in the frisson he aroused by declaring himself to be a communist, he kept himself to a small circle of like spirits and, as ever, read extensively. He had the qualities for undergraduate success. He was quick-witted, had an inquiring mind, was very widely read for his age and was notably argumentative. His family's taste for argument, his skill acquired at school in debating and his training in essay-writing at Bootham combined to make Taylor well equipped to write incisively and cogently.

As for his becoming a historian, this is not so surprising if one considers the most obvious alternatives. It was improbable that he would follow his father into the cotton trade, or enter any other aspect of Manchester's commercial life. For one thing he could not succeed to his father's role in the family business as his father had sold his share, thereby causing some family friction. For another he preferred books, was full of anti-capitalist sentiment and showed no eagerness to earn money through commerce. Another opportunity was to work for or with his former conscientious objector uncle, Harry, who was a hero in the eyes of his mother. Harry Thompson's work was 'politically correct' in that his solicitors' firm undertook work mostly for the Labour movement. Harry had spoken to Alan about the possibility of training as a barrister soon after he had first gone to Oxford. Accordingly, Alan had put his name down at the Inner Temple and eaten dinners there during his last two student years. In his final year his uncle had proposed that instead Alan should work for him and in due course become his partner. In 1927–28 Alan Taylor did spend six months working for his uncle. It did not work out. This was due in part to a clash of personalities. However, this may have stemmed from Taylor's being temperamentally disinclined to adapt and fit into office routines, being impatient of learning what he deemed intellectually undemanding tasks and preferring his books.

In his autobiography he commented: 'The work, such as it was, bored me and I spent most of the day in a corner of the office reading Dickens and books from the Times Book Club.'

After his six months in London Alan Taylor returned to Oxford. There he unsuccessfully worked for a prize essay. One of his former tutors, G N Clark, advised him to learn German if he wished to become a historian. H W C Davis, the Regius Professor of History, put him in contact with the Austrian professor A F Pribram as a possible supervisor for research. This resulted in him studying in the archives in Vienna from 1928 to 1930 and laying the foundations of his expertise in diplomatic and central European history. In 1930 Pribram's support secured him an assistant lectureship in the History Department at Manchester University. While there he continued his research into the problem of northern Italy in 1848 as seen by the Austrian, French and British governments, research which was published as *The Italian Problem in European Diplomacy 1847–1849* (Manchester, Manchester University Press, 1934).

Alan Taylor's entry into a career in history had more than a little of the gentleman scholar about it. Throughout he had been funded lavishly by his parents. They paid for his return to Oxford in 1928 and much of the expense of his two years in Vienna; though in his final year in Austria he did have the benefit of a Rockefeller research fellowship.

At Manchester University (1930–38) his lifestyle was funded well above that of an assistant lecturer's £300 per annum or a lecturer's £400 per annum. By this time some of the money came from his first wife's family. From 1933 he and Margaret lived in some style out at the edge of the Peak District at Higher Disley. He could afford the £500 for the house (two cottages knocked into one) and, unlike most professors at that time, he ran a car. In his autobiography he commented:

. . . I loved my open cars, particularly an enormous V-8 which I drove before the war and during it. It ate up petrol, but petrol was then very cheap and, as a sop to my conscience, I always bought ROP or ZIP, the two grades of Soviet petrol.

There in the country he could put on the airs of a man of means, who walked on the fells, grew vegetables and derived some income from a few days' university teaching per week in term time. Alan Taylor aspired to be a man living off investments, in the manner of his father. He began investing in 1931, using £2,000 from an insurance policy given to him by his father. This sum he more than quadrupled by early 1940.

He also aspired to write history that would have a wide appeal. From at least his mid-thirties he aimed to write books which should secure large and steady sales. Steeped in the classics of both English literature and history, he sought to become the modern Gibbon or Macaulay. Part of him craved a wide public recognition for his history just as it did for his activities in current public affairs.

Yet the competitive part of him made him anxious also to gain academic recognition and respect. For all his persona as the plucky, radical northerner, which was genuine enough, he was nevertheless eager to return to Oxford. Later when asked if he had ever been inclined to return to a northern university he would reply: 'I have done my bit at Manchester.' He applied for Oxford posts from as early as 1931. In 1938 he was successful, becoming a Fellow of Magdalen College.

* * *

Between 1928 and the publication in 1961 of *The Origins of the Second World War* (London, Hamish Hamilton) the focus of Alan Taylor's work was on the history of European diplomacy and of central Europe. When he began his researches in 1928 diplomatic history was very much in vogue, as scholars tried to satisfy public interest in and concern about what had gone wrong before 1914. He later wrote:

it would be foolish to pretend that their sudden interest in contemporary history was detached and 'scientific'. It was a political interest, forced upon them . . . by the event of the First World War. The twentieth century would have shown less concern with diplomatic history if the Bismarckian peace had endured. The diplomatic history of our time has always been a study of war origins, by no means to its advantage.

Throughout his career the study of war was central to his interests. This was so with his major diplomatic surveys, *The Struggle for Mastery in Europe 1848–1918* (Oxford, Clarendon Press, 1954) and *The Origins of the Second World War*. It remained so when, from about 1958, he moved to working more on British history. His volume in the Oxford History of England – *English History 1914–1945* – covered the two world wars. He wrote excellent short histories of both of them: *The First World War* (London, Hamish Hamilton, 1963) and *The Second World War* (London, Hamish Hamilton, 1975). His main biographical work was of figures with substantial wartime reputations: Bismarck, Lloyd George, Churchill and even Beaverbrook. (This selection includes his best essays on the two wartime British premiers.)

Alan Taylor moved away from the radical or Marxist interpretations of the causes of the First World War in the 1930s. In 1933 he bought a set of the fifty-four volumes of *Die grosse Politik der europaischen Kabinette* (1922–26) from a Jewish refugee from Nazi Germany. Working through these German diplomatic documents and those published of other countries he became increasingly convinced that German expansionism had caused that war. This view was reinforced by the writings of a radical German historian. Taylor, later commenting in *The Course of German History*, wrote: 'I learnt most of my approach from Eckart Kehr, a brilliant and at that time neglected historian, who had developed in detail the evil consequences of the marriage between the Junkers and heavy industry and who died before Hitler came to power.' Taylor's views on the causes of the First World War influenced, and were influenced by (a two-way process), his changing attitude to the international crises of the 1930s. In February 1936, when it was apparent that Hitler was about to reoccupy the Rhineland, he threw aside his own past arguments, breaking with the views of his parents and Henry Sara, and called for rearmament.

Alan Taylor's period in Vienna also disposed him to take a dim view of German expansionism. He later wrote that he 'saw German history from outside – partly as an Englishman, partly as an Austrian'. He had been unfavourably impressed when he had visited Berlin in 1924 and 1928 and he had thought even less of upper Bavaria in 1932 when the growing strength of the Nazis was much in evidence. His and Lewis Namier's historical work before the Second World War, plus his contact with refugees from Germany and Austria, brought him to condemn nearly all Germans for at least passively supporting Hitler's territorial ambitions. Hence for him, while Hitler's domestic policy was of unparalleled evil, his foreign policy was a German norm. The course of German history, for him, led to 'the struggle for world supremacy in 1941'; Hitler's attack on Soviet Russia being 'the climax, the logical conclusion, of German history'. In *The Course of German History* he firmly coupled the failure of democracy in Germany with his belief in the German people's preference for supremacy beyond their borders; the invasion of Russia being 'the cause for which the German people had sacrificed liberty, religion, prosperity, law'. In his Preface he rightly stated: 'This book is a *pièce d'occasion.*' Yet he held his view of the fundamental expansionist drive of German external policy until at least the mid-1960s, and this attitude underlay *The Struggle for Mastery in Europe* and *The Origins of the Second World War*. It was ironic indeed that some critics of the latter book denounced him for whitewashing Hitler over war origins whereas Taylor was eager not to allow Hitler and a few other Nazis to be scapegoats and all other Germans to be exculpated.

Alan Taylor's taste for Marxism did not last long. He was full of crude Marxism as a teenager and in politics could take a conventional hard-left line well into the 1930s. However, while attentive to the broad economic and social forces at work in the periods he studied, his writing of history was not Marxist. He later explained: 'I suppose my mind is too anarchic to be fitted into any system of thought. Like Johnson's friend Edwards, I, too, have tried to be a Marxist but common sense kept breaking in.' He added: 'When I write, I have no loyalty except to historical truth as I see it and care no more about British achievements or mistakes than about any others.'

Indeed one of the characteristic features of Alan Taylor's writing became his emphasis on historical accidents, the reverse of historical inevitability. This is well illustrated in his book *The First World War*, where the summary of the book's themes is expressed in its Preface in a manner close to a parody of his own style. This summary included:

The statesmen were overwhelmed by the magnitude of events. The generals were overwhelmed also. Mass, they believed, was the secret of victory. The mass they evoked was beyond their control. All fumbled more or less helplessly. They were pilots without a chart, blown before the storm and not knowing where to seek harbour. The unknown soldier was the hero of the First World War . . .

In the first chapter of *The First World War* he portrayed the opening of the war as a matter of chance. Franz Ferdinand's assassination led to the First World War. He was in Sarajevo in his military capacity. This enabled his wife to be publicly recognized, regardless of his morganatic marriage. Therefore, Taylor started his book with their wedding fourteen years earlier because 'this wedding day ultimately set the fuse to the First World War'. He went on to argue:

Men are reluctant to believe that great events have small causes. Therefore, once the Great War started, they were convinced that it must be the outcome of profound forces. It is hard to discover these when we examine details. Nowhere was there a conscious decision to provoke a war. Statesmen miscalculated. They used the instruments of bluff and threat which had proved effective on previous occasions. This time things went wrong. The deterrent on which they relied failed to deter; the statesmen became the prisoners of their own weapons. The great armies, accumulated to provide security and preserve the peace, carried the nations to war by their own weight.

Alan Taylor's most refined examination of the outbreak of the First World War in such terms is reprinted in this volume. *War by Time-Table: How the First World War Began* (London, Macdonald, 1969) was first published as a slender, heavily illustrated paperback. It has become the classic statement of this view of his that 'the great armies . . . carried the nations to war by their own weight'. His emphasis is on the short-term causes, on explaining why war broke out in Europe in late July and early August 1914 rather than in some other month or year. In this account Germany remains 'the most dangerous power in Europe', but his argument is that the war was not premeditated.

Yet, as is immediately apparent both in the passage above from *The First World War* and in *War by Time-Table*, there is a clear contemporary moral: beware of nuclear weapons. For all Alan Taylor's insistence that history taught no lessons, his writing often contained warnings for contemporaries. In 1961, when his *The Course of German History* was republished in paperback (London, Methuen), he was still warning of the dangers of a united Germany and asserting 'only a divided Germany can be a free Germany'. But he was forced, albeit reluctantly, to admit: 'I have almost reached the point of believing that I shall not live to see a third German war; but events have an awkward trick of running in the wrong direction, just when you least expect it.' Thereafter his major theme was to warn that one day nuclear weapons would not deter, a message he kept repeating up to his final public lecture, the Romanes Lecture for 1981: 'War in Our Time' (reprinted in his *An Old Man's Diary*, London, Hamish Hamilton, 1984). It is a moral he drew in several of the essays in this collection.

Alan Taylor's emphasis on chance in history did help him in his handling of the historiographical issue of the weight to be assigned to individuals' actions in history. He depicted Bismarck, the Kaiser and even Hitler as responders to the forces of their time. In this way in his major works, if not in some of his slighter, he avoided making crude claims that one person on their own could determine a nation's fate. So German diplomacy, whether under Bismarck, the Kaiser or Hitler, was likely to follow certain courses. For if the other powers permitted it, Germany would dominate Europe because of its geographic, demographic and economic advantages.

Power fascinated Alan Taylor. This appears to have been so in his life as well as in his history. He was attracted by men who had held high office, from Michael Karolyi, the Hungarian statesman, to Lord Beaverbrook. Similarly, as a historian he wrote mostly of men such as Metternich, Bismarck, Louis Napoleon, Lloyd George and Churchill. Indeed men generally dominate his writing; very few women intrude into his work. His choice of topic was traditional. For all his radical comments that his heroes were 'Captain Swing' or the Chartists, he wrote relatively little of such working-class movements. His history usually dealt with High Politics and used orthodox sources; indeed he relied heavily on published documents, memoirs and secondary sources. His was not 'history from below', that is grass-roots history dealing with the lives and aspirations of ordinary people. What was striking was not the novelty of his topic but the brilliance of his treatment.

* * *

Alan Taylor's career from the time of his return to Oxford in 1938 was marked on his part by something of a love–hate relationship with the university. Part of him determined to play the role of the northern radical outsider, thwarted by the effete southern Establishment; a man who could appeal beyond the walls of academe to the great popular audiences. Yet part of him wished to belong and to be recognized, and to have bestowed on him the glittering prizes of his profession.

Alan Taylor took great delight in his populist role in the media. He loved being on the radio and on television, writing regular columns for the popular press and being recognized in the street. On one occasion he confessed:

I used to take part in a discussion programme on television. At first I was surprised and a bit worried when people recognized me in the streets. But soon I was anxious and unhappy unless people waved at me and called me by my Christian name all the time I was out. Publicity became a craving worse than alcohol and more exciting. I had only a mild attack.

By 1951 he was making more money from the media and his books than from his university work. In addition, between 1958 and 1961, he devoted much time to campaigning for nuclear disarmament, as usual in a high-profile role.

Yet alongside this Alan Taylor was competitive as an academic. He was delighted to be invited to write the 1848–1918 diplomatic history volume in the Oxford History of Modern Europe and his volume, *The Struggle for Mastery in Europe 1848–1918,* appeared twelve years before the next volume in the series. When others faltered he was considered to write the diplomatic volume for 1789–1848. After he had been sounded out, it was reported: 'AJP says that he is prepared to write all the volumes in the series provided that it be called Taylor's History of Modern Europe.' He was also delighted to be invited to write the Oxford History of England volume on 1914–1945 and to give prestigious public lectures. Whatever else, Alan Taylor was very productive as a historian, even during his years as a star of the media.

Hence, for all his later disclaimers, he was mortified when he was passed over when the Regius Chair of Modern History became vacant in 1957. He clearly saw himself as the front runner for the post. There was further friction in 1963 when he came to the end of a fixed-period special lectureship which involved less teaching and more time for research. He released to the press the bare facts, which implied he had lost his job following the controversies over his *The Origins of the Second World War.* In fact the situation was more complex. The special lectureships were for five years, renewable once. He had had the full ten years, with his college funding the resulting loss of part of his teaching during that time. Another university might well have either promoted him to a Readership or Personal Chair or made some special arrangement; the outcome at Oxford was that Taylor declined to return to the teaching commitments of an ordinary lectureship. So his regular university lecturing career ended then, though he remained a Fellow, then Honorary Fellow, of Magdalen College until his death.

Though Taylor felt slighted by Oxford he nevertheless chose not to secure a chair at another British university. He declined all offers, even to succeed Namier at Manchester. Provincial universities were not Oxford and most were inconveniently far from London for his media and personal interests. He enjoyed Magdalen College and was proud of his administrative role in it during Sir Henry Tizard's time as president (1942–46) and even more so of his period as vice-president during the college's quincentenary celebrations in 1958. He was punctilious in observing Magdalen's traditions. For all the legends of Oxford hostility to Taylor, many in Oxford University admired him. His lectures were packed even when held at the least appealing hours of the day. His writing and his lecturing technique were much admired by his younger colleagues. Yet there were those who frowned on his media activities, his radical views and even his collecting together in book form his better essays and book reviews.

The end of his special lectureship gave Alan Taylor more time for writing and for his media activities in London. From the late 1950s he had been increasingly writing about British history and, generally, twentieth-century history as he prepared *English History 1914–1945*. Soon after he completed it in the summer of 1964 his friend Lord Beaverbrook died. Alan Taylor took on writing the official biography. This assignment took him back to archival work, using Beaverbrook's huge collection of papers. The resulting biography, *Beaverbrook* (London, Hamish Hamilton, 1972) was Alan Taylor's last substantial book. It was much criticized for being unduly kind to its subject, for relying too much on Beaverbrook's own accounts of events and for not being based on other archives. Yet it had the merits of Taylor's interest in his subject, his grasp of twentieth-century British history and his mature style.

The Beaverbrook connection provided Alan Taylor with the last major role of his career: as honorary director of the Beaverbrook Library during its short existence from 1967 to 1975. Here, just off Fleet Street, researchers worked on the various collections of papers that Beaverbrook had acquired, notably those of the British premiers Lloyd George and Bonar Law. Alan Taylor encouraged researchers by the interest he showed in their work and by running a research seminar there in university vacations. He drew on the archival resources of the library not only for his biography of Beaverbrook but also for editing three books drawing on records of Frances Stevenson, Lloyd George's mistress and second wife, and of W P Crozier, editor of the *Manchester Guardian*, 1932–44.

By the time he was in charge of the Beaverbrook Library Alan Taylor was revered by many of the younger generation of scholars as the Grand Old Man of History. At the seminars he often dazzled with the brilliance of his comments on the topic of that day's research paper. As with the best of his written work he surprised by the originality of his insights. This quality is present in the best of his essays. He continued to write reviews until the autumn of 1984 and some of his best later ones are reprinted in this collection.

For many of the general public during the last three decades of his life he was the History Man. He was the best-known historian in Britain. When he gave public lectures, people packed into the halls to hear them. He mostly restricted such activity to the branches of the Historical Association. In his later years he attracted audiences of several hundred to these lectures as he made periodic progresses round the country. Sadly the onset of Parkinson's disease eventually affected the delivery of both his public and television lectures from about 1980 onwards.

Following Taylor's death in 1990, some writers of obituaries or appreciations were surprisingly cool about his achievements. As in his lifetime there were strikingly divergent assessments of his contributions to history. Perhaps more surprising was that in the few years after his death several who wrote about him and were favourably disposed to his history were critical of him as a person. He could be self-centred, egotistical and much else, but for those who knew him reasonably well the blunt, even testy, front that he displayed in public seemed something of a shield. He was a kindly man, somewhat shy and, when not busy, prone to self-doubt. In talking about history he was charismatic. Even in his final illness his eyes would light up when his favourite topics were mentioned.

'History,' he wrote in his autobiography, 'has always been my consuming passion: reading history, writing the subject lecturing about history.' He was always enthusiastic about the subject and he was aware of the need to be able to communicate this enthusiasm. As he commented on one occasion: 'A lot of historians forget that one purpose at any rate of writing a book is that someone should read it.' For him history was one of the great humanities:

History is the one way in which you can experience at second hand all kinds of varieties of human behaviour, and after all the greatest problem in life is to understand how other people behave, and this is what history enables us to do: to see people in all kinds of situations and in all kinds of walks of life ... It makes the reader, and to a certain extent the historian too, aware of a fuller, much wider life than somebody could possibly have merely by his own private experience.

In his life he wrote history that was never dull and presented it with style in print, on the radio and on television. Thereby he provided many thousands of people with pleasurable insights into the past which may have enriched their lives. He left behind a substantial legacy, of which these essays are a part.

The Rise and Fall of 'Pure' Diplomatic History

This essay was first published in 'Historical Writing', a supplement to The Times Literary Supplement, *6 January 1956.*

* * *

Historians have been writing diplomatic history for a long time, indeed ever since they penetrated into the archives of state. Ranke spent his happiest and most profitable years examining the papers of the republic of Venice. Sorel wrote a masterpiece, *Europe and the French Revolution*, which bears in its title the evidence that it is in part diplomatic history. Vandal reached the same supreme level in his study of *Napoleon and Alexander I*. These themes were relatively remote from the date when the books were published. Moreover, the evidence from the diplomatic papers was subordinated to a general narrative. Political ideas and the personalities of statesmen counted for more than 'what one clerk said to another clerk'. The novelty some forty years ago was twofold. Historians set out to write the history of international relations purely from Foreign Office archives. More important, they claimed to be able to write about contemporary events with as much detachment as they had written about more distant periods. Their claim may have been justified. But it would be foolish to pretend that their sudden interest in contemporary history was detached and 'scientific'. It was a political interest, forced upon them by events and in particular by the event of the First World War. The twentieth century would have shown less concern with diplomatic history if the Bismarckian peace had endured. The diplomatic history of our time has always been a study of war origins, by no means to its advantage.

Historians seek to be detached, dispassionate, impartial. In fact no historian starts out with his mind a blank, to be gradually filled by the evidence. Is it conceivable, for example, that any document would have induced Macaulay to confess that the Glorious Revolution had been after all a great mistake? Or even conceivable that Ranke might have come to regret the rise of Prussia as a Great Power? The historians of the early twentieth century had lived through the First World War; and nearly all of them lamented it. Their reaction took different forms. German, and to some extent French, historians were anxious to prove that their governments had been right. British and American historians were anxious to prove that their governments had been wrong. Soviet historians were a class apart. They were delighted to distribute the blame among all 'imperialist' governments, the old Russian government perhaps most of all. But even they trimmed their sails to political convenience.

Diplomatic history was pushed to the front both by the way that the First World War started and by the way that it ended. The European crisis of July 1914 was peculiarly an affair of diplomacy. Few maintained then, and fewer would maintain now, that the outbreak of war was deliberately foreseen and planned by any Power or even by any general staff. Lloyd George expressed the general opinion: 'We muddled into war.' The outcome had been determined by what diplomatists said, or failed to say, to each other. Moreover, what they said seemed to have been shaped by the existing diplomatic structure – the Triple Alliance, the Franco-Russian alliance, or the vaguer commitments of Great Britain to France. Every Great Power sought to justify itself by publishing a selection of its diplomatic papers; and the very inadequacy of some of these suggested that the truth would emerge from a fuller, franker publication. The peace settlement reinforced the demand for impartial inquiry. The Treaty of Versailles followed on the defeat of Germany; but its moral justification was that Germany had been solely 'responsible' for the outbreak of war, either deliberately or from negligence. No doubt the statesmen at Paris would have made much the same arrangements even if they had been convinced that all the Great Powers were equally at fault; but they would have had a harder time with their consciences, and still more with those of others.

It is not surprising therefore that German historians took up the struggle against 'the lie of war-guilt'. They did not need to prove that Germany had always been right; it was enough for them to show that she had not always been wrong. The first republican government employed Kautsky to make a very full publication of the German records on the events immediately preceding the outbreak of war. This did not serve the German purpose. For it seemed to show that, whatever the faults of others, the German government was very much to blame. The German historians therefore shifted their ground back from July 1914 to the diplomacy of the preceding years and ultimately even to the epoch of Bismarck. Within less than a decade after the peace treaty Thimme published fifty-four volumes of diplomatic documents running from 1871 to June 1914. It was not the first publication of the kind. The French were doing it for the origins of the Franco-Prussian War. But the French proceeded slowly – they finished their task only in 1930; the events with which they were concerned were already distant and somewhat parochial. The German publication eclipsed the French series in size and excitement. Historians all over the world, and not only in Germany, took their version of events from it. Even today a historian will catch himself following its pattern even when he resolves not to do so; and the 'received idea' of the world before 1914 still rests on *Die Grosse Politik*, though this origin is forgotten.

Die Grosse Politik was the first and most grandiose publication of documents on the origins of the First World War. There is another reason for its success. The interpretation underlying it corresponded to that which British and American historians had already formed in their minds. It is perhaps a special Anglo-Saxon characteristic to see the virtue in the other side of the case, and even to start out with a prejudice against one's own government. The official case had been challenged in England from the beginning. The Union of Democratic Control had been founded in September 1914; and its central doctrine was that 'secret diplomacy' caused the war. E D Morel, who inspired and led it, had already exposed secret diplomacy in Morocco; his *Truth about the War* soon followed, with the clear implication that earlier versions had been lies. Some of the diplomatic historians in England, such as Lowes Dickinson and Dr G P Gooch, were members of the UDC; none escaped its influence. The Englishmen who wrote on contemporary history were as much cut from E D Morel's cloak as the Russian novelists were from Gogol's. This spirit soon spread to the United States. There was the same desire for fair play; the same readiness to distrust the national government; and American historians had always been more closely linked to German scholarship. Apart from this, the American people as a whole shook off sooner the passions of the war years and came to distrust an outlook associated with the spirit of Versailles. American historians were following a national trend; British historians were helping to make it.

The years between the peace settlement and Hitler's victory were great days for the 'pure' diplomatic historian. Men wanted to understand the contemporary world; and historians assured them that they could do so if all diplomatic secrets were 'revealed'. The British documents were published from 1898 to 1914; the French plodded laboriously on (as they are still doing) with a publication of documents from 1871 to 1914. The Italians asserted themselves as a Great Power by refusing to publish anything. More recently they have turned round and made the same assertion by proposing to publish everything from 1861 to 1943. Even the Russians abandoned their traditional secrecy and began to publish on a grand scale; then, repenting their frankness, abandoned the enterprise and tried to suppress what they had revealed already. If the diplomatic archives really contain the key to history, then the door was decisively unlocked. Yet the result was curiously disappointing. For the most part the spate of documents confirmed what men thought already. The Germans and the former members of the UDC demonstrated that Germany had not caused the war; Soviet historians continued to blame capitalist imperialism; and the cynical were still convinced that all statesmen lurched in a fog from one blunder to the next. What was wrong? Why had the golden key jammed in the lock? Perhaps the revelations had not been complete enough. Some discovered defects in the *Grosse Politik*; and these existed, though dwarfed by its great merits. The British government confirmed half-formed suspicions by imposing a hocus-pocus of secrecy on the so-called 'cabinet papers'; and some future generation of historians will be disappointed to find what trivialities these contain.

The doubts about diplomatic history went deeper. It was not merely that we had missed some revelation or were being denied some material. We were asking the wrong questions, using the wrong method. We must turn from the Foreign Offices to the more profound forces which shape the destinies of men. Even Professor Renouvin, the leading French diplomatic historian of the day, has done this recently, though with some backsliding. There was from the start an undercurrent of opinion which tried to give diplomacy an economic interpretation – an opinion partly Marxist, but also stemming from English radicals such as J A Hobson. Markets and raw materials, not alliances, had caused the war. This view, though also held by some members of the UDC, took longer to become respectable. Teachers of history put the works of Dr Gooch or Professor S B Fay on the top of their table and consulted Brailsford's *War of Steel and Gold* under the desk. The economic interpretation did not win the field until the days of the Left Book Club; and even then it was not much applied in detail. Historians setting out to describe an 'imperialist' conflict, lost their balance in the flood of diplomatic documents. Some of them even reached the conclusion, perhaps correctly, that conflicts such as Morocco or the Baghdad railway had more to do with power and less with profits than they had originally supposed. Certainly it is difficult to point to any really successful work of scholarship applying this economic interpretation, even by a Russian. There is, of course, always the excuse that, whereas Foreign Office secrets have been revealed, those of the counting-house and the company promoter have not; and the unknown is always a safe source to look to for further enlightenment.

There have been other and wider forms of retreat from 'pure' diplomatic history. It is fitting that historians in what is called the age of the masses should abandon the archives for the study of public opinion – a study, however, more easily preached than practised. How can we take a Gallup poll among the dead? The study of public opinion has changed only too often into a study of newspapers – a subject also of great interest but one attended with more difficulties than the unworldly historian supposes. Do newspapers voice public opinion or make it? Do they lead or follow? Often neither. They obey the directive of a government agent; dance to the whims of a proprietor; or, more rarely, express the policy of a great editor. Most frequently of all, they put in enough news and articles to fill the space. Little of this was recognized by the earnest scholars, usually American, who pursued the trail of public opinion. How surprised Frank Harris would have been, for instance, to learn that he had supplied the evidence for British hostility to Germany by a single leader in the *Saturday Review*. Some outstanding work has indeed been done in this field. Eckart Kehr wrote an amazingly brilliant book years ago on the building of the German Navy and party politics – so brilliant indeed as almost to make one forget that the German admirals must have had something to do with it. More recently Professor Chabod has dissected with infinite subtlety what the Italians thought of foreign affairs in the year 1870. The intellectual achievement could hardly be bettered. But our shelves will groan if every nation is to require 600 pages for each year of its public thoughts.

Historians have run too eagerly after some subjects, and passed others by. It is curious that a generation which experienced two world wars should still neglect the papers of the service departments. No muckraking radical has penetrated their secrets; even respectable historians have only been allowed a selective glance. The generals and admirals have defended the secrets of their enemies as zealously as they defend their own. The records of the German Admiralty have been reposing in London since 1945, inviolate from any prying eye. The Americans have not done much better with the records of the German General Staff which they carried off to Washington. We know what Hitler planned to do in war; how far was the German Army equipped to carry out his intentions? The answer would be not without interest. Solidarity, worthy of a trade union, ensures that we shall not learn the answer.

Wars are the eclipse of diplomacy, and therefore of diplomatic history. This, no doubt, explains why there are few books on the diplomacy of the First World War and why the archives for this period are still rigorously sealed, even though the documents of the interwar period are being published. More specifically we continue to live in a war atmosphere in the immediate present – first the Second World War against Germany, then the more insidious 'Cold War', which seems equally impervious to diplomacy. The arguments and manoeuvres of diplomatists have become little more than an entertainment, imperfectly cloaking the 'outdoor relief' for members of the ruling class which John Bright regarded as the object of all foreign policy. What goes on at Lake Success is of little moment; therefore, we think, diplomacy never mattered, and the diplomatic historian is wasting his time as well as ours.

This depreciation of diplomacy started even before the Second World War. The dictators, Hitler and Mussolini, refused to play according to the accepted rules. What was the sense of negotiating, still less of making agreements with them? And therefore, even more, what sense is there in writing about these barren negotiations and meaningless pacts? The 'pure' diplomatic historian has been perhaps too readily discouraged. It was the outbreak of the Second World War, not the First, which led Sir Lewis Namier to write a masterpiece – largely from diplomatic documents of the most formal, dreary kind.

Foreign policy of a sort will go on so long as there are sovereign states, even though its instrument may be an atomic test instead of a dispatch. Diplomatic historians may have to learn new tricks and to lament their vanished 'purity'. Certainly the records of Foreign Offices no longer arouse much curiosity. Once it was believed that they contained as much explosive matter as Pandora's box. Now it appears that the patron saint of the archives is Joanna Southcott.

The Traditions of British Foreign Policy

This was a BBC Third Programme radio broadcast, transmitted at 10 pm on Saturday 6 January 1951 as a twenty-minute review of James Joll's book Britain and Europe: Pitt to Churchill 1793–1940 (*Oxford, Clarendon Press, 1950*). *Alan Taylor was paid a fee of 25 guineas.*

*   *   *

The great thing about foreign policy is that it is a matter of talk, of general principles. In most public affairs, there comes a point when you proceed from talk to action. When you have talked about education, you go on to build schools – though not to paying schoolteachers enough: and when you talk about socialism, you end up by nationalizing steel. But foreign policy is essentially a matter of saying what you are going to do. When you do it, it becomes something else. If you go to war, it becomes a matter for the War Office and the Admiralty; if you cooperate economically, the Treasury or the Board of Trade see to it. The only *action* that a foreign secretary ever takes is to sign treaties; and treaties (though people often forget this) are not action – they are only promises to act like this or that in a given set of circumstances. Foreign policy is displayed in discussion – either in parliament or with foreigners – and therefore it is a good topic for an anthology in a series on the British political tradition. It is much easier to show in this way than, say, housing policy, which would have to be shown in a collection of plans and photographs – very boring for those of us who would still rather read books than look at pictures, whether still or moving.

James Joll has put together a collection of extracts – speeches, pamphlets, newspaper articles – to illustrate the theme Britain and Europe, from Pitt to Churchill. It starts with Pitt explaining in 1793 why England was going to war with revolutionary France; it ends with Winston Churchill in 1940 looking forward to an ever closer cooperation with the United States. In between are some of the best-known episodes in British foreign policy, and some not so well known; Castlereagh refusing to join the continental Powers in a reactionary policing of Europe; Canning keeping out of intervention in Spain; Palmerston defending his intervention in Greece; and Lord John

Russell blessing the revolutionary unification of Italy. You can guess what it ends up with just before Churchill: Munich and the argument over appeasement, which still supplies superficial parallels and superficial terms of abuse for the present day.

Throughout the nineteenth century – and indeed ever since the wars with Spain in the sixteenth century – British foreign policy rested on the assumption that it had a choice, even if only a choice of evils. You could cooperate with the Holy Alliance to maintain the existing settlement of Europe or you could work with France to revise it; you could help Turkey to resist Russia or you could work with Russia to impose reforms on Turkey, or even to partition her; you could reconcile Germany, even Hitler, by appeasement, or you could build up a system of collective security to resist Hitler. These were not always good choices; but they were respectable choices, honestly advocated by intelligent and well-informed men. There was a choice, because we had, or thought we had, freedom to choose. I do not say it did not matter which policy was chosen; all I say is that it was a balance of advantages. There's a remarkable passage in Sir Edward Grey's speech at the time of the outbreak of war with Germany in 1914. That might seem a matter of life and death. But Grey says, 'if we are engaged in war, we shall suffer but little more than we shall suffer even if we stand aside'. And he goes on to say that, in any case, we shall only suffer by the loss of our trade with the Continent.

We have been so used to this freedom of choice over a long period that we perhaps fail to see how unusual it is. Most countries have their foreign policy dictated to them by their situation and by the behaviour of their neighbours. Very often they have only the choice between resisting or being overrun without a fight. For instance, this country chose deliberately to go to war with Germany in September 1939: we declared war and we could have kept out of it if we had wanted to – no doubt only for the time being. Russia had no such choice in June 1941: war was imposed upon her by Hitler and would have been imposed whatever policy Stalin had tried to follow. It is worth while trying to understand why we had this freedom of choice in the past: it casts a good deal of light on our policy, and still more American policy, in the present. Primarily it came from our being a bit further off: the straits which divide us from Europe gave us that extra time for deliberation. But it is a mistake to think that British security rested only on sea power or ever has. The fiercest and most prolonged debate over British foreign policy has always gone on between those, usually a minority, who regard sea power as enough in itself; and those, usually in control of policy, who have insisted that sea power was only the beginning, the foundation of British security. Curiously enough, it has usually been the Left in British history who have been isolationists, wanting to rely solely on the strength of the British Navy – from Charles James Fox opposing the war against Napoleon to John Bright opposing any active foreign policy at all, and finally to the radicals before 1914 who opposed the ententes with France and Russia. In fact, if you pushed the question a little nearer our times, you would find the opponents of collective security and advocates of a straight deal with Germany at the time of Munich were mostly radicals gone sour from Neville Chamberlain downwards. Nevertheless isolationism, based on sea power, has been by and large the voice of a minority in British history.

The classical basis of British security – as established at the Glorious Revolution and practised throughout the eighteenth and early nineteenth centuries – was the balance of power. In those days English people prized control of the seas simply because it enabled them to play their part in maintaining this balance. Observe the phrase 'maintaining the balance of power'. The old school of English statesmen, from Somers and Montague in William III's reign to Palmerston in Queen Victoria's, did not think that there was an automatic balance of power on the Continent of Europe, by which the Great Powers cancelled each other out and so left us alone. They thought that the balance had to be constantly adjusted by changes in British policy; in fact they recognized that it demanded a more active foreign policy, even involved Great Britain more in wars, than if they had done without it. Mr Joll remarks, quite rightly, that the balance of power in Europe has broken down. The old-fashioned British statesmen would have answered, 'then put it back again; make it the object of British policy to restore the balance'. It is worth while considering why this answer does not appeal to us; the answer will tell us a lot about the change in British political thinking.

The first part of the answer is that in the second half of the nineteenth century English people got the balance of power theory wrong. They came to think that it worked automatically, like the law of supply and demand or any other of the famous economic 'laws' that the Victorians imagined they had discovered. In international affairs, as in economic affairs, you only had to look after your own interests and everything would be perfect; when this did not happen and the balance broke down, at the time of the first German war, people thought that the policy of the balance of power was no good. People also came to think that it was wicked, cynical. This is a very old radical attitude. But not all radicals were satisfied with isolationism. They wanted to substitute something for the balance of power; and they thought – the idea was invented by Gladstone – that they had discovered this substitute in the 'Concert of Europe'. The League of Nations and the United Nations are later versions of the same outlook. Not rivalry, but harmony; not conflict of interests, but cooperation in improvement were to be the determining motives in international affairs. Most of all, disputes between nations were to be settled by judging rights and wrongs, not by weighing the strength of the opposing sides. This theory sounds morally superior to the balance of power; and so it is, so long as the same international morality is accepted by all the Great Powers. Gladstone would never have preached the Concert of Europe unless he held – rightly or wrongly – that Russia was 'a great Christian power' – that is, had the same moral outlook as himself. It is a very different matter when you set up institutions based on international harmony, not because this harmony exists, but because you hope that these institutions will create it. This was done both with the League of Nations and with the United Nations. It is as though a man and woman who did not care for each other got married in the hope that they would then fall in love. This sometimes happens between individuals, not, I think, in the world of international relations.

To go back to the point of Great Britain's having freedom of choice; consider the consequence. That consequence is simple: it is a sensation of being morally superior. If you do things because you have to, as most continental nations have done, you cannot waste time thinking about right and wrong: you act. When you have time to weigh advantages, you also weigh moral claims. Ever since Great Britain had an independent foreign policy, this has always had a moral element. First it was the defence of the Protestant religion: then it was the defence of the kings and princes of Europe against the encroachments of the French Revolution; and in the nineteenth century it became the encouraging of national liberty, and not merely of the independence of states. It would have been very difficult for

English people to conduct either the first or the second war against Germany – or for that matter the present Cold War against Russia – unless they had felt, and now feel, morally superior to their opponents. But in the old days British statesmen knew how to keep their moral sentiments within practical bounds. Canning defended Spanish independence against Napoleon; he did not think it worth while defending Spanish liberalism against the intervention of conservative France. Palmerston welcomed the liberation of Italy and helped to promote it; he would do nothing for Poland or for Hungary – the one was beyond his reach, the liberation of the other he supposed would have been against British interests. I do not commend this attitude; I record it. C P Scott, a great British liberal, once said, 'Truth like everything else should be economized.' This sensible attitude looks very different when seen through foreign eyes. And those who believe in the moral superiority of British, or now of Anglo-American, foreign policy, should ask themselves why this country has always been known abroad as perfidious Albion. Is it merely the jealousy of rival and less successful Powers? I doubt it. It is rather the price you have to pay for having freedom of choice. Compared to continental countries, England has been a bad ally. She has always assumed, rightly in the past, that her allies needed her more than she needed them – that is what the phrase 'natural allies' really means. This was expressed in Salisbury's proud sentence, 'England does not solicit alliances; she grants them.' And Palmerston meant much the same when he said that alliances were impossible between equals: one Power has to be dependent on the other and to need protection.

It may be that these considerations are now all out of date and that there is very little to be learnt from the study of past foreign policy. I would not easily dismiss that view. Indeed I have long thought that we learn too much from history rather than the reverse. For instance the appeasement of Germany would not have been tried so obstinately in the 1930s if it had not been for the recollection or myth or legend that the appeasement of France had worked in the 1830s. And similarly a conciliatory policy towards Russia would not be rejected so firmly now if it were not for the recollection of the appeasement towards Germany that failed a decade ago. Both historical analogies were profoundly misleading and did nothing but harm. All the same you cannot escape so simply from the factors that have shaped British foreign policy in the past. At the present time we seem committed to the doctrine that we have no longer a freedom of choice and that policy is determined for us by the actions of others – by the actions of either the Russians or the Americans – at any rate not by our initiative. If this were true then indeed every tradition in British policy would have to go overboard. But is it really true? Or do we perversely want it to be true in order to escape our responsibilities? Have the Straits of Dover ceased to exist as a military factor? Has sea power ceased to count in the world? Even the balance of power is not so hopelessly destroyed, if anyone had the courage to juggle the weights round. And even the Concert of Great Powers, or harmony of interests, might occasionally sound a note in unison, if British diplomatists were more concerned to act as piano-tuners. Certainly the theory of British policy nowadays is that we have lost freedom of choice. The practice of British policy – from our attitude towards the Council of Europe to our attempt to follow a more reasonable line towards China – asserts that we are still an independent Power. Here again I do not commend; I record. Almost the last words in James Joll's book are from the speech by Churchill in which he said that the organizations of the British Empire and the United States will have to be somewhat mixed up . . . for mutual and general advantage. 'Let it roll on full flood, inexorable, irresistible, benignant.' I wonder whether history will show that Churchill was right.

War and Peace

This essay first appeared in the London Review of Books, *2 October 1980, as a review of Geoffrey Best's* Humanity in Warfare: The Modern History of the International Law of Armed Conflicts (*London, Weidenfeld and Nicolson, 1980*) *and Martin Ceadel's* Pacifism in Britain 1914–1945: The Defining of a Faith (*Oxford, Clarendon Press, 1980*). *Best and Ceadel wrote on themes close to Alan Taylor's heart. In March 1982 he wrote, 'For fifty years I had been teaching history and writing books about it. All my books and lectures had been implicitly about war; from the Napoleonic Wars to the shadow of final war under which we now live.'*

*   *   *

War has been throughout history the curse and inspiration of mankind. The sufferings and destruction that accompany it rival those caused by famine, plague and natural catastrophes. Yet in nearly every civilization war has been the noblest of professions, and among the heroes of every age those distinguished in war have always ranked first, as a visit to St Paul's Cathedral will bear witness. In many civilizations, war has been a once-for-all affair: the conquest of neighbouring territory or the repulse of an invader. In some, however, war between contending states has gone on for generations – the Times of Trouble, in Toynbee's phrase. Ancient Greece experienced such a Time, and there followed one of the first attempts to limit the sufferings of war, as the Olympic Games indicate. But the Greek wars were not ended by moderation and wise agreement. They were ended by the Roman conquest, which provided one solution to the problem of war: the establishment of a single dominant power that subdued or eliminated all other contenders.

Europe, too, has known attempts at a single universal state from the early days of the Holy Roman Empire to the brief domination of Hitler's Nazi Germany. But broadly speaking European history has been a continual Time of Troubles, interrupted by occasional periods of armed peace. The realization that war was here to stay produced a unique development in European thought: attempts to eliminate war altogether, or, if these failed, to lessen its horrific consequences. The first type of attempt lay behind the medieval pursuit of 'the just war', a pursuit as elusive as that of the Holy Grail. For it is almost universally true that in war each side thinks itself in the right, and there is no arbiter except victory to decide between them. Until recently, most historians have endorsed this verdict by applauding the victory or blessing the cause of their own state. Thus English historians saw little to question in the plundering raids of Henry V or even of William the Conqueror. French historians saw little to question in the Empire of Napoleon. The *jus ad bellum* has proved a will o' the wisp, though still actively pursued by some. The lesser attempt to moderate or even to civilize war has been more rewarding. This *jus in bello* is the topic of Geoffrey Best's fascinating book, a volume replete with scholarship and brilliant presentation.

Moderate or civilized wars can only operate within certain limitations. They are almost impossible when there is a conflict of creeds as well as of state power. The wars of religion or the crusade against the Albigensians were as savage as the wars of ancient Rome. Even the most civilized powers observe the rules only when at war with another civilized power. The British did not observe the rules when they blew Indian mutineers from the mouths of cannon. The Americans did not observe the rules when at war with the Red Indians, and of course the Red Indians also did not observe them. In fact, the laws of war were until recently confined to Europe, though Best ends by chronicling the present-day attempts to extend them more widely.

In more precise terms, the laws of war began when the European states contended over their respective ambitions, not over their fundamental beliefs, religious or political. Vattel was their acknowledged father. He sought for laws that the antagonists could accept without forfeiting their chance of victory. Ideally, wars should be conducted between professional armies without injury or disturbance to the civil population. Rousseau carried this view to extremes when he wrote: 'War, then, is not a relationship between man and man, but between State and State, in which private persons are only enemies accidentally.' Most theorists were more moderate and recognized that the laws of war must sometimes bow to 'necessity'. Indeed, far from necessity knowing no law, it became itself part of the law. Thus the soldier should not loot or plunder but he cannot be required to respect hen roosts when he is hungry. The bombardment of a town is deplorable but may be necessary in order to enforce its surrender, though only the necessary minimum should be used. Despite these exceptions, the Enlightened eighteenth century did pretty well with the laws of war. Armies carried their commissariat train with them instead of living off the countryside. Destruction was not operated for its own sake. There was little attempt to shake the morale of the civilian population. Combatants wore recognized uniforms and did not prolong a hopeless resistance.

There was one curious flaw which exasperated continental Europeans. This was the problem of how far the rules of war applied at sea. The continentals held that they should be applied unchanged. The British argued that the differing maritime circumstances fundamentally affected the laws of war. For instance, bombardments of towns were to be deplored but how else could the Royal Navy employ its strength against a land power?

Still graver was the problem of blockade. Continentals were clear as to the answer: neutral ships and neutral goods must be respected unless they were 'absolute' contraband. The British did not share this view. For them, blockade was a weapon with which to strangle an enemy and the rights of neutrals were of little account. This rigorous attitude weakened a little when Great Britain was faced with a powerful league of Armed Neutrality. But it was a hint of greater difficulties that were to arise in the future.

The French Revolution signalled the breakdown of Enlightenment in the laws of war as in other matters, though its original intention was the precise opposite. The early revolutionaries certainly aspired to spread their example abroad, but they imagined that the instruments of liberation would be Jacobin chants and floral wreaths rather than muskets and cannon. Even when forced to fight they insisted that their antagonists were few: 'war to the castles, peace to the cottages'. But who were to pay the liberators? Revolutionary France could not do so with its finances in chaos. The liberated peoples must pay. Soon the revolutionary armies were expected to work at a profit. Add to this the revolutionary strategy of speed, carried to its highest point by Napoleon. There was no time to waste on commissariat trains. The French armies lived off the country and often did very well out of it.

These revolutionary wars lessened and in time almost obliterated the distinction between soldiers and civilians. The Jacobins proclaimed 'the nation in arms'. How then could the civilian claim immunity? Things grew still more troublesome when civilians in the shape of partisans or guerillas took up arms themselves. In Spain, for instance, the French attempted to treat all partisans as criminals, an action they repeated in Russia. The British took the same attitude in 1798 when they accorded to the French invaders of Ireland the honours of war and massacred the Irish rebels whom the French had come to liberate. Even those such as the British in Spain who were in alliance with partisans agreed afterwards that this was an episode better forgotten.

Neutrals came off as badly as civilians. Nelson's assault on Copenhagen in 1801 brought him almost as much honour as the battle of Trafalgar. Two years after his death the Danes had their fleet ruthlessly snatched away from them. During the French wars the British blockade gradually eroded the securities for neutral trade established during the eighteenth century. This culminated in the Anglo-American war of 1812–14, a war fought, ironically enough, after the British had conceded the main point at issue. Once more the British appealed to necessity: relying on maritime power, it was necessary for them to do things which land powers did not need to do – though Napoleon also disregarded neutral rights and imposed a fictitious blockade. By the end of the Napoleonic Wars neutral rights had almost ceased to exist.

More fundamentally, the revolutionary and Napoleonic Wars demonstrated that the laws of war demanded some basis of common principles if they were to operate successfully. The Jacobins despised their enemies as tyrants. The tyrants responded by treating the Jacobins as subverters of civilization. Napoleon was given a half-hearted welcome as the restorer of law and order. But the victorious Powers showed their true opinion of Napoleon when they proclaimed him the enemy of mankind. Even so, it is surprising how much of the laws of war survived the impact of the French Revolution. Prisoners-of-war were still taken and were interned, usually under tolerable conditions. Flags of truce were generally respected and it was thought immoral to use them deceptively as a stratagem of war. The laws of blockade continued to provide matter for argument even if the British preferred maritime power to high principles. Enlightenment and Revolution produced conflicting impacts – a legacy that Geoffrey Best has analysed with admirable clarity and frankness.

For forty years after the Napoleonic Wars the laws of war did not advance. Their renewal came with the Congress of Paris in 1856, perhaps because the Congress had nothing better to do. The Congress celebrated the end of a war predominantly on land by wrestling with the laws of war at sea, a topic where even the British representatives proved for once slightly conciliatory. From the Congress of Paris stemmed further international discussions culminating in the two peace conferences at The Hague. Despite this accumulation of pointless oratory and ingenious drafting, the greatest advance in the laws of war ever made was the achievement of one man, Henri Dunant, seconded by that impractical dreamer, Napoleon III. The Red Cross began with individual initiative and was continued by it. Great Powers did not sponsor the Red Cross: they succumbed to it until it became as acceptable an element of international society as war itself. Further, the Red Cross did not grow out of the existing laws of war: it imposed itself upon them.

What was the cause of this universal acceptance? Did each Power see advantage for itself in the Red Cross? Did the principles of humanity and civilization for once triumph? There is no easy answer. Certainly the triumph was not repeated elsewhere. Geoffrey Best again shows his powers of exposition as he traces the advance in the laws of war during the nineteenth century. Certainly there was a more conscious and official application to the subject than there had been earlier. During the Enlightenment, aloof philosophers enunciated general principles which each state and each soldier, almost, was expected to work out in practice for himself. The nineteenth century saw the arrival of the international lawyer, of whom the Russian Martens was the chief. Martens would have liked to formulate laws of war which should be at once wise and acceptable. In practice, this meant discovering laws that should have at least some humanity in them and that would despite this be tolerated by the military. The intellectual agility required to produce this was confined almost to Martens alone. The various conferences laboured productively. But there was always the shadow of 'necessity', sharply raised whenever the military saw some encroachment on their powers.

Broadly, the laws of war improved most in their application to actual fighting on land, which took on almost the medieval character of armed combat under chivalrous conditions. There was less advance over the problems that had arisen during the Napoleonic Wars: requisitions, reprisals, partisans and the treatment of civilians. The practices of the Royal Navy suffered further encroachments even though

Fisher dismissed them as 'nonsense' which would be 'ditched' if war came. The European legalists averted their eyes from bombardment as practised by the British at Alexandria, and still more from the Union operations in the American Civil War, particularly Sherman's demonstration to the inhabitants of the South that war was hell.

The laws of war improved more in appearance than in reality. For, as Geoffrey Best points out, there were two flourishing movements during the nineteenth century: the peace movement, which everyone noticed and commended, and the war movement, which many people ignored and which yet proved more powerful. Best has found a wonderful quotation from Joseph Conrad, who described the Hague Tribunal as 'a solemnly official recognition of the Earth as a House of Strife'. Conrad continued: 'War has made peace altogether in its own image; a martial, overbearing, war-lord sort of peace ... eloquent with allusions to glorious feats of arms.'

The nineteenth century formulated the laws of war; the twentieth century was expected to apply them. Geoffrey Best discusses in his powerful concluding chapter how far this has proved true. The answers, drawn from both world wars, are contradictory. The laws have been best observed in fighting between regular land forces, particularly on the Western Front and in such 'professional' areas as North Africa. It seems that soldiers have higher standards when they are not being criticized and provoked by civilians. On the Eastern Front Soviet Russia observed the laws of war more nearly than did Nazi Germany, despite allegations to the contrary. The laws of war came off less happily at sea and in the air. This sprang partly from the British reversion to the ruthless application of blockade which she had developed in earlier wars. The deeper cause was the development of weapons of war which could not be covered by the existing laws.

The first of these, already effective in the First World War, was the submarine, which, as the Germans showed, had to sink its victims without warning if it were to operate successfully. The Germans pleaded that they were retaliating to the British blockade. The true situation was that the submarine had been projected as an additional naval weapon and that its role as a commerce-destroyer had not been foreseen. This was even truer of the Zeppelin, which first set the practice, however ineffectually, of indiscriminate bombardment. This problem was exacerbated with the arrival of bombing aircraft. Best makes two striking remarks about air experiences in the First World

War. The first is that Trenchard enunciated the doctrine of indiscriminate bombardment, quite without practical experience. The second is that the Royal Naval Air Service developed precision bombing during its short life. This achievement was subsequently ignored, partly as impractical and partly as being not aggressive or terrifying enough.

Best continues the problems of air warfare, when he reaches the Second World War. Here the Trenchard legacy came to fruition. It is often not appreciated that indiscriminate or area bombing was a British speciality. The American Air Force disliked it; the German Luftwaffe operated it sceptically and reluctantly. British obsession with area bombing was an extension of British reliance on blockade – the weapon of a power reluctant to develop a great army. Best traces Sir Arthur Harris's persistent and unjustified defence of area bombardment, which culminated in the unnecessary attack on Dresden in 1945 – not that this attack was any more reprehensible than earlier attacks except that it came towards the end of the war. Air warfare as practised during the Second World War, and particularly with its last achievements at Hiroshima and Nagasaki, left two profound holes in the restraining laws of war: the first that indiscriminate destruction, however horrible, was a legitimate means of war; the second that with 'the nation at war' there was no longer any distinction between the military and civilians and that therefore civilians were legitimate targets. The same moral was drawn from the extension of partisan warfare, which led to the conclusion that every civilian who was not a collaborator of the invaders was a concealed or potential partisan, a moral the partisan forces applied the other way round. The logical consequence was that every inhabitant of a conquered country should be massacred or at the very least dispatched to slave labour, as the Germans demonstrated.

And so Best arrives at the present day. There have been even more conferences and regulations. The profession of international lawyer is more active than ever. There are two black clouds. The first is air warfare, which with the development of nuclear weapons transgresses all the laws of war ever known. The second is the attempt to extend the laws of war to cover colonial revolts or social revolutions, an attempt further confused by the Marxist insistence that Marxist acts of violence are always right and resistance to these acts always wrong. Despite these portents, Best remains mildly optimistic. He welcomes the persistent discussion of the laws of war as evidence that there is some desire to limit and restrain armed conflicts. He even hints a hope that this desire may be fulfilled. To my mind, the experiences of the past eighty years are not encouraging. Fortunately, the past is not always a guide to the future.

The experts in the laws of war claimed to be practical men, resigned to the fact that war, somewhat humanized, would go on for a long time, if not for ever. The search for an end to war has been of more recent origin, being almost confined to Great Britain during the last hundred years, with some echoes in the United States. Martin Ceadel approaches this search with a sharp distinction between pacificism (a word which he claims to have borrowed from me and which I gladly lend him) and pacifism. Pacificists are those who favour peaceful foreign policies and who seek to develop international institutions for the promotion of peace. Pacifism in its pure form is a total rejection of war as an instrument of policy.

The distinction is clear to Ceadel and will be clear to his readers. It has been less clear in the historical record. Pacifism is the older, in that there have always been a few men who refused to take part in war, but this was an individual gesture of abstention and not a contribution to solving the problem of war. The early Christians refused to serve in the Roman armies, but this sprang from their refusal to accord divine honours to the emperor. Once they could serve under the sign of the cross the Christians fought vigorously enough, not only against pagans and barbarians, but against each other.

Modern pacifism was part of the humanitarian outlook which characterized the philanthropists of the nineteenth century: peaceful aims went along with anti-slavery and prison reform. Quakers tended to take up a pacifist position, but this did not prevent their becoming advocates of a peaceful policy. A Quaker delegation visited Nicholas I at St Petersburg in an attempt to prevent the Crimean War. John Bright opposed that war in his greatest speeches, but he was clearly not a pacifist: he supported the armed suppression of the Indian Mutiny and applauded the Union victory in the American Civil War. With Great Britain not involved in a European war for nearly a century, the question for humanitarians was not, 'What do we do in the event of war?' but: 'How do we discourage or prevent war elsewhere?'

There was a further obstacle to the development of a clear-cut pacifism in Great Britain: even when at war, as in the Anglo-Boer War of 1899–1902, Great Britain fought with professional volunteer forces. The potential pacifist did not have to resolve what he would do if called upon to fight. On the contrary, his difficulty was to find outlets for his humanitarianism either by providing medical services or by conducting political agitation against the policy and operations of war. The pro-Boers were often stigmatized as pacifists, but it is clear that they were nothing of the kind, and Lloyd George, one of the most assertive pro-Boers, became later an outstanding war minister. Ceadel is therefore right in taking the outbreak of war in August 1914 as the starting-point for his theme: pacifism in Britain. Even so, the emergence of pacifism remained obscure.

Ceadel is pretty firm in dealing with those who opposed the First World War as being a mistaken policy or even as fought against the wrong enemy. The Union of Democratic Control was clearly not pacifist. But what about the Fellowship of Reconciliation, which Ceadel specifies as 'quietist'? Even the No-Conscription Fellowship began as a political movement to oppose the legislative introduction of conscription, and continued on a practical basis after conscription operated. Conscription certainly made some people ask themselves whether they were pacifists or merely high-minded. There were few clear responses. Only 16,500 of those called up pleaded conscientious objection; only 6,000 of these refused to accept the tribunal's verdict, and only 1,298 of these resisted 'absolutely'. Nor were even the absolutists all of a kind. Some were religious pacifists; some were humanitarian pacifists. But a number were solely against the Great War which was raging: some as socialists, some as critics of British foreign policy, some as defenders of individual liberty. The experiences of war strengthened the confusion: conscientious objectors did not inquire into the theoretical basis on which the conviction of their comrades rested. All could be numbered as opponents of war, from the pure pacifist to the Marxist champion of war on the barricades.

The confusion which had developed during the Great War increased when the war was over. Many who had been combatants now regarded the war as mistaken in either its aims or its conduct or perhaps both together. Ceadel analyses this confusion with admirable clarity. Perhaps he is a little too rigorous. The man who defines his convictions with absolute accuracy is very rare and rarest of all in the world of politics. Ceadel tends to imply that all such confusions are foolish, and that pacifists and near-pacifists are peculiarly prone to them. Indeed, there is even a hint that those who reject the methods and arguments of pacifism are eminently sane − a strange view. How are we to describe the rulers of great states and their technical advisers who propose to defend civilization by blowing the peoples and cities of the world to pieces? 'Sane' is not a word that would occur to me.

The 1920s were the heyday of pacificism and pacifism in a tangle. The former absolutists did not reproach those who had served in the war, and these latter for the most part did not reproach the absolutists. Many who had preached and even practised individual rejection felt that this was too self-centred and cooperated with others in the search for means of preventing war. The former conscientious objector might join the No More War movement, but he recognized no contradiction in joining the League of Nations Union as well. Yet the basis of the League of Nations was 'collective security', which implied in the last resort military sanctions, or, as the American historian Harry Elmer Barnes expressed it, 'perpetual war for the sake of perpetual peace'. This was not a problem of any practical relevance when the prospect of another Great War seemed remote.

The hard core of Ceadel's book concerns the great transformation which began in the early thirties with the realization that perpetual peace would not come of itself or perhaps was not on offer at all. Some of the one-time pacifists decided that with the rapid approach of social revolution they were not pacifists after all. Since social revolution failed to arrive, this conversion had little practical application except to remove a rather disruptive element from the pacifist movement. Fascism, or, to be more precise, the appearance of Hitler, was a different matter. Comparatively few recognized Hitler's threat from the first. On the contrary, pacifists like nearly everyone else argued that the wisest as well as the most moral course was the redress of German grievances. It is curious to read of a time when former conscientious objectors applauded Neville Chamberlain.

The final years before the Second World War saw the rise of a pacifist movement that was political rather than ethical: the Peace Pledge Union. The Union was virtually the creation of one man, Canon Dick Sheppard, and a very erratic shepherd he proved. The origins of the Union went back, I think, to the spate of anti-war literature that characterized the end of the twenties. Not surprisingly, the Union was an assembly of prima donnas, as Ceadel entertainingly demonstrates. Perhaps there is nothing more absurd than gifted writers earnestly believing in some cause. Quite a number were members of the League of Nations as well as the Peace Pledge Union; many moved from one Union to the other and back again. Ceadel does not fail to add that many were vegetarians while some had a high track record in plurality of wives. The Peace Pledge Union enlisted an impressive total of pledges against war. Comparatively few of these pledges were honoured when war actually arrived. Though there were many more conscientious objectors than in the First World War – 60,000 against 16,000 – their impact was much less. Instead of being persecuted, they were tolerated or even admired. Some 5,000 were sent to prison, more in sorrow than in anger: most of these took up some form of humanitarian work before the war was over. Only Christians – 'Christadelphians, Plymouth Brethren, Elimites, Particular People' – stuck to their belief. Ceadel concludes that pacifism has been reduced to a religious belief, rather than a solution to the problems of war.

Though never a pacifist, I had more patience with the pacifists of that age than he has now. In my view, they were, though often foolish, a good deal more sensible than their opponents. Martin Ceadel has a great future before him as a historian, particularly when he becomes more tolerant of human follies.

Moving with the Times

This essay first appeared as a review of E H Carr's What is History? *(London, Macmillan, 1961) in the* Observer, *22 October 1961. Alan Taylor admired the work of Edward Hallett Carr (1892–1982) both before the Second World War and once Carr had progressed beyond the first two volumes of his history of Russia 1917–29 (published in fourteen volumes between 1950 and 1978). He selected a work by Carr as his book of the year for the* Manchester Guardian *in both 1937 and 1939: in the former year his choice was* Michael Bakunin *(London, Macmillan, 1937); in the latter year it was* The Twenty Years' Crisis *(London, Macmillan, 1939), which he deemed 'the most important book on world politics published this year, learned, witty and free from hollow phrases'. However, in the 1950s he was uneasy at Carr's sympathetic treatment of communism. He wrote in 1950 of Carr's* Studies in Revolution *(London, Macmillan, 1950): 'There is no moral condemnation of communism; and no suggestion that the failure of communism may be due to the moral revolt of mankind, not to the blunders in tactics.'*

* * *

Those who can, do; those who can't, pontificate. A chef is more interested in taste than in vitamins; a vintner more interested in aroma than in alcoholic content. Like Goering with culture, I reach for my revolver when offered philosophies of history. But there are exceptions. Occasionally a practising historian turns aside from his work in order to explain to himself and others what he is up to. Then we listen with respect, and no one is entitled to greater respect than E H Carr.

He is without rival among contemporary historians. His history of Soviet Russia is a masterpiece of scholarship and narration. No man knows better the problems which a historian encounters; no man has a higher sense both of the historian's responsibilities and of his limitations. He can range from meticulous detail to wide generalization. He sees both the furniture of his own study and the stir of the great world. As well, he has a beautiful gift for exposition which makes his lectures a delight to read. Who can resist a lecture which begins with the words: 'If milk is set to boil in a saucepan, it boils over. I do not know, and have never wanted to know, why this happens'?

*

There are many fine things in this set of lectures. The layman tends to imagine that the historian first accumulates facts and then generalizes from them. Carr points out that the general picture comes first and that the facts acquire significance only in relation to this general picture. New 'facts' emerge whenever we look at history in a different way. As Carr says, 'the relation between the historian and his facts is one of equality, of give-and-take'. The historian sometimes shifts his standpoint because he finds new facts; he is more likely to shift it because of new experiences.

Increased knowledge of the present increases our understanding of the past quite as much as the other way round. Every historian belongs to his age, and each age gets the historians it deserves. Thus Mommsen, disillusioned by the failure of the revolutions of 1848, could dissect the last sad years of the Roman republic. At this point Carr seems to push his argument too far. Mommsen, he says, stopped at the fall of the republic because 'the problem of what happened once the strong man had taken over was not yet actual'. No Hitler; hence no history of the Roman Empire. I doubt whether things were quite so simple.

Even the general principle that each age gets the historians it deserves does not work out in practice or works so haphazardly as to be no principle at all. The present day in England, when the educated classes have lost faith in the future and in themselves, no doubt deserves conservative historians, as Carr suggests: historians like the great Sir Lewis Namier and his lesser followers, who insist that history has no meaning and that it ought now to stop. How then does our disillusioned age come to deserve Carr or even me? Are we merely an antiquated hangover from the Victorians?

Carr would be cross at any such suggestion. He places himself in the vanguard of progress and runs over with an optimism which might have daunted even Macaulay. Though he accuses others of confusion, he is himself not without sleight-of-hand. History, he insists, is movement. This is well said. But then he goes on to assert that the movement is all in one direction: upwards. Individuals, classes, nations may suffer; for the mass of mankind the march of events is set fair. Since things are getting better all the time, it follows that whatever produces these things should be welcomed by the historian.

Hence, for example, Stalin's extermination of the kulaks was justified because it helped to produce what has happened, that is, the present strength of the Soviet Union. (By analogy, though Carr does not say so, Hitler's extermination of the Jews was not justified because Germany now is not a world power.) Carr's message is even more cheerful. Since things have got better in the past, it follows that they are bound to get better in the future. This, if I understand him, is what he means by learning from history. The duty of the historian is to keep up with the times – so much so that Carr makes Robinson Crusoe a citizen of New York.

I find all this bewildering. I sympathize with so much that Carr says – particularly with his criticism of those historians who spend their time extolling the plundering monarchs and nobles of the past. But I cannot understand how knowledge of the past provides us with morality, let alone with knowledge of the future. How can the fact that something happened prove it right or, for that matter, wrong? Again, why should knowledge of where I came from tell me where I am going to? Carr is not alone in holding that knowledge of the past enables us to behave more sensibly in the present and to foresee the future.

To me this is all sales talk: History makes the future brighter. It does not work when tested against the facts: historians are not wiser politicians or more sensible in their private lives than other men – often indeed the reverse. Was Sir Charles Oman, for instance, a particularly enlightened MP? Yet he was quite a good historian. At the present time, it is possible to guess with Carr that, by the end of the century, countless millions will be living in unparalleled happiness all over the world. It is also possible to guess, as I am inclined to do, that by the end of the century a few thousand maimed human beings will be living, near to starvation, in caves.

All history tells us is that something will happen, though probably what we do not expect. My view of history is more modest than Carr's. The task of the historian is to explain the past; neither to justify nor to condemn it. Study of history enables us to understand the past; no more and no less. Perhaps even this is too high a claim. In most European languages 'history' and 'story' are the same word. So history deserves Carr's condemnation as 'literature' after all: 'a collection of stories and legends about the past without meaning or significance'.

Economic Imperialism

This essay was first published in the New Statesman and Nation, *26 March 1955, in a series entitled 'Reassessments'.*

*   *   *

These reflections on J A Hobson's *Imperialism* (1902) came fifty years after the original publication of the book.

Ideas live longer than men, and the writer who can attach his name to an idea is safe for immortality. Darwin will live as long as evolution, Marx be forgotten only when there are no class-struggles. In the same way, no survey of the international history of the twentieth century can be complete without the name of J A Hobson. He it was who found an economic motive for imperialism. Lenin took over Hobson's explanation, which thus became the basis for communist foreign policy to the present day. Non-Marxists were equally convinced, and contemporary history has been written largely in the light of Hobson's discovery. This discovery was an offshoot from his general doctrine of underconsumption. The capitalists cannot spend their share of the national production. Saving makes their predicament worse. They demand openings for investment outside their saturated national market, and they find these openings in the undeveloped parts of the world. This is imperialism. In Hobson's words, 'the modern foreign policy of Great Britain has been primarily a struggle for profitable markets of investment' – and what applied to Great Britain was equally true of France or Germany. Brailsford put it a few years later in a sharper way:

Working men may proceed to slay each other in order to decide whether it shall be French or German financiers who shall export the surplus capital (saved from their own wages bill) destined to subdue and exploit the peasants of Morocco.

This idea is now so embedded in our thought that we cannot imagine a time when it did not exist. Yet the earlier radical opponents of imperialism knew nothing of it. They supposed that imperialism sprang from a primitive greed for territory or a lust for conquest. The more sophisticated held that it was designed to provide jobs for the younger sons of the governing classes (a theory which James Mill invented and himself practised and which Hobson did not discard). Marx had no theory of imperialism. In classical Marxist theory, the state exists solely to oppress the working classes – to silence their grievances, destroy their trade unions and force them ever nearer to the point of absolute starvation. Marx jeered at the 'night-watchman' theory of the state, but the only difference in his conception was that it stayed awake in the daytime. Hobson added a true Marxist refinement. Marx had demonstrated that the capitalist, however benevolent personally, was condemned by economic law to rob the worker at the point of production. Similarly Hobson showed that the capitalist, however pacific, must seek foreign investment and therefore be driven into imperialist rivalry with the capitalists of other states. Previously Marxists had condemned capitalism as being pacific and particularly for preventing the great war of liberation against Russia. Now all wars became 'capitalistic', and war the inevitable outcome of the capitalist system. It is not surprising that, when the First World War had broken out, Lenin seized on Hobson's 'bourgeois-pacifist' theory and made it the cornerstone of his neo-Marxism. Like most prophets, he boasted of his foresight only when his visions had become facts.

Hobson wrote his book immediately after the partition of Africa and when the experiences of the Boer War were fresh in everyone's mind. For him, imperialism was mainly the acquisition of tropical lands, and what he foresaw next was the partition, or perhaps the joint exploitation, of China. In the spring of 1914 Brailsford applied similar doctrines to a wider field. *The War of Steel and Gold* (1914) is a more brilliant book than Hobson's, written with a more trenchant pen and with a deeper knowledge of international affairs. Though less remembered now, it had probably a stronger influence on its own generation, and American historians between the wars, in particular, could hardly have got on without it. Our own thought is still unconsciously shaped by it. Brailsford speaks more to our condition. The aggressive, self-confident imperialism of the Boer War seems remote to us; the competition of great armaments is ever-present in our lives.

Both writers wrote with radical passion. The first sensation in re-reading them is to cry out: 'Would that we had such writers nowadays!' Take Hobson's peroration:

Imperialism is a depraved choice of national life, imposed by self-seeking interests which appeal to the lusts of quantitative acquisition and of forceful domination surviving in a nation from early centuries of animal struggle for existence ... It is the besetting sin of all successful States, and its penalty is unalterable in the order of nature.

Or Brailsford's:

Let a people once perceive for what purposes its patriotism is prostituted, and its resources misused, and the end is already in sight. When that illumination comes to the masses of the three Western Powers, the fears which fill their barracks and stoke their furnaces will have lost the power to drive. A clear-sighted generation will scan the horizon and find no enemy. It will drop its armour, and walk the world's highways safe.

These are heavyweights of political combat. The intellectual diet of the mid-twentieth century cannot nourish such stamina. But we must stay the flood of our admiration with some doubting questions. Was the Hobsonian–Leninist analysis of international capitalism a true picture either then or now? Has the struggle for overseas investments ever been the mainspring of international politics?

The export of capital was certainly a striking feature of British economic life in the fifty years before 1914. But its greatest periods were before and after the time of ostensible imperialism. What is more, there was little correspondence between the areas of capitalist investment and political annexation. Hobson cheats on this, and Lenin after him. They show, in one table, that there has been a great increase in British investments overseas; in another that there has been a great increase in the territory of the British Empire. Therefore, they say, the one caused the other. But did it? Might not both have been independent products of British confidence and strength? If openings for investment were the motive of British imperialism, we should surely find evidence for this in the speeches of British imperialists, or, if not in their public statements, at any rate in their private letters and opinions. We don't. They talked, no doubt quite mistakenly, about securing new markets and, even more mistakenly, about new openings for emigration; they regarded investment as a casual instrument. Their measuring-stick was power, not profit. When they disputed over tropical African territory or scrambled for railway concessions in China, their aim was to strengthen their respective empires, not to benefit the financiers of the City. Hobson showed that imperialism did not pay the nation. With longer experience, we can even say that it does not pay the investors. But the proof, even if convincing, would not have deterred the advocates of imperialism. They were thinking in different terms.

The economic analysis breaks down in almost every case which has been examined in detail. Morocco has often been treated as a classical case of finance-imperialism, by Brailsford himself and in more detail by E D Morel. In fact, the French financiers were forced to invest in Morocco, much against their will, in order to prepare the way for French political control. They knew they would lose their money, and they did. But Morocco became a French protectorate. Again, Brailsford made much play with the British investment in Egypt, which Cromer had promoted. But Cromer promoted these investments in order to strengthen British political control, and not the other way round. The British held on to Egypt for the sake of their empire; they did not hold their empire for the sake of Egypt. Even the Boer War was not purely a war for financial gain. British policy in South Africa would have been exactly the same if there had been no gold-mines. The only difference is that, without the profits from the dynamite monopoly, the Boers would have been unable to put up much resistance. Rhodes was a great scoundrel in radical eyes, and quite rightly. But not for the reasons that they supposed. Rhodes wanted wealth for the power that it brought, not for its own sake. Hence he understood the realities of politics better than they did.

Those who explained imperialism in terms of economics were rationalists themselves and therefore sought a rational explanation for the behaviour of others. If capitalists and politicians were as rational as Hobson and Brailsford, this is how they would behave. And of course a minority did. They took their profits, agreed with their enemy on the way and died quietly in their beds. But they did not set the pattern of events. It is disturbing that, while Hobson and Brailsford were so penetrating about the present, they were wrong about the future. Hobson ignored Europe altogether – rightly, since he was discussing colonial affairs. He expected the international capitalists to join in the exploitation of China and even to recruit Chinese armies with which to hold down the workers of Europe. Brailsford looked to Europe only to reject it. He wrote – this in March 1914: 'the dangers which forced our ancestors into European coalitions and continental wars have gone never to return'. And again, 'it is as certain as anything in politics can be, that the frontiers of our modern national states are finally drawn. My own belief is that there will be no more wars among the six Great Powers.' Even if there were a war, 'it is hard to believe that . . . German Socialists would show any ardour in shooting down French workmen. The spirit which marched through Sedan to Paris could not be revived in our generation.' It may be unfair to judge any writer in the light of what came after. Yet men with far less of Brailsford's knowledge and intellectual equipment foresaw the conflict of 1914, and even the shape that it would take. The true vision of the future was with Robert Blatchford, when he wrote his pamphlet, 'Germany and England', for the *Daily Mail*.

This is a sad confession. Hobson and Brailsford are our sort. We think like them, judge like them, admire their style and their moral values. We should be ashamed to write like Blatchford, though he was in fact the greatest popular journalist since Cobbett. Yet he was right, and they were wrong. Their virtues were their undoing. They expected reason to triumph. He knew that men love power above all else. This, not imperialism, is the besetting sin. Lenin knew it also. Hence, though a rationalist by origin, he turned himself into a wielder of power. Thanks to him, there is nothing to choose between Rhodes and a Soviet commissar. Nothing except this: the capitalist may be sometimes corrupted and softened by his wealth; the Soviet dictators have nothing to wear them down. If the evils which Hobson and Brailsford discovered in capitalism had been in fact the greatest of public vices, we should now be living in an easier world. It is the high-minded and inspired, the missionaries not the capitalists, who cause most of the trouble. Worst of all are the men of power who are missionaries as well.

The Jameson Raid

This essay was first published as a review of Jean van der Poel's The Jameson Raid *(Oxford, Clarendon Press, 1951) in the* Manchester Guardian, *24 January 1952.*

* * *

The Jameson Raid of 29 December 1895 is one of the most controversial episodes in recent British history. Was Joseph Chamberlain implicated in it? For many years it was thought that the answer might be found in the 'missing' telegrams, exchanged between Cecil Rhodes and his London agents, which were produced before the Select Committee of Inquiry. Garvin published extracts from these in the third volume of his *Life of Chamberlain* and argued that while Chamberlain knew that a revolution against Boer rule was being prepared at Johannesburg (a revolution which never came off) he did not know that Rhodes and Jameson were gathering a force outside the Transvaal to go to the aid of the rising. This, though damning enough, was still inconclusive and it was supposed that a final verdict could never be reached. A South African scholar has now opened a new source. Sir Graham Bower, imperial secretary to Robinson, the high commissioner, was the 'fall-guy' of the Jameson affair. His official superiors persuaded him to admit his own complicity but to deny that of Robinson or of Chamberlain. He had his career ruined as a reward. Though he loyally kept silence until death, he left his papers and a full record for future historians. They are decisive: the mud sticks to Chamberlain and to others besides.

The idea of engineering a rising in Johannesburg was devised by Rhodes in the days of the Liberal government. It was approved by Rosebery, and Sir Hercules Robinson, a shareholder and director of Rhodes's concerns, was appointed high commissioner in the belief that he would be clay in Rhodes's hands. Bower was sent out with him to keep the technical side of things in order. When Chamberlain took over the Colonial Office in July 1895, Rhodes was in high hopes. It was the essence of his plan that a force should be stationed outside the Transvaal, ready to make a dash for Johannesburg, and territory in Bechuanaland Protectorate had to be handed over to Rhodes's company in order to make this possible. This is the key point: if Robinson and Chamberlain knew why Rhodes wanted this land, they condoned and encouraged the raid.

It is now clear that they both knew. Robinson said to Bower after a talk with Rhodes: 'The less you and I have to do with those damned conspiracies of Rhodes and Chamberlain the better. I know nothing about them.' But, adds Bower, 'he ordered me to allow the troops to come down to Pitsani' (the jumping-off ground for the raid). As to Chamberlain, he wrote to Robinson on 2 October asking for his views on a rising at Johannesburg, 'with or without assistance from outside'.

In December 1895 the conspirators at Johannesburg began to falter. Fairfield, assistant undersecretary at the Colonial Office, told Bower later 'he had written to Mr Chamberlain at Birmingham suggesting that the revolution be damped down. Chamberlain had replied telling him to hurry it up on account of the Venezuela dispute [with the United States]. He had therefore instructed Lord Grey and Maguire accordingly and they had telegraphed in the sense I have given.' Bower saw Rhodes show this telegram to Robinson on 20 December. It has been alleged by Garvin and others that the telegrams urging Rhodes to hurry came only from Rutherford Harris, his shady man-of-affairs, and that they were designed to blackmail Chamberlain. This will not do for Earl Grey and Maguire, a fellow of All Souls. Chamberlain later intended to put the blame on Fairfield, who wrote to Bower that 'he was to be the scapegoat of the Colonial Office and was to be disavowed'; he would be required 'to conform his evidence to that of the others'. Fairfield, however, died suddenly before he could have the pleasure of perjuring himself for the sake of Joseph Chamberlain. Rhodes, at any rate, had no doubts. When Bower expostulated, Rhodes replied, 'Then you are disloyal to your chief, Chamberlain, who is hurrying me up.'

Of course part of Chamberlain's defence is technically true. He did not know that there would be a raid without a revolution. But no one knew this, neither Rhodes nor Jameson himself. The latter decided on it spontaneously when the revolution in Johannesburg 'fizzled out'. But that there was to be a raid as well as a revolution was planned by Rhodes, authorized by Chamberlain, and known to Robinson. The raid did immeasurable harm in South Africa. More than any other single event it caused the Boer War, and it left an estrangement between Boer and Briton which is not yet removed. The authors of the Jameson Raid were those two builders of empire Cecil Rhodes and Joseph Chamberlain.

Why did this not come out at the time? Far from Rhodes blackmailing Chamberlain, it was Chamberlain who blackmailed Rhodes. He threatened to take away the charter of the British South Africa Company if the telegrams came out, and Rhodes paid the price of silence. According to Bower the attorney-general thought that the only telegram that 'could not be explained away' was the Grey–Maguire message. It was not produced at the inquiry, nor has it been published by Garvin. Bower would not 'fling all the mud at Rhodes and Jameson'. Therefore he was instructed to confess that he had known of the preparations for the raid but had not told either Robinson or the Colonial Office. Rhodes said to him: 'If you branch off and divulge this correspondence old Robinson will be carried into the box in his bandages like the dying Chatham and will give you the lie. He will be backed by Chamberlain, and at the day of judgement those two old men will shake hands and say they did the right thing.'

Why did the Liberals on the Select Committee swallow this suppression? Miss van der Poel suggests that they knew that Rosebery had been involved in the original plans for a rising and were afraid to discredit their former leader. This seems unlikely. It appears from Harcourt's *Life* that they were content to have secured a unanimous condemnation of Rhodes. No doubt they did not realize the weight of evidence against Chamberlain or appreciate how he had behaved. For, in fact, Chamberlain stood in exactly the same relation to Rhodes and Jameson as Hitler stood to Henlein and the Sudeten Germans in 1938. Perhaps it was this which made Neville Chamberlain listen so sympathetically to Hitler's tales of innocence. They were no worse than those which Joseph Chamberlain had dished up to the Committee of Inquiry.

The Boer War

This essay was first published as ' The Boer War: The Issues after Fifty Years' in the Manchester Guardian, *11 October 1949.*

* * *

On 11 October 1899 the Boer ultimatum expired and Boer forces crossed the frontier into Natal. The Boers hoped to overrun all South Africa before British forces arrived; more remotely, they had hoped for the intervention of European powers. The British, on their side, had expected the Boers to give way without a struggle; at worst, in Milner's words, 'an apology for a fight' would be necessary. 'A slap in the face' would do the business. Though Boer hopes were disappointed, British hopes were disappointed also. The war dragged on for three years, and by the end the eclipse of Boer independence was of less importance than the deflation of British imperialism. In fact, the Boer War had a more decisive effect on British politics than on imperial history. It brought first the culmination and then the end of an arrogant, boastful epoch, in which British public opinion seemed to have abandoned principles for power – the political equivalent of that *fin de siècle* spirit in art and literature which produced decadence and Oscar Wilde.

The Boer War caused a bitterness in British politics without parallel since the great Reform Bill and never equalled since except in 1914 during the Ulster rebellion (and perhaps, briefly, at the time of Munich). 'Pro-Boer' was a more opprobrious epithet than ever 'pro-German' became in either German war. No minister during these later world conflicts openly regretted the escape of an opponent from physical violence or even death as Chamberlain regretted Lloyd George's escape from Birmingham Town Hall. His comment was: 'What is everyone's business is nobody's business.'

This bitterness had many causes. Every dispute in which Chamberlain was involved was conducted in a savage, scurrilous way (on both sides); the Boer War gave the cheap press its first chance to display its quality; most of all, the war had the bitterness of a family quarrel – not merely a quarrel within the empire but a quarrel in England between politicians of the same party origin. Imperialism and anti-imperialism were both advocated by men of Liberal background. Even Disraeli had been originally a radical; Milner, Chamberlain, and their associates had all started as Liberals; and Milner's friends were still mostly Liberals – it was Grey, Haldane, and Asquith whom he visited when he came to England. In the same way Rosebery, not Salisbury, had been the most imperialist of prime ministers. Old Toryism, with its roots in the countryside, had little sympathy with the aggressive and optimistic spirit of imperialism. In August 1899 Salisbury passed this verdict on the coming war: 'We have to act upon a moral field prepared for us by Milner and his Jingo supporters. And therefore I see before us the necessity for considerable military effort – and all for people whom we despise and for territory which will bring no profit and no power to England.'

Salisbury was dragged into war by Chamberlain; and Chamberlain was dragged into war by Milner. Certainly Chamberlain wanted to establish British supremacy in South Africa; this he had hoped to do gradually, by persuasion and the passage of time. But Chamberlain was fatally compromised by his association with the Jameson Raid, the greatest blunder in his career. The raid ruined the chance of the Boer moderates and made it certain that Milner would have to deal with Kruger and his associates, men as violent and as obstinate as himself. Milner was a great administrator, but no statesman and no diplomatist. He hated inefficiency and delay; most of all, he hated compromise. With German dogmatism he wrote on 16 August 1899: 'They will collapse if we don't weaken, or rather if we go on steadily turning the screw.' Milner had a great vision of a British South Africa, which would escape dependence on the gold-mines by wise economic planning and by raising the standard of life of the native population: he destroyed this vision by his impatience with the Boers. After the Jameson Raid the Boer War was probably inevitable, but it was Milner who determined that it should come when it did and in the way it did.

Milner made a mistake not uncommon among civilian politicians: he supposed that the soldiers would conduct the war as competently as he had brought it about. The early disasters could be repaired; what could never be repaired was the prestige of imperialism, on which Milner and Chamberlain had staked their political existence. Even worse than the blow to prestige was the damage to England's moral position on the continent of Europe. No war has been so

unanimously condemned by enlightened European opinion. Even forty
years afterwards, every European, though few Englishmen, recognized
the taunt in the Nazi 'concentration camps', which deliberately paro-
died in name and nature the British 'methods of barbarism'. Yet it will
not do for the later historian to react against this by idealizing the
Boers, as the pro-Boers did at the time. Though the Boers fought to
preserve their independence they were even more concerned to preserve
other, and less admirable, things: their policy of racial exclusion; their
share of gold profits; and their tyranny over the natives.

Fifty years afterwards, it is clear that victory has gone to the worst
elements on both sides. Milner got his war without achieving his
vision; the Boers lost their independence without being won for
progress and civilization; soon the British citizen in South Africa will
be again an *uitlander*, as he was before the Boer War. The mining
houses and the most narrow-minded Boers, Johannesburg and Pre-
toria, have joined hands to oppress and exploit the native peoples who
are the overwhelming majority of the population, and Smuts, the last
general of the Boer War, lived to accuse the prime minister of South
Africa of using 'the methods of Fascism'. If Milner could see the
results of victory, or Campbell-Bannerman the results of Boer self-
government, would either have reason to be proud of his handiwork?

The pro-Boers were wrong about the Boers; they were right about the
war. The great underlying issue at stake was not whether the Boers stood
for a moral cause but whether the British Empire stood for one. Milner
and Chamberlain had appealed from principles to power; the pro-Boers
reasserted the claims of principle, and four years after the end of the war
this despised minority received at the polls the greatest majority that any
party had won since the Reform Act. Many men fought bravely in the
Boer War, but none acted more bravely or served his country better than
the politician who declared in the St James's Hall on 15 September 1899:

You may make thousands of women widows and thousands of children
fatherless. It will be wrong. You may add a new province to your Empire. It
will still be wrong. You may give greater buoyancy to the South African
stock and share market. You may create South African booms. You may
send the price of Mr Rhodes's Chartereds up to a point beyond the dreams
of avarice. Yes, even then it will be wrong.

The outbreak of the Boer War were better passed over in silence, were
it not for the occasion it gives for reprinting Morley's words.

Milner: The Man of No Luck

This essay on Lord Milner (1854–1925) first appeared as a review of John Evelyn Wrench's Alfred Lord Milner. The Man of No Illusions *(London, Eyre and Spottiswoode, 1958) in the* Observer, *24 August 1958. Milner, whose early politics were Liberal then Liberal Unionist, was created a viscount in 1902 at the recommendation of Lord Salisbury's Conservative and Unionist government. After he had left office in 1921 he married Lady Violet Cecil (the widow of Lord Salisbury's fourth son). In reviewing another book on Milner in 1964 Alan Taylor drew the conclusion: 'The Right was a real danger to British democracy, the Left never.'*

*   *   *

Alfred Milner had great abilities and many devoted admirers. He achieved great things. He established British supremacy in South Africa. He played a decisive part in the war cabinet during the First World War, particularly when he took the lead in making Foch Allied commander-in-chief. He was honoured by the Crown and by the University of Oxford.

Yet there was some flaw in him. Things always went wrong at the point of triumphant success. In South Africa he manoeuvred Kruger into declaring war, only to discover that the British generals were unready for it. His work of reconstruction after the Boer War began to bear fruit just when the Liberals won the general election of 1906 and tore his work to pieces. He cooperated with Lloyd George loyally throughout the war, only to be publicly humiliated by him within a month of the armistice.

It was the same in his private life. When he shared a house with his cousin, she turned out to be a dipsomaniac. He fell in love with Margot Tennant, only to be told that an unfortunate love-affair had destroyed her capacity for feeling (this did not prevent her marrying Asquith less than two years later). The final episode of his life had the same character. He was 'deemed to be duly elected' Chancellor of Oxford University as from 25 May 1925. He died on May 13.

Napoleon used to ask of a man: 'Has he Luck?' It is tempting to suggest that this was the quality which Milner lacked. Yet there was also something missing in his personality. Mrs Barnett wrote of him when young: 'Tall, dignified, and grave beyond his years . . . eager to organize rather than to influence, and fearful to give generous impulses free rein.' Elinor Glyn noted many years later: 'I cannot love him – I love only one. But . . . we shall write. That side of me he can safely have, the intellectual. He shall be the friend of my ideals.'

Milner himself decided, soon after leaving Oxford, that since he could not afford both a wife and public service, he would remain celibate. This was curiously calculating, and wrongheaded at the same time; for the man who became High Commissioner in South Africa and could have been Viceroy of India need not have found a wife beyond his means.

Sir Evelyn Wrench calls him 'the man of no illusions'. But in fact he was always being diddled by people perhaps less intelligent but certainly more adroit than he was. Margot Tennant, for instance, with all her parade of a broken heart, clearly wanted to keep a distinguished admirer safely dangling; and got her wish for almost nothing. Asquith behaved as badly somewhat later. In 1903 Milner wished to introduce Chinese coolies into South Africa. Even Joseph Chamberlain demurred. Milner undertook to square the Liberals. He saw his Liberal friends – Asquith, Grey, Haldane; and all three agreed with his proposal. This did not prevent their joining in the outcry against 'Chinese slavery' a couple of years later; and all three sat silent in the House of Commons while the youthful Winston Churchill defended Milner in terms of contemptuous patronage. The breach with Lloyd George was also characteristic. Sir Evelyn Wrench puts it down to the tiredness general at the end of the war. But it surely had advantages for Lloyd George to shake Milner off once the war was won.

Perhaps what was really wrong with Milner was that he despised everyone less able than himself. His letters are full of phrases about 'our rotten political system'. I find this bewildering. Milner was a great 'imperialist'. Surely this means extending the British system of government with all its freedom and political controversy. Milner not only disliked parties. He disliked 'democracy'. This is really why he disliked the Boers, despite his claim that he wished to protect (paternally) the natives.

His violent opposition to home rule shows the same attitude. It sprang from dislike of the Irish rather than fondness for Ulster. Sir Evelyn Wrench reveals that Milner was to have become head of the Ulster movement if Carson had been arrested. Again, why? He was not an Irishman. He was not a Presbyterian nor even a zealous Protestant. He was merely a 'loyalist'. And of course, if he had succeeded Carson, he would have been once more the 'fall-guy', as with South Africa or the unpopular acts of the war cabinet. Bonar Law and F E Smith would have made violent speeches; Milner would have carried the blame.

He was at once too honest, too narrow, and too able to succeed in British politics. Like all the Milner kindergarten – Philip Kerr, Curtis, Geoffrey Dawson – he wanted to run things, without paying the democratic price. My own feeling is that he and his followers did immeasurable harm; but many judges whose opinion I respect think very differently.

It cannot be claimed that Sir Evelyn Wrench has written a particularly telling defence or even an effective biography. But it is full of valuable information, much of it new. Sir Evelyn Wrench has been carefully through Milner's papers, now at New College, and has made unrestrained use of them. No nonsense for him about the 'fifty-year rule'. For instance, he quotes passages from a memorandum which Milner wrote about the appointment of Foch as supreme commander. This is clear defiance of the ban on publishing 'cabinet papers'; and there is no statement that the permission of the cabinet office has been obtained. Will Sir Evelyn Wrench be prosecuted? I should guess not. In which case he, if not Milner, will have deserved well of 'the democracy'. Others will be free to follow the path which he has somewhat erratically blazed.

Hunting Slim Jannie

This essay on Jan Christian Smuts (1870–1950) first appeared as a review of W K Hancock's Smuts, Vol. I *(Cambridge, Cambridge University Press, 1962) in the* Observer, *28 October 1962. Smuts became prime minister of the Union of South Africa after Botha's death in 1919 until 1924 and again from 1939 to 1948. When reviewing the second volume in 1968 Alan Taylor wrote of Smuts: 'His principles were noble. His methods were devious and sometimes worse. Like Lloyd George he was a liberal who took the long way round.'*

*　　*　　*

Smuts was a hard man to catch. British troops found this when they were trying to keep up with his commando during the Boer War. Others found it later on occasions of high politics. Time and again Smuts seemed to be committed beyond escape. He always discovered some loophole of evasion or compromise.

He was the supreme Trimmer of his age, winning golden opinions from men who were in bitter conflict with each other, or from nearly all of them. He was a Boer nationalist and a British imperialist; the friend of generals and of Quakers. He outdid even Gandhi in subtlety. He was impervious to the wiles of Lloyd George. He played an important part in many great affairs from the Boer War to the Second World War, always with a slight air of philosophic detachment. A few distrusted him. Patrick Duncan wrote of him:

I only wish I thought that his fine sentiments were more intimately hitched on to the springs which govern his actions. They do sometimes get turned on, but they spend much of their time in the cupboard of his soul.

Smuts has found the biographer he deserved. Sir Keith Hancock is a historian of faultless grasp. He is a beautiful writer. Also he is not without guile. There is in this book no concealment of the charges against Smuts, no extenuation of his failings. There is only a soft blurring of outline, like the haze which comes up over the veldt or which comes up whenever Smuts was required to define his philosophy or his political intent with precision.

The first part of the book, dealing with the Boer War and its background, is the most outspoken, though at the expense of Milner, not of Smuts. Milner was one of the few men who ever 'made a war'; and it is welcome to have this set down clearly after some recent exercises in his favour. Smuts favoured compromise before the war; fought resolutely, though evasively, while it was on; and again favoured compromise afterwards. The British found him 'pleasant, plausible and cunning'. The outcome, indeed, was something of a miracle. The Boers lost the war and won the peace. When Botha became prime minister of the Transvaal, Smuts wrote: 'The British people have paid 250 million in cash and thousands in lives in order to make him prime minister.'

Sir Keith Hancock is very good on all this; very good too on the complicated diplomacy with which Smuts cajoled the Union of South Africa into being. Smuts wanted the union of races – by which he meant of course union of Briton and Boer. He kept quiet about the African or, as it was then called, 'the native question', perhaps because he hoped a future generation would solve it, perhaps for other reasons. This is one of the occasions on which Sir Keith Hancock walks softly – frank, one may say, without being brutal.

The question of the Indians in South Africa is a different matter. Here another saint of empire has to be allowed for. According to the blurb, 'Smuts stands with his friends Churchill and Gandhi in the front rank of Commonwealth and World statesmen.' A strange trio; it leads to the strange conclusion that Smuts tried to cheat Gandhi and almost succeeded. Gandhi, however, had the last word: he presented Smuts to Lord Irwin, yet another saint of empire as a realpolitiker, and so discredited both just a little.

Smuts reached world politics with the First World War, when he became a member of the British war cabinet. His position was characteristically vague or, a less friendly critic might say, two-faced. He was not a representative of the Commonwealth, and yet did not sit in either British house of parliament – a unique case in modern times, or perhaps ever. His acts were also supple. On Lloyd George's request, he investigated military prospects. He listed the advantages of an Eastern campaign; pressed the claims of attacking in Palestine, particularly if he were in command; and then came down on the side of Haig and the Western Front after all – to Lloyd George's intense disappointment.

He negotiated for peace with a representative of Austria-Hungary, and got nowhere. Thus he had the double gain of advocating the maintenance of Austria-Hungary and yet of showing that this was impossible. Lloyd George says that Smuts conducted the final, barren negotiations; his own records, according to Sir Keith Hancock, show that he was not in Switzerland at all. Here again is a competition in vagueness which Smuts won.

Smuts attended the peace conference as representative of South Africa, not as a member of the war cabinet. He secured German South West Africa, and was then free to criticize the appetites of others. His ingenuity devised the idea of including war pensions in the claim for reparations. His noble principles led him to condemn the harshness of the final treaty. He signed it as 'one sinner among many'. He encouraged Keynes to write against the treaty; and later advised him not to publish what he had written. His attitude was always finely balanced. He lived among Quakers at weekends, and regretted that his workaday commitments as a fighting man prevented his joining their Society.

This book is a model of political biography, clear, perceptive, judicious. There are no revelations. Lloyd George, Milner, Law, went off with their cabinet papers. So no doubt did Smuts. Sir Keith Hancock does not use them. Though he repudiates the title of 'official biographer', he respects the 'official' closing date of fifty years ago. The photograph on the dust-cover shows a Smuts appropriately quizzical. He has still not been caught.

Prince of Storytellers

This essay first appeared in the Observer, *13 April 1980, as a review of Guy Arnold's* Held Fast for England: G A Henty, Imperialist Boys' Writer *(London, Hamish Hamilton, 1980). In his autobiography Alan Taylor recalled that as a boy he had greatly enjoyed books by George Alfred Henty (1832–1900) and Harrison Ainsworth, contrasting them favourably with those by Stanley Weyman, who he felt 'used history as a sort of fancy dress'. He reminisced:*

At the opposite extreme were the books – you can hardly call them novels – of G A Henty. They were my favourites. I acquired many of them myself instead of depending on the public library. The best of them, still very good in my opinion, was *A Roving Commission* which, though blatantly anti-black as I noticed even at the time, gives a wonderful feeling of what a slave rebellion, or for that matter any rebellion, is like. I did not read any of Henty's books about the British Empire, having already written off that institution. That left me with one book after another about the Thirty Years War, each one if I remember aright turning on a single obscure battle. The best feature was the battle diagrams with the oblongs for the opposing forces of cavalry and infantry. I reproduced them on the attic floor with my toy soldiers, setting up one dreary battle after another. As a result of this craze, whether Henty's or mine I am not sure, the Thirty Years War is the only stretch of European history before the French Revolution I am safe on. I suppose my view of it is not much like that of adult historians.

*   *   *

At first retrospect G A Henty appears as a figure of fun: writer of eighty-two historical novels, not one of which contains a genuinely living character. His heroes are always impeccably moral and, what is more important, always emerge from their adventures triumphant. Even his villains would rank as heroes nowadays. There are virtually no heroines, only modest, slightly tomboyish girls, who provide an ending to the book by marrying the hero.

The British Empire is extolled. The coloured races come off badly except when they provide a faithful servant for some brave young Englishman. For that matter no foreigner except an occasional king attains the highest rank of excellence. The vocabulary is stilted, the narrative pedestrian. Guy Arnold's entertaining analysis of the eighty-two books provokes the embarrassing question, 'How on earth did I ever manage to read them?'

The reader of Henty must dream himself back into the golden years before the First World War if he is to find an answer to the question. Then all becomes clear. Henty's books are not novels in the accepted sense at all. They are tales of adventure such as have been told from the beginning of time. Developed characters would get in the way of the narrative. All the reader wanted was a slightly idealized version of himself – moral integrity combined with physical prowess, quick in mind and body, and success guaranteed after the occasional setback.

Guy Arnold implies that Henty was not above preaching lessons, whether of imperialism or morality. I think rather that Henty was concerned to reproduce ideas and outlooks that his readers already possessed. Henty was a storyteller first and a preacher second if at all. Once the reader identified with the hero events could move at a rattling pace. The novels are sociological documents in that they show what boys of the time were thinking rather than what they were being taught. I regarded Henty's imperialism and most of his morality as very great nonsense. But they seemed to me how most of my contemporaries saw things. I have one reservation to this. Even the most devoted admirers of Henty's books found them comic as well as exciting: they were too good to be true, but very good (my own opinion) all the same.

The essential merit of the Henty corpus for me was not so much the adventures, let alone the morality. It was the historical information that it provided with such clarity. Henty himself was a conscientious amateur historian. Before starting a novel he sent for ten books on its subject from the London Library. The result may seem dull to a later generation brought up on instant history. I can only answer that it was a great deal livelier than most of the textbooks then current or even than many of the works by respected historians.

Other writers of historical novels may be better novelists but they are not such good historians. Stanley Weyman provides romantic tushery; Harrison Ainsworth has a taste for horrors. Scott of course is incomparable in the role, but he has too many real characters for the teenage reader, or had in my day. Henty's history is on the whole rather good history. The conflicts are presented fairly. The battles are described effectively. The battle plans are clearer than many that appear nowadays in books of technical military history.

I liked the volumes on various aspects of the Thirty Years War the best, if only because I did not expect ever to concern myself with that dreary subject again. As a matter of fact, however, vague recollections from Henty carried me through when I had to lecture on the Thirty Years' War at Manchester University.

The Henty books stir an agreeable nostalgia. Their world is admirably simple, everything black or white as it should be. The information required comes in an acceptable form. When Guy Arnold deprecates the flatness of Henty's narrative, he has not realized how drab the history textbooks were at that time. Henty in comparison is exciting, almost intoxicating.

He had been a successful war correspondent before he took to writing historical novels and displayed in his novels the virtues of a newspaper correspondent – direct, clear and with no literary frills. Henty never aspired to be a 'writer'. He was merely doing an artisan's job. That won him 25 million readers. Probably it also deprived him of immortality. A journeyman, by definition, has no long-staying power.

Long, long ago I read the works of Henty with more eagerness, more enjoyment and more application than I did those of any other historical writer, perhaps even with more profit. I should not mind being acclaimed the Henty *de nos jours*. But I must confess that I do not want to read the works of Henty ever again. They belong to a vanished Arcadia.

Joseph Chamberlain

The first of these two essays, '"Joe" at his Zenith', first appeared in the Manchester Guardian, *8 June 1951, as a review of* The Life of Joseph Chamberlain, *Vol. IV, by Julian Amery (London, Macmillan, 1951).*

The second, 'Imperial Miscalculations', first appeared in the Observer, *13 July 1969, as a review of Vols. V and VI of Amery's* Life, *dealing with the periods 1901–3 and 1903–8 respectively (London, Macmillan, 1969).*

*   *   *

'Joe' at his Zenith

We have had to wait a long time for the *Life of Joseph Chamberlain*. The late J L Garvin gave up after publishing three volumes which carried the story to the end of 1900. Mr Julian Amery is to complete the task in the present and a subsequent volume. 'Joe' will receive five volumes where Mr Gladstone had to be content with three and most prime ministers with two or even one. Though Chamberlain's political importance does not justify this excessive length it was inevitable once Garvin was given the job; he was incapable of writing concisely, and the three volumes were composed in the oracular style of his famous *Observer* articles. Mr Amery was bound to follow the Garvin pattern of treatment, though not, fortunately, the Garvin style. The best that can be said of his book is this: since someone had to wield Garvin's bow, Mr Amery is to be congratulated on having done it successfully.

The present volume runs only from the end of 1900 until the spring of 1903, when Chamberlain returned from his visit to South Africa. He was overworked and getting old; as a result, the revelations in this volume are fewer and less interesting than previously. For instance, in spite of a valiant attempt by Mr Amery to build up Chamberlain as 'the chief author of the revolution in British foreign policy', there is nothing of importance on foreign affairs; the bulk of the story is taken from German documents long published. There is one document of interest: a memorandum of 10 September 1900 naïvely proposing to play off Germany against Russia in the Far East:

Both in China and elsewhere it is our interest that Germany should throw herself across the path of Russia ... the clash of German and Russian interests, whether in China or Asia Minor, would be a guarantee for our safety.

The other curiosity is the comment of Paul Cambon when he learnt that Chamberlain had become the advocate of friendship with France:

It must not be forgotten that Mr Chamberlain has no political principles. He lives in the present and changes his opinions with incredible ease; he is not in the least embarrassed by his own statements and contradicts himself with extraordinary ease. He has a very accurate sense of what public opinion wants and follows its fluctuations while having the air of guiding them – hence his popularity.

Mr Amery calls this judgement 'myopic'.

The two principal themes of the volume are South Africa and the origins of tariff reform. South Africa bulks the larger, though here again there is not much to add, especially to the material published from the Milner papers. It is clear that Chamberlain meant ultimately to give self-government to the Boers, equally clear that he meant to humiliate them first. There is an account here of the lamentable scene when he met the Boer generals who had come to Europe to seek help for their women and children:

A launch swept them out to *Nigeria* [the Colonial Secretary's ship]. There, on the deck, they came face to face, for the first time, with Chamberlain. The Colonial Secretary, immaculately dressed as ever, was accompanied by Roberts and the colonial dignitaries assembled for the Coronation. Behind him the battle fleet of Britain stretched out in four grey lines to the horizon. Amid the pageantry of Empire, the generals seemed awkward in their crumpled country clothes. For all their valour and cunning they were only simple farmers seeing the world for the first time.

This is how German historians used to write of Bismarck, but one of the Boer generals was called Botha. Would it have increased their faith in Chamberlain if they had known that Milner, his chosen pro-consul to whom he gave 'a Roman welcome', was writing in 1902: 'What I have seen of the working of "responsible government" in South Africa makes it wholly impossible for me to labour for its extension with any sort of zeal'; or that Chamberlain himself, who had once denounced the population of Johannesburg as 'devoted to money-making and their own interests', should write after his visit there: 'The population of this city . . . is keen, intelligent, and responsive, with an inclination to be too impatient and critical but still at the bottom intensely loyal and Imperialist.'

In fact, Chamberlain, once a social reformer, even – as Mr Amery calls him – a revolutionary, had energy without principle and became the willing prisoner of the most energetic men of his time, the great capitalist magnates, whether in London or Johannesburg. He thought of the empire as power or as an undeveloped estate, not as a moral cause, and he said, with profound misjudgement: 'The days are for great empires and not for little states.'

This led him to imperial preference and so, ultimately, to tariff reform. Mr Amery has been able to use the unpublished minutes of the Colonial Conference of 1902, and these show how Chamberlain's plans for imperial federation and for military unity broke on colonial resistance. The great colonies, Canada in particular, wished to be equal nations, not daughters of the mother country, and Chamberlain, without sentiment himself, could not conceive of a Commonwealth held together by sentiment alone. Imperial preference seemed to be the answer and it suited Canada's needs.

But there were also motives of domestic politics. As Mr Amery shows in the most interesting part of his book, imperial preference was taken up by Chamberlain in order to put new life into the dying party of Liberal Unionism. This had been essentially the party of the industrial middle class, which needed a separate organization so long as the Tory Party was 'a predominantly landed interest'. But now the Tory Party, too, had become a party of businessmen; they could promote their interests there without paying the price of social reform, on which Chamberlain had previously insisted. Hence, as Mr Amery points out, Chamberlain had to drop his advocacy of old-age pensions if he was to keep his followers. The one thing which discriminated the Liberal Unionists from the Tories was their Nonconformity, and here the Education Bill of 1902 was decisive. Chamberlain supported the Bill so as to have his hands free for South Africa, and he rammed it down the throats of his Nonconformist followers. Also, in part, he wanted to pay the Nonconformists out for having supported Gladstone. He said to a leading Nonconformist Liberal:

Had the Nonconformists supported me, they would have had Disestablishment long ago. Now they have got nothing. When Mr Gladstone suddenly sprang his Irish policy upon the country after consulting Morley, it was not so much to satisfy Ireland that he did so as to prevent me placing the Disestablishment of the Church of England in the forefront of the Liberal programme, as Mr Gladstone knew and feared I meant to do.

Since Chamberlain could no longer use a sectarian appeal for his party, he sought something else, and believed that imperial preference would do the trick. In the words of Lord George Hamilton, 'If we had had no Education Bill of 1902, we should have had no tariff reform in 1903.' The move was not designed only to salvage the Liberal Unionist Party; it was designed ultimately to oust Balfour from the leadership of a great party of imperial union. As it was, Chamberlain only managed to destroy the Unionist Party, as he had earlier destroyed the old Liberal Party. Like all men who split their party, he was a failure, slightly above the level of Ramsay MacDonald, a great deal below that of Lloyd George.

Imperial Miscalculations

Though I have written about Joseph Chamberlain before, the topic of these two volumes [the tariff reform campaign] seemed different enough from its predecessors as to justify inclusion.

Joseph Chamberlain was the greatest force in British politics between the decline of Gladstone and the rise of Lloyd George. He was a pioneer in social reform and municipal enterprise. He defeated Irish home rule. He inspired a new era in British imperialism and directed its triumph in the Boer War. When old age was already upon him, he challenged the accepted dogmas of free trade and launched the movement for tariff reform, which was to transform British economic life a generation after his death.

Despite these achievements, nothing went right with him. He stands pre-eminent as a splendid failure. Only the six counties of Northern Ireland remain in the United Kingdom, and even they have home rule. South Africa is a republic, dominated by the Boers. The British Empire is little more than a memory, and the last fragments of imperial preference survive only as an embarrassment for those who are clamouring to make Great Britain part of Europe. Chamberlain, it seems, was successful only in destruction, bringing ruin first to the Liberal, and then to the Unionist Party. Was he too impatient, too self-centred? Did he misjudge the climate of the times? These are riddles perhaps without an answer.

He has triumphed belatedly in one field. No man not a prime minister has had a biographical monument of such grandeur raised to his memory. J L Garvin, the famous editor of the *Observer*, produced three volumes of Chamberlain's life more than thirty years ago. Julian Amery, taking over the unfinished task, added a further volume and was then distracted by political activities. Electoral defeat has at last freed him to finish the work and with a grandiose conclusion. The two volumes now presented run to more than a thousand pages, though they cover only three years of Chamberlain's fully active life. The first hundred pages, it is true, are taken over from Volume IV, in order to make the story of tariff reform complete, and the last seventy pages continue this story from Chamberlain's death to the present day. Still, there is a formidable amount of reading.

The enthusiast for political biography would not have the book a page shorter. The details have the fascination provided by the analysis of a game of chess. Each pawn has its significance. Each move helps to determine the future. Chamberlain does not stand alone. All the great names in British politics pass before us. The Duke of Devonshire confesses: 'My knowledge of political economy is small, and I should find it very difficult to argue with either an expert free-trader or protectionist, and I am too old to begin.' Balfour of course is the key figure, perhaps concerned, as Mr Amery suggests, to hold the Unionist Party together, perhaps, however, even more concerned to defeat Chamberlain without caring much about either free-trade or protection.

Chamberlain set out to undo the work of Richard Cobden seventy years before. The Anti-Corn Law League was much better run, with better organization and more skilful speakers. Cobden gave the impression that he was really conducting a crusade. Chamberlain presented tariff reform as the offshoot of a cabinet squabble, which indeed it was. The campaign was started without adequate preparation. Chamberlain and his followers were not clear what British industries would benefit from colonial preference. They could not determine how much British food prices would rise – if at all. There were few reliable statistics and little practical information. The current talk was of 'a scientific tariff', but the only science involved was guesswork such as is shown at the gaming tables. In all the arguments, summarized by Mr Amery, the critics not surprisingly came off best. Chamberlain scored off Balfour; Asquith scored off Chamberlain; the sophisticated ingenuities went round and round.

Chamberlain had a vision of a united empire. Reading his speeches one after another, it is hard to feel that he ever translated this vision into practical terms. He initiated his campaign for colonial preference as a matter of imperial sentiment. This led him to advocate taxes on imported foodstuffs as the only counterpart which Great Britain could offer to the colonies. But the colonial advocates of preference were industrialists. The colonial farmers were free-traders, who in any case were already exporting all their wheat. In exchange they wanted cheap industrial goods and did not care whether these goods were British or American. Next, talk of food taxes raised the claims of British agriculture, a deserving cause which had little to do with imperial sentiment – and where Chamberlain was ignorant. Then, if British agriculture needed protection, why not British industry also? Yet Chamberlain asserted: 'I am not a protectionist.' He favoured tariffs only against dumping or, as Balfour did, for purposes of retaliation – putting them on in order to compel other countries to take them off.

The bewilderment of the voters was not surprising. This was an argument where the protagonists knew only that they disagreed with one another and hardly knew why. The practical decision sprang from 'stomach taxes'. It was the feeling against these which defeated tariff reform. Balfour recognized this, as Bonar Law and Baldwin did after him. The latter-day outcome has been paradoxical. Though we are still without food taxes, British agriculture now flourishes as never before, and such imperial preference as remains provides us with cheap food. Once the British people were asked to accept dear food for the sake of the empire. Now they are asked to accept it for the sake of Europe. Maybe the fear of stomach taxes will work its old magic and keep us out of the Common Market. All this is far from Chamberlain. His campaign, despite Mr Amery's epilogue, has become a historical curiosity.

*

Chamberlain's personality remains a puzzle even after six volumes of biography. He commanded great devotion, inspired great enthusiasm. He also provoked great hostility, perhaps more than any other British political figure in modern times. Even Lloyd George got off more easily. Mr Amery suggests correctly that he was never accepted by the political Establishment, and this was particularly tough in the Tory Party. He had also an arrogance which provoked and almost justified dislike. He had virtually no friends in politics – certainly not Balfour, despite their exchange of polite phrases, maybe only John Morley, and that friendship was little more than a reminiscence.

Fate worked against all the Chamberlains. Joseph, Austen and Neville in their different ways deserved better of their times than they achieved. Evidently bad luck becomes a habit, much like anything else. Now, however, the run is broken. Joseph Chamberlain has at least been lucky in his biographer.

Balfour: Odd Man In

This essay on A J Balfour (1848–1930), prime minister 1902–5, was first published in the New Statesman, *15 March 1963, as a review of Kenneth Young's* Arthur James Balfour *(London, Bell, 1963). The Mrs Dugdale referred to was the former Blanche Balfour, Balfour's niece. Alan Taylor often disapproved of Balfour, much as he did of Disraeli. Thus he wrote five years later of Balfour that he came over as 'a detestable man, cynical, unprincipled and frivolous'.*

* * *

Men in politics often profess a wish to be out of them. If anyone takes this seriously, they react, as Baldwin did, with the ferocity of a tiger. Balfour took a more elegant course. He spent his life in politics, and paraded an indifference which he often felt. He was fifty-five years in parliament, for twenty-six years a minister of the Crown. Few men have set a deeper mark on the history of their times. Balfour's Education Act, Balfour's Licensing Act, the Balfour declaration of Palestine as a national home for the Jews, the Balfour note on war-debts, the Balfour formula on Dominion status, make up an achievement second to none. He created the Committee of Imperial Defence; was largely responsible for the Anglo-Japanese alliance and the Anglo-French entente. He destroyed rivals with feline cunning. Both Randolph Churchill and Joseph Chamberlain were brought down by him. Yet his career was marked by failure. He was repudiated by his own followers. The experience gave him his first sleepless night since he left Eton.

Though Balfour loved power, he could not take the ordinary contentions of politics seriously. He was more curious to observe the fight than eager to win it. Most politicians would have been depressed by the crushing electoral defeat of 1906. Balfour was merely fascinated to watch the consequences which would follow the rise of the Labour Party. He wrote cheerfully: 'I am profoundly interested in what is *now* going on.' Photographed in a group of politicians, Balfour stands out by his detachment. Where other men strike imposing attitudes, Balfour's eyes are fixed on a speculative horizon. Mr Kenneth Young, in his excellent though occasionally sententious new biography, makes a wise remark. Balfour had passions, but they were low-powered. He had passion for philosophy, passion for politics, even, in a restrained way, passion for a woman. His intellect dominated these passions, and kept them under control. Clemenceau called Balfour 'an old maid'; and many people suspected that he had only an intellectual interest in the opposite sex. Mr Young reveals that this was not true. Balfour had a love-affair for many years with Mary, Lady Elcho, later Countess of Wemyss. He wrote to her constantly, saw her often, experienced 'intimacy' with her (her word) occasionally.

He brushed off sharply any suggestion that she might divorce her husband and marry Balfour. When she sent him a letter, now lost, apparently of physical endearment, he returned the letter, and wrote: 'If I am to speak all my mind, the mention of topics of such kind with shooting invitations, bicycles, cures for obesity and current literature is to my mind [word illegible] repulsion.' Evidently he made love to Mary Elcho just enough to discover what other men made such a fuss about. He was content to be the only bachelor prime minister since the younger Pitt.

Success came easily to Balfour. As Mr Young says, 'there was nothing that Balfour wanted that he could not have, nothing that he wanted to do that he did not do'. If he ever made an effort, he did not show it. He would have agreed with his sister Nora, married to an impotent man, who liked winking because 'it is the least tiring expression of emotion'. He inherited four million pounds from his grandfather, an Indian nabob. His uncle, the great Lord Salisbury, brought him early into politics, and soon placed him near the top. Balfour did not serve the arduous apprenticeship as either foreign secretary or chancellor of the exchequer which has been the lot of every other Conservative prime minister (and of nearly every Liberal prime minister) for the last century. He had a few years – arduous enough – as Irish secretary, then passed straight to be leader of the House of Commons, and never held a great executive office until he had become an elder statesman.

He criticized the work of others, and sometimes seconded it. He was less forthcoming with initiatives of his own. He was caught up, as prime minister, in the great row which Joseph Chamberlain provoked by demanding tariff reform. Balfour obviously thought that the row was folly. He wrote: 'I am not a protectionist'; nor was he, in any serious sense, a free-trader. The dispute had for him little intellectual interest. It was one of those delightful cases in which much should be said ingeniously on both sides, and to no purpose. 'Half a sheet of notepaper' was the contemptuous phrase with which he dismissed the merits of the controversy. He claimed to have held his party together. He did it only at the price of unbearable confusion.

It would be wrong to think of Balfour as a negative statesman. He was indeed unmoved by the ordinary topics of party dispute. These were, for him, a game, an intellectual diversion. As Irish secretary, he got as much satisfaction from exposing the inconsistencies of the home-rulers as from restoring order in Ireland. Mr Young writes: 'Campbell-Bannerman had always disliked Balfour, mainly because of Balfour's habit of making rings round him in Commons debate.' In fact, Campbell-Bannerman administered to Balfour perhaps the most crushing rebuke ever directed against a statesman: 'Enough of this foolery.'

Intellectual foolery was Balfour's incurable weakness. Intellectual policy was intermittently his strength. Birkenhead said that his was 'the finest brain that has been applied to politics in our time'. The remark was just, particularly when coming from Balfour's only intellectual peer. Balfour was that rare thing in politics, an intellectual extremist. Compromise has been the dominant theme in British politics: an illogical muddle between conflicting points of view. Balfour was incapable of it. He was an all-or-nothing man. He often evaded an issue. He sometimes settled one. He never sought a halfway house. He told the members of the Manchester Athenaeum: 'Of two evils it is better, perhaps, that our ship shall go nowhere than that it shall go wrong, that it should stand still than that it should run upon the rocks.' Yet no man hesitated less when he saw a course where the ship could go right.

This happened, for instance, with his Education Act of 1902. This could bring no party advantage – indeed much the reverse. Balfour did not count the cost, once he had recognized the need to get sectarianism out of education. He drove through one of the most ruthless and successful reforms of the century. Sir Harold Nicolson tells a characteristic story of Balfour as foreign secretary. The Foreign Office submitted two alternative policies, and asked: 'Which of these two courses do you wish us to adopt?' Balfour merely minuted: 'Yes. AJB.' When told that this was not a very helpful answer, Balfour replied: 'But when I wrote Yes I only meant that I agreed that there

were two courses open. I still agree with the proposition.' Sir Harold
Nicolson adds: 'And then something would happen and Mr Balfour
would be seized with galvanic energy and decision.' What happened
was the blinding flash of intellectual conviction. Balfour had the
intellectual courage to preserve an open mind and, more occasionally,
to undertake resolute action. This made him a powerful critic and,
sometimes, a great statesman. It was disastrous in a party leader.

Balfour's extremism appeared clearly in his attitude towards nationalism. He took the lead, for instance, against home rule. He gave
Ireland 'twenty years of resolute government'. Yet he was not fighting
the same battle as most Unionists. They were resisting Irish separatism.
Balfour was opposing home rule as neither one thing nor the other.
He believed that Ireland must either remain in complete subjection to
the imperial parliament, or else achieve an equally complete independence. When it proved impossible to maintain the first, he was not
greatly dismayed at the arrival of the second. He showed the same
extremism as foreign secretary during the First World War. Balfour
had not previously been distinguished by any enthusiasm for national
freedom. His heart did not beat with generous emotion during the
Midlothian campaign. Indeed, his only contribution then was to play
'a part, however small, in the acquisition of Cyprus'. Once set on the
defeat of Austria-Hungary, he became the most devoted advocate of
her subject nationalities, pressing their cause on a reluctant Lloyd
George. He became, even more urgently, the champion of the Jews.

Here his sceptical spirit was, for once, overcome by a belief which
had remained unshaken for two thousand years. His reason was on
the same side. He had always doubted whether there was a certain
and secure place for Jews in Gentile society. His Zionism was a form
of anti-Semitism: the Jews should go to their own place. Zionism, in
his mind, was a logical arrangement; and Balfour, in sponsoring it,
gave no more thought to the Arabs than he had done at an earlier
point in his career to the native Irish.

Balfour was a great political figure, also a great failure. He was
great in organization, great in achievement which brought no party
advantage, hopeless in holding a party together. Opposition after
1906 showed his worst qualities. The shattered Unionist Party needed
the inspiration of some mighty cause. Balfour offered it only the
entertainment of intellectual contradiction. He delighted in entangling
the Liberal government over speculations about how many Dread-

noughts Germany might have in some hypothetical circumstances. He had no answer to Lloyd George's programme of welfare. He refused to join a coalition in 1910, yet did not know why he had refused. His resistance to the Parliament Act was again a game. He ran resistance to the last moment, then dropped it as a matter of no importance.

There is a fascinating exchange of letters in this book between Balfour and the king's private secretary, Stamfordham. Balfour asked: 'Has the king agreed to create an unlimited number of peers?' Stamfordham replied: 'No, only enough to carry the Parliament Bill.' Balfour asked again: 'Does this mean then a limited number, say 120?' Stamfordham again: 'No, enough to carry the Bill.' And so on, Stamfordham becoming increasingly impatient, Balfour increasingly contemptuous. In the end, Balfour dismissed further resistance as 'the music-hall attitude of mind'. This may have been a correct description. It was not a tactful one. And it is not surprising that soon afterwards Balfour's followers turned against him. Mr Young thinks that this was the moment when the businessmen took over the Conservative Party from the landed gentry. I doubt it. Balfour never showed any concern for the landed interest, despite being a large landowner himself. He showed little taste for the society of landed gentry. He preferred clever women and academic philosophers. He speculated about life after death, not about the price of wheat. Bonar Law and his backer Max Aitken, 'the little Canadian adventurer who sits for Ashton-under-Lyne', did not want the rule of businessmen. They wanted a Conservative Party which would fight hard for simple ends.

Balfour has had to wait long for an adequate biography. The two volumes by Mrs Dugdale, though not without charm, were restrained by family piety. Mr Young has now done the work properly. His book will take a permanent place among political biographies. It covers every aspect of Balfour's life: his philosophy, his scientific interests, his social life, even his obsession with turning peat into a profitable fuel. There are many good stories, ranging over half a century. In the early pages, Bismarck displays a knowledge of the works of Sir Walter Scott. Bismarck said: 'When we were young we all had to read Sir Walter. He was considered so very proper.' Towards the end, George V complains to Balfour, as Chancellor of Cambridge University, that 'a certain tutor is a Communist propagandist and is no doubt sowing seeds of sedition'. Balfour replied tactfully 'that the man concerned did not seem to be particularly pressing his views'. Mr Maurice Dobb may be relieved at this acquittal.

Mr Young's book provokes two grumbles. Though his book is a work of scholarship, he is ashamed of being a scholar. The references are tucked away at the end; and there is no indication in the text that they exist. A reader can go right through the book without appreciating that it is carefully based on documents. This is a tiresome trick, which is becoming increasingly common. Mr Young is not to be blamed for the other failing. Balfour's papers were divided after his death into personal and political-cum-philosophical. The personal papers remained at Whittinghame; most of the other papers were deposited in the British Museum. When Mr Young came to work on these papers, he learnt that 'about a third of the material has been barred to the historian by the Cabinet Office and other government departments on so-called "security" grounds'. This is an absurd position. The papers are the property of Balfour's family; yet even a historian authorized by the family cannot see them. Mr Young says well:

From the historian's point of view, owners of political papers cannot be too strongly urged in present circumstances to keep control of their property for once it is handed to the British Museum they are not even allowed to give permission for historians to see their own property.

The United States government is already making available 'top secret' material from the war of 1939–45. Lord Avon was allowed to exploit indiscriminately the records of the Foreign Office during the thirties. A qualified historian is unable to study adequately Balfour's work as foreign secretary. What can there be so disgraceful in British foreign policy during, and after, the First World War, which it is still necessary to hide?

Shaw: The Court Jester

First published in the Observer, *22 July 1956.*

* * *

An article written for the centenary of Shaw's birth on 26 July 1856. Perhaps this essay is a little ungrateful in view of the pleasure and intellectual stimulus I derived from Shaw's writing. Even if he had nothing to say, he said it incomparably well.

Bernard Shaw lived to be ninety-four, and we are still dominated by personal memories on the hundredth anniversary of his birth. In time these will fade. The rich brogue and challenging beard, the homespun knickerbocker suit and the infectious laugh, the inexhaustible appetite for jest and controversy – they will become incidents in volumes of reminiscences. Sooner or later we must ask – what of Shaw as a writer? Still more, what of Shaw as he claimed to be, a sage and philosopher? Will he last as long as Shakespeare? Or will he be forgotten like his contemporary Stephen Phillips?

We ought to be able to answer these questions even now. For though Shaw the man was with us until just the other day, Shaw the writer had worn out long before. Indeed, the creative Shaw had a curiously short run. He wrote his first play when he was nearly forty. *Saint Joan*, his last serious achievement, came out in 1924 – a working span of less than thirty years and an ironic comment on his view that men would achieve more by living longer.

Shaw had one superlative quality. He was the greatest arguer there has ever been. All Irishmen have the gift of the gab. Shaw out-talked everyone for fifty years. He was greater than Burke, greater than Swift, in the art of political advocacy. Start reading a preface or play at any point, and you are swept away by the torrent of words, all criticism or doubt bludgeoned down. But scramble to the bank, recover your sense, and look around. Shaw was marvellous over a short distance; he could not sustain an argument for more than a paragraph.

This is why plays suited him so well. A second character could always interrupt when the first ran dry. There is no development; only statement and counter-statement. All Shaw's plays anticipate the round-table discussions which are now a stock-in-trade of radio – discussions without shape or conclusion, designed to show off the personality of the four distinguished contributors.

The Intelligent Woman's Guide showed most clearly Shaw's lack of staying-power. Though no one else could have written such dazzling pages, any intelligent woman could have written a better guide to almost anything – as one intelligent woman, Beatrice Webb, remarked.

Shaw was an Irishman of the ascendancy, stradding between England and Ireland, and despising both. He had the arrogance which comes of belonging to a master-race – always ready to assert his own opinion and to reject authority. But he had also the sycophancy which comes of being a poor relation. Just as Burke always curried favour with his patron, the Marquis of Rockingham, so Shaw never offended his patrons, the enlightened *rentiers* of Edwardian England who filled the stalls for his plays and bought his books. He was outrageous only on things that were too silly to matter – defending the flat earth theory or jeering at medical science. Fine stuff to make a boy think when he is working for a scholarship, but not dangerous.

On all serious questions Shaw came down firmly on the side of the stronger, though satisfying his conscience by the use of perverse arguments, much like Sir Henry Wilson – his fellow Irishman. He supported the Boer War and welcomed the first war against Germany as 'the last spring of the old Lion'; the neutrality of Belgium was, he held, a fiction, and British policy a trap for Germany deliberately laid by Sir Edward Grey. He worshipped strong men. In his prime he chose Julius Caesar and Napoleon as the heroes of his historical plays; and he outdid all contemporaries in his admiration for Mussolini and Stalin. Even when he glorified a heretic he took care to choose Joan of Arc – someone safely canonized and not associated with any really dangerous idea. William Morris dreamt of John Ball. But Morris had really burnt his boats so far as the governing classes were concerned. Shaw was a court jester who never lost his place at the high table.

He was certainly a socialist, and a hard-working one. But his socialism was 'off-stage', like Rigoletto's life with his daughter. And even this socialism sprang from intellectual arrogance, not from sympathy. To Shaw every working man was a Caliban, to be despised or, sometimes, feared. The working classes were brought into his plays as comic relief – dustmen or chauffeurs, caricatured and debauched to make sport for their betters. Shaw was the most snobbish of all English writers; the more offensive when he disguised his snobbery as worship of the superman.

Revealed religion had lost its force in the England of his day, and instead every literary man was expected to have a 'message'. Shaw did his best to oblige; he, too, would be a moral teacher. A comparison with Wells shows how tawdry Shaw's message was. Wells really understood the barrenness and frustration of contemporary society, and he had a vision of a more constructive, hopeful future. Shaw was merely impatient with human stupidity, and supposed that this would be cured if men tried to live longer. He learnt a twaddle of biology secondhand from Samuel Butler, and the only man who has ever applied this Shavian biology is Lysenko, hardly a disciple to be proud of.

Shaw despised humanity, despite his desire to prolong men's days. He was himself always rational, never knew passion either for good or ill. He was incapable of resentment, but also incapable of love. This gives his plays their peculiar character. The essence of drama is human tension: there is no tension in Shaw's play, only debate. What playgoer has sat forward in his stall, racked with anxiety whether Ann Whitefield will marry John Tanner?

Shaw was a materialist in the strictest sense – a true representative of the Edwardian age in which he flourished best. He loved money, and the things that money would buy – tasteless comfort in de luxe hotels, swimming in heated baths and warm southern seas. He was a teetotaller, a vegetarian, a non-smoker, not from asceticism, but in order to savour the pleasures of life more. One has the feeling that Shaw was never unhappy, and therefore he was never happy either. He knew only pleasure, a very different thing.

At the end of his life Shaw confessed that he stood for nothing. He, the missionary, the advocate, the socialist, might have been expected to bequeath his hoarded wealth to some great cause. The only one he could think of was the promotion of a new alphabet – not even words, but letters. The magic of Shaw's words may still bewitch posterity. It will applaud the last sentence of *Man and Superman*: 'Go on talking.' But it will find that he has nothing to say.

The Man Who Tried to Work Miracles

First broadcast as a radio talk on the BBC's Third Programme, 7 July 1966,
and published in the Listener, *21 July 1966.*

*   *   *

An article for the centenary of H G Wells's birth on 21 September 1866. Though I owe more to Bernard Shaw than to any other single writer, I owe more to H G Wells's *Outline of History* than to any other single book.

H G Wells did not expect to last. He did not even want to last, or so he claimed: 'What I write goes now – and will presently die.' He was not interested in being a literary artist, though he had in fact great literary gifts. He was, he insisted, a journalist, someone who wrote for the day and who 'delivered the goods'. He would be disappointed if the hundredth anniversary of his birth were marked only by discussions of Wells as a novelist. He would want to know what had happened to his ideas. Had men listened to his message? Had they taken what he believed to be the only way to salvation? The answer would be at first sight even more disappointing for him. His novels and scientific romances survive as entertainment – widely read in paperbacks. Hardly anyone bothers about Wells as a thinker, perhaps no one except a devoted young American, W Warren Wager, who has written a book about *H G Wells and the World State* and has produced more recently an anthology of Wells's prophetic writings.

Still I would not dismiss Wells lightly. Going back to his books after not reading them for many years, I found all sorts of ideas which are running round the world with little appreciation that Wells started them. Not that his ideas were as original as he claimed. Wells was more a representative man than an originator. This does not make him any the less interesting. Of course his literary gifts are what really count, whatever Wells said in depreciation of them. Taken simply as a writer, Wells had two qualities, and these keep him alive. The first was a gift for social comedy. His best book, *The History of Mr Polly*, is a work of irresistible fun. I would say the same, with some reservations, about *Tono-Bungay* and, with more, about *Kipps*. But even his least inspired books have occasional flashes of the same spirit. None of his characters is real – and that goes, to my mind, even for the much-vaunted *Ann Veronica*. They are caricatures or Humours in the Jonsonian sense. Mr Pooter, also a comic figure, is a hundred times more real than Mr Polly – you can still meet him in many a suburban street. Does anyone believe in Mr Polly, in Uncle Ponderevo or in Kipps? They are creatures of fantasy to whom comic things happen.

And not only comic things. Each book by Wells begins more or less realistically, usually in rather depressing surroundings, and then the principal character escapes by a miracle. I do not mean merely by an unlikely twist. I mean by something preposterously impossible. Mr Polly finds an impossible plump middle-aged woman, who owns an impossible riverside inn. Uncle Ponderevo invents an impossible patent medicine and makes an impossible fortune. Kipps comes into an impossible fortune not once but twice. None of Wells's characters gets out of his difficulties by his own strength. The escape comes from outside. It happens to him. The characters who do not escape go off at the end of the book to 'think things out', an implication that they will rescue themselves. But if they have not managed to 'think things out' during the course of a long book – and they never have – why should they succeed afterwards? Thinking things out only means waiting for a miracle instead of experiencing one.

The need for a miracle even in Wells's apparently realistic novels was of course much greater in his scientific fantasies, was indeed the essence of them. This was Wells's other great gift, one still more unusual – I would venture to say unique. He could pretend and then take the pretence seriously. He would postulate one simple impossible step – a food which produced giants, a man who slept for 200 years, a war of the worlds – and then he would work out calmly, realistically, what would follow. The overwhelming feature of his scientific fantasies is that they are not fantasies, except for the one impossible twist. They are exactly what would happen 'if only . . .'

Wells could really live in the imaginary situation which he had created and sometimes, to his dismay, his imagination took him prisoner. He always wanted a glowing future, but the future of his fantasies often turned out to be most unpleasant. At any rate, for good or ill, Wells in these fantasies was 'the man who could work miracles' – the title of one of his stories which was later made into a film.

Wells, the thinker and prophet, was the same: he could work miracles, or at any rate wanted to work them. Here again he had the right patter and often the right imagination. He made many inspired guesses about the future developments of machines. For instance he described full-scale battles in the air almost before heavier-than-air machines had got off the ground. He announced more than fifty years ago that men would get to the moon, though he did not foretell correctly what they would find when they got there – but this is hardly surprising, for it seems that they found precisely nothing. At a time when motor cars had hardly started, Wells foresaw that the traffic in cities would grind to a halt, as we all know it is doing, and he anticipated other, more sensible forms of transport, such as moving platforms – an idea which is just being aired now. He also foresaw that, thanks to the motor car, everyone would desert cities for the country and that, in this way, the country would disappear, another gloomy and correct prophecy. He had unbounded faith in the beneficent effects of electricity, a faith which he shared with Lenin, and expected that electrical devices would end the drudgery of housework. And so they have, though only at the price of turning the housewife into their slave. He was sure that one day we should all live on a scientific diet of pills, another prophecy which threatens to come true.

These prophecies were wrapped up in scientific jargon. Underneath they were merely inspired guesses and just as likely to be wrong as right. Wells did not really understand what he was talking about. If he wanted something, he assumed that there was a way in which it would happen. For instance, in 1903 he foresaw mechanical monsters fighting each other in a future war and was later aggrieved when the credit for inventing the tank was denied to him. But he had never faced the technical problems involved in building tanks. He merely described what he wanted and left someone else to work it out. And, though he was right about tanks, he was wrong about the answer to them. Writing in the 1930s about the next war, he imagined that tanks would be stopped by vast ditches dug across Europe and filled with slime. The more prosaic, successful answer was the anti-tank gun. Wells's inventions for the future brought him much reputation, but of course they were the product of a lively imagination, not the serious work of a disciplined technician. This hardly mattered. They were fun, and the books built round them made good reading.

But the mix-up between what could be and what Wells wanted mattered a good deal more when he came to deal with man. This was Wells's serious concern as a thinker. He was amused to speculate on the ways in which machines could develop. He was passionately resolved on changing man's behaviour, and he believed that this could be done only by changing man himself – changing him in a specifically biological way. Wells claimed that the miracle could be worked by Science, very much with a capital S. Actually it was his own obstinate will: an impatient insistence that the change must happen. The word science was used simply as an incantation. Wells himself claimed to be a scientist. At any rate he had had some elementary training in biology under the great T H Huxley. He learnt the doctrine of evolution at its most confident. But he does not seem to have understood what he learnt. If evolution teaches anything, it is that the process of biological change is very slow. It took millions of years to evolve mammals; hundreds of thousands, if not millions, to evolve man. It is surely inconceivable that there should have been any biological evolution in man – any change in his natural make-up – during the few thousand years of civilization, and still more inconceivable that man should have changed during the 150 years or so since the French Revolution and the coming of modern industry.

Wells seems to have expected that men would change, you cannot call it evolve, more or less overnight, say in a couple of centuries; and of course men do change their behaviour and even, to some extent, their physical character quite quickly. For instance, the average height of Englishmen has increased markedly in the last fifty years, but such changes have nothing to do with biological evolution. They occur because of what happens to men after they are born, not because of a change in their nature. Englishmen are taller because they, and particularly the lower classes, are better fed than they used to be. Put them back on their old, inferior diet, and the next generation would be back where they started. It is the same with behaviour. Men are warlike or peaceful, brutal or tolerant, religious or atheistic, because that is what they have been taught to be, not because of something in their nature. Wells's appeal to evolution was sales talk, irrelevant to what really happened. At best it provided him with analogies and dangerous analogies at that.

The danger was greater still when Wells shifted from man to society and treated even this in biological terms. He regarded society as a sort of animal, subject to the laws of evolution. This is a common trick of historians or, I would prefer to say, of writers who make sweeping generalizations about the past. They talk about old societies, mature societies, even about decaying societies – useful analogies perhaps, but no more. If a man has been around on the earth for a long time, he will really be 'old' – his bones will creak, his physical powers will be failing, within a fairly limited time he will die. But there is no reason whatever to suppose that any of this will apply to a society. It may amuse us, it certainly amuses me, to make out that Great Britain is a mature society, wise, experienced, sensible, while the United States are brash, new, blundering, just because our history starts with Boadicea and theirs with George Washington. But we know that it is nonsense, good for a laugh and no more. Wells took the claptrap seriously, as other pontificators about history do. All his thought, if it can be dignified with that word, revolves round the analogy with evolution. Animals adapted themselves to their surroundings, and those who adapted themselves best survived. Men will do the same in their social behaviour. Wells believed that he had only to point out what was wrong in society and evolution would step in to put it right. Things had been getting better up to now and therefore we were bound to arrive at Utopia.

Wells condemned the contemporary world in every novel and other sort of book that he wrote. The first words uttered by Mr Polly, as he sat on a stile, can serve as the theme for all Wells's writing: 'Hole! *'Ole!* Oh! *Beastly* Silly Wheeze of a hole!' But why was the world a hole? It is easy to understand why Mr Polly felt so that afternoon. He owned a shop which did not pay and his wife produced meals which gave him indigestion. These are individual misfortunes which happen to many individuals. Wells insists on generalizing them. He writes solemnly that Mr Polly was 'one of those ill-adjusted units that abound in a society that has failed to develop a collective intelligence and a collective will for order commensurate with its complexities'. There is an implication, you see, that in a well-ordered society there will be no inefficient shopkeepers and of course no indigestion.

Wells was not only generalizing from Mr Polly. He was generalizing from himself. He had been a shop assistant. He had hated it. He escaped to become a writer. Very considerately, he wanted this to happen to all other shop assistants – a miracle, in fact; and, though considerate, like so much of Wells's or any other high-minded kindness, very wrongheaded. There are writers, potential or otherwise, who would hate to be shopkeepers. But there are far more shopkeepers who would hate to be writers. Wells had the snobbishness which nearly always goes with intellectual activities. He thought his way of life superior and he wanted to provide it for others.

This was the 'confusion' which he saw in society – too many shopkeepers, not enough devoted thinkers. There was another confusion which bulked large in Wells's novels and which indeed bulked large in his life – the relations between men and women. Somehow they rarely hit it off. Wells seems to have thought that, in a well-ordered society, all would come right of itself, by which he really meant that women would fit in with men's moods. Sometimes they would be satisfied with casual relations; when required, they would settle for something more permanent. But they would never try to hold a man if he wanted to move off. The modern state, as he put it, 'must refuse absolutely to recognize or enforce any kind of sexual ownership'. This deserves a top prize for Utopia. I suspect Meredith was wiser when he said that woman would be the last thing to be civilized by man.

Wells started before the First World War by wanting to put society right. That war led him into wanting to put the world right as well. At once he jumped the whole way: there must be a world-state, and that without delay. The final illustration in his *Outline of History* is a map of the world, and scrawled across it in bold letters the words: The United States of the World. He often implied that this would come of itself, according to the supposed laws of evolution. For instance, he says in his *Experiment in Autobiography*:

A planned world-state ... is, we perceive, as much a part of the frame in which our lives are set as the roundness and rotation of the earth, as the pressure of the atmosphere or the force of gravitation at the sea level.

And again:

The modern world-state which was a mere dream in 1900 is today a practicable objective; it towers high above the times. The socialist world-state has now become a tomorrow as real as today. Thither we go.

But sometimes he had qualms that we were not going there at all.

Wells always bounced easily from optimism to despair. In *Boon*, a book which he wrote in 1915, he discovered the Mind of the Race, which was working for salvation. But he concluded also that the Wild Asses of the Devil were loose – a more likely verdict on the twentieth century.

If the world-state was not coming of itself, what were we to do? Sometimes Wells implied that there was a superior moral force, pulling things the way in which he wanted them to go – in a phrase borrowed from Matthew Arnold 'that something not ourselves that makes for righteousness'. But he soon confessed that God, in his view, was merely another name for his own wishes. He wrote:

My deity was far less like the Heavenly Father of a devout Catholic . . . than he was like a personification of, let us say, the Five Year Plan.

Wells admitted, indeed boasted, that he was very near the communist outlook. Just as the five-year plan was imposed on Russia by Stalin, the world-state was to be imposed by Wells and a few other enlightened intellectuals – what he called the Open Conspiracy. In his own words: 'If Russia has done nothing else for mankind, the experiment of the Communist Party is alone sufficient to justify her revolution.' He insisted however that there was one great difference. Communism was based on class war and sought to set up the dictatorship of the proletariat. The Open Conspiracy would be composed of anyone intelligent enough to accept Wells's ideas, and principally by the men with real power. Wells thought that the captains of industry and finance would save the world. William Clissold, one of his fictional mouthpieces, announces: 'I shall travel on the Blue Train to the end of the chapter.' This seems to me another fantasy, more Utopian than the rest. All experience teaches that, if an élite run affairs, they do so in their own interests, and this is perhaps truer of businessmen than of any other so-called élite.

Wells became more and more convinced that knowledge would transform the world, if only there were enough of it. In *The Canford Visitation*, which he wrote in 1937, he imagines a supernatural voice, pointing the way of salvation:

There can be no escape for your world, for all mankind, from the ages of tragic conflict ahead of you, except so heroic an ordering of knowledge, so valiant a beating out of opinions, such a refreshment of teaching and such an organization of brains as will constitute a real and living world university, head, eyes and purpose of Man. That is the primary need of your species now. It is your world's primary want. It must come now – if it ever is to come.

In *Babes in the Darkling Wood*, published in 1940, the hero says much the same:

The Right Thing to Do will be to have a vast, ordered, encyclopedia of fact and thought for its Bible, and a gigantic organization not only of research and record, but of devoted teachers and interpreters. A World Church, a World Brain, and a World Will . . . We have to find out all that there is to be known and what is afoot in those various movements for documentation, for bibliography, for indexing, for all that micro-photographic recording one hears about distantly and dimly. Make understandings and more understandings. That is the reality of life for every human being.

This is the great contemporary delusion at its wildest: the belief that if only we accumulate enough facts, enough knowledge, the answer will emerge of itself. The facts will provide their own solution. Think of the pundits all over the world who are writing long solemn books about the problem of nuclear warfare and they are no nearer a solution. Yet any child could tell them what to do with nuclear weapons: 'Don't have them.'

Wells not only demanded ideas; he provided them. He had an unlimited faith in the power of education, and himself wrote books with an educational purpose – an outline of biology, an outline of economics, and, his most successful, an *Outline of History*. This at any rate is not only still read; it is the best general survey of man's history that there is. Wells wrote it to demonstrate that knowledge was superior to art and literature. He remarked slightingly: 'An industrious treatment of early nineteenth-century records would make Balzac's *Comédie Humaine* seem flighty stuff' – a view which Karl Marx would not have agreed with. The *Outline of History* was supposed to demonstrate that all recorded history had been moving fumblingly forward towards a planned world-state. It totally fails to demonstrate anything of the kind. It shows that men have always been in conflict and that the rich have always exploited the poor. Sometimes one state or one group in a civilization has come to dominate all the others. This is done by superior force and nothing else. Most people, including

Wells, sentimentalize their view of the past. They like to think that the better side wins. It doesn't. The stronger side wins. The Romans were not more civilized or more enlightened than the Greeks. They merely possessed a more efficient fighting machine. When Europeans established their authority throughout the world in the nineteenth century this was not because they were more civilized. It was because, in Hilaire Belloc's words: 'We have the Maxim gun, and they have not.' One conqueror, one potential uniter of Europe, perhaps represented a superior cause to the states he conquered. This was Napoleon. No one comes in for rougher treatment in Wells's *Outline of History*.

The *Outline* has a drawing of various national symbols, entitled Tribal Gods for which men would die. This is a true verdict on the history of the last 150 years. More men have died willingly for national loyalty than for any other cause. There is no heroism, and also practically no crime, which they will not perform in its name. If we draw any historical moral from this, it can only be that national states are not likely to vanish, though they may be conquered. Wells repudiated this moral: it did not accord with the world-state. He condemned men for their national loyalties. Though he wrote the *Outline* in order to show that history was going his way, in fact he demanded that men should abandon all their historical habits and behave in exactly the opposite fashion to that in which they had behaved throughout all recorded time. And of course they may. This is why it is so pointless to ask a historian to foretell the future. He can only say what will happen if men go on behaving as they have done in the past. For instance, if the past is any guide, the deterrent will one day fail to deter. There will be nuclear war, and all mankind will be destroyed. If you want the future to be different, the best thing is to forget history, not to try to extract morals from it.

Wells wanted a miracle, that men should change their nature. As he put it in *The Croquet Player*: 'Only giants can save the world from complete relapse and so we – we who care for civilization – have to become giants.' He was far from becoming a giant himself. Though he condemned the tribal gods of nationalism in theory, no one was a more fervent patriot when it came to war against Germany. In the First World War he wanted to bomb Essen – 'a daily service of destruction to Germany'. In the Second World War he declared that afterwards 'a few score thousand [German] criminals need to be shot', and then the world would be all right. Underneath he was too honest to imagine that his Utopia would really work. When he really imagined the future, in his scientific romances, he foresaw that a few clever men would still be exploiting all the rest. When the Sleeper awakes, for instance, 200 years hence, he discovers that the mass of mankind have become slaves, and the Sleeper raises an insurrection in the cause of old-fashioned freedom.

The contradiction was typical of Wells and rather endearing. He was by nature a radical, a rebel – one of the few Englishmen incidentally who still wrote diatribes against the monarchy. He knew instinctively that dictatorship, ordering people about, would not save them, and yet he could not think of any other way of doing it. In his ideal state, only one set of ideas would be allowed – his own:

Only one body of philosophy and only one religion, only one statement of men's relation to the universe and the community, can exist in a unified world-state.

This is a recipe for stagnation and disaster. Besides, if men turned to the writings of the master for instruction, what would they find? Instead of clear guidance, they would find chaos and confusion. Wells insisted, times without number, on the need for hard precise thinking. He was himself incapable of it. Every attempt at discussion in his books tails off with four dots in a row – a sort of 'to be continued in our next'. The great prophets of mankind are remembered by a single book, even if they wrote many. Rousseau is remembered by *The Social Contract*; Marx by *Capital*; Darwin by *The Origin of Species*. Wells put himself in their class. Indeed he claimed to be a better thinker than any of them. He wrote more than a hundred books. But when we ask: in which of them is the gospel according to Wells to be found? the answer is always: in the next book that Wells is going to write.

Actually his last book announced that there was no answer. Men had failed to listen to his teaching. Therefore they were doomed. He wanted his epitaph to be: 'God damn you all. I told you so.' He had imagined himself as God and was embittered when others did not acknowledge his divinity. But Wells was not God, was not even an inspired prophet. He was a spluttering imaginative little man in a hurry, bouncing from one contradiction to the next. His writings reflected the confusions and delusions of his age. There is not much wisdom in them, but there is a good deal of humanity. Maybe no one reads Wells any more for guidance – there are newer, equally muddled thinkers who provide that. We read Wells now for fun – the fun of the scientific romances, the fun of *Mr Polly*, even the fun to be found in *The Outline of History*. And fun is a great deal better than worshipping the golden calf of knowledge.

The Rogue Elephant

This essay was first published as a review of Robert Speaight's The Life of Hilaire Belloc (*London, Hollis and Carter, 1957*) *and Eleanor and Reginald Jebb's* Testimony to Hilaire Belloc (*London, Methuen, 1956*) *in the* Observer, *27 January 1957.*

*   *   *

Literature has its fashions, like dress; and Hilaire Belloc is neglected at present along with his contemporaries. Will he survive at all? I find myself almost alone in the opinion that he and Wells are the writers of their generation safe for immortality. And this though I dislike most of his opinions – on history, on religion, sometimes on politics. I can feel nothing real in his serious verse, and even his prose style often irritates me. It is easier to catalogue his defects than his virtues. Yet there are no books that I look back to with more gratitude or read again with more pleasure.

Belloc exploded sham when it was more secure than it is now; but he resented the price he had to pay. He was a rogue elephant who enjoyed trampling down other people's fences and yet expected society to provide him with rewards. He was Lucky Jim born at a less suitable time. For nowadays Lucky Jim is happy enough at the devastation he causes and even achieves modest security as lecturer at a provincial university. Belloc missed election at All Souls and complained about it ever afterwards. When a young journalist asked his rule for happiness, Belloc replied: 'I have none. You can't be happy. Don't try. Cut it out. Make up your mind to be miserable.'

Belloc was always restless and always shouting – perhaps to silence his doubts and disappointments. He could not sit through a single act of a play; and, on arriving in a strange town, he immediately looked up the time of a train to take him away. His impatient assertiveness was a failure in the House of Commons and he wore his voice out on the hustings almost before the campaign began. One has the feeling that he could not drink a pint of beer without exclaiming: 'Look, I am drinking beer.' His best book, *The Path to Rome*, takes place in the open air; all his books have to be read out of doors – you feel battered by them in a room. He had a rather tiresome trick of despising his readers, and not them only. When taking the chair at a debate between Shaw and Chesterton, he announced: 'They are about to debate. You are about to listen. I am about to sneer.'

His own dogmatism was ruthless. When asked how he could possibly believe that the bread and wine were really changed into the body and blood of Christ, he replied that he would believe that they were changed into an elephant, if the Church told him so. It is not surprising that he made few converts. Mr Speaight says rather that he restored the self-confidence of English Roman Catholics – and this may well be true.

Mr Speaight has written what is described as the official biography – that is, it was written at the request of Belloc's literary executors. The book is admirably full and surprisingly critical. Indeed it is rather odd that I should have to defend Belloc against his chosen biographer. Mr Speaight admires Belloc, but he is also rather embarrassed by him. He extols Belloc the sincere Roman Catholic and Belloc the romantic poet. He is less happy about Belloc the politician and social critic. His account of the Marconi scandal, for instance, is as cautious and non-committal as any speculator could wish. The reader who wants to know what all the fuss was about must turn to the memoir of Belloc by his daughter and son-in-law, published last year. Suppose the affair had gone to a special tribunal, such as dealt with J H Thomas and Sidney Stanley; what would have been the verdict? My guess is that a future prime minister and a future Lord Chief Justice would have seen their careers sharply interrupted. The trouble with Mr Speaight is that he thinks there is nothing wrong with the English upper classes. Belloc slipped into this view later in life; and how relieved Mr Speaight is when Belloc strikes up a friendship with Lord Derby. But earlier on Belloc was savagely opposed to the system of influence and corruption by which our affairs are conducted.

Mr Speaight slides over Belloc's political novels. To my mind they are the best of their kind in English, as well as being very funny. You can see Mr Speaight, in his respectable, latter-day Roman Catholicism, puzzling what they are all about. They seem to him pure fantasy, and antiquated fantasy at that. Yet *Emmanuel Burden* throws a piercing light on the imperialism which caused the Boer War; and, as to their being out of date, anyone who wants to know how our present government was constructed will find a precise and detailed account of it in *A Change in the Cabinet*, which Belloc published in 1909. Of course, there is now a real difference between the Conservative and Labour parties, as Mr Speaight says. It is the difference between Eton and Winchester.

Mr Speaight is more effective in his appreciation of Belloc's historical writings, though their vision was more creative and the facts perhaps shakier than he makes out. He is warm, as other friends have been, in personal affection. Yet the full power of Belloc is somehow muted. One gets the impression that homecoming is the best part of a stormy voyage. No doubt Belloc felt this himself towards the end of his life; but he had done much navigating in rough weather before that. The Belloc of tumult and conflict is the one who is still alive.

The Entente Cordiale

This essay was first published in the Manchester Guardian, *8 April 1944.
In the midst of the Second World War, shortly before the Normandy landings, it
was especially appropriate to mark the entente's fortieth anniversary.*

*In February 1944 Alan Taylor, who had appeared seven times in 1942 on the
BBC Forces Network radio programme* The World at War: Your Questions
Answered, *suggested to the BBC that he should give a talk on the Anglo-
French entente. Trevor Blewitt, who was responsible for foreign affairs broadcasts, commented that if they made a broadcast on that topic 'we should want to
use a speaker who had practical experience of Anglo-French relations before the
last war and, if possible, at the time of the conclusion of the entente'. Having
failed to secure a commission at the BBC, Alan Taylor instead prepared his
piece for the* Manchester Guardian.

*   *   *

The agreements which gave formal expression to the Anglo-French
entente were published on 8 April 1904. British opinion welcomed the
agreements enthusiastically, but saw in them colonial arrangements
and nothing more. 'We have settled our differences with France' was
the common phrase. England had made a good bargain: apart from
the sorting out of many minor disputes she had made her control of
the two ends of the Mediterranean secure from French interference
for ever. At the one end France recognized British predominance in
Egypt and finally renounced her own claims; at the other end France
gave new guarantees for the invulnerability of Gibraltar, for she
agreed, as the condition of her bringing Morocco into the French
Empire, that the Moorish coastline opposite Gibraltar should pass to
Spain and should be preserved unfortified by the three Powers.

No wonder the British welcomed the agreements: in cheering the
French they were, in characteristic British fashion, cheering a good
loser. The heirs of Napoleon were acknowledging finally the victory of
Nelson. There was on the British side hardly a shade of precaution
against Germany. The British were, of course, glad to escape from the
attitude of dependence on Germany into which the danger of conflict
with France had sometimes led them. But they did not fear Germany,
nor had they any cause of conflict with her: the trivial colonial

disputes were long ended, and although the building of the German fleet was a nuisance the British were confident that they could always hold their own at sea unaided – after all, in 1905 the British Navy attained a superiority over the combined naval forces of all other Powers unparalleled in our history.

Still less was there on the British side any great principle, any idea of cooperation between the Western democracies against German militarism. Lord Lansdowne, the foreign secretary, had worked as hard in 1901 for an alliance with Germany as in 1903 and 1904 for an entente with France. It would be difficult to see in the Irish landowner who resigned from Gladstone's government in 1880 rather than acquiesce in Irish land reform and the Tory die-hard who defended the House of Lords in 1910 a champion of democracy; and the author of the Lansdowne peace letter, who in 1917 advocated a status quo peace (for the sake of social order) and even then saw no need for Germany to atone for her crimes, detected no threat to civilization in the Germany of 1904.

With the French it was far otherwise: there the advocates of the entente knew what they were doing, knew that they were staking the future of France for the sake of Western democratic civilization. For more than two hundred years the French had carried on colonial conflicts with England, and for more than two hundred years French ambitions in Europe had made her the loser in these colonial conflicts. French domination in Europe was ended at Leipzig and Waterloo, and its last echoes were silenced at Sedan. After 1871 necessity left France free as never before to pursue colonial aims and to find a substitute for lost European glory in the Mediterranean empire which was the legacy of Bonaparte's expedition to Egypt in 1798. Germany, as Bismarck was constantly urging, was eager for reconciliation, and if France had been reconciled with Germany as Austria-Hungary had been after 1866 she could have had German support against England in Egypt as Austria-Hungary had it against Russia in the Near East.

Reconciliation was the logical, easy course, but it was not taken. Only a small unpopular minority advocated revenge. The great majority recognized that France had been irretrievably defeated, yet they would not accept German patronage. For almost thirty years France refused to acknowledge the inevitable; she tried to oust the British from Egypt without German support. The Fashoda crisis of 1898 showed that the attempt was impossible, and Delcassé, then newly foreign minister, determined the future destinies of France when, without appealing for German assistance, he ordered Marchand to withdraw.

For the English the entente had no anti-German point, but the French knew that in making the entente they were becoming the hostage of democracy on the continent of Europe. They had no hope of winning British assistance for a war of revenge. Indeed in the then state of the British Army they did not even value British assistance for a defensive war; the army of their Russian ally remained their sole military support. But the French were determined not to become partners in the German order. To renounce Egypt was a crime against the memory of Bonaparte; to renounce Alsace and Lorraine would be a crime against the national principle, an infringement of the Rights of Man.

The French hesitated for thirty years, but at the crisis of their destiny they remained faithful to the ideas of the Revolution. Relinquishing material gain and Mediterranean empire, they chose to remain independent and to remain democratic; they continued to be the standard-bearers of Western civilization against militarism and autocracy. They chose with their eyes open; they knew that if they held out against German temptation it was on them that the German blow would fall. By making the Anglo-French entente the French brought on themselves the sufferings of 1914–18 and of 1940–44, but in 1904 the prospect of a German hegemony of Europe achieved by peaceful means vanished for ever.

Small wonder that the French hesitated. Small wonder that the entente was not received on the French side with the easy popularity which it evoked in England. Small wonder that at first the nerve of the French almost failed and that, fifteen months after the conclusion of the entente, Delcassé, its author, was driven from office on German orders. Yet the work of Delcassé was not undone. France looked the dangers in the face and, when the time came, accepted them. Many Frenchmen contributed to this decision. Yet Delcassé was more than their spokesman. He was not a great man; indeed, in some ways he was foolish and hot-headed. He offended his own colleagues and injured his own cause. But he had in him the flame of loyalty to the ideas of 1789, to the principles of national independence and of human equality. He was determined to keep France free, both at home and abroad. The entente was perhaps no more than a new expression of the unity of Western democratic civilization, but Delcassé gave it that expression. Forty years after, all those Englishmen who recognize the difference between French civilization and German order may well say: 'Homage to Théophile Delcassé!'

The Anglo-Russian Entente

This essay, written for the entente's fiftieth anniversary, was first published as 'Forgotten Anniversary: The Anglo-Russian Entente' in the Manchester Guardian, *31 August 1957.*

*　　*　　*

The Anglo-Russian entente was formally concluded on 31 August 1907. Unlike the Entente Cordiale with France, it has vanished into the mists of history. Yet, for good or ill, it ranks high among the significant events of the century. Its making and its ten years of existence changed the face of the world. The Anglo-French entente, though sentimentally admirable, was no more than a renewal of good relations which had been temporarily interrupted by rivalry in the Nile valley. The entente with Russia was a revolution. Great Britain and Russia had never been on close terms before, at any rate not since the end of the Napoleonic Wars. Usually, indeed, they had been on bad terms – at war in the Crimea, and on the brink of war over Pendjeh in 1885. Continental statesmen, especially German, based their plans on the expected clash between the elephant and the whale. Instead the two countries composed their differences, cooperated diplomatically, and finally, to their mutual surprise, found themselves partners in a great European war.

The agreement of 31 August was modest in form. The two Powers merely promised to keep their hands off the buffer states of Central Asia. Afghanistan and Tibet were to be left alone. Even in regard to Persia, which is often described as 'partitioned', the bargain was negative. The British were to keep out of the north, the Russians out of the south; the centre lay neutral between them. Sir Edward Grey boasted that, unlike some earlier agreements, this contained no secret clauses. He spoke the truth, yet there were understandings unwritten but binding.

The Russians received a hint that they would get concessions at the Straits if they behaved well for a few years. As a matter of fact they had to wait until 1915 before they secured the promise of Constantinople, and then they proved unable to cash the cheque. More broadly, the two countries were committed to diplomatic cooperation. The

Triple Entente came into existence, though both Grey and Izvolski tried to avoid using the phrase. Neither side liked its implications. The British had no wish to support Russia's ambitions in the Balkans (so far as she had any); the Russians managed, more successfully, to keep clear of the naval dispute between England and Germany. All the same, the consequences were inescapable. Germany could no longer exploit her policy of 'the free hand', once England and Russia were on good terms. Henceforward the Germans aimed to disrupt the Triple Entente and when they failed flung themselves in exasperation against it.

The Anglo-Russian entente was a business deal, not a matter of sentiment. In England it was unpopular as no diplomatic step has been except the policy of 'appeasement'. Most Conservatives swallowed it cynically as strengthening the balance against Germany. Liberal ministers – Grey and Morley, for example – excused it on the ground that otherwise large forces would have to be provided for the defence of India. The radical rank and file abhorred the friendship with an autocratic Power, the more so when Russia's only democratic Duma had been recently dissolved. In 1908 the Labour Party protested, with some radical support, against Edward VII's visit to the Tsar at Reval; and their renewed protests kept the Tsar confined to Cowes when he wished to visit England the following year. The betrayal of Persia made them yet more indignant. English radicals believed that Persia could maintain her own independence of Russia if she received some British backing, and they were probably right. It was additionally tiresome that, whatever the professions of the Russian ministers at St Petersburg – and they were perhaps sincere – the representative at Tehran went cheerfully on encroaching as he had done for years. Persia caused Grey more trouble than any other question in foreign affairs. Exasperation with Russian behaviour made him threaten to resign and to make way for a pro-German foreign secretary – a step that would have been welcome to the Liberal majority in the House.

At the outset the radical critics complained that Persia had been sacrificed to 'that foul idol, the balance of power'; it had been the price for Russian backing against Germany. Later they turned the accusation the other way round and made out that the peace of Europe was being endangered for the sake of imperialist gains in Persia and elsewhere. These charges were too simple. The entente was a bargain of mutual advantage, and, if this weakened Germany's position, Great Powers cannot be expected to bicker merely to please some third party.

The real British commitment was to France, not to Russia, but undoubtedly Great Britain had to be somewhat complaisant towards Russia in order to ensure that France could count firmly on her Eastern ally. The British government decided, rightly or wrongly, not to tolerate a German hegemony of the Continent. Once having decided this, they had to go along with Russia in the last resort. In peacetime Russia benefited more than Great Britain from the entente. When war came it was the other way round. It was the Russian army which ensured that there should be a Western Front in the First World War and which, moreover, ensured that the Germans could never put their whole weight on that front until too late.

In Russia, too, the policy of the entente was not without its critics, though occupying almost exactly reverse positions from those in England. The Russian liberals wanted to turn towards Europe and away from Asia. Therefore they welcomed the compromise over imperial interests and, still more, friendship with the Western Powers. The realists of the extreme Right deplored being involved in European affairs, and, paradoxically, Lenin shared their view. Lenin and Witte both regarded the entente as the root of all evil. Both wanted the European Powers to destroy themselves in a great war, while Russia developed the riches of her Asiatic empire.

The first Russian revolution of March 1917 would have marked the triumph of the entente, if it had been a triumph for anything. The Bolshevik revolution ended the entente and led logically not only to the peace of Brest-Litovsk but to the Nazi–Soviet pact. The Anglo-Russian entente has been forgotten by both partners. Yet, oddly enough, it has been more successful than the Anglo-French entente as a practical arrangement. England is no longer paramount in Egypt, nor France in Morocco. But the buffer states of Asia survive. Tibet is safe from Russia or the British Empire. Afghanistan is still neutral and independent. Most remarkable of all, Persia still defies imperialist encroachment from every quarter with supreme self-confidence.

'We Want Eight, and We Won't Wait'

This essay was first published as 'The Dreadnought Programme: "We Want Eight, and We Won't Wait"' in the Manchester Guardian, *23 February 1959.*

*   *   *

Written to mark the fiftieth anniversary of the great controversy over naval building in March 1909. The German naval archives have now been returned to Germany but the secrets of German anticipation have not yet been adequately revealed.

Armament programmes have often been the subject of controversy in British politics from the 'French panic' of 1860 to nuclear weapons at the present day. No controversy has been fiercer than that over naval building in March 1909. The phrase then coined still rings down the avenues of time. 'We want eight, and we won't wait.' The Liberal Party, with its great majority, was deeply divided on this question; the cabinet itself threatened to disintegrate. The Unionists saw their chance to reverse the electoral defeat of 1906. They exploited popular passion and believed office to be again within their grasp.

The origin of the crisis lay in 1906 when Sir John Fisher, first sea lord, introduced the Dreadnought, the first all-big-gun ship. The Dreadnought made all existing navies out of date; it was more powerful than three of its immediate predecessors put together. For the time being the Dreadnought increased British superiority and upset all other programmes; the Germans did not lay down a single battleship for nearly two years. But the superiority, though greater, rested on a narrower margin. In March 1909 the British had forty-three pre-Dreadnought battleships as against twenty-two German. They had two of Dreadnought type completed and three battle-cruisers; the Germans had none. But the Germans had fourteen ships projected; the British only seven. The gap between the two navies might close ominously when the Germans began to build.

Here was the second and more dangerous point. It had always been assumed that Great Britain, as the greatest industrial Power, could build more ships than any other Power and could build them faster. Even if another country stole a march on the British, they could catch up before the danger point was reached. Gladstone had said it in 1894: 'Our means of construction are overwhelming . . . Our methods of construction are far more rapid.' Goschen, Unionist first lord, repeated this confidence in 1898. Ten years later it was ceasing to be true in the opinion of many experts. Germany, too, was now an industrial Power of the first rank. Though still inferior in the number of her shipyards, she was equal, if not ahead, in the armament factories producing the guns, gun-mountings, turrets and armourplate which a battleship needed. The Germans could, if they put themselves to it, build up to the British programme and, what was more, with their industrial efficiency, they could build as fast, if not faster.

It was the duty of the expert advisers to tell the government how British supremacy could be maintained. By 1909 they had reached the conclusion that the yardstick should no longer be German ships, built or projected, but German capacity. This opened the door to fantastic calculations. The needs of the German Army were ignored, all budgetary considerations disregarded. The only question was: how many battleships can the Germans have if they concentrate on this and nothing else? According to the published programme, the Germans would have ten battleships completed in the spring of 1911. Asquith, the prime minister, striking a moderate note, held that they would have thirteen or at most seventeen. Balfour, leader of the Opposition, excelled in these speculative subtleties; according to him, the Germans would have at least twenty-one battleships in 1911, but more probably twenty-five.

In face of these imagined perils the Board of Admiralty wished to increase the British building programme for 1909 from four battleships to six, and to maintain this rate for the two years following. The Unionists, supported by the popular press, raged that eight should be laid down at once. Two members of the cabinet, Lloyd George and Winston Churchill, stood out against the clamour. They pointed to the published German figure of ten for March 1911; four British battleships a year, added to the existing number, would be adequate to meet this. Germany, they argued, was a constitutional country. Battleships could not be built without the financial authorization of the Reichstag. What evidence, they asked, was there that the German Admiralty was cheating either the Reichstag or the British experts?

The question could be given a theoretical answer. Germany, it could be alleged, was not a constitutional country in the British sense. The Reichstag would forgive a breach of the rules – as the Prussian parliament had forgiven Bismarck in 1866 – if it brought strategic gain, and of course the German government had no moral obligation towards Great Britain to observe its published programme, whatever it might have towards the Reichstag. But there was also a more practical answer. There was evidence that some of the contracts for the German 1909–10 programme had been given out in the autumn of 1908, and evidence too that material for the projected ships had been collected in advance.

This is the most puzzling part of the story. We do not know to this day why the Germans 'anticipated' their 1909 programme. It may have been to break the ring of contractors or to provide continuity of employment. To suspicious British eyes it looked like an attempt to steal a march. The information came from secret sources. It could not be used publicly. But Fisher saw to it that it did not stay with the government; it reached, probably in exaggerated form, the leaders of the Opposition and the press. Thus there were two supposed dangers: the theoretical possibility of German 'acceleration', the actual probability of German 'anticipation'. The argument plunged into inextricable confusion – men hinting at the second when they were ostensibly talking of the first.

Asquith handled the crisis with his customary adroitness, apparently doing one thing with the intention later of being forced to do the other. In the debates of March 1909 he stood solid with Lloyd George, Churchill and the bulk of Liberal MPs. There was, he insisted, no danger, no need for panic; the building programme would remain at four battleships. But he asked also for authorization to lay down four 'contingent' ships later in the year, if this proved necessary. Both parties were satisfied. The Liberals thought that agitation had been defied; the Unionists found that their thunder had been stolen. In July McKenna, first lord of the admiralty, announced that the four contingent ships would be built. He made no reference to German acceleration or anticipation; his new excuse was that Germany's two allies, Austria-Hungary and Italy, were proposing to build four Dreadnoughts at some time in the future. Everyone knew the real 'contingency': the Liberals had just suffered resounding defeat in a by-election at Croydon.

Only seventy-nine Liberals voted vainly against the contingent ships. Thus the British public got their eight ships and did not wait. But the panic did the Unionists no good. To meet the increased naval bill Lloyd George devised the People's Budget, and soon his Limehouse speech drowned the cry of 'We want eight'. As to the supposed danger period of spring 1911, the Germans did not then have twenty-five battleships or twenty-one or seventeen or thirteen; they had six. A year later they had nine, against the British sixteen. Had they ever planned to have more? The answer might be found in the German naval records which, for some years after the Second World War, reposed at Admiralty House and maybe are there still. No curious eye has looked upon them. British admirals guard the secrets of their German colleagues as carefully as they guard their own, or perhaps, considering Fisher's constant leakages, rather better.

A Great Man?

This essay first appeared in the New Statesman and Nation, *22 December 1956, as a review of Arthur J Marder, ed.,* Fear God and Dread Nought: The Correspondence of Admiral of the Fleet Lord Fisher of Kilverstone, Vol. II, The Years of Power 1904–1914 *(London, Jonathan Cape, 1956). Sir John Arbuthnot Fisher (1841–1920) was first sea lord 1903–10 and 1914–15 (when he resigned over the Dardanelles). He was created Baron Fisher of Kilverstone in 1909.*

*   *   *

The correspondence of generals and admirals has a peculiar fascination. No one expects these men of action to possess much in the way of literary gifts; but they often develop a spluttering explosiveness as they wrestle with this unaccustomed and, to them, distasteful medium of words. The fighting men before 1914 were particularly choice – perhaps because they had so little real conception of the Armageddon which they were always prophesying. Sir Henry Wilson comes out top of the bunch. Every sentence of his reveals an arrogant fatuity and a political frivolity such as one would find only in an Irishman. It now appears from the letters which Professor Marder has so laboriously and devotedly edited that 'Jackie' Fisher can give Wilson a close run. Every letter is a peach. There are rather too many of them; and he was too fond of repeating himself, in accordance with one of his favourite tags: 'Reiteration is the Secret of Conviction!' Reading them straight through is almost as shattering as a broadside from one of Fisher's beloved Dreadnoughts. Exclamation marks, whole sentences in capital letters, inarticulate bellows, bestrew the pages. Add to this a glance at the Herkomer portrait of Fisher, and it is difficult to believe that he was altogether sane.

Still, perhaps it would have been a good thing if he had bitten some of the others. The serious theme of the book is Fisher's remaking of the British Navy which ensured its adequacy in the First World War. He scrapped old ships; made the fleet an effective fighting force; ran after every invention from wireless telegraphy to oil-firing. Most remarkable of all, these reforms, though they improved the navy enormously, actually saved money. On occasion, the government had even to put forward reduced estimates, much to its embarrassment. All this is now old stuff. The long lines of Dreadnoughts are as obsolete as the Spanish Armada. Tested by later events, Fisher made many good guesses and a few wrong ones. He foresaw the submarine, though not the answer to it: indeed he advocated a Channel tunnel as the only way of breaking a submarine blockade. He imagined that the Germans would oblige him by sallying forth to undertake a great naval engagement, and was much at a loss when they stayed in port. His one really foolish idea was that it would be possible to land an expeditionary force on some sandy beach in north Germany – even the generals knew this was wrong. But, by and large, he was more farsighted and certainly more creative than his service contemporaries. Who can blame him for being wrong now and then, seeing that, like all the other fire-eaters, he had never heard a shot fired in anger?

The topic of more lasting interest is how he did it – how he put his ideas over on the politicians and on the ruling circles of the day. Fisher knew how to flatter: he won the heart of every first lord, and Asquith's into the bargain. It is particularly curious how he landed the politicians in a mess, through his overconfidence, during the 'acceleration' crisis of 1909; and then compelled them to get out of it, himself looking as innocent as could be all the while. His dealings with the Court merit special notice. He charmed Edward VII and played royal backing hard to secure his success. George V was a different matter – a sailor with many friends among the stuffier admirals whom Fisher detested. So Fisher turned round and became a democrat, insisting that the navy was a parliamentary force and even applauding John Ward's attack on the army officers after the Curragh mutiny. Fisher, in short, was convinced that he was always right, others always wrong; and he was not troubled with scruples in carrying this view through. He was supposed, perhaps correctly, to be the greatest admiral since Nelson. But it did not add up to much. Nelson's domination of the seas lasted a hundred years; Fisher's about ten. Now he has only the wistful charm of yesterday's music-hall comedian.

H H Asquith

The first essay on Herbert Henry Asquith (1852–1928), prime minister 1908–16, was a review of Asquith, *by Roy Jenkins (London, Collins, 1964) which appeared in the* Observer, *1 November 1964. It originally ended with a passage which raised the question whether there were further secrets in Asquith's correspondence with Venetia Stanley (1887–1948). The second essay reviews the published correspondence between them:* H H Asquith: Letters to Venetia Stanley, *selected and edited by Michael and Eleanor Brock (Oxford, Clarendon Press, 1982). This was first published in the* Guardian, *25 November 1982.*

* * *

A Toga Somewhat Tattered

Asquith presents something of a puzzle for the historian. He was always cool and rational, answering abuse with argument. His finely chiselled features breathed serenity. 'A rock', his admirers called him and 'the last of the Romans'. He was never rattled, never impatient. Though leader of a radical party, he sustained the noblest traditions of British politics. He had great triumphs. He was prime minister for eight and a half years – the longest continuous tenure since the Reform Bill – and presided over perhaps the most brilliant cabinet in British history. He broke the power of the House of Lords. Against all expectations, he led an almost united country, and even more surprisingly, a united Liberal Party, into the First World War.

Yet not only was he driven from power – that happens ultimately to most prime ministers. He also provoked a peculiarly bitter and lasting hostility. Some of this no doubt was caused by his skill. When the Unionists in 1911 shouted him down in the House of Commons, they were expressing their resentment at having been outmanoeuvred, in the words of Mr Jenkins, 'according to the classic rules of nineteenth-century politics'. This resentment, still lingering, may explain, though it cannot excuse, the rejection of Asquith in 1925 as Chancellor of Oxford University.

But the hostility extended to his own associates. The feud between his supporters and those of Lloyd George tore the Liberal Party asunder and was never assuaged. Its echoes rumble to the present day. Was Asquith really too noble for the rough world of politics? Or were there in him hidden weaknesses which provoked, or even justified, the outbursts against him? Was the Roman statue a true portrait of the man or a stage-prop?

The official biography by J A Spender and Cyril Asquith, published in 1932, did not face these questions. It was a partisan work of glorification. To quote the dust-cover of the present book, 'it sets Asquith on a somewhat remote pedestal'. The time was ripe for a fresh assessment which would serve no purpose other than historical truth. The political battles, once fought so fiercely, are now remote, all passion surely spent. There are many new sources of information, beginning with Asquith's own papers now in the Bodleian Library.

Mr Jenkins, the present biographer, has high qualifications. He has written admirable books of political history, including an excellent account of the conflict with the House of Lords, a central episode in Asquith's career. It is sad to record that Mr Jenkins, despite many revelations, has ended by drawing round Asquith the folds of a somewhat tattered toga.

The key to the mystery is to be found perhaps at the beginning. Asquith was no Roman. He was a Gallo-Roman: son of a Yorkshire wool manufacturer, not scion of the aristocracy. Asquith sought worldly success. He took on, and even exaggerated, the attitudes of the society which he aspired to enter. Mr Jenkins does not conceal the growing estrangement between Asquith and his first unworldly wife. She died in September 1891. For once Asquith did not show his usual procrastination. Before the end of the year he was writing to the rich and socially distinguished Margot Tennant: 'You tell me not to stop loving you, as if you thought I had done or would or could do so.'

His second marriage, to Miss Tennant, brought its reward. He had a house with fourteen servants, 'including a butler and two footmen, who were occupied with a continuous round of luncheon and dinner parties'. Asquith now lived in high society, his visits to the mansions of the great and wealthy interrupted only in the afternoon, when he browsed in the library of the Athenaeum. It was characteristic that, when Campbell-Bannerman was forming his government in December 1905, Asquith had to be summoned from Hatfield, the seat of the Marquess of Salisbury. From this unlikely base, Asquith presented, and failed to carry, his ultimatum that Campbell-Bannerman should go to the House of Lords.

Asquith had a double belief in his own superiority: it was both intellectual and social. Once he became prime minister, he regarded both associates and opponents from an Olympian height. He accepted only Balfour as an equal. Otherwise he was always ready with a condescending comment, many of them recorded by Mr Jenkins. Thus, repeating Bolingbroke's remark about Bishop Warburton: 'I never wrestle with a chimney-sweep,' Asquith added: 'A good saying, which I sometimes call to mind when I am confronting Bonar Law.' After the Marconi scandal, he remarked cheerfully of Lloyd George: 'I think the idol's wings are a bit clipped,' and repeated: 'a bit clipped' with a shrug of the shoulders. A little later he found that Lloyd George lacked 'the best sort of courage'. He wrote of Churchill: 'It is a pity that Winston hasn't a better sense of proportion, and also a larger endowment of the instinct of loyalty . . . He will never get to the top in English politics, with all his wonderful gifts.'

Asquith's own courage was in procrastination. He held his ground quietly and waited for the opposition to exhaust itself. This strategy worked over the House of Lords, and Asquith deserves full credit. Its wisdom was not finally tested in regard to home rule. The Great War intervened. Then Asquith once more allowed events to happen. He waited this time for the Germans to exhaust themselves. According to Mr Jenkins: 'He was happier as prime minister than he had ever been.' He watched his brawling colleagues with detached amusement. When a coalition government was formed in May 1915, in order to conceal the failure at Gallipoli from the public, Asquith did not repine. He let his oldest political ally, Haldane, go without a word of regret and ingeniously kept the Unionists from all the key posts. He still did not doubt that his main duty was to hold on to the highest office himself.

Thereafter Asquith was concerned to ward off criticism, not to find the best way of winning the war. Thus over conscription, he wrote impatiently of McKenna, its leading opponent: 'the Dickens is that I so agree with him'. But Asquith carried conscription all the same. The decisive conflict came at the end of 1916. Lloyd George, Law and Carson demanded a more efficient system for running the war.

Asquith thought only in terms of holding his supreme position.

On this vital episode, Mr Jenkins, though without new evidence, challenges the version of Lord Beaverbrook. According to Beaverbrook, the leading Unionists resigned as much in impatience with Lloyd George as with Asquith. According to Mr Jenkins, their resignation was directed solely against Asquith. Even if true, this was not creditable to Asquith. It means that not only the Unionist backbenchers, the majority of Liberal back-benchers, and all the press except the *Daily News* (including even the *Manchester Guardian*) preferred Lloyd George to Asquith, but that even aristocratic Unionists, such as Balfour, Curzon, and Lord Robert Cecil, did so too. Mr Jenkins makes this case because he wishes to argue that Asquith was driven from office and did not resign as a tactical manoeuvre. There is decisive evidence the other way, not referred to by Mr Jenkins. Robert Donald, editor of the *Daily Chronicle*, a Liberal paper, has recorded that Asquith expected Lloyd George to fail: 'then he would have to come in on *my* terms'.

It was not only Asquith's superiority, nor even his negations in policy, which turned men against him. He had other flaws. Mr Jenkins refers to one in a tactful footnote:

For the last 10 or 15 years of his life, at least, he was a fairly heavy drinker. Occasionally this made him look a little unsteady (even in the House of Commons) late at night. But no one ever suggested that his mind lost its precision or that there was any faltering in his command over what he did or did not want to say.

On the contrary, many witnesses have suggested precisely this. As well, Asquith was regarded as indiscreet. Kitchener complained that the cabinet ministers told military secrets to their wives, except X who told them to the wives of other people. Sir Philip Magnus, Kitchener's biographer, identifies X as Asquith. There is evidence for this charge. Between 1912 and 1915 Asquith wrote voluminous letters to Venetia Stanley, a young woman of an aristocratic family: often three letters a day, and a daily total of more than 1,000 words. Many of the letters were written during cabinet meetings and contain cutting comments on ministers, as well as details of the proceedings. It has also been rumoured that they contain military secrets, such as the sinking of the battleship *Audacious* and the numbers of divisions in France or Gallipoli.

Mr Asquith in Love

One day early in 1912 Herbert Henry Asquith, British prime minister since 1908 and now rising sixty, was struck down by Cupid's dart: suddenly he realized that he was in love with Venetia Stanley, a smart society girl not half his age. This love affair became an infatuation, a consuming passion which dominated Asquith's life.

Asquith was a lover by correspondence. Between 1912 and 1915, when the affair ended, he wrote to Venetia nearly every day except when they met. Over 550 of these letters survive of which some 460 are reproduced in this book.

The editors think that 'it is almost certain that Asquith never became Venetia's lover in the physical sense'. Probably they are right, though who can say? At all events Asquith would have saved himself a mint of trouble if he had become Venetia's lover in the physical sense instead of finding his expression of love in writing letters and holding her hand under the rug while driving in an opulent motor car. As it is, historians and observers of human nature are the gainers.

Asquith's letters make up a unique series. Here is a prime minister with considerable gifts as a writer, describing one political crisis after another from the threat of civil war in Ireland to the outbreak of the Great War and ending with the military failures in Flanders and the Dardanelles which provoked the end of Asquith's government, the last Liberal government in British history.

Nor are the letters made up of detached political disquisition. As time passed and Asquith's obsession became more consuming he poured out to Venetia all the secrets of the day.

Until the outbreak of war these were mainly political manoeuvres: who was to occupy which governmental posts, what new offer had been made to Carson or Redmond and so on. With war came increasing indiscretion. Venetia learnt many things that were concealed from the cabinet: the departure of the British Expeditionary Force to Flanders, the offensive plans of Sir John French in 1915 and the plans and projects in Gallipoli.

Venetia was an immature girl, much given to rash political gossip in many different circles. The only precaution Asquith took was to write an occasional *secret* or even *very secret* before setting down information that should never have been written at all. Letters of this kind would ruin the most junior minister these days, let alone a prime minister. Yet Asquith presided complacently over cabinet, writing page after page to Venetia and pausing only for an occasional remark. No colleague ever asked him what he was writing.

Maybe this is the explanation for this extraordinary situation. Asquith regarded all his colleagues with Olympian aloofness. Some few who had been with him for a long time he accepted, as fellow mortals. The newcomers were dismissed with a condescending wave of the hand. Most of them were awarded nicknames; the Impeccable, the Arch-Colonel, Sweetheart, and so on.

It was perhaps unfortunate that Asquith wrote off one junior minister, Edwin Montagu, as 'the Assyrian'. For Montagu shattered Asquith's romance. In May 1915 he induced Venetia to marry him. Venetia was not oblivious of the fact that Montagu inherited over one million pounds from his father Lord Swaythling. There was a condition attached: anyone marrying into the Montagu family had to become a Jew. This did not perturb Venetia at all.

On 12 May 1915 Asquith's love letters came to an abrupt end. He wrote: 'As you know well, *this* breaks my heart.' Later he resumed his letter writing, first to Venetia's sister and then to a war widow, Mrs Harrison. But there was no new affair of the heart and no more communicating secrets.

Years later when Asquith wrote his *Memories and Reflections* he asked Venetia to return his wartime letters which she did. They appear in Asquith's *Memories* as excerpts from his 'diary'. As such they have been used by many historians. Nor was this the only appearance of Asquith's letters. Venetia passed on to Lord Beaverbrook many copies in pencil of Asquith's wartime letters and Beaverbrook used the copies without acknowledgement in his *Politicians and the War*.

Many of the book's best passages come from this surprising source. Beaverbrook paid for a few of the passages. Most of the excerpts Venetia gave to him in exchange for the favours, financial and perhaps sexual, that Beaverbrook bestowed upon her.

The full publication of Asquith's letters to Venetia was long delayed. Edwin Montagu died in 1924, Venetia Montagu in 1948. The letters then passed to their daughter Judith Montagu who did not know of them until she looked through her mother's papers. Judith proposed to enlist Randolph Churchill as editor of the letters, a project which fell down. Randolph died and so did Judith.

Lady Violet Bonham Carter, who held the Asquith copyrights, was implacably opposed to the publication of her father's letters. After Lady Violet's death, the copyrights passed to Mark Bonham Carter. The letters themselves had meanwhile passed to Milton Gendel who had married Judith. At last agreement was reached and the way was clear for the complete publication of the Asquith–Venetia letters.

The two editors, Michael and Eleanor Brock, were an inspired choice. Theirs is a work of impeccable scholarship which it is a delight to read. I cannot think of any collection of letters that I have enjoyed more. The letters tell the very human story of a distinguished statesman who was led by vanity into folly.

They contain much new information. Here are two fragments. If war had not broken out in August 1914 it is more than likely that the Irish question would have been settled that autumn. And if the Germans had gone only through southern Belgium the Liberal government would not have gone to war.

Finally a quotation of Asquith on Churchill: 'He will never get to the top in English politics, with all his wonderful gifts: to speak with the tongues of men & angels, and to spend laborious days & nights in administration, is no good, if a man does not inspire trust.'

At least Churchill did not spend his time writing letters to his girlfriend.

Farce before Tragedy

This essay first appeared as a review of Geoffrey Barraclough's From Agadir to Armageddon: Anatomy of a Crisis *(London, Weidenfeld and Nicolson, 1982) in the* Observer, *31 October 1982. The book was one of Barraclough's last. He and Alan Taylor had known each other since their days at Bootham and Oriel, though Barraclough was younger (1908–84).*

*   *   *

In May 1911 some ingenious members of the French government launched a plan to transform Morocco into a French protectorate. Kiderlen, the German secretary of state, answered by sending a gunboat, the *Panther*, to Agadir. His object was to acquire some compensation for Germany in Morocco or elsewhere. The British government imagined that France and perhaps Great Britain were threatened in their vital interests. The answer was a bellicose speech at the Mansion House by Lloyd George and the dispatch of the Home Fleet to its war stations. Such was the crisis of Agadir which is presented by Geoffrey Barraclough as the harbinger of the First World War.

Professor Barraclough, who has a lifetime of experience in writing historical narrative, provides a vivid account of the political man-oeuvres accompanying the Agadir crisis. The story inclines to the dramatic side. The leading actors – Kiderlen in Germany and Caillaux, the premier, in France – were not building up a situation leading to a war ultimatum; they were conducting skilful though unscrupulous negotiations which achieved a bargain as they had expected from the first. France duly got its protectorate over Morocco. Germany got some rather trivial slices of the French Congo which Kiderlen imagined would open the way to the larger prize of the Belgian Congo as well. The crisis of Agadir was not, in my opinion, the first stage to world war but rather a last episode in an age of European rivalries in Africa which had been running for the previous forty years. None of the participants, not even Lloyd George, projected a war: they were showing off, as they had done for years past.

In so far as the Agadir crisis had any sense, it was as a struggle, not between France and Germany, but between Schneider-Creusot, the

Franco-German combine, which already had a monopoly of Morocco's iron ore, and German interlopers, Mannesmann Brothers,
who tried to stir German national passions. The combine won after a
certain amount of uproar. Barraclough passes over one point of
relevance. At the opening of the crisis, the French High Command
informed its government that the army was not fit to fight Germany.
On top of this the Russians refused to support their French ally and
the British lacked an army equipped to support France however
much they might want to do so. Everything military and financial
points to a sham crisis, designed to rouse the Reichstag and the
French chambers.

Karl Marx once said that history repeats itself – the first time it is
tragedy, the second time farce. The reverse is true about the Agadir
crisis: the first time it was farce, what followed was tragedy. Few
people except the English radicals expected the Agadir crisis to turn
into war. But a great European war broke out three years later. This
is Barraclough's main theme. Even before the *Panther* arrived in
Agadir the leading European countries were in a state of economic
crisis: increasing unemployment, trade union activity, and social
violence. In Great Britain the suffragettes were active; there was
political conflict over Ireland and the House of Lords; in Liverpool
soldiers opened fire on mobs of striking workers. Stable European
civilization was breaking down.

Barraclough lays down a clear thread of events from Agadir to the
outbreak of war in August 1914. Once the French acquired Morocco,
the Italians decided they must occupy Libya, then part of the Ottoman Empire. The Turks were not cooperative; the Italians invaded
Libya and, when the Turks proved obstinate, threatened the Aegean
islands as well. The Balkan states believed that with Turkey already
in difficulties their chance had come to overthrow Turkey-in-Europe,
which they duly proceeded to do. This success went to the heads of
the Serbs who tried to overthrow Austria-Hungary as well. Here is
Barraclough's analogy with the present day. For the Aegean, read the
Persian Gulf; for the Triple Entente and the Triple Alliance, read the
Soviet Union and the United States and here we are: world war in
three years, nuclear this time.

I distrust these analogies. The relations between the Great Powers
were exceptionally friendly between 1911 and 1914. The future of the
Baghdad railway was amicably settled. Germany and Great Britain

arranged a partition of the Portuguese colonies. Throughout 1913 a conference of ambassadors meeting in London kept the peace more successfully than the Council of the United Nations has ever done. The Great War of 1914 did not begin as a conflict between the Great Powers but as a conflict between Austria-Hungary and Serbia, the one a declining power, the other a small power which had just arrived. Foreign Offices and foreign ministers did not provoke the war of 1914. It was the offspring of the rival General Staffs.

I have long held that great wars are first designed by military commanders and then launched by them. This will happen next time except that it will happen more quickly.

Holstein: The Mystery Man

This first appeared as a review of The Holstein Papers, Vol. I, Memoirs, *edited by Norman Rich and M H Fisher (Cambridge, Cambridge University Press, 1955) under the title 'Evil Genius of the Wilhelmstrasse?' in the* Listener, *21 July 1955.*

*   *   *

The First World War has always been a happy hunting ground for theories of the 'Hidden Hand' – men of mystery behind the scenes who manoeuvred human destiny. Even before 1914, many English radicals held that Sir Edward Grey was the prisoner, perhaps unwitting but certainly helpless, of the Foreign Office. The Foreign Office was not condemned alone. The Quai d'Orsay and, still more, the Wilhelmstrasse fell under the same verdict. The Wilhelmstrasse had a special feature. All its members were wicked, but one was more wicked than others. Friedrich von Holstein – the spectre, the evil genius of the Wilhelmstrasse, the man with hyena eyes, blackmailer and psychopath, the perfect man of mystery.

Holstein died in 1909, five years before the outbreak of war. He had retired from the Foreign Office in 1906. He could hardly, therefore, be blamed for the war itself. What he got was the blame for the decline in Germany's position: she was the decisive factor in Europe when Bismarck left office in 1890 – 'the tongue in the balance', he called her. By 1906 she had become isolated and 'encircled', no ally except the moribund Habsburg monarchy, war soon to be forced on her, and defeat following. And Holstein had done it. He manoeuvred himself into the dominant position in the foreign ministry; planted his creatures out in the leading embassies; and then ruined everything by his insane suspicions. His first act as adviser in 1890, when Bismarck went, was to stop the renewal of the Reinsurance Treaty with Russia and so force her into the arms of France. Then he followed a policy of irritating pinpricks towards England, trying to blackmail her into a formal alliance; but when the British statesmen came along with an offer in 1901, he answered with, according to the title of one book about him, 'Holstein's Great No'. So there we are: the Anglo-French entente as well as the Franco-Russian alliance was all his doing.

His evil influence was not shown only in affairs of grand policy; he was also a corrupter of individuals. Sitting at the centre of his spider's web in Berlin, corresponding privately with ambassadors and spying on them, he taught them to be servile – as though Germans needed any teaching in that – uncritical, unreliable. He got hold of scandalous secrets about Princess Bülow, the chancellor's wife, or, according to another account, about Bülow himself, and he used these secrets to blackmail the chancellor, not only keeping himself in office but dictating policy to suit his whims. Even when he was got rid of, he released scandal against Prince Eulenberg, the Kaiser's closest friend. The scandals ruined Eulenberg and discredited William II into the bargain. Certainly a fine record of destruction. The papers from the German foreign ministry did not show much of this when they were published in the 1920s. Holstein appeared as a hard-working official, very competent technically, perhaps rather inclined to see the weak points in any policy rather than its advantages, but not malignant or destructive. Still, the legend survived. It was known that Holstein had carried off most of his private papers; and these hung like a dark cloud over the record, scholars rubbing their hands and saying: 'Wait until they are published. Then we shall see something!'

I have no doubt about the importance of Holstein's career. The years between 1890 and 1906 were vital in the history of Germany, years of decision at their most intense. 1906, I am tempted to think, is the real beginning of contemporary history so far as Europe is concerned; certainly it began the era of the German wars, an era perhaps now closed. The real question of interest in regard to Holstein is not whether he blackmailed people, but how far he contributed to the changes in Germany's position. On the personal side the first volume of his papers, which has just been published, is disappointing. There may be more excitement in the later volumes which will contain his private letters.

This one turns out to be very much a damp squib. It contains his so-called 'memoirs', partly scraps of recollections, from his early years, some amusing anecdotes about Bismarck, spiteful and less amusing remarks about his colleagues; and partly reflections on policy put down after his retirement – German relations with the principal Great Powers, the influence of William II, and so on. There is nothing new here, certainly nothing sensational. Holstein had always been an assiduous worker. Thrown out of his job, he was bored,

restless, perhaps resentful; and he obviously meant to write a vindication of his career, much as Bismarck had done in similar circumstances
fifteen years before. But, like most professional diplomatists, like
Bismarck himself, he could not manage a sustained narrative. It is all
a rigmarole, just like all the other memoirs by professional diplomatists
since the world – their world – began: gossip; personal trivialities; the
same grievance or episode repeated again and again. You end by
being sorry for Holstein. He obviously had not much idea of what was
going on in the world beyond his official desk. But then it has always
puzzled me why people should expect members of a Foreign Office,
German or other, to understand what is going on in the world. They
are a monastic order – cut off from their own country by always
having to deal with foreigners and foreign questions, and yet cut off
from the foreigners by belonging to their own country. They have to
translate hard, often unpleasant, facts into artificial, fine-spun formulas; and they often mistake the formulas for the reality. It is a
profession that both attracts neurotics and produces them. They have
their uses so long as we remember this, so long as we accept them as
advisers and experts, never as the men who determine policy.

Holstein perhaps stepped over the line here, though I am not sure
about this. If you look at the advice he gave, it does not seem to me
markedly more suspect, pathological, destructive – whatever you like
– than the advice given by similar diplomatic officers in other countries: by Eyre Crowe, for example, his contemporary in the British
Foreign Office. In fact, I think Eyre Crowe was even quicker on the
draw in spotting traps and frauds in every seemingly innocent German
proposal than Holstein was with English ones – perhaps justifiably, of
course. To make a case against Holstein you need something more
than his advice, however pathological; you have to get him on the
charge of deciding and directing policy, without being officially responsible for it. And there is something in it – though Holstein was not by
any means the only one. He did sometimes go behind the back of the
chancellor, particularly in the days of Bülow; he certainly tried to
keep affairs away from William II, who was theoretically the supreme
authority. But for the most part he stuck to advice; and if his superiors
usually swallowed his advice, it was because they were not capable of
anything better on their own.

Bülow, for instance, the man whom the liberals wanted as the
saviour of Germany as late as 1917, though a brilliant orator in his

way, had to have every word written out for him beforehand; even his celebrated impromptu replies to interruptions had to be rehearsed. There was no guiding hand in Germany, no one truly responsible, between 1890 and the outbreak of the First World War (nor, for that matter, after it). But the blame, if you want to put it at someone's door, does not rest with Holstein. It was Bismarck who had destroyed every independent, outstanding figure in politics except himself; or perhaps there never were any. It certainly must have been nerve-racking to work under William II; and I have little doubt that Holstein would have liked to turn the Kaiser into a harmless constitutional monarch, but I do not think he did much more than grumble. And I cannot get up much interest in the other personal affairs that Holstein was supposed to be involved in.

The real interest of Holstein's career, it seems to me, is of quite a different kind: not the mystery, the shady stories, the melodrama, but the policy he advised and perhaps conducted. There certainly was a great change in Germany's European position between 1890, when Bismarck was overthrown, and 1906, when Holstein left office. Her relations with Russia and with England were certainly less intimate. But was this change really owing to personal whims and misunder-standings on one side or the other? Did Holstein help to wreck the Reinsurance Treaty simply because it was associated with Bismarck and he wanted to prevent the Bismarck family returning to office? Did England and Germany drift apart in 1895, as Holstein suggests in one of the present essays, simply because Lord Salisbury failed to keep an appointment with William II one summer morning at Cowes? Or, to take the biggest point of all, was the alliance of England and Germany, which was constantly proposed by British statesmen, especially Joseph Chamberlain, between 1898 and 1901, prevented simply by Holstein's unbalanced suspicions? I do not believe a word of it. Look at the Anglo-German alliance which British and German liberals so lamented when the story became known. What the British wanted was an ally against Russia in the Far East. They would provide a navy; and the ally would provide the men. Very nice for the British. But from the German point of view it was an insane proposition – to use that favourite word again – to commit themselves to a large-scale war, a war of life and death, for the sake of British investments in Shanghai and the Yangtse valley.

The key to Holstein's policy is simple. His attitude, like Bismarck's before him, was purely European. Though he knew the outside world unusually well – spoke perfect English and lived for some years in the United States and in South America – he had no sympathy whatever with what contemporaries called 'World Policy'. Most Germans, indeed most people all over Europe, thought that European conflicts were finished and Europe was settled for good. The future conflicts were going to be for world markets. Holstein would have agreed with Bismarck when he said to a colonial enthusiast: 'Here is Russia, and here is France. That is my map of Africa.' Bismarck had kept German ambitions under control. Holstein could not. But he claimed quite rightly to have opposed every step of Germany's world policy which estranged the two world powers, England and Russia. Perhaps 'opposed' is too strong. Holstein was not in a position of power where he could oppose anything. But he did not have anything to do with these steps, and he warned against them. He did not favour the Baghdad railway, which helped to estrange Russia. He was in no way responsible for the Kruger telegram, which challenged the British in South Africa. And he did what he could against the plans for a great German Navy. Of course, his opposition was futile; and even more futile was his line with British statesmen and journalists that, since he disliked Germany's world policy, they should not resent it – even though it was happening. He was a brake that failed to work, a melancholy position, as he himself came to recognize.

He wanted solely to rely on the German Army and to give Germany security in Europe by means of 'the free hand'. This really was not very different from Bismarck's policy, though he used rather different ways of doing it. I do not believe that he ever intended for a moment to make a binding alliance with either England or Russia, whatever his talk of making them bid higher. He held – quite rightly from Germany's point of view – that she had everything to gain by letting England and Russia quarrel and remaining uncommitted in the middle. As European policy this was foolproof. What wrecked it was the German insistence on having a world policy as well: to be a great imperial power in the Far East, in Africa, and on the seas. For this annoyed England and Russia, and pushed them together. Alliance between Russia and the Western Powers is the worst of situations for Germany, just as estrangement between them is the best.

There was, and is, only one way out for Germany. If she is going to challenge the world powers, she must become not *a* European but *the*

European power. She must start with the whole continent under her control. Hitler held this doctrine; so, I think, do the present German advocates of European unification. Holstein arrived at it also, towards the end of his life. Since he could not prevent world policy, he would make it possible. In 1905 he launched the first Moroccan crisis with France with the deliberate object of turning her into a German satellite – perhaps by threats, if not by war. Again, in 1909, he pushed Bülow into standing 100 per cent behind Austria-Hungary in the Bosnian crisis, with the object of making Mitteleuropa at any rate a solid military block. His policy did not come off. But it was the only way out for Germany if she wanted to be a world power.

The moral of the story? A personal one: it is a sad life being a private adviser who cannot direct events, but that is a risk private advisers always take. A literary one: the secrets of the archives are mostly humbug. Government departments guard their records because it flatters their self-importance, not because there is anything startling to be revealed. Most of all, a political moral: when Russia and the Western Powers are on bad terms, Germany is the only gainer. Holstein could play his tricks at the beginning of the century; the present rulers of Germany do much the same now. Very nice for the Germans no doubt, but I have never been able to understand why we or the Russians should get any pleasure from it.

The Ruler in Berlin

This essay first appeared as a review of Erich Eyck's Das Persönliche Regiment Wilhems II *(Erlenbach-Zwich, Rentsch, 1948) in* The Times Literary Supplement, *11 December 1948. In his comments on the book Alan Taylor argued that Eyck gave a disproportionate amount of space to foreign policy at the expense of domestic history 'which should have dominated the book'.*

* * *

On 31 July 1914, Berchtold, Austro-Hungarian foreign minister, was dismayed by advice from Bethmann, the German chancellor, to act with restraint and not to give the signal for war. His distraction was interrupted by Conrad, chief of the Austrian General Staff. Conrad showed him a telegram from Moltke, chief of the German General Staff, which urged that Austria-Hungary should at once mobilize against Russia and so launch a European war. Berchtold, with his irresponsible giggle, exclaimed: 'That beats everything. Who rules then in Berlin?' This flippant remark was a profound judgement on the Germany of William II, and for that matter on the work of Bismarck. The question baffled contemporaries and has baffled later observers.

Between 1871 and 1890 it had seemed possible to answer the question. Bismarck ruled in Berlin. He devised legislation, determined policy, controlled even the military leaders; his decisions settled Germany's course. Yet Bismarck himself did not give this answer. He always insisted that Germany was ruled by the king of Prussia; and claimed that this was the core of his achievement. Bismarck's answer was not a mere pretence; even he, the greatest of political Germans, shrank from ultimate responsibility and shouldered it on to a 'king by the grace of God'. All the same, the version was nonsense in practice, and largely even in theory. Germany could not be ruled by the king-emperor, as Prussia had been ruled by Frederick the Great or even by Frederick William IV. Men may obey their king, even in a period when monarchical sentiment is declining; they will not obey someone else's king, and the king of Prussia was the king of others for the majority of Germans. The king of Prussia was German emperor by conquest, by invitation of the German princes, by political intrigue, by constitutional arrangement, by everything except 'the grace of God'. The German emperor had no coronation – hence no religious sanction. Right still counted for much in Germany; and the emperor's right rested on national sentiment, not on divine appointment.

Bismarck's creation deserved its name of 'the second empire'; its spirit was, in truth, nearer to the demagogy of Napoleon III than to the mystic tradition of 'the Holy Roman Empire of the German nation'. After 1806, when the Holy Roman Empire ended, German authority could rest only on the masses. Bismarck had concealed this fact, as the titanic figure of Napoleon I had concealed it in France in similar circumstances. With the fall of Bismarck it could be concealed no longer. The question, 'Who rules in Berlin?' was stated with ever-increasing urgency, until it found an answer in 1933.

William II had perhaps supposed in 1890 that he himself would rule in Berlin. This view was held later by those who wished 'to hang the Kaiser'. The fault of William was his failure to rule, not that he ruled wrongly. Dr Eyck, his latest historian, is nearer the truth when he draws a parallel with the system of English government in the reign of George III. George III, too, used to be accused of personal rule; this is a myth no longer believed by anyone. On the personal side it is unfair to compare William II with George III. William had considerable political gifts, to say nothing of his gift for phrase-making. Theodore Roosevelt said to him in 1910: 'In America you would have your ward behind you and would lead your delegation at your party's national convention.' In fact, William was a first-rate 'keynote' speaker. On the great issues of politics he often saw farther than his professional advisers. In 1890 he was right to reject Bismarck's programme of a *coup d'état* in favour of reconciling the working classes to the Reich; in 1905 he was right in opposing Holstein's policy of the Tangier visit; he was right (from the German point of view) in promoting the Baghdad railway; he was right in distrusting the moribund Habsburg monarchy and, at the end, in advocating concessions to Romania as the one way of staving off disaster; even his advances to both Russia and England did more good than harm – without such a gesture, for example, as his visit to the deathbed of Queen Victoria, estrangement between England and Germany would have come even sooner than it did. While the German Foreign Office was confidently snubbing all the Great Powers in turn, William II saw the dangers of 'the free hand' and never ceased, though by erratic impulses, to seek for some great political combination.

His immediate reactions, no doubt, were often as wild as his longer vision was sound. He would scribble, 'We must mobilize at once' on the news of some colonial dispute; and even proposed to arrest the transference of the British Fleet to the North Sea by an ultimatum. He exploded repeatedly against Austrian failure to destroy Serbia; yet he realized more clearly than any German diplomatist that this was a futile programme and, in his serious moments, urged reconciliation. His marginal notes, which made so much stir when published, were written for pleasure, not for action; and no action ever followed from them. They were the outbreaks of a man knowing himself, and known to be, irresponsible. The Kruger telegram is a case in point. This was certainly a watering-down of William's original idea of landing marines at Delagoa Bay. All the same, it would never have been sent, had it not suited Holstein's scheme of frightening England with the shadow of a Continental League. When this scheme failed, Marschall and Holstein shifted the blame to William, though the policy underlying it was theirs. So later, in the great crisis of the reign, Germans of all classes, from Bülow downwards, used the *Daily Telegraph* affair as a means for shifting on to William II all the consequences of German arrogance and power.

William II was not a ruler; he was a medium. He reflected the political mind of Germany and expressed it with genius. Contemporary observers were much at fault when they attributed the great German Navy to a personal whim of William II. The navy was a demagogic cause, promoted by liberal professors and popular even among socialist and Roman Catholic voters. Had William surrendered altogether to his demagogic impulses, he would have anticipated Hitler's undisputed power. As it was, his upbringing and conscience reined him in; the king of Prussia restrained the German emperor, as Prussia, in Bismarck's conception, restrained Germany. These negations were not a solution; and since William failed to lead, the problem was returned to the chancellors. Here, indeed, is the profound political interest of the reign of William II – the search for a principle of authority and responsibility when this could no longer be provided by the Crown. To return to the analogy with George III: Dr Eyck supposes that George III was defeated by 'the opposition of Charles Fox', and blames the Germans for not producing a liberal figure of similar eminence. This does that charming gambler too much honour. Growth of a sense of responsibility, not of an opposition, transformed the British constitution; and this responsibility rested on a governing class which was truly representative of 'the political nation'. In Bismarckian Germany the governing classes, military and civil, were not merely out of touch with the masses who had become the nation: they were actively and consciously opposed to everything that was dearest to national ambition. Bismarck's greatest achievement was his defeat of Greater Germany: he preserved the Habsburg monarchy and insisted that his truncated Germany was a 'satiated state'. This flew in the face of national sentiment. The only binding force in the governing classes was resistance to the popular will. Liberal observers, misled by Western analogies, thought that this implied principally resistance to a constitutional system; but the national masses demanded most of all a truly united Germany.

The reign of William II saw two attempts to break the deadlock between the governing classes and the nation; in different ways both Caprivi and Bülow aspired 'to rule in Berlin'. Caprivi took the way of liberalism; Bülow attempted to wield the bow of Bismarck and to create a new Bismarckian compromise by agility and intrigue. Caprivi, who followed Bismarck as chancellor, has been neglected by historians; yet he was the most significant of Bismarck's successors, for he conducted the experiment in liberalism which later writers often suggested as the 'solution' of the German problem. In fact Caprivi was the only parliamentary chancellor of imperial Germany. Though appointed by the emperor, he thought in terms of a parliamentary majority, and this could be created only by means of a 'national' programme. Hence Caprivi gave up Bismarck's negative foreign policy and supported the German cause in south-eastern Europe: domestic and foreign demagogy went hand in hand. Caprivi justified the imperial military programme by reference to Russia, instead of to France; and the climax of his policy came in 1893 when he carried the increased army grant with the votes of Roman Catholics, Poles and some progressives. As Dr Eyck rightly says, the split in the Progressive Party which followed this vote marked the end of liberalism as a political force in Germany. Dr Eyck calls it suicide; suicide is sometimes the only solution. Liberalism had no future if it failed to support Caprivi; equally it had no future if it supported him. For Caprivi himself had no future. In 1894 he ran into conflict with Botho

Eulenberg, prime minister of Prussia. Caprivi wanted a democratic reform of the Prussian suffrage, Eulenberg a revival of the anti-socialist laws. William II took the only course and dismissed them both. The decisive answer was given: no one could rule in Berlin.

This answer was accepted by Hohenlohe, the next chancellor. Dr Eyck speaks contemptuously of his age and feebleness; these were the necessary conditions of his existence. As a Bavarian, he would not restrain Germany for the sake of Prussia; as a conservative, he would not break Prussia for the sake of Germany. With little power over events and no influence in the Reichstag, he tolerated all the decisive lurches in German policy: the Baghdad railway, the great navy, the establishment in China were all Hohenlohe's doing, or rather consequences of his lack of doing. He deliberately avoided asking the great question, let alone attempting to answer it. Yet it was a question which demanded an answer. The man who attempted to answer it in the reign of William II was Bülow, chancellor from 1900 to 1909. Bülow's name is weighed down by his *Memoirs*, the most trivial record ever left by a man who has occupied high position. Nevertheless he dominated the history of Wilhelmine Germany. Bülow was the only imperial chancellor after Bismarck to count in German politics – the only one who made effective speeches and to whom men looked for a 'policy'. Still more, 'the Bülow bloc' of 1906 was the first stable parliamentary combination behind the chancellor since Bismarck broke with the National Liberals in 1879, and it was a more reliable coalition than any created under the Weimar Republic. Finally, in 1908, Bülow – whether deliberately or not – used the *Daily Telegraph* affair to eject William II from politics and to impose upon him the limitations of a constitutional monarch. William II never recovered from this blow; it ended whatever fragments of 'personal rule' remained.

Bülow's success was barren. It served only to reveal that the problem of German government lay deeper than in William's character; it was rooted in the foundations of Bismarck's Reich. The humiliation of William II left Bülow face to face with the Prussian conservatives; and once more, as with Caprivi, it became clear that the twin causes of 'world policy' and internal democracy could be achieved only after the defeat of the classes which Bismarck had preserved, the forces of old Prussia. Bülow declared to the conservatives who brought him down: 'We shall meet again at Philippi.' The engagement was not fought in Bülow's lifetime; it was won by his demagogic heir in 1933 and completed by the massacres which followed 20 July 1944. Bülow's fall led to another, more fateful, interregnum, the chancellorship of Bethmann Hollweg. Hohenlohe had allowed policy to be made without him; Bethmann Hollweg had it made against him. It was a grotesque, though inevitable, conclusion to Bismarck's work that the chancellor should be helpless both in the Reichstag and in the Prussian Landtag; universal suffrage and privileged class-franchise alike rejected him. Yet for this very reason he was the only possible chancellor. As in Metternich's Austria, 'administration had taken the place of government'.

A solution of a sort was found, perhaps against Bethmann Hollweg's will: a solution of foreign policy. German foreign policy of the 1890s had been 'cabinet diplomacy', even though it made an occasional demagogic gesture. The last display of this 'cabinet diplomacy' was the first Moroccan crisis of 1905; a crisis deliberately engineered by Holstein without any preparation of public opinion and hence ending in failure for Germany. Once more, in the Bosnian crisis, Bülow was the man of the transition: demagogue enough to back the German cause in south-eastern Europe, Bismarckian enough to regret having done so. In 1911 national opinion came into its own: the Agadir crisis was fought with public backing from start to finish. Nevertheless, Agadir was a false start, a red herring: it was deliberately designed by Kiderlen, last of the Bismarckians, to distract German chauvinism from eastern Europe and so from the mortal conflict with Russia. Until Agadir, Germany had remained a Power which, if not 'satiated', could still be satisfied with colonial gains; after Agadir, Germany had to bid for the mastery of Europe. This inescapable fate determined the diplomacy of 1913 and 1914, which Dr Eyck describes in full detail: German policy sought in vain to avoid the mission of conquest which was being thrust upon it. Few historians will quarrel with Dr Eyck's verdict that the German statesmen and generals did not deliberately plan the outbreak of world war in July 1914; yet a war of conquest was the only possible outcome of German history. Bethmann Hollweg had been the only imperial chancellor to be censured by the Reichstag; he was also the only chancellor to receive from the Reichstag a unanimous vote of confidence. Certainly in August 1914 Bethmann Hollweg did not 'rule in Berlin'; what ruled at last in Berlin was the will of the German people for power.

The German problem, past and present, is the problem of German unity. Though this does not exist now, we are tempted to think that it existed in some Golden Age of the past. Dr Eyck's book is a reminder that this Golden Age cannot be found in the age of William II. Imperial Germany was never a united national state, in the sense that France was united and made a nation by the Great Revolution. In imperial Germany, almost as much as in the Holy Roman Empire, there was a balance of authorities and classes; instead of authoritarian rule there was 'organized anarchy'. Germany had, in some sort, a 'governing class' – the Prussian army officers and Prussian administrators. Though this class held Germany together, it was even more concerned to hold Germany back; while offering Germany a corset, it strapped on a straitjacket. The first German war weakened this class; the Hitler revolution completed its destruction. There are now no forces within Germany to resist the full programme of German unification, and the present partition rests solely on the occupying armies. This gives it a unique and precarious character. A Germany free from foreign control will seek to restore the united Greater Germany which Hitler achieved in 1938; nor will democracy provide an automatic safeguard against a new German aggression. In the reign of William II every step towards democracy was a step towards general war. The navy was popular, 'world policy' was popular, support for the German cause in eastern Europe was popular. Attempts at reconciliation with others were unpopular; and William's prestige was ruined in 1908 when it became known that he favoured friendship with England.

The harsh truth of German history is that the solution of the German question cannot be found within Germany. Partition cannot be maintained as a permanent policy; yet a united Germany will keep Europe in apprehension, and would be tolerable only in a world of United Nations. Wilhelmine Germany overshadowed her neighbours by playing off East and West; any future Germany will seek to do the same. If the Great Powers were on friendly terms, there would even now be no German problem; so long as they remain estranged, Germany will offer the occasion, and may be the originator of future wars. 'Who rules in Berlin?' The question once dominated German history; now it torments all the world. In our impatience and anxiety we are led to hope that one day the German people may rule in Berlin. That outcome is, in the long run, unavoidable; it will be tolerable only if there also rules in Berlin awareness of a community of nations. It is for the Germans to seek unity on a democratic and pacific basis; the Great Powers must ensure that the Germans do not promote unity by a programme of foreign aggression. At the present time, both the Germans and the Great Powers are failing in their task; and the question, 'Who rules in Berlin?' has lost nothing of its menacing character.

War by Time-Table

These essays were first published in a small book, War by Time-table: How the First World War Began (*London, Macdonald, 1969*), *in the Macdonald Library of the Twentieth Century, edited by John Roberts. An earlier version was given in October and November 1968 as a series of lectures in University College, London University.*

* * *

The Making of the Time-Tables

When the twentieth century opened, there were six Great Powers in Europe. They were, in alphabetical order, Austria-Hungary, France, Germany, Great Britain or more accurately the British Empire, Italy, and Russia. Though they were not equally powerful, even the least of them – probably Italy – was decisively stronger than the most considerable of the powers in the middle rank. Russia was the greatest in population; Great Britain the greatest in financial resources; Germany the greatest in economic strength, with Great Britain not far behind. There had been no war between any of these Great Powers since the Franco-German war of 1870–71. There had been disputes between them, usually over questions outside Europe. Threats had been exchanged, but there had been no serious mobilization of rival forces since the conflict between Russia and Great Britain over Constantinople in 1878 had brought the two Powers close to war.

This remarkable run of peace had been achieved virtually without formal organization. The Concert of Europe was a phrase, not an institution, and even as a phrase had not much reality. The Powers maintained ambassadors at one another's capitals, and ambassadors and foreign ministers talked together at length, sometimes amicably, sometimes the reverse. The crowned heads, who still had a large say in determining policy, were all personally acquainted and even included the president of the French Republic, a little condescendingly, in their social rounds. Apart from this, there were few international meetings. The great exception was the Congress of Berlin in 1878, but even this, unlike earlier congresses, discussed few general questions and was content to revise the peace treaty which Russia had imposed on Turkey earlier in the year. There was a conference at Berlin in 1884 over central Africa and another at Algeciras in 1906 over Morocco. During the Balkan Wars, the ambassadors in London met regularly under the chairmanship of Sir Edward Grey, the British foreign secretary, in order to ensure that they were not dragged into war by the doings of the belligerents. For most of the time, however, international relations seemed to run themselves.

In this liberal age, men came to assume that political relations between states, like economic relations between individuals, were governed by a beneficent law of nature, and that if each state, like each individual, pursued its own interests, the good of all would be achieved. In international affairs there was a special law, known as the balance of power. This, too, was supposed to be self-operating. An unknown providence ensured that, if one Power became too strong, the others would automatically shift their weight, without knowing what they were doing, and the balance would thus be safely restored.

The civilization of the later nineteenth century rested on the belief that certainty, and therefore security, could be indefinitely prolonged into the future. The most obvious example of this was the railway time-table. With its aid, a man could state, down to the minute, precisely where he would be a month or a year from now. Similarly, an investor would lay out his money in government bonds, with the absolute confidence that these would retain their full value for fifty or a hundred years ahead. In England landowners granted leases for 99 or even 999 years, equally confident that society and money would remain exactly the same throughout that time. International relations operated under the same expectations. Statesmen drew up arrangements with each other which were to last for an indefinite future. These arrangements produced the system of alliances which seemed to shape the politics of the early twentieth century.

The system had been there so long that it was treated as though it had been there for ever. In fact, like so many traditions, it was of nineteenth-century invention. Statesmen had of course referred to their 'allies' for generations past. All they meant was a vague friendship towards the allied country and perhaps a hope that they might work together in time of war. Alliances, in the form of precise written engagements, were made only in wartime or when a war was about to break out, and they dissolved into generalities when the particular war was over. Bismarck inaugurated the new system when he made a peacetime alliance with Austria-Hungary in 1879. Ironically, the inventor of the system did not like it. He included a clause that the alliance was to last for five years, unless renewed. He added that every alliance included the unwritten clause, *rebus sic stantibus* – as long as things remain the same. However, his successors did not follow his maxim, and the Austro-German alliance was generally assumed to have become a fixture in the international law of Europe. The provisions of the alliance were simple. If either party were attacked by Russia, the other would come to its aid; in any other war (most probably a war between Germany and France) the second ally would remain neutral.

In 1882 Bismarck also brought Italy into his system which thus became the Triple Alliance. This too was simple. Germany and Italy would aid each other in case France attacked either; Italy would remain neutral if either of her allies were at war with Russia. Other clauses of a more temporary nature were tacked on as the years went by, but essentially the Triple Alliance remained the same. Few people, however, took it very seriously. Italy had laid down the condition that she would not go against Great Britain and therefore moved away from her Triple Alliance partners when Great Britain was reconciled with France. Moreover Italy and Austria-Hungary were on bad terms. Italy coveted Austrian territory, and Austrian generals often pined for a war against Italy, the only war which they were likely to win.

Bismarck's system was designed to provide security against the supposedly aggressive Powers, France and Russia. These two were, however, equally apprehensive of an attack by Germany and after many hesitations concluded an alliance on their side in 1894. Oddly enough there was no precise political agreement, only a military convention. This provided that at least a third of the Russian Army would act against Germany, if Germany attacked France. It also provided that France would mobilize, though not necessarily go to war, if Austria-Hungary did so. Strangest of all, the convention was to last as long as the Triple Alliance, though neither France nor Russia knew the latter's terms. This last provision was cancelled in 1899.

There were other alliances between Great Powers and lesser ones: an Austro-German alliance with Romania, for example, directed against a Russian attack; a British alliance of long standing with

Portugal; and three general treaties of guarantee, involving all the Great Powers, for the benefit of Switzerland, Belgium, and, more vaguely, Luxembourg. Outside Europe there was an alliance between Great Britain and Japan, by which after 1905 each promised to aid the other in the event of attack by any one Power. After 1911 this alliance did not apply against the United States. But all these were extras. The essential European balance was between the Franco-Russian or Dual Alliance on the one side and the Triple Alliance, or more realistically the Austro-German alliance, on the other. Both sets of alliances were strictly defensive if taken literally: they were to operate only in case of attack, and since every Great Power declared that it was exclusively concerned with defence, war was theoretically impossible.

The Great Powers had comparatively few direct causes of conflict with each other. Germany did not desire any additional territory in Europe: neither the Baltic Germans nor the Austrian Germans interested her. France would seek to recover Alsace and Lorraine if war came about, but most Frenchmen agreed that they would not start a war to recover them. Russia would have liked to control Constantinople and the Straits, but was reasonably content so long as no other Great Power did so. Some Austrian militarists had fantasies of recovering the Italian lands which had been lost in 1859 and 1866, but these fantasies had no reality. Many Italians wished more urgently to liberate the irredentas of South Tyrol and Trieste, but they lacked the strength to do it.

Conflict could, however, arise by accident or from questions apparently trivial and remote from Europe. Great Britain and France nearly went to war over Siam in 1893 and over the upper Nile in 1898. Germany and France got fairly close to war over Morocco in 1905 and 1911. Russia and Great Britain had repeated alarms – over the Near East, over Persia, over Afghanistan, and over the Far East. Russia and Austria-Hungary had alarms over the Balkans – at first over Bulgaria and later over Serbia. These conflicts often threatened to bring the alliances into play. For example, if Russia attacked Austria-Hungary as the result of a quarrel over Bulgaria, would Germany be obliged to aid Austria-Hungary, as she had undertaken to do in the Austro-German alliance? Or if Germany attacked France as the result of a quarrel over Morocco, would Russia have to fulfil her promise under the Franco-Russian alliance? On the whole, the various Powers rejected such consequences. An attack which brought the conditions of the alliance into play would really have to be 'unprovoked aggression', in the later twentieth-century phrase. Thus Bismarck steadfastly refused to promise support for Austria-Hungary in the Bulgarian troubles during the 1880s. If she wanted to oppose Russia, he said, she must find other allies – Great Britain and Italy. Later, Russia refused to support France in the two Moroccan crises of 1905 and 1911. France refused to support Russia in the Bosnian crisis of 1908.

In ordinary day-to-day affairs, the precise written alliances seemed to count for comparatively little and were no more than a last resource. What really mattered were vaguer unwritten associations of the old sort. Here again the main groups were the same: Triple Alliance against Dual Alliance. But there were many exceptions to this generalization. France, for instance, was of all the Powers the most opposed to the establishment of Russian control over Constantinople and the Straits and, while she gave a vague approval to Russia's ambitions in the Far East, did so only in order to divert Russian interest from the Near East. On the other side, though German and Austro-Hungarian interests did not conflict, they did not coincide. Germany cared little or nothing for the Balkans, which were Austria-Hungary's sole preoccupation. Austria-Hungary was totally aloof from Germany's world policy of a great navy and colonial acquisitions.

Great Britain always refused to make any binding alliance in peace-time, except for the historical relic of her alliance with Portugal. But she played an active part in the vaguer understandings. After all, friendships, if not alliances, were needed for many lesser purposes than war – particularly for such things as the international supervision of finance in the derelict empires, Turkey, China, and Egypt. At one time Great Britain cooperated with Austria-Hungary and Italy against Russia in regard to Turkey. She cooperated with Germany and Italy against France in regard to Egypt. She tried unsuccessfully to cooperate with Germany against Russia in regard to China. Later she made up her quarrels with both France and Russia in agreements known as ententes. Were these ententes merely settlements of differences, as they claimed to be? Or did they imply a more general partnership? Sometimes the one, and sometimes the other. After 1904, when the

Anglo-French entente was made, Great Britain was always on good terms with France and was even ready to say that the maintenance of French independence was an important British interest. But she gave no firm promise of military support. With Russia, Great Britain was often on cool terms even after making the Anglo-Russian entente in 1907, and she certainly did not declare that the maintenance of Russia as a Great Power was vital to her.

Though all the Powers relied on the alliances for their security and power, they relied even more essentially on their own strength. After all, they were no good as allies unless they were strong. The strength of the continental Powers took a common form. All had vast armies composed mainly of infantry and based on universal military service. This system had been adopted by all the Great Powers, and most small ones also, after Germany's victories in the Franco-German War. In theory, every young man received intensive military training for either two or three years and remained liable for recall for some years thereafter. Then he was placed in the reserve, and these reservists, in the judgement of all military authorities except the German, were not fit for war until they had received a new period of training. The system was by no means watertight. In most countries, those proceeding to a university or to other higher education got off with one year's military service, and in countries with more population than industrial resources, such as Russia, many men escaped without serious training of any kind. Still, every country could count on having some millions of men under arms within a few weeks of the outbreak of war.

This was the great operation known as mobilization. At a given signal – usually the display of placards on public notice-boards – every man recently discharged would proceed to rejoin his unit at a centre designated on his card. These units would in turn proceed to some higher formation until the structure of armies was complete. Not only would men be on the move. The light and heavy guns and their shells had also to be assembled from their peacetime parks. Most conspicuous of all would be the horses, most of them also mobilized from their peacetime tasks. Quite apart from the cavalry and their remounts, there would be horses for the artillery and their supply wagons, horses to transport everything needed by the infantry from first-aid stations to field kitchens, and, above all, horses by which officers could carry messages or direct the march of their men. Every railway wagon in France had long been labelled: '40 men or 8 horses', and the wagons in other countries bore similar designations. The entire process would be conducted by rail, until the armies had reached the assumed point of battle, and General Staffs had been labouring for years past to perfect their time-tables. It was universal doctrine that speed was essential. Whichever Power completed its mobilization first would strike first and might even win the war before the other side was ready. Hence the time-tables became ever more ingenious and ever more complicated.

Major-General Sir Edward Spears, who himself watched the French mobilization in August 1914, has left a classic account of the problems involved:

If the mobilization is delayed or slow, the enemy will be enabled to advance with a fully equipped army against an unprepared one, which would be disastrous.

The time factor also makes it essential that the armies, once mobilized, should find themselves exactly where they can at once take up the role assigned to them. There is no opportunity for extensive manoeuvres: mobilization is in itself a manoeuvre at the end of which the armies must be ready to strike according to the pre-arranged plan.

The plan is therefore obviously of vital importance. It has of necessity to be somewhat rigid, for it has to be worked out in every detail beforehand. From the moment mobilization is ordered, every man must know where he has to join, and must get there in a given time. Each unit, once complete and fully equipped, must be ready to proceed on a given day at the appointed hour to a pre-arranged destination in a train awaiting it, which in its turn must move according to a carefully prepared railway scheme. Each unit has also to drop into its place in the higher formations, and these again must find themselves grouped in position according to the fundamental plan. No change, no alteration is possible during mobilization. Improvisation when dealing with nearly three million men and the movements of 4,278 trains, as the French had to do, is out of the question.

There were some curious features about these wonderful plans for universal mobilization. Though they had been worked on and elaborated for many years, they had never been tried in practice. Russia was the only Great Power which had ever mobilized its great army, and this was for the Russo-Japanese War, not a relevant experience. In that war the Russian armies had to be trickled slowly across the interminable wastes of Siberia, and there could be no question of flinging them all simultaneously into battle. In other countries there were of course manoeuvres and occasional sample tests to see how the time-tables worked. But no one had any idea what would happen when the time really came to mobilize and move men by the million. Some General Staffs, especially the German, trusted the efficiency of the railways as well as their own and confidently assumed that no margin need be left for error or misfortune. Others, especially the Russian and the Austrian, expected that things would often go wrong and allowed for this in the time-table.

One interruption was not postulated in any plan for mobilization: the enemy. It was assumed that, while rates of mobilization might vary, no Power would be allowed a head start on its rivals. But the assumption was carried further, and the plans went on developing with no allowance for enemy interference when weeks might have passed or even when, as in the exceptional German case, the mobilization was to be completed in some foreign or enemy country. An anecdote from the Crimean War comes to mind. The British surgeon general, when faced with complaints about the breakdown of the medical services, replied: 'The medical services would have been perfectly adequate if it had not been for the casualties.' Similarly the General Staffs could say before 1914: 'Our plans are perfect unless the enemy interferes with them.' Even the manoeuvres which tested the plans to some extent were determined by special moves as in a game. Once a decisive position was occupied, the manoeuvres were over.

Real fighting was difficult, if not impossible, to simulate, and no staff officers outside Russia had fighting experience of a relevant kind. The Russians had faced problems of logistics during the Russo-Japanese War, but they had learnt little except that war was a chaos. They concluded that the only method was somehow to get the armies together and then to send them lurching forward – a method they applied throughout the First World War. The British Army had considerable fighting experience during the Boer War, but this was experience of fast-moving warfare against an elusive enemy, skilled but with small forces. The Italians had got some fighting experience in Abyssinia and Libya, campaigns which did them little credit. The French and Germans had virtually no experience at all. Colonial campaigns in Morocco or against the Hereros of South-West Africa taught few lessons of value. It was peculiarly ironical that Schlieffen, the most influential of all German planners, never took part in any fighting – not even during the Franco-German War, though he was already a serving officer.

These inexperienced strategists all held firmly to the dogma that their plans were immutable to the last detail and that improvisation of any kind was impossible. With each elaboration, they became still more the prisoners of their own time-tables. Mobilization appeared to them a once-for-all operation. It had to be performed in a particular way and would then determine the entire shape of the war which followed. Moreover, since the plans were prepared and occasionally tested in peacetime, they assumed unconsciously that peacetime conditions would continue after the outbreak of war. The war would be, as it were, imposed on a peacetime society which would pursue its usual habits. The army trains therefore had to be fitted in not only with each other, but also with the normal traffic in passengers and freight.

Politically the plans for mobilization were all made in the void. They aimed at the best technical result without allowing for either the political conditions from which war might spring or the political consequences which might follow from any particular plan. There was little consultation between military planners and civilian statesmen. The statesmen assumed that the General Staffs were doing their best to ensure that they would win a war if one came, and there was no speculation how policy could be seconded by military action. The dogma of the great Clausewitz that 'war is a continuation of policy by other means' had lost its hold. War had now become a theoretical operation conducted for its own sake. This attitude persisted even when war came. Hence the belligerents fought simply for victory, not to gain any precise, specified advantage.

The military planners were a little more forthcoming towards their allied colleagues, but not to the extent of coordinating their plans. The British were the one exception for an obvious reason. Mobilization within the British Isles would not of itself lead on to war. The army would have to go somewhere outside the country, and the British staff drew up elaborate plans by which it should go to France. In this way, Great Britain, which was supposed from her maritime position to possess the most flexible strategy, acquired the most inflexible. The French made no answering gesture and merely tacked on the British forces to their own. The great French preoccupation lay elsewhere in the fear that, while the Germans were invading France, the Russians would throw all their strength against Austria-Hungary. From the moment when the Franco-Russian alliance was concluded, the French insisted that a considerable proportion of the Russian Army should be directed against Germany.

The Russians willingly produced fanciful figures showing the vast armies available for the German theatre. They were less forthcoming in the practical consideration of building strategic railways to the German frontier. Time and again, the French provided loans to Russia, on condition that part of the money should be spent on such railways. Time and again, the condition was evaded. The Russian time-table, though impressive on paper, thus remained largely a figment of the imagination.

The absence of coordination between Germany and Austria-Hungary was even more striking, especially as these were reputed to be 'the military monarchies'. The Germans drew up elaborate plans for moving Italian forces to the French front, and the Italians enjoyed this planning greatly. They did not intend, however, to take part in a war against France and when the time came did not do so. The prolonged discussions were therefore without purpose. Between Germany and Austria-Hungary there was little more than vague talk of making war in common. The Germans suspected that the Austrians might divert all their strength to the Balkans instead of fighting against Russia, but there was little they could do to change this, and they made no attempt to plan a joint campaign against Russia. Certainly the Germans did not rely on the Austrians for the defence of German territory in the east. Instead they relied on time – that is to say, the superior speed of their own mobilization. They assumed that they would have defeated France before the Russians were prepared to move against East Prussia on any great scale at all.

On a more technical level there was no coordination at all. The British and French armies in the west, the German and Austrian armies in the east, would presumably fight side by side. Yet there was no attempt to coordinate equipment or intelligence services. No one had thought out a system of liaison between the various allied armies. The Germans had the advantage that they spoke the same language as the Austrians, at any rate at the higher levels of society, but they took few steps to use this advantage in practice. The British and French had made no preparations at all and, when they found themselves fighting side by side, had to rely on any bilingual officer who happened to be available. Even so, when Joffre, the French commander-in-chief, wished to communicate with Sir John French, who commanded the British Expeditionary Force, he usually did so via the British ambassador in Paris.

There were thus half a dozen separate plans for mobilization, none designed to fit in with any other, except in the British case, and all merging to a greater or lesser extent into plans for actual war. The Russian and Austro-Hungarian plans were the least linked with the war which might actually follow. The Russians merely provided that the armies would gather at their centres of mobilization. Then the commanders would decide what to do next, whether in fact to attack Austria-Hungary or Germany. Even so, only one type of mobilization was possible. If the Russians resolved on a limited mobilization, say of the forces nearest to Austria-Hungary, they could not switch over to a larger mobilization later. For that would mean that some trains would be running according to the time-table of Day 6 or 10, when others would be running according to the time-table of Day 1. This sort of confusion would be unthinkable.

The Austrians had prepared in theory a more flexible strategy. Even if they operated a general mobilization, some of the armies were placed in such a position and provided with such alternative time-tables that they could proceed to different fields of battle. The bulk of the army was pointed towards Galicia, where it would encounter the Russians. But three groups could turn against either Serbia or Russia, and two against either Serbia or Italy. The ingenuity with which this was planned gave Conrad, chief of the Austro-Hungarian General Staff, the reputation of being the best strategist in Europe. But the ingenuity was mainly on paper. When the time came, the Austrians put off mobilizing as long as they could and then improvised in an atmosphere of chaos.

The Russian and Austrian plans had one feature in common: they provided that, after mobilization, the commanders would look around and decide what to do. In other words, the dogma often heard before the First World War and repeated parrot-like by many historians after it that 'mobilization means war' did not apply so far as Russia and Austria-Hungary were concerned. For them mobilization meant mobilization: greater readiness to fight a war, but not a final decision to fight it, and still less a decision where and how it would be fought. The distinction between mobilization and war was less clear on the Western Front.

The French had no doubt where their war would be fought. Indeed they were the one country for whom any choice of strategy was inconceivable. Their only possible war was against Germany, and the only possible place for the French to fight it was on the short Franco-German frontier of the Vosges. The French plans were designed to ensure that all their armies would be in a position to fight this great battle of the frontiers as soon as possible after the beginning of mobilization. For many years, the French had planned a purely defensive battle – to keep the Germans out of France. Latterly their commanders had come to believe that a defensive strategy was bound to fail and that an offensive one was bound to succeed. They therefore proposed to rush bull-headed against the Germans.

There was a further reason for this change of strategy. The French suspected that the Germans might try to turn their northern flank by going through Belgium. The French could not plan to violate Belgian neutrality first, if only for fear of offending British feeling, and any move into Belgium after the Germans had entered it would be that impossible thing – improvisation. However, the French were undismayed. They thought that they knew the answer. Since they refused to believe that the Germans could use reservists as front-line soldiers, they greatly underestimated the forces at Germany's disposal and assumed that the Germans could send armies into Belgium only by weakening their centre. Hence a victory for the French offensive was even more certain.

French mobilization was very near to war, but not quite war. Once the French armies were assembled on the frontier, they could wait for the signal to attack. Indeed they had to wait until they knew whether the Germans were going through Belgium or not. This news would determine both the weight and the place of their own attack. With the Germans, and only with the Germans, there was no breathing space between mobilization and war. One merged inevitably into the other, and this proved the decisive impulse towards war in August 1914. This unique feature of German planning had been developing for a generation past. It sprang from Germany's unique position. Alone among the Great Powers she had two potentially hostile Great Powers, France and Russia, as neighbours and would have to fight two great wars with one army. The elder Moltke, victor of the Franco-German War, had proposed to hold the narrow French frontier with its strong fortifications, while the bulk of the German Army defeated the Russian. His successor, Schlieffen, rejected this strategy. Like everyone else, he doubted whether a defensive stance could succeed. In any case, the defeat of Russia would not be decisive. Great Russian armies would remain somewhere in Russia's vast space, and the Germans would be entangled in a prolonged campaign, while the French broke through in the west.

Schlieffen therefore proposed to fight the western battle first. France would be defeated, Paris would be taken, and the Germans could then turn all their strength against Russia. Originally, when Schlieffen switched the weight of German attack from east to west, he thought only of a battle of the frontiers, just as the French did. Soon he decided that the French line of fortresses was too strong to be broken in a hurry, and, with Russian armies massing in the east, the Germans would have no time to spare. The French line would therefore have to be outflanked on either south or north. A southern flanking movement through Switzerland would not put the Germans across the French lines of communication, nor would it lead to any centres of French strength. Schlieffen therefore rejected it. A northern advance through Luxembourg and Belgium offered greater rewards. The German armies would move through easy country. They would soon be in a position to encircle the French armies and to threaten Paris, or so Schlieffen imagined.

Schlieffen was a professor of strategy, not a practical general. He played with his plan for many years, making it ever more elaborate. At first he intended to go only through Luxembourg and a corner of Belgium. Later he became more ambitious and proposed to sweep right through Belgium into northern France. Ultimately he allotted four armies, two-thirds of Germany's strength in the west, for this great stroke. There was only a narrow gap of eighty miles between the supposedly impassable Ardennes and the frontier of Holland, which the Germans proposed to respect. The four armies must pass through Aachen, the only railway junction, and then be pumped through this narrow gap before the French realized what was happening. It was impossible for all four armies to mobilize at Aachen and then wait for the declaration of war. The first army must mobilize and be on its way before the second arrived, and so on. Schlieffen therefore included the invasion of Belgium in his plans for mobilization. More correctly, he had no plans for mobilization. Once the

Germans began to mobilize, war inevitably followed on the second or third day, unless of course the Belgians gave the German armies a free run.

Schlieffen never worried about the political problem of Belgian neutrality. He did not speculate as to whether the Belgians would resist. He did not reflect that the infringement of Belgian neutrality might bring Great Britain into a war against Germany – a consideration which, in view of the small size of the British Army, did not interest him. His anxieties were purely technical. For instance, the Belgians had a great fortress, Liège, immediately barring the way against the Germans. This, far from making Schlieffen hesitate, determined him to act even more at a rush and to take Liège almost before the Belgians knew what was happening. Again, in his remorselessly academic way, he pushed on to consider remote contingencies, which might arise on the twentieth or even the fortieth day. He would need one army to seal off Antwerp, another to guard the German lines of communication, and still more fresh armies when the Germans arrived in front of Paris. The only contingency he never considered was that the French might at some time realize what was happening and get in his way. The entire Schlieffen plan was conceived as a peacetime manoeuvre. In the end, he decided that he could not provide enough forces for a decisive victory. His plan was 'an enterprise beyond our strength', and his only practical conclusion was that the government must raise larger forces.

Still, the Schlieffen plan was all the Germans had. When Schlieffen retired, he was succeeded by Moltke's nephew, and this younger Moltke, a courtier not a strategist, simply relied on the drafts which he found in Schlieffen's drawer. The marshalling yards at Aachen were increased still more. The time-tables went on being elaborated. The German General Staff did not tell the civilian statesmen what was being prepared, and the statesmen tactfully did not ask. It was not, they thought, their affair. They conducted German policy or tried to. If war came, the generals would win it, and there was no overlap between one task and the other.

After this grandiose plan, which envisaged the greatest battle in history, British intentions seem on a small scale. Yet they too were to have immense consequences. Until after the Boer War, the British had no army for continental purposes. Their armed forces existed only for colonial warfare and for the defence of India. In the first decade of the twentieth century, the British built up an expeditionary force of three army corps for use on the continent of Europe. Their original intention, so far as it existed, was to send this force on some kind of independent venture, sustained by British sea power. Mobilization would be completed in England, and any decision what to do with the expeditionary force would be made later. As time went by, the French began to press for a promise of British support. The British would not give this promise, but they saw no harm in answering that they could actually provide the support if they decided to do so. There were staff conversations with the French, which worked out a time-table for the BEF to arrive on the left of the French line. The civilian statesmen insisted that there was no firm promise involved in these conversations, and their insistence was accepted. The statesmen did not realize that, in a sense, they were committed all the same. They could decide whether or not to go to war. But if they decided for war, then the plans established with the French were the only ones which could operate. Once at war, the BEF must go to Maubeuge in north-eastern France and nowhere else in the wide expanses of Europe.

Every Great Power also possessed a navy of some size, and there were plans for naval mobilization. Here, with one exception, the time-tables stopped. The fleets would assemble in their bases and then, for the most part, conduct a defensive strategy, mainly protecting the coasts from invasion and coastal shipping from interference. None of the navies except one had any offensive intention. Their purpose was to ward off the enemy ships rather than to challenge and join combat with them. The one exception was Great Britain. Certainly the Royal Navy had many cruisers and smaller ships for policing trade routes all over the world. But its pride was the Grand Fleet, the greatest assembly of the most powerful ships ever known. On mobilization, the Grand Fleet would proceed to its wartime base at Scapa Flow. Shortly afterwards, according to Admiral Lord Fisher, its principal creator, it would sally forth into the North Sea and would there destroy the German fleet at a true Armageddon. This plan was in curious contrast with most army ones, which were assumed to operate without any interference by the enemy. Fisher's plan was the exact opposite. It assumed that the enemy fleet would conveniently attend on its destruction, whenever it suited the Royal Navy.

This assumption was unfounded. The Germans, too, had a battle fleet on which they had lavished much money and for the sake of which they had jeopardized their relations with Great Britain. But they had no plan for using it in wartime. The German fleet was supposed to present the Royal Navy with some vague menace and thus to secure British neutrality, if not friendship. Once war broke out, it would have failed in its purpose, and it must be kept safe until some other possibility of menace was restored. The only German naval plan was therefore that the fleet should remain in harbour. Yet the Germans could have caused great damage to the British if they had forgotten about the British Grand Fleet away at Scapa Flow. They could for instance have raided the British sea communications with France and been safely back in harbour before the British Grand Fleet could come south. But the Germans never thought of it. They were as convinced as the British that the one purpose of a battle fleet was to engage another and, in a sense, they defeated the entire purpose of the British simply by keeping out of the way.

To judge solely from the military and naval plans, all the Great Powers were in imminent peril and on the brink of war. It seems astonishing that the generals and admirals had not pulled the lever long before. In truth, their plans had become a habit. Few of these great warriors had ever heard a shot fired in anger, and they hardly connected this experience with their plans. On the surface at least, all the plans were defensive. All, even that of the Germans, were designed to win a war if one happened, not to bring one about. Though many generals and some admirals talked of war as desirable in order to clear the air or to improve the national character, none of them tried to turn their talk into action. They waited for the civilian statesmen to give the warning that the country was in danger, when no doubt they would save it. The statesmen, not the commanders, brought on the outbreak of war in 1914.

Yet few, if any, of the statesmen were more eager for war than they had been earlier. They all wanted their particular country to be secure and even to triumph in diplomatic encounters. But they had not changed their patterns of general behaviour which had somehow kept Europe at peace for more than thirty years past. The particular statesmen who happened to be in power in 1914 were not markedly more incompetent than their predecessors and certainly not more bellicose. The international situation was no more tense in the summer of 1914 than it had been previously, indeed in many ways a good deal less so. European relations had changed with remarkable rapidity in the previous few years. The alliances, though still rigid in theory, appeared much less so in practice. Almost every power played with the idea of changing its partners. The atmosphere of reshuffle began in 1911. In that year the French set out to establish a protectorate over Morocco. The Germans claimed compensation for the rights which they possessed under the agreement of Algeciras, made in 1906. Caillaux, the French premier, was willing to pay the German price. He knew that he could expect no support from his nominal ally, Russia. In any case, he hoped to escape by a reconciliation between France and Germany. The protests came from Great Britain. British statesmen were afraid that France would appease Germany by concessions at their expense. British statesmen, not French, turned the confrontation into a war crisis. The British fleet was mobilized, not the French or German armies. In the end, Germany and France reached agreement despite British protests.

This crisis had curious results. French opinion was offended by the agreement with Germany, British opinion was offended by the nearness of armed conflict. In France, there was a revival of national spirit, more assertively patriotic than at any time since the establishment of the Third Republic. French statesmen put aside the reserve with which they had previously treated their Russian ally. Now the Russians were told that they could count on French support, however the conflict happened to start. There was of course an implicit moral that the Russians should make the same assurances the other way round.

The British on the other hand laboured to redress the grievances from which Germany was supposed to be suffering. Reconciliation with Germany was pursued as steadfastly as reconciliation with France and Russia had been pursued earlier. The British laid aside their own grievance against the German challenge of naval rivalry and accepted the German Navy as a given fact of the international scene. The Germans claimed to be short of colonies, and the British earnestly pressed the Portuguese colonies upon them – not forgetting of course to take a cut for themselves. The Germans also wanted British approval for the railway which they were building across Asia Minor, ultimately to Baghdad. The British dropped their old objections, again after securing their own interests. These were somewhat sordid transactions, buying Anglo-German friendship at the expense of other people. But the purchase was successful. Great Britain and Germany moved on to closer terms than for ten or fifteen years past.

The first European war of the twentieth century broke out in the autumn of 1912, when all the Balkan states except Romania attacked the Ottoman or Turkish Empire and carried off most of Turkey-in-Europe. This war was both a humiliation and a success for the Concert of Europe. On the one hand, small powers defied great ones. The Great Powers forbade the Balkan states to attack Turkey and warned them that if they did so they would not be allowed to acquire any Turkish territory. The Balkan states took no notice, went to war, and annexed Turkish territory without any attempt being made to stop them. On the other hand, the Great Powers remained at peace among themselves. For years past diplomats had been saying that a great European war would break out 'when the snow melted on the Balkan mountains'. The snow melted metaphorically, yet no great war followed.

The Great Powers kept in touch by means of a conference of ambassadors which met regularly under Grey's chairmanship in London. The two Powers most closely concerned with the Balkans, Russia and Austria-Hungary, laid down their irreducible minimum. Russia would not tolerate the Bulgarians in Constantinople; Austria-Hungary would not tolerate the Serbs on the Adriatic. Both conditions were met, partly by the accidents of war, partly by demonstrations of force on the part of the Great Powers. The nationalities of the Balkans were liberated. The great Balkan question which had racked international relations for a couple of centuries seemed to have been solved without provoking a general disturbance.

Of course there were still problems left over. The Ottoman Empire seemed on the point of disintegration, and the Russians were bound to worry about the future of Constantinople and the Straits. The victory of nationalism in the Balkans provoked a stir among the subject nationalities of Austria-Hungary, especially among the Serbs. But these were problems for the future. The Turks were still alive and in fact recovering some of their military strength now that they had lost most of Turkey-in-Europe. The Serbs were exhausted by the Balkan War and in no position to face a new war against Austria-Hungary. The greatest fear which had haunted Europe – a war between Russia and Austria-Hungary – seemed to have been removed. The so-called prizes of the Balkans were no longer there for them to fight over. The Balkan states had taken the prizes for themselves.

Historians, enjoying the advantage of hindsight, have discovered all sorts of indications in the spring of 1914 that a great European war was about to break out. The Great Powers were spending more on armaments than ever before, though economists of a more sophisticated age might have pointed out that in these boom years the Powers were not spending on armaments a greater proportion of their national income. Violence was in the air – strikes in Russia, suffragettes in England, chaos in the Austrian parliament, Futurists in Italy. Even the ethereal world of the ballet was disturbed, and riots broke out in Paris whenever *Le Sacre du Printemps* was performed. Yet was this violence new or unusual? Wagner's music had once provoked as many riots as ever Stravinsky's did. The Austrian parliament had seen worse chaos seventeen years before. The suffragettes were less destructive than the Fenians. For the ordinary person, Europe was more peaceful than it had ever been before or was to be afterwards. For the only time in history, the private citizen could wander almost anywhere across Europe without check from the police or danger from brigands. Again for the only time in history, the private citizen could count on a reasonably free trial almost anywhere in Europe even for a political offence.

Contemporary observers, who did not know what was going to happen, often guessed in an exactly contrary way. It looked as though the system of alliances was breaking up. Now that the Balkan question was settled, there seemed little reason why Germany should need to back Austria-Hungary, or why France, and still less Great Britain, should back Russia any more. French financiers were reconciled with German, and Franco-German heavy industry was as much a combine as it became later in the Common Market. Great Britain and Germany were each other's best customers. The three advanced industrial countries of western Europe were drawing together for a cooperative exploitation of the rest of the world. Enlightened Frenchmen were glad to be rid of Russia. Even German diplomats believed that the Austrian alliance was an encumbrance which should be shaken off.

There still seemed plenty of room in the world for the imperialist Powers. Germany had plans for building an empire in central Africa from one ocean to another, and there was no objection except from the helpless Belgians – many even of whom would be glad to give up the Congo. Turkey-in-Asia was ripe for partition into economic spheres of influence, and only Russia would object if the remnants of the Ottoman Empire were at last modernized. China offered a still larger field for imperialist partnership, with Germany and the United States already cooperating against the two reactionary Powers, Japan and Russia, while Great Britain tardily moved towards the side of progress. Industrial and financial interests were everywhere pulling the rich together against the poor and backward, and economic factors which have been blamed for the First World War were in fact the greatest security of peace. The capitalists of every country cried against war in the crisis of July 1914. Capitalism did not rule the world in any political sense. This negative fact ranks high among the causes of the First World War.

The people were supposed to rule. There was universal suffrage in France, Germany, Italy (only since 1912), and Austria, though not in Hungary. There was household suffrage in the United Kingdom. There was suffrage of a sort even in Russia, though the Duma had few powers. There had certainly been times when the people had responded to the call of imperialism and even of war. The British people had been eager to go to war with France during the Fashoda crisis of 1898 and had exploded into jingoism during the Boer War. The French people had resented the compromise with Germany after the Agadir affair. The German people had resented the same crisis even more sharply.

By 1914 the tide was running the other way. Jingoism and imperial rhetoric were no longer winning cries at the polls. The Social Democrats were the largest single party in the German Reichstag, and they were pledged in theory to an attitude of war resistance. In France a general election of April 1914 produced a majority of radicals and socialists who repudiated the previous policy of militarism and aggressive alliance with Russia. Caillaux, the radical leader, was an advocate of cooperation with Germany. Jaurès, the socialist leader, was the greatest advocate in Europe of conciliation and international friendship. President Poincaré, champion of revenge, gloomily faced the prospect of having to appoint a pro-German pacific prime minister. A stroke of luck, bad or good, saved him from the worst. Caillaux's second wife, pursued with libellous hostility by his first, shot dead the editor of a Paris newspaper. The scandal ruled out Caillaux as prime minister. Viviani, the substitute, was less clearheaded and less competent. Poincaré could count for something after all.

Tory imperialism was on the run in the United Kingdom. British army officers in Ireland, prodded on by the Unionist Party, had staged a near-mutiny rather than coerce the Protestants of Ulster. The resultant outcry made the Tories for once the unpatriotic party. Liberals and Labour drew together in a common programme of peace and social reform. Lloyd George, chancellor of the exchequer, announced confidently that hostility between Germany and Great Britain was at an end, and this announcement seemed likely to be a winning card at the next election. This was a springtime of radical confidence. It is tempting to suggest that the old ruling classes of Europe launched a great war in the realization that otherwise power would slip from their grasp. But this would credit them with too much intelligence and directive ability. The old gang had little idea what they were doing and drifted haphazardly from one problem to the next. Though their prestige was declining, their wealth was increasing, and this was no situation for dangerous general revolution. On the other hand, even fewer believed that war would prevent revolution. The balance between the factors maintaining peace and those pulling towards war seemed no different in 1914 than it had been throughout the previous generation, and war therefore was no more likely to occur than it had been previously.

There was perhaps one difference in 1914, a difference of emphasis rather than of nature. In nearly all European countries the forces making for war were much what they had always been – silly old generals who had never seen fighting, pedantic diplomats who had been told by someone or other that they should guard the national honour, hack journalists who could pull in an odd penny by writing a jingoistic piece. These were diseases of an endemic nature present in every modern society and did no harm except to themselves. In Germany militarism went deeper. Here was the only society where army officers determined the moral tone of public life as well as of their own military circle. University professors and bank directors took pride in their rank as army reservists, a quirk rarely encountered in England or France. Military values determined the tone of German policy in a way that was not true elsewhere. Of course Russia too would have been a 'military monarchy', if it had been capable of being anything. But in the general deliquescence of the tsarist regime, the Russian system had ceased to have any character.

Germany had displayed a peculiarly militaristic character ever since the foundation of the Second Reich in 1871. Generals had always set the social tone, and the constitution had always been twisted in favour of the army. But in earlier years, particularly during Bismarck's time, the army and its leaders had existed for defensive purposes. Bismarck had certainly taught that Germany would perish unless she were the most militaristic of the Great Powers, but that was all he had taught. Indeed, in Bismarck's view, Germany had to be militaristic because she was weak. Since then Germany had grown increasingly strong. Few Germans doubted that their country was the greatest of European Powers. From this it was an easy step to feeling that she was receiving less than her due. Germans were aggrieved that they had come late to the distribution of colonies. Hence their demand for 'a place in the sun'. This was comparatively harmless. There were plenty of sunny places still waiting to be allotted, and Germany could have had them. But many Germans slipped into the habit of believing that Germany should exercise a sort of general control over Europe, as France had done or was supposed to have done in the reign of Louis XIV and had certainly done during the Napoleonic Empire. Berlin should succeed Paris as the political, and London as the economic, capital of Europe. When this did not happen, Germans came near to thinking that German power should be used to exact the tribute which others refused to pay voluntarily. Assertiveness, though not perhaps open aggressiveness, had become a predominant German characteristic before 1914. When this was added to the traditional respect which Germans accorded to their military chiefs, Germany became the most dangerous Power in Europe.

Comparatively few Germans had conscious plans for a German domination of Europe, and still fewer tried to give such plans practical shape. Most Germans in positions of high authority did not appreciate how far they had drifted from the general European outlook. They were aggrieved and bewildered when others rejected the proffered hand which they supposed they were holding out. In their view, they would be delighted to protect the British Empire as they had long protected the Austrian Empire; delighted to patronize France as they patronized Italy; delighted, most of all, to assist the Russian tsar against his revolutionary subjects. It was strange and exasperating when others did not share this view. They inclined more and more to rely on Germany's 'sharp sword' – the sort of out-of-date military phrase used by public men in every country. All imagined a war of glamour and heroics, with swords and cavalry charges. They got something quite different.

It is the fashion nowadays to seek profound causes for great events. But perhaps the war which broke out in 1914 had no profound causes. For thirty years past, international diplomacy, the balance of power, the alliances, and the accumulation of armed might produced peace. Suddenly the situation was turned round, and the very forces which had produced the long peace now produced a great war. In much the same way, a motorist who for thirty years has been doing the right thing to avoid accidents makes a mistake one day and has a crash. In July 1914 things went wrong. The only safe explanation in history is that things happen because they happen.

Meeting at Sarajevo

The occasion for the First World War was provided by two shots fired at Sarajevo, capital of Bosnia, on 28 June 1914. With these shots Gavrilo Princip, a Bosnian student, killed Archduke Franz Ferdinand and his morganatic wife Sophie, Duchess of Hohenberg. The archduke and the student were symbolic figures. Franz Ferdinand was the nephew and presumptive heir of Francis Joseph, emperor of Austria, apostolic king of Hungary, king, archduke, grand duke, count, and lord of this, that and the other – to say nothing of being titular king of Jerusalem. The archduke was also inspector general of the Austro-Hungarian Army. He personified the Habsburg Monarchy, which had ranked high among the Great Powers of Europe for almost five hundred years. Throughout that time, though rarely successful in wars, it had somehow survived. It had championed Christendom against the Turks and the counter-reformation against the Protestants. It had resisted the French Revolution and the great Napoleon. Now, with its conglomeration of eleven different nationalities (or, with the Jews, twelve), it seemed to represent historic right against national freedom. In practice, this worked out as German and Magyar, or Hungarian, domination over the rest. Franz Ferdinand, an absolutist by nature, disliked the two dominant nationalities as much as he disliked the other peoples over whom he was destined never to rule.

The student was the son of a Bosnian farmer. When Bosnia was under the Turks, some of his ancestors had been Turkish gendarmes. His grandfather had taken part in the rebellion of 1875 against them. Princip followed in his grandfather's footsteps. Though a Bosnian subject, he was a Serb by nationality and sentiment. When he first crossed the border into Serbia, he fell on his knees and kissed the national soil. In 1912, when Serbia launched a war of liberation against Turkey, Princip tried to enlist as a Serb guerilla. He was rejected as too young and too puny. Now he had just finished at secondary school.

He ranked as a student in the sense that he had left school and not started on any career. He wanted to do something great for the cause of national liberation. Not, however, for the Serbs alone. Like other young idealists, Princip hoped for a union of all the South Slavs. His nationalism was only part of his revolutionary spirit. He was half-anarchist, half-socialist. He and his friends claimed to belong to 'Young Bosnia', an echo of Mazzini's 'Young Italy' in the previous century. They were close in spirit to the Irish enthusiasts who made the Easter rising in 1916. Vladimir Dedijer, the modern Yugoslav historian who understands Princip and his friends best, calls them 'primitive rebels'. Perhaps they were not so primitive. Twenty years later they would have fought in the Spanish Civil War. Today they would be at home among the rebellious students who have recently caused a general European turmoil. Princip was in fact the eternal student with the particular grievance that his nation was denied national freedom under the Habsburg yoke.

The encounter between the archduke and the student had been fixed for some time, at least since the previous March, when it had been decided to hold the principal summer manoeuvres of the Austro-Hungarian Army in Bosnia and the archduke had decided to attend them. This was an obvious political gesture. The Serbs under Turkish rule had been liberated by the Balkan Wars of 1912 and 1913. Talk of liberating the Serbs or even the South Slavs under Habsburg rule naturally followed, though more in Bosnia than in Serbia, which had been exhausted by the previous war. The Austro-Hungarian government had declared that it would not tolerate any acquisition of

Turkish territory by Serbia. When this happened all the same, Austria-Hungary had done little except to limit Serb claims against Albania. The Habsburgs seemed to be losing in their stand against nationalism. The moment for defiance had come. The Austro-Hungarian Army would demonstrate its might in Bosnia, and the heir to the throne himself would add political weight to the demonstration.

It is tempting to suggest that the date for the fatal meeting had been fixed further back in history: 28 June was the day of St Vitus, patron saint of Serbia. On that day in 1389 the last army of old Serbia had been destroyed by the Ottoman Turks at the battle of Kosovo Field. Revenge came only in the autumn of 1912 when the army of new Serbia defeated the Turks at the battle of Kumanovo. It would have been strikingly appropriate if the archduke had defied Serb feeling by visiting Sarajevo on their sacred national day. There is no evidence that the connection was made. The Habsburgs knew nothing of the national traditions of the peoples over whom they ruled. Probably the archduke and his advisers had never heard of Kosovo. At most, they were vaguely aware that 28 June was some sort of holiday in Bosnia and therefore suitable for a ceremonial visit.

However, 28 June had another significance. In 1900 the archduke married on that day. His bride, Sophie Chotek, belonged to an old and aristocratic Bohemian family, but she did not come within the 'permitted degrees' suitable for a member of the Habsburg house. She was merely aristocratic, not royal or imperial, and therefore was not allowed to share her husband's rank. Their children were disinherited. At court ceremonies, she had to follow the youngest archduchess. Franz Ferdinand bitterly resented these humiliations to his wife. If he came to Bosnia, it would be as inspector general and field-marshal, not as archduke. It would be a purely military occasion, and his wife would ride by his side. There could be no better celebration for their wedding anniversary. Once more, there is no evidence that the connection was made. Perhaps the coincidence with the archduke's wedding-day, like that with the day of Kosovo, was an accident, which no one noticed at the time. The archduke had simply decided to defy Serb feeling, and his wife loyally went with him.

Princip was in Belgrade, waiting for the results of his final examination, when a Bosnian friend sent him a cutting from a Sarajevo newspaper. It contained the announcement of the archduke's coming visit. This was a great moment for Princip. He had long wished to strike a blow for national freedom, if not by fighting in war, then by assassinating somebody. He had talked of assassinating General Poti-orek, the governor of Bosnia. Franz Ferdinand was an even more attractive target.

Contrary to the common belief, Princip was not a member of any secret society, except those he invented with other Bosnian schoolboys. But he had a contact, though he probably did not know it, with one such secret nationalist society, the Black Hand.

This had been originally an association of Serb officers, who had something to do with the assassination of King Alexander Obrenović in 1903. After this, it ran guerillas into Macedonia, not so much to injure the Turks as to compete with the Bulgarians who also claimed Macedonia. This activity gave out in 1913, when Macedonia was liberated and most of it seized, in defiance of Bulgaria, by Serbia. Now the Black Hand was in conflict with the Serbian government. It wanted army officers to control Macedonia, whereas the government determined to establish civilian rule. The conflict was the odder in that 'Apis', head of the Black Hand, was in real life Colonel Dimitri-jević, head of the Serbian military intelligence. Apis managed to engineer the dismissal of his enemy Pašić, the prime minister. Then things went wrong. King Peter, who had backed Apis, wearied of public life and handed over power to Crown Prince Alexander, who hated Apis. At the same time, Hartvig, the Russian minister in Belgrade, who had previously backed Apis also, announced that Russia wanted no new troubles in the Balkans. Pašić returned to power and determined on a general election, which would silence the Black Hand for good.

In such circumstances, the thoughts of Apis were directed towards Pašić, not towards the remote Habsburg archduke. All the specula-tions that Apis arranged the assassination of the archduke as the man who might conciliate the South Slavs when he came to the throne and so thwart plans for a great Yugoslavia are so much poppycock, if only because Apis cared solely for the Serbs, not for the South Slavs. Here again, it is tempting to suggest that Apis wanted to make trouble for Pašić. If there was an attempt at assassination in Sarajevo, the Austrians would protest to Belgrade, particularly if they knew that the assassins had come from there. If Pašić gave way, he would be discredited in Serb eyes; if he defied Austria-Hungary, he would again need the support of the nationalist Black Hand. Unfortunately there is no evidence that Apis knew of the plans to assassinate Franz Ferdinand until they were well launched. The connection between Princip and the Black Hand was yet another accident.

Princip himself never knew that he had been in contact with the Black Hand. He only knew that in 1912, when he had tried to enlist, he had been directed to a Major Tankosić, who turned him down. Now he went to Tankosić again, as the only Serb he knew, and so stumbled on the right person. For Tankosić, as the organizer of guerillas, kept the stock of weapons with which these guerillas were equipped for Macedonia. Now, though he had no use for them, he had a few left. He agreed to let Princip have half a dozen bombs and revolvers. Later he said that he did this 'to embarrass Pašić'. It is more likely that, having worked himself out of a job in Macedonia, he was glad to stir up trouble in Bosnia. In any case, handing out weapons was a routine operation for Tankosić, and it did not occur to him to consult Apis or any other member of the Black Hand.

Princip enlisted two other Bosnian students with whom he went around in Belgrade. He also wrote to a slightly older friend called Ilić in Sarajevo that they needed three more, whom Ilić duly found. In this way Ilić became the organizer of the affair. It is possible that he really was a member of the Black Hand, though the only evidence for this was provided by Ilić himself when he was trying to save his neck. But his instructions came only from Princip. Tankosić gave the three conspirators further assistance by helping to smuggle them across the Bosnian frontier with their weapons – again a routine operation like the old Macedonian days. The three young men talked indiscreetly about their mission, to the subsequent ruin of those who sheltered them.

No news of the crossing reached the Austrian authorities. The police and the civil officials were in any case not trying very hard. They thought that the archduke's visit was a risky project and would have advised against it if they had been consulted. But they were not. The visit was laid on as a purely military affair, and the army authorities were confident there would be no trouble. The civil officials were therefore sulking. They took no precautions. When Francis Joseph visited Sarajevo in 1910, hundreds of political suspects were imprisoned for the day and thousands of extra police were brought in. Now no one was arrested, and 120 police provided the only security in a town of 50,000 inhabitants. The military held that it was unnecessary to line the archduke's route with soldiers. He was to travel unprotected except by Habsburg prestige.

The Serbian government learnt that some men with arms had crossed the Bosnian frontier. It had its agents in the Black Hand and called Apis to order. He, in his turn, learnt from Tankosić what had happened. The committee of the Black Hand resolved that the attempt on the archduke must be stopped. Apis sent an agent into Bosnia, and this agent summoned Ilić, the only contact he had. Ilić was told that the attempt must not take place. He returned to Sarajevo and told Princip, who, not being a member of the Black Hand, took no notice. Ilić reluctantly went on with his friends. It is possible that Apis was two-timing. On the day of the assassination, another of his agents appeared in Sarajevo and may have told the conspirators to go ahead. The point has little significance one way or the other. Princip and his friends made their own decisions and did not take orders from the Black Hand.

The Serbian government also attempted to give a warning in Vienna. This was a tricky business. The Serbian government did not know the names of the conspirators and in any case could not actually betray Serb patriots. The Serbian minister in Vienna had therefore to fall back on vague hints of trouble. A Serb soldier in the Austro-Hungarian Army, for instance, might load his rifle with live ammunition and kill the archduke by mistake. Naturally such hints only gave offence. Moreover, the Serbian minister got on to the wrong man – not that there was a right one. He spoke to Biliński, the Austro-Hungarian minister of finance. Biliński was certainly in charge of Bosnia, for want of anything better to do. But he was merely head of the civil administration and had no authority over the army. Also he was on bad terms with Franz Ferdinand. Biliński therefore did not pass on the warning, though again it would have made no difference if he had. Any threat of danger at Sarajevo would have made the archduke even more determined to go.

So the stage was set. On 27 June Franz Ferdinand and his wife arrived at Ilidže, a spa outside Sarajevo, which served as military headquarters. The archduke inspected troops and attended man-oeuvres. He and his wife drove informally into Sarajevo, where they

visited the ethnographical museum and had a drink at the principal
hotel. They were received with cheers. Everything augured well for
the ceremonial visit on the following day. According to schedule, the
archduke and his wife were to leave Ilidže by special train at 9.25 am.
They would be met at Sarajevo by six open cars. They would inspect
a nearby barracks. At 10 sharp they would drive along the quayside
of the River Miljacka to the town hall. There the archduke would
receive an address. After this, the procession of cars would drive
through the narrow streets of the old town to the museum, where the
archduke would officially open a new wing. There was a good deal
more to the programme which was never carried out. Ilić had also
made his dispositions: three conspirators on the river side of the quay,
three on the land side, with himself unarmed to watch what was
happening.

The conspirators were in their places by 9 am. The archduke was
also punctual. The only slip occurred at Sarajevo station where the
leading automobile, which was supposed to be occupied by security
officers from Vienna, drove off without them. The archduke visited
the barracks, and the drive along the quay then began. Of the six
conspirators, five failed to do anything. They had never experienced a
moving target and were also taken aback by the crowds. The first boy
imagined that there was a policeman behind him and that, if he tried
to pull out his bomb, the plot would be revealed. The second felt
sorry for the archduke's wife. Čabrinović, the third, was regarded as
the least reliable and had only been given a bomb at the last moment.
However, he was the only one to act. He asked a policeman: 'Which
is His Majesty's car?' The policeman obligingly told him. He then
knocked the detonator off against a lamp-post and threw his bomb.

The detonator hit the archduke's wife on the neck and bruised her.
The bomb landed on the back of the archduke's car, bounced off, and
exploded under the next car, damaging a wheel and injuring a dozen
people. The damaged car was pushed out of the way, and the
procession went on. Princip, hearing the explosion, left his post and
saw Čabrinović being taken away. He thought of killing Čabrinović
in order to keep the secret of the conspiracy, decided it was too
difficult, and sat down in a café, contemplating suicide. The fifth boy
was too shortsighted to see the archduke and in any case lost his
nerve. The last of them was still puzzling whether to follow Ilić's
earlier instruction and call off the attempt. Also he feared that his

bomb might injure people in the crowd. He, too, did absolutely nothing.

The archduke arrived at the town hall in a bad temper. He said to the mayor: 'I come on a friendly visit, and someone throws a bomb at me.' Then, recovering himself, he listened to the mayor's address and made a more or less gracious answer. The archduke asked Potiorek: 'Do you think other attempts will be made?' Potiorek answered: 'Go at ease. I accept all responsibility.' The archduke decided to visit the wounded men in hospital before going to the museum. The procession would therefore drive straight down the quay instead of turning into the old town. Count Harrach, who had lent his car to the archduke for the day, stood on the running-board to ward off any further bombs from the river side. The drivers had not been told of the change of plan. The first two cars turned into the old town. The archduke's driver followed them. Potiorek called out: 'Stop! You are going the wrong way.' The driver stopped and began to back into the quay.

Princip was sitting in the café exactly at this corner. To his astonishment, he saw the archduke immediately before him. He pulled out his revolver. A policeman tried to strike up his hand and was kicked on the knee by a friend of Princip's who was standing by. Princip fired twice. One shot hit the archduke. The other, perhaps intended for Potiorek who was sitting at the front, hit the archduke's wife who was sitting at the back. She died at once. The archduke murmured: 'Sophie, live for the children'; then: 'It is nothing' and fell back dead also.

Princip, like Čabrinović, was arrested. Both talked freely, and all but one of the other conspirators were soon arrested, along with many who had helped them to cross the frontier. After a laboriously fair trial, all those who were of age were sentenced to death. Čabrinović, Princip, and one other died in prison during the war, more from neglect than from ill-treatment. The other two were released after the war. One became curator of the Sarajevo museum; the other professor of history at Belgrade. The one who had escaped later returned to Sarajevo and ran a market garden. The archduke and his wife were buried on his private estate without imperial honours. There were other victims. In 1917 Pašić framed Apis who was with the Serbian Army at Salonika. Apis tried to save his associates by claiming that he had organized the Sarajevo assassination. This did not save him or them. They were all shot on a trumped-up charge.

Such was the spark which fired the First World War. It is ironical that it would not have gone off if the archduke had stuck to his time-table. There was to be no further deviation.

Decision in Vienna

An imperial power must do something when the heir to its throne is assassinated. That was obvious to everyone in Europe. The Habsburg Monarchy had been losing prestige for a long time. Now it had a wonderful chance to assert itself. All the peoples of the monarchy except the Serbs demonstrated their loyalty with enthusiam – the Hungarians, who had no reason to regret Franz Ferdinand, as enthusi-astically as any other. The crowned heads of Europe were indignant at the killing of one of their number. A strong line by Austria-Hungry would meet with universal approval. But what line? The trial of the conspirators, even reprisals against the Serbs of Bosnia, were not enough. Something had to be done against Serbia herself.

Austrian officials looked for proof of Serbian complicity in the assassination. They never found any. They did not get on to the Black Hand at all, and in any case Princip's connection with it was tenuous. The reason for Austrian ignorance of the Black Hand was curious. In 1908 Austrian Intelligence had blundered. Forgách, the minister in Belgrade, acquired evidence of treasonable behaviour by Serbo-Croat leaders in Zagreb. The evidence turned out to be forged – some of it in the basement of Forgách's own house. Henceforth the Austrians relied on German Intelligence in Serbia, not on their own; and the Germans derived much of their information, in the agreeable way of intelligence services, from none other than Apis. Naturally he did not mention the Black Hand.

Evidence was a secondary affair in any case. Serbia's real crime in Habsburg eyes was to exist. Serbia did not need to enlist conspirators. She kept the Serbs, and to a lesser extent the Croats, of Austria-Hungary in a turmoil merely by representing the national principle. There was no solution short of Serbia ceasing to exist, and this was impossible. The Serbs could not be exterminated, as might have happened in a more barbaric age or as Hitler might have attempted

later. Annexation of Serbia to Austria-Hungary was equally impossible, even if the other Powers had allowed it. It would merely have
added more to Francis Joseph's discontented subjects. Humiliation of
Serbia was the only answer. If the Habsburg Monarchy displayed its
might, it would temporarily restore its prestige.

Theoretically, the decision lay with Francis Joseph himself. He had
so arranged the successive constitutional concessions of his reign that
he kept foreign policy in his own hands. There was no Austro-Hungarian government. Occasionally, Francis Joseph held a gathering of the
common ministers and other dignitaries, but this meeting only advised
– it had no powers. In practice, Francis Joseph left foreign affairs to
his foreign minister, who in 1914 was Count Berchtold, a rich Bohemian count, formal in manner, smart in appearance, short in ideas
and resolution. Berchtold consulted Forgách, now running Balkan
affairs at the foreign ministry. Forgách was naturally for strong action
against the Serbs who had deceived and humiliated him. Berchtold
next consulted Conrad, chief of the General Staff. Conrad, too, was
for war, as he was on every occasion. But he explained, to Berchtold's
dismay, that the peacetime forces, even if strong enough to deal with
Serbia, could not be moved. Their movement would cut across the
plans for mobilization and make them unworkable. Austria-Hungary
would therefore be helpless in case of a threat from Russia or even of
powerful Serbian resistance. The time-tables dictated that there must
be full mobilization or nothing. Finally Berchtold consulted Tisza,
prime minister of Hungary and the most forceful character in the
monarchy. Tisza disliked the Serbs, but he did not fear them. He was
much more fearful that a successful action against the Serbs would
restore Habsburg prestige, to Hungary's disadvantage. He insisted
that action should be taken only if Germany approved.

This suited Berchtold. He could demonstrate to his ally that
Austria-Hungary did not merit the reproaches of feebleness levelled
against her. At the same time, he could shift the responsibility for
decision on to someone else. He drafted a note that Serbia 'must be
eliminated as a power factor in the Balkans' and sent it to Berlin by
special messenger. In Germany, too, there was no imperial government – only the Kaiser William II and such ministers as he chose to
consult. William was at Potsdam, where the Austrian ambassador
came for lunch on 5 July. William did not hesitate. He was upset by
the assassination of the archduke, who had been within the imperial

limits a friend of his. His first reactions, though not his later ones, were always violent. William at once agreed that Austria-Hungary should act against Serbia. He also promised that Germany would stand by Austria-Hungary if Russia tried to intervene. In after years, these seemed shocking things to say. They were natural and inevitable in the atmosphere of the time. No crowned head, the German emperor least of all, could have told the Austrians that they should disregard the archduke's assassination. No German statesman at this moment, and least of all the emperor, could have left Austria-Hungary at the mercy of Russia. German diplomats had complained for years past that Austria-Hungary had been fearful and irresolute. Here for once the Austrians were trying to be firm, and Germany could do no other than encourage them.

William showed more sense in the course of the afternoon. He consulted such German generals as happened to be available and asked them whether this was a suitable moment to back Austria-Hungary. The available generals were mostly court officials. They had picked up from more serious military authorities talk about a preventive war. They agreed that this was a good, even a desirable, moment for war. William also insisted that he could make no firm decision without the approval of his chancellor, Bethmann Hollweg – a most admirable respect for constitutional principle. Bethmann arrived at Potsdam in the course of the afternoon. In character and perhaps in intellect he was ranked above most other statesmen of the day. He played Beethoven where Berchtold went to the races and Grey went fishing. In his grave appearance there was an impressive sense of responsibility. During past alarms he had sometimes restrained William II, and he often tried to lessen the roughness of German policy. On the other hand he had got into his head the idea that Germany was about to run downhill. Like the generals who talked of preventive war, Bethmann believed that it was 'now or never'. There seems a special disease among statesmen which makes them feel that their highly prosperous country is on the brink of ruin. Bethmann had this disease strongly.

Bethmann knew, before he left for Potsdam, that the question of Austro-Hungarian policy and of Germany's attitude towards it would come up. Yet he made no preparations. Jagow, the secretary of state, was away on holiday, and Bethmann did not seek advice from anyone else in the foreign ministry. Nor did he enquire of the General Staff – a practice he had never followed. His lack of precise information did not, however, deter him. As soon as William had outlined his answer to the Austrians, Bethmann endorsed it. This was not from timidity or subservience. Indeed Bethmann provided some new arguments of his own to show how strongly he agreed with his imperial master. He, too, had little appreciation of what he was doing. It seemed obvious to him that Austria-Hungary should be supported and equally obvious that Russia would make no effective protest. Confidence that Russia would back down at the last moment had become a habit with German diplomats, and Bethmann had no means of knowing whether Russian resolution or the state of Russian armaments might have changed. He guessed blindly in the void. There was a sort of competition in 'dares' – what the Americans call playing chicken. First the Austrians showed how brave they were to talk of going to war and dared the Germans to restrain them. Now the Germans showed how brave they were by encouraging the Austrians and so dared the Austrians to pull back. Vienna wanted to impress Berlin. Berlin wanted to impress Vienna. No one in either capital seriously contemplated the chances of general war.

After the momentous conversations at Potsdam, William II went on holiday, and most of the generals departed also. This was not an act of deception. William II and the rest assumed that somehow war could be fitted in between a couple of vacations. Though they had talked of war, they could not imagine it. Their only military experience was on manoeuvres, where action could be conveniently broken off at dinner time. William II and Bethmann soon forgot, or very nearly, the formidable promises which they had made to Austria-Hungary. If they recalled these promises at all it was with the consoling reflection that the Austrians never stuck to any firm resolution for long. Thus the two men who were responsible for German policy gave Berchtold a blank cheque, told him to fill it in for a large sum, and yet were confident that he would not present it at all.

They were very nearly right. Berchtold was enthusiastic for war only so long as he knew that someone would restrain him. He became more and more hesitant as the obstacles to war disappeared. When the German encouragements arrived in Vienna, even Tisza wavered. If the German rulers thought Austria-Hungary should go to war, then perhaps the risk was worth while. Tisza disputed the necessity for war over nearly a week. Finally he yielded, because of the need to come up to German expectations. But he still made a condition: Austria-Hungary should not acquire any Serbian territory, however great the victory of her arms. Berchtold agreed to this condition though it made nonsense of his policy. For there was no purpose in war if Serbia was to be merely harassed, not dismembered. By this time, Berchtold had lost his enthusiasm for war, and the staff in the foreign ministry at the Ballhausplatz shared his hesitations. As one of them wrote later, they were like 'someone who is to undergo an operation and hopes more or less confidently to be able to escape it'. Forgotten were the days when Berchtold was pushing Tisza into war. Now Berchtold was finding excuses why war should be postponed.

The European Powers might have tolerated an immediate strike against Serbia in the first flush of indignation. All idea of this had long been abandoned. In true bureaucratic fashion, the Austrian diplomats wished to justify their own prejudices and laboriously sought evidence that the Serbian government had been involved. A legal official was sent to Belgrade. After a couple of days, he reported correctly that there was no evidence against the Serbian government. This was irrelevant, though slightly awkward. The Austrians had resolved to act somehow against Serbia for reasons remote from the archduke's assassination. Their real problem was in drafting the ultimatum. They had to devise conditions which would bring some sort of advantage, even though their real aim was that Serbia would reject them. By 14 July the note was ready. Ministers came to Berchtold's private house secretly at night in order to discuss it. Apparently they wanted to give the impression that nothing was happening. Berchtold himself was by now hoping that nothing would happen. Even if Serbia did not accept the Austro-Hungarian demands, she might well do so when faced by a mobilization – a dream project to which Berchtold had reverted, even though Conrad had told him that it was impossible.

A new pretext for delay now emerged. President Poincaré of France was on the point of visiting St Petersburg along with Viviani, who combined the posts of French premier and foreign minister. It would never do for the Russian and French statesmen to discuss the Austro-Hungarian note face to face. Presentation of the note was therefore put off until Poincaré and Viviani left St Petersburg for the voyage home. In this way, almost a month passed. The archduke had been assassinated. Austria-Hungary took no action, even diplomatic. The question was not quite forgotten in the other European capitals, but it lost any sense of urgency. Most people assumed that the Austrians would do nothing serious in their usual ineffective way.

The other Powers could not decide on a policy until Austria-Hungary did something, but the Russians at any rate did some thinking. Sazonov, the Russian foreign minister, was a gentle, puzzled man, not very bright, with a romantic Slav devotion to his duty. He had been admirably cautious during the Balkan Wars and now asked nothing better than that the Balkans should be left to the Balkan peoples. Pan-Slavs may once have dreamt of extending Russian power into the Balkans. Now Russia's anxiety was that no European Great Power should control the Bosporus and the Dardanelles – Russia's outlet to the world. Through these straits Russian wheat went out to pay her debts, and steel and machinery for her heavy industry came in. Without security at the Straits, Russia could hardly exist as a Great Power. The Russians feared rightly that Germany was building up influence in Turkey. They also feared with less justification that this influence would be used to close the Straits against them.

The prospect of Austro-Hungarian domination over Serbia threw the Russians into a state of alarm. They imagined that this would bring Germany that much nearer to Constantinople. This was a misconception. Germany's economic route to Turkey was by sea – from Hamburg or Rotterdam, and the Balkans meant nothing to her. Even Austria-Hungary's interest was mainly political, except for the railway line to Salonika. But if Allied statesmen during the First World War, such as Churchill, could imagine that Constantinople and the Balkans provided a back door into Germany, the Russians may be forgiven for believing beforehand that the back door could be used the other way round. There were simpler impulses at work in Sazonov's mind. Russia was no longer a despotism. The liberal politicians now counted for something, and they would be offended if nothing was done to uphold the Slav cause.

The French statesmen were more remotely involved. The prospect of a general European war was the least of their worries. They were far more anxious that Russia might quarrel with Great Britain over Persia and then abandon the Triple Entente in favour of Germany. Hence they stressed their own loyalty to the Russian alliance – exactly as William II and Bethmann had stressed their loyalty to the Austro-German alliance. At least, this was Poincaré's view. In normal circumstances, the French president had little to say in foreign policy. But the circumstances were not normal. Viviani, though foreign minister, was merely the stop-gap premier of a radical-socialist coalition, the real leader, Caillaux, being temporarily out of the running because his wife had just shot and killed a Parisian newspaper editor. Viviani knew nothing of foreign affairs and left them to Poincaré. However, there is no evidence that the Russian and French statesmen ever discussed the Serbian affair. It was fourteenth on the agenda which the French had brought with them and was never reached. Of course Poincaré talked about the glories of the Franco-Russian alliance and gave the Russians general encouragement. But his real concern was to keep Russia on good terms with Great Britain.

The British were the least involved at all. Even the few who feared that the archduke's assassination might provoke a war did not foresee that Great Britain would be involved in it. Serbia had a bad press in Great Britain. 'The least worthy member of the European family' was the general verdict. The *Manchester Guardian* wished that Serbia could be towed out to sea and sunk. Horatio Bottomley, the demagogue, produced the headline: 'To Hell with Servia'. Sir Edward Grey, the foreign secretary, took the same line more decorously. In his view, peace was more important than justice, and the lesser power must yield, however humiliatingly, so that peace could be preserved. This was the usual British outlook – repeated with Greece in 1923 and with Czechoslovakia in 1938. Of course Grey issued warnings against any violent action. He talked vaguely of mediation, but who between? If between Serbia and Austria-Hungary, the Austrians would reject any outside interference, and Grey, as foreign secretary of a Great Power which had often disciplined some small one, would be inclined to agree with them. If the suggested mediation was to be between Austria-Hungary and Russia, the Austrians could reply with equal plausibility that Russia was not involved. Until Austria-Hungary acted in some way, the Russians could not react, and it was of course easy to assume that, since the Austrians had taken one month to think of an action, the Russians would take another to think of an answer.

It was a strange crisis – everyone waiting for some sort of explosion, with the Serbian government waiting most anxiously of all. They were in bad trouble: their army was exhausted by the Balkan Wars and they knew that, whatever happened, Serbia could not gain. They were also without a trusted counsellor. For years past they had relied on Hartvig, the Russian minister in Belgrade. On 10 July they lost him under strange circumstances. Hartvig, once an extremist, was now a moderate. He called on the Austro-Hungarian minister in order to propose a common front against nationalist conspirators such as the Black Hand. The excitement was too much for him. In the middle of making his proposal, which would no doubt have prevented the war, he fell dead. Russia was virtually unrepresented thereafter. The Russian government received no information, and the Serbian government received little advice.

On 23 July President Poincaré ended his state visit to St Petersburg. The Austrians had ascertained the precise moment when the French cruiser, taking him home, would cast off. One hour afterwards, Giesl, the Austro-Hungarian minister at Belgrade, presented his government's ultimatum. This was tight timing. The Serbs were given forty-eight hours in which to reply. By then, 6 pm on 25 July, it would be Saturday evening, and the Austrians wanted to start mobilizing on the Sunday morning. The Serbian government were summoned to repudiate the nationalist societies and to proceed against those accessories to the assassination who were on Serb soil – Austrian officials were to collaborate in this. There were ten points in all, but the collaboration of Austrian officials seemed the essential one. If the Serbian government agreed to this, it would be confessing its inability to keep assassins under control. Even so, the agreement was very nearly given.

Pašić, the prime minister, had left on an election tour when the Austrian note arrived. Evidently he hoped to escape responsibility for decision one way or the other. When summoned to return, he left for a holiday in Greece and had to be pulled off the train to receive a telegram of recall from the Prince Regent. By the time he got back, the Serbian ministers had decided to accept the Austrian demands almost unconditionally. There were slight changes of phrasing so as to imply the innocence of the Serbian government. Even so, it would have been almost impossible for the Austrians to declare that their terms had not been met. They would have had to make do with boasting instead of war. Acceptance of such terms would be humiliating for Serbia. It would weaken national enthusiasm for the time being. But Serbia would survive and be free to resume the South Slav cause later.

At the last minute the Serbian ministers changed their minds. They decided to make difficulties over some of the Austrian demands and to reject the collaboration with Austrian officials outright. It is not known what swung them round. Pašić may have feared that Austrian officials would find out about the Black Hand. The Sarajevo investigation had already uncovered Tankosić, and from him the trail led straight to Apis. Perhaps Pašić was himself threatened by the Black Hand. A more popular hypothesis claims that there was some message from St Petersburg, urging the Serbian government to stand firm. The written record fails us. However, there was one Russian action, or preliminary to action, which spoke louder than words.

On 24 July, when first news of the Austro-Hungarian ultimatum came through, Sazonov urged on the Tsar and the council of ministers that Russia could not stand entirely aside. She must show that she was involved. But how? An immediate protest to Vienna would be too provocative, especially when it was not known whether the Serbs intended to refuse the Austrian demands. A promise of support in Belgrade would commit Russia too much. But what about a mobilization in the military districts adjacent to Austria-Hungary? This would show that Russia was not sleeping. At the same time, it would be an assurance that towards Germany Russia had no warlike intentions. Sazonov's colleagues were delighted with the idea. It seemed to offer exactly what they wanted: a gesture of support for Serbia without firm commitment or risk of general war. Sazonov did not consult the chief-of-staff or any other military spokesman. If he had done, he would have learnt that this partial mobilization was unworkable – it would cut across the plans for general mobilization and make them impossible. It could be tried only if there were a firm pledge of German neutrality, and that was not likely to happen. However, the chief-of-staff had not been long in office and did not venture to wrangle with the foreign minister. Sazonov went on believing he had a safe weapon when he cared to use it.

For the moment, the Russian government were content to take only preliminary steps – recall of technical officers and so on; seemingly harmless though involving nearly a million men by the end of the month. The Serbians seem to have learnt Sazonov's further intentions.

Here was an assurance that Serbia would not be left totally friendless. The prospect stirred the Serbians to more resolute behaviour. Unless they showed their spirit, Russia might shift her favour to some other Balkan country. Though still anxious to avoid war, the Serbian ministers walked a little nearer the edge. They aimed to keep the dispute with Austria-Hungary going so that, in the subsequent diplomatic wrangling, Russian prestige could be asserted. Throughout Saturday, 25 July, the Serbian ministers worked on their answer, inserting reservations on the original typescript until the last moment. The changes of phrase were sometimes plausibly conciliatory, sometimes insolent. The refusal to admit Austrian officials at the Serb enquiry was the only point which gave excuse for a breach.

The Serbian ministers also decided to mobilize the army and to withdraw the government to Niš, further from the Austro-Hungarian frontier. Pašić himself delivered the answer at the Austro-Hungarian legation with five minutes to spare, at 5.55 pm. He then caught the official train to Niš, also by a narrow margin. Giesl took a quick look at the Serbian note; saw that it was not an unconditional acceptance; and at once sent back a note he had already prepared, announcing that he was leaving Belgrade and that diplomatic relations between Austria-Hungary and Serbia were broken off. He was just in time to catch the 6.30 pm train from Belgrade and ten minutes later was on Hungarian soil. He telephoned to Tisza who asked: 'Did it have to be?' Giesl answered: 'Yes.' His news was telegraphed to Vienna. Francis Joseph was on holiday at Ischl, where Berchtold had joined him. Giesl's news was telegraphed on to them. When Francis Joseph learnt it, he remarked untranslatably: 'Also doch' – meaning something like: 'Berchtold told me things would not go wrong, but they have.' He added: 'However, breaking off diplomatic relations does not necessarily mean war.' Berchtold's comments are not recorded. When the news arrived, he was out taking a walk. Later in the evening he persuaded Francis Joseph to sign the order for mobilization against Serbia. But he shared much of Francis Joseph's optimism and added the further consolation: 'Mobilization does not mean war.'

Berchtold's resolution was by now exhausted. This silly gentleman had never intended to go to war. He had been assured by everyone from Forgách to William II that if he showed an unshakeable spirit Serbia would at some point give way – perhaps when the Austrian note was presented, perhaps when relations were broken off, or

perhaps with the threat of Austro-Hungarian mobilization. Berchtold
had little desire to go further. The bluff, to which others had encouraged him, was not succeeding and, in the usual way of those who get
into this position, he proposed to play for time, in other words to do
nothing. This was not a bad idea. The other powers still had no desire
to be involved in war for Serbia's sake. Both Sazonov and Grey were
tumbling over themselves to get Berchtold out of his mess. July 25 was
of course a Saturday, and it was too much to expect that Sir Edward
Grey would give up his weekend's fishing for a remote Balkan crisis.
However, he approved a suggestion from the Foreign Office that
Great Britain should propose an international conference similar to
the ambassadors' meetings during the Balkan Wars. At the same time,
Sazonov was cutting across this proposal by seeking direct talks with
Austria-Hungary.

Both proposals were made to Germany, on the assumption that
Bethmann, like Grey and Sazonov, was anxious to avoid war. This
assumption was mistaken. Bethmann probably wanted to avoid a
general European war. On the other hand, he consciously wanted a
'localized' war – that is, a war between Austria-Hungary and Serbia.
This, he thought, would solve all his problems. It would restore
Austro-Hungarian prestige. It would demonstrate Germany's loyalty
to her ally and so increase her prestige also. The conciliatory pleadings
from Sazonov and Grey convinced him that neither of them would go
to war merely for the sake of Serbia, and the lack of any decisive
French policy while Poincaré and Viviani were still absent strengthened his confidence. But he was in a hurry. The statesmen of the
entente Powers might change their minds. Still worse, William II was
returning home against Bethmann's advice, and he, as Bethmann well
knew, was likely to turn soft when faced with a real danger of war.
This indeed was exactly what happened. As soon as he got back, he
declared that the Serbian answer was a triumph for Vienna and
ought to have been accepted. His conversion was too late. By then,
Bethmann's insistence had pushed Austria-Hungary into war.

Berchtold was repeatedly prodded by urgings from Berlin. Grey's
proposals for mediation or an international conference were sent on to
him belatedly, with an assurance that Germany had already turned
them down, but also with a warning that they could not be resisted
indefinitely. Austria-Hungary must present Europe with a *fait accompli*.
Grey must be met with the answer: 'Too late.' Berchtold summoned

Conrad, the chief-of-staff. An odd situation was revealed. The timid pacific diplomat wanted to declare war. The fire-eating general was against it. Conrad explained that mobilization, even against Serbia, would take some time. The Austro-Hungarian Army could not be ready until 12 August, and a declaration of war before then would expose it to derision. This was music in Berchtold's ears. A declaration of war would after all mean nothing. It would be merely another diplomatic move, a further gesture of bluff which might make the Serbs give way. Meanwhile he would have displayed his own resolve anew and would have satisfied his German ally. He rejected Conrad's advocacy of 12 August with the words: 'The diplomatic situation will not hold so long.'

Berchtold, now back in Vienna, wired Francis Joseph at Ischl that Serbian troops had fired on the Austrians. Francis Joseph wired back his approval of a declaration of war on Serbia. By this time, the report of the Serbian troops having opened fire had turned out to be false. Berchtold struck the reference to it out of the declaration of war, though he did not inform Francis Joseph of this until after the declaration had gone. In later years Berchtold asserted that he had not intended to deceive his imperial master, so perhaps duplicity had merely become a habit with him. One problem remained: how to deliver the declaration of war, in view of the fact that relations had already been broken off. The Germans, who were looking after Austro-Hungarian interests in Serbia, refused to act as postmen, since, in Jagow's words, 'it might give the impression that we had hounded Austria-Hungary into war'. However, Berchtold or his officials found a simple answer. The declaration of war was sent to Belgrade by the ordinary telegraph via Bucharest.

Pašić received the telegram at 1 pm on 28 July. He thought it might be an Austrian trick, designed to provoke a Serbian attack. He telegraphed to the Serbian ministers at London, Paris, and St Petersburg, asking whether Austria-Hungary had really declared war on Serbia. The answers came back during the afternoon. It was true. The war had started, at any rate in theory. But nothing real seemed to have happened. Berchtold was soon saying that a declaration of war was not the same as war, and events almost proved him right. There was no serious fighting between Serbia and Austria-Hungary until the autumn of 1914, when Potiorek, in command, mismanaged the invasion of Serbia as badly as he had mismanaged the archduke's visit to Sarajevo. Yet war, even ineffective and unfought, was basically different from the sternest diplomatic threats. The Great Powers had waged plenty of wars with countries outside Europe and with one, Turkey, on the fringe. But no Great Power had issued a declaration of war against another European country since 1870. Berchtold did not mean to start a war, even against Serbia. He merely wanted to show that he was not an impossibly weak foreign minister and to find some means of stopping the flow of reproaches, rebukes, and proddings which came to him from Berlin. Having deceived everyone in turn – Tisza, Conrad, Francis Joseph, the Germans, the entente statesmen – he ended by deceiving himself. But what Berchtold intended or desired was no longer of importance. By declaring war on Serbia, Berchtold fired the second shot in the First World War as surely, if as unintentionally, as Princip fired the first.

Decision in Berlin

Men in Vienna started a Balkan war or at least made the gesture of doing so. This was the utmost they were capable of. It depended on the rulers of the really Great Powers whether this would grow into a European war, and it depended most of all on men in Berlin. All the others were eager to compromise. The British and French cared nothing at all for Serbia. Even the Russians were willing that Austria-Hungary should obtain some satisfaction, though not all she sought. There was a way out which, curiously enough, was grasped most clearly by a man in Potsdam, if not in Berlin. William II had lost his bellicose ardour. He remained convinced that the Serbian reply gave Austria-Hungary all she needed. His erratic intellect pointed to a solution. The Austrians should occupy Belgrade as a pledge that Serbia would fulfil her promises. At the same time, they would declare that they had no designs against Serbian sovereignty. This was the Halt in Belgrade, a solution which any capable diplomat might have devised and which could have ended the crisis.

The Austrians did not like it. They hesitated to move against Serbia until 12 August when their mobilization would be theoretically complete. Ironically their apprehensions were unfounded. The Serbs had resolved not to defend Belgrade, and the Austrians could have occupied it almost without firing a shot. They had a larger objection.

Once war with Serbia really started, the Austrians did not intend to keep their promise of respecting Serbian integrity. If Tisza's objections could be overcome, Austria-Hungary herself would annex Serbian territory; if not, chunks of it could be thrown to Bulgaria and Albania. Later events were to make the object look foolish. For, in the autumn of 1914, it was the Serbs who ended in occupation of Hungarian territory and not the other way round. Such however were the calculations which led Berchtold to turn a deaf ear to all projects for a halt in Belgrade.

Berchtold's evasions and silences mattered little. The decisive opposition to William II's conciliatory diplomacy came from Bethmann, who displayed a surprising disregard for his imperial master except when it suited him. Bethmann was obstinately set on a localized war. All along he had wanted a violent reassertion of Austro-Hungarian prestige, with German support, so that the standing of the central Powers would be increased. If Austria-Hungary compromised or weakened, Germany's prestige would be shaken also. Bethmann was convinced that Serbia would yield at some point, preferably after a war. He was also committed to the doctrine that Russia would not intervene, if faced with the threat of war with Germany. He had laid down this doctrine on 5 July. He continued to hold it on 28 July. He had virtually no choice. For if Russia failed to back down, what happened to the belief in Germany's strong right arm? What would be said by all the patriotic Germans who had been told for a generation that their army was the most powerful in the world? Bethmann liked to think that he acted as a brake on German nationalism, and of course a brake can work only when the vehicle is moving. A check, if not a humiliation, for Russia was an essential part of Bethmann's policy.

Bethmann had a secondary aim which gradually moved up to first place. His constant refrain had been: 'War will be averted if Germany stands firm. But if war comes after all, the responsibility for it must lie with Russia.' In his anxiety to shift the blame on to Russia, Bethmann came almost to forget his original objective. Putting the blame on to Russia had for Bethmann great attractions. Russian initiative might make the French hesitate, as they had done during the Bosnian crisis. More important from Bethmann's point of view, it would keep Great Britain neutral – or so Bethmann believed. Bethmann was not thinking

in terms of armies, where the British counted but little. Perhaps he
doubted whether the German Army could win at a single blow and
therefore looked forward to a long war. More probably, as a conservative but civilized German, Bethmann regarded Great Britain as his
touchstone and needed her neutrality to maintain his psychological
confidence.

Bethmann had also a domestic calculation. As chancellor, he tried
to straddle between Left and Right. Though himself conservative, he
hoped for a time when the social democrats, now the largest single
party in the Reichstag, would join the government side instead of
remaining permanently in opposition. The process was already happening. Though still theoretically Marxist internationalists, the
German social democrats were, in fact, becoming day-to-day opportunists with a strong dose of German sentiment. A threat from Russia
would push them over the edge. They had made an exception about
Russia in their anti-war principles from the days of Marx and Engels
onwards. Bebel, their leader, had declared long ago: 'Against Russia
the social democrats would march as one man.' Thus, if the situation
could be presented as a Russian aggression against Germany, Bethmann would accomplish the miracle which had escaped every German
statesman since 1848. He would produce a united Germany, and so
he did.

A tame ending to the crisis was therefore unwelcome to Bethmann.
It was easy for him to run William II's well-meaning efforts into the
sand. William II was at Potsdam and absurdly had no telephone line
to Berlin. Every message from him had to be delivered by hand, and
each time Bethmann was able to reply that it was too late. It had
been superseded by events. Similarly, William II only learnt of
diplomatic developments some hours after they had happened. At a
time when every minute counted, the most powerful ruler in Europe
was always a day behind events.

The situation was moving faster than Bethmann or anyone else
expected. By declaring war against Serbia, the Austrians had turned
everything upside down. Where previously they had drifted with
intolerable slowness, they had now fixed a final date, 12 August,
before which everything must be settled or get out of hand. Even this
date soon proved too far ahead. Berchtold assumed that he had a
fortnight in hand before anything real happened. Conrad shattered

this illusion. He explained that until 1 August mobilization could proceed against Serbia alone. On that day he must decide whether to continue mobilizing solely against Serbia or whether, as provided by his flexible planning, the remaining four army corps should be directed towards the Russian front. In other words, Austria-Hungary must have a guarantee of Russian neutrality by 1 August. The Austrians could not obtain this themselves, for any approach to Russia by them would imply a recognition that their dealings with Serbia were not a simple localized war. It was time, in fact, for Germany to fulfil her promise and to keep Russia neutral by threat of war.

At exactly the same time the Russians were facing the need for decision. They had resolved to give Serbia support which they still hoped would be only diplomatic. They did not know that the Austrians dared not go on with their mobilization against Serbia without a guarantee of Russian neutrality. On the contrary, the Russians assumed that they, too, must negotiate arms in hand. It never occurred to them that, merely by doing nothing, they could prevent Austria-Hungary's acting against Serbia or, at worst, compel Germany to act openly as the aggressor – which Bethmann was determined not to do. The most difficult thing in a crisis is to wait upon events, and the Russians could not bring themselves to do it. Uncertainty weighed them down and, as well, Sazonov, like others, wished to show that he was not the weak, irresolute character that he was alleged to be – and was.

Sazonov believed that there was still a safe way out: a partial Russian mobilization directed solely against Austria-Hungary. Grey had telegraphed that he found this quite natural. Jagow, the German secretary of state, had said on 26 July that Germany would make no objection. Here was the secret card on which Sazonov had relied all along. On 28 July he learnt of the Austro-Hungarian declaration of war against Serbia and at once went to see Nicholas II at Peterhof, seventeen miles from St Petersburg. Sazonov produced his solution. The Russian generals objected. Now, and apparently not before, they explained that partial mobilization was impossible. There were no plans prepared for it. It would be a hastily improvised operation. Still worse, once it began, general mobilization would become impossible, and Russia would be at Germany's mercy. Nicholas II and Sazonov hesitated once more and finally decided to avoid a decision. Two orders or *ukazes* should be prepared – one for partial, one for general mobilization. The further formalities were important. First the *ukaze* must be signed by the Tsar. Then it must be signed by the ministers for war and the navy. Finally the Tsar must again give his approval.

The next morning Sazonov, back in St Petersburg, had a discussion with Janushkevich, the chief-of-staff. He was shaken by the military arguments against partial mobilization. He therefore agreed that Janushkevich should take both *ukazes* to Peterhof for the Tsar's signature, which Janushkevich did. Nicholas II signed both, without however finally committing himself to either. Janushkevich had no interest in the *ukaze* for partial mobilization. Back in St Petersburg, he took the *ukaze* for general mobilization to Sukhomlinov, minister for war, who declared that Russia was unready for war. Maklahov, the minister of the interior, who was also present, added that war would lead to revolution. Sukhomlinov exclaimed: 'We cannot escape our fate,' crossed himself, and signed the *ukaze*. Janushkevich took the *ukaze* on to the minister for the navy and then waited impatiently for the Tsar's final approval.

This was given and then snatched away again. In both cases the motive came from Berlin. On 29 July Bethmann began to lose his nerve. It became clear to him that, if Austria-Hungary went ahead against Serbia without any attempt at compromise, the diplomatic situation would not move in Germany's favour. Germany would have to threaten Russia and would be displayed as the aggressor. The social democrats would not be won over; Great Britain would not pledge her neutrality. Yet the German generals were insisting that, with the rumours of mobilization coming out of Russia, German mobilization could not long be delayed. Shortly after midday on 29 July Bethmann therefore sent a message to Sazonov that 'further progress of Russian mobilization would compel us to mobilize'. This was meant as a warning, not as a threat. Bethmann did not grasp the difference between Russian partial and general mobilization, which indeed to all military men was non-existent. But for Sazonov the message was shattering. It destroyed his faith that there was a way of checking Austria-Hungary without bringing on war with Germany.

Once more Sazonov conferred with the Russian military leaders. They again argued for general mobilization, and now he agreed with them. After the message from Bethmann, the difference between partial and general mobilization seemed to have disappeared. In this way, Sazonov, having been bewitched by the escape hatch of partial mobilization, drifted into the general mobilization which he had never intended to promote. The recommendation for general mobilization was telephoned to Nicholas II, and he agreed to it. But both Nicholas II and Sazonov went on believing that they were merely increasing the bid, not committing themselves to war. The typewriters began to tap out the necessary telegrams. Later in the evening Nicholas received a telegram from his cousin, William II. William implied, sincerely though inaccurately, that his proposal for the Halt in Belgrade was within sight of accomplishment. Russian mobilization, even against Austria-Hungary, would throw it out.

Nicholas II was shaken. Clad in his nightshirt, he stumbled downstairs in the empty palace and telephoned to Sukhomlinov that the general mobilization should be stopped. He and Janushkevich tried to argue that this was impossible, but the Tsar answered: 'Stop it', and the generals prepared to obey. Transmission of military telegrams stopped for the night. Did the Tsar intend that partial mobilization should be stopped also? Apparently not, for he wired back to William II that the military measures now coming into force had been decided on for reasons of defence because of Austria's preparations. The generals however deplored partial mobilization, so it may be that they in fact held up all action, while the Tsar presumed that partial mobilization was going ahead.

Sazonov made the same assumption, though he drew a different conclusion from it. After his prolonged discussions with the generals, he had now grasped that partial mobilization was impossible. But, instead of abandoning all mobilization for the moment, he became an advocate of general mobilization. On the morning of 30 July, he telephoned the Tsar, who refused to be moved. Finally, the Tsar agreed to see Sazonov at three o'clock that afternoon. Once more Sazonov journeyed to Peterhof, bearing with him a message from the president of the Duma that 'as head of the representatives of the Russian people he would never forgive a delay which might precipitate the country into fatal confusion'. For over an hour Sazonov argued in vain. The Tsar would not commit himself to war. The Tsar's aide-de-camp said sympathetically: 'Yes, it is hard to decide.' The Tsar snapped: 'I will decide' and did so. He told Sazonov to authorize general mobilization. Sazonov telephoned Janushkevich with the news and ended: 'Now you can smash your telephone.' The orders went out at 4 pm. The red call-up notices appeared on the walls during the night. Yet once again this was not intended as a decision for war. Nicholas II believed correctly that the mobilized Russian armies could remain at their post for an indefinite time. On the following afternoon he promised William II that Russian troops would not move so long as negotiations were going on between Austria-Hungary and Serbia. This promise was sincere and could have been kept.

The Austrians, however, did not mean to negotiate. They began to develop enthusiasm for a localized war just when others, including Bethmann, lost faith in it. Berchtold was timid so long as he was being pushed by the Germans. He developed a new obstinacy when Bethmann instead began to display doubts. By 30 July Bethmann had come round to the Halt in Belgrade. This was the moment when Berchtold resolved to wreck the idea. There was an obvious course for him to take. An Austro-Hungarian general mobilization would be the repudiation of a localized war. It would imply that war with Russia was inevitable and so force Bethmann to abandon his belated attempts at conciliation. More practically, it would at last relieve Conrad's anxieties.

This new bellicosity by Berchtold received support from an unexpected source. Until now Moltke, the German chief-of-staff, had left diplomacy to Bethmann and in any case, knowing his own insufficiency, was anxious to avoid war. As the crisis deepened, he, too, wanted to show that he was a strong man. Moreover, it seemed that William II, failing to get conciliatory answers from the Tsar, was also swinging round to violence again. Moltke therefore telegraphed to Conrad: 'Mobilize at once against Russia.' On the morning of 31 July, Conrad showed this telegram to Berchtold, who was himself waving the telegrams in an opposite sense from Bethmann. Berchtold exclaimed: 'That's rich. Who rules in Berlin: Moltke or Bethmann?' He decided to follow the Moltke line. Austro-Hungarian general mobilization was proclaimed later in the morning. Neither the Russians nor the Austrians knew that the other had started general mobilization. In this way, each provided justification for the other's act without knowing that they were doing so. But, as with Russian mobilization, Austro-Hungarian mobilization merely raised the tension. It was not a decision for a general war.

This decision was taken in Berlin on 31 July, and almost without debate. Bethmann had been told often enough by Moltke and others that mobilization meant war, as indeed it did for Germany. He therefore assumed that the same was true for Russia and that with Russia's general mobilization all hope for peace had vanished. His hope that Great Britain and perhaps even France would be estranged from Russia if she mobilized had been belied. Therefore he ceased to be interested in avoiding war and was concerned only to win it. Far from being pushed on by Moltke, Bethmann now wanted to know how quickly the fatherland could go to war. Moltke, for his part, was bewitched by the time-table which he had inherited from Schlieffen. He was convinced that, once Russia started to mobilize, Germany could not waste a day. Yet he knew that Russian mobilization would lurch along for many weeks and that Germany had plenty of time in hand. Instead he sounded the alarm of French mobilization, which had, in fact, not yet started. Even this alarm was misplaced. For the object of the Schlieffen plan was to encircle the French armies in their advanced positions on the frontier. Therefore the more advanced and mobilized they were, the greater the catastrophe.

None of these calculations was made. With combined despair, Bethmann and Moltke hurried each other into war, both convinced that all chance of peace was over and both also believing, with a mixture of patriotic illusion and personal gloom, that Germany could win the coming war. Diplomacy now became the servant of strategy. In a last flash of legality, the Germans wanted to document that somehow their resort to war was justified. Hence there must be a dispatch of ultimatums to Russia and France before an actual declaration of war, though not with any expectation that the ultimatums would be accepted. The ultimatum to Russia was easy: she was simply called upon to stop mobilizing and to undo the steps already taken. Sazonov still did not understand that refusal of the German demand meant immediate war. He supposed only that the Germans would mobilize in their turn, and the Germans did not enlighten him, for fear that he might back down. Thus even on this last day of peace, 31 July, Sazonov thought only in terms of strong nerves and going nearer the edge. He explained that Russia's measures were merely precautionary. He was not to know that historians later, in their anxiety to exonerate Germany, would accept the German apology

and accuse Sazonov of starting the war by taking defensive
precautions.

The German approach to France was trickier still. The French had
played no active part in the crisis – a modesty which was to be made
an accusation against them by some historians later. There had been
neither encouragement nor restraint from Paris to St Petersburg. In
France there had been nothing beyond preliminary measures without
general mobilization. The Germans would have been highly embarrassed if the French had answered that they had not mobilized and
did not mean to do so. For the Germans had only a plan for defeating
France and no other. The Germans had therefore made up their
minds that, if the French returned a conciliatory answer, they would
go on to demand the surrender of France's two frontier fortresses,
Toul and Verdun, for the duration of the war, and this demand
would surely provoke the French to a refusal. However, when the
German ambassador presented the demand that France should promise not to mobilize, Viviani merely replied that she would consult her
own interests. The Germans did not renew their demand. It occurred
to them that France might agree, if only for a few days, and this
would throw out Germany's offensive plans.

However, by 1 August the Germans decided that their two ultimatums
would not be accepted. The time had come for general mobilization,
which was in fact proclaimed before war was actually declared on
France. William II appreciated that this was the decisive act and
made the most of it. Wearing full-dress Guards uniform he drove in
an open carriage from Potsdam to the royal palace in Berlin, where
he proposed to sign the order for general mobilization before an
audience of glittering generals. There was a bizarre interruption.
Bethmann, who could attire himself only as a major, pushed through
the dazzling throng. He brought the astonishing news that Sir Edward
Grey had offered to stand surety for French neutrality. William II
reacted with optimistic excitement and declared that the preparations
against France must be stopped. Moltke answered that this was
impossible. It would involve the rerouting of 11,000 trains. He sulkily
agreed to hold up movement over the western frontier for a few hours,
and by then it turned out that Grey's message was a blunder or had
been misunderstood. Grey now asserted that he had offered French
and British neutrality only if Germany would refrain also from attack-

ing Russia. More probably he had forgotten Russia as British statesmen often did and do.

Yet here again a slight change of time-table would have sent events
quite a different way. Grey's offer was potential dynamite. The
French were pledged by their alliance to attack Germany if Germany
attacked Russia. Had the Germans assented quickly enough to Grey's
proposal, France would have been compelled to appear as the aggressor. Or maybe not. For the Germans had no plan for attacking
Russia. If therefore they did not move in the west, there would be no
war. And since the Russians had no offensive intentions, the war in
the east would have been stuck also. These are idle speculations. Once
the rulers of Germany decided that general mobilization was their
only means of safety, war had begun for all practical purposes.

On 1 August, failing a promise to stop mobilization, Germany
declared war on France on the quite unfounded pretext that French
aviators had bombed Nuremberg. The bombs, if any, were dropped
from German aeroplanes, or possibly there were no bombs at all. In
an odd way, neither of these declarations was urgent. The Germans
had no offensive plans against Russia, and therefore it was foolish of
them to hurry the eastern war on. Nor had they offensive plans for
attacking France directly. Their intention was to go through Belgium
and to take the French armies in the rear. The ultimatum demanding
free passage through Belgium for the German armies had been pulled
out of a drawer by Moltke on 26 July and sent to Brussels. It was
quite unsuited to the circumstances, containing a rigmarole of how
French troops were preparing to invade Belgium. However, the
pretext was of no importance. The ultimatum was delivered on the
evening of 2 August, actually twenty-four hours before the declaration
of war against France which was supposed to justify it. By the time
the Germans actually declared war on Belgium their troops were
already on Belgian soil.

Between 28 July and 3 August there were many decisions in the
sense of answering the question: what shall we do or say next? But
there was only one decision which turned the little Balkan conflict
between Austria-Hungary and Serbia into a European war. That was
the German decision to start general mobilization on 31 July, and
that was in its turn decisive because of the academic ingenuity with
which Schlieffen, now in his grave, had attempted to solve the
problem of a two-front war. One final step remained to be taken. The

Germans had decided on a European war. It remained for the British to decide whether the war would spread beyond the Continent and become worldwide.

Decision in London

There was war between the two great alliances, as had long been expected. Two Great Powers settled their course on less precise terms. Italy was tied by contradictory promises, which in fact freed her from any embarrassing action. As a member of the Triple Alliance, she was pledged to support Germany in case of French aggression. She was also secretly pledged to France not to support Germany in an attack on France. She was pledged to remain neutral in a war between Russia and Austria-Hungary. On the other hand, she was pledged to join in if her Triple Alliance partners were at war with two other Great Powers. In all this, the Italians heard only the word neutrality. The Austrians for their part were determined not to have Italy as an ally.

Under such circumstances, it should have been easy for the Italians to follow a neutral and even a mediating path. But the Italians were also obsessed with the idea of compensation. They wanted to profit from action without taking it. It was too soon for them openly to abandon the Triple Alliance and to offer themselves to the other side. They therefore spent the entire crisis trying to extract from Vienna and Berlin statements of what rewards they would receive if they entered the war, which they had resolved not to do. Not surprisingly, their diplomacy proved barren. It had importance only as foreshadowing the search for rewards which finally brought Italy into the war in the following year.

The greatest decision in the crisis lay with the British government. It determined the future fate both of the British Empire and of Europe. For fifty years past, the British had followed a policy of detachment from continental affairs. Their relations with the continental Powers, though intense and sometimes hostile, had been shaped by events outside Europe. There was one step which came near to a commitment. The British General Staff had discussed with the French how their army could be used in case Great Britain entered a European war, and agreement had been reached. But there was no pledge that the army would be used. There were those, particularly among the Conservatives, who would have liked a formal alliance with France. There were others, particularly among the radicals, who thought that Anglo-French relations were already too close. The majority of politicians were reasonably content with Great Britain's equivocal position – half-in, half-out.

There was one striking difference between the way in which British policy was determined and how it happened elsewhere. On the Continent the decision lay in the hands of individuals: the foreign minister, the ruler, and to some extent the chief-of-staff. In Austria-Hungary, it was Berchtold and Francis Joseph; in Russia, Sazonov and the Tsar; in Germany, Bethmann and William II. The question hardly arose in France where there was no decision to make. But even here Viviani settled policy so far as there was one, with encouragement from Poincaré. If any of these foreign ministers had acted differently, the decisions would have been different. The councils of ministers, where they existed, were rarely informed and never consulted. For all practical purposes, they played no part in the crisis.

In Great Britain decision lay with the cabinet and beyond that with parliament. Grey could not conduct an independent foreign policy even if he had wished to do so. He had to carry the cabinet with him. Most of its members had little interest in European affairs. They expected Great Britain to stay out, the more so when the war seemed to originate in a remote Balkan struggle. In the first days, Grey agreed with them. He had no doubt that, whatever the rights and wrongs of the matter, it was Serbia's duty to give way. Some infringement of Serbian independence was better than a European war. He was prepared to mediate. He was not prepared to threaten. He did not warn Germany that Great Britain would go to war if Germany took the aggressive approach against France and Russia. He did not warn France, still less Russia, that Great Britain would remain neutral if they were unreasonable. He left both sides to make up their own minds. He pleaded later that the cabinet would not have allowed him to do anything else. The truth is rather that he did not know what Great Britain would do or what course he himself would favour.

The British had one anxiety. They were pledged to maintain the neutrality of Belgium, and they regarded this as an essential British interest. Being good Liberals, they looked up what Gladstone had done at the outbreak of the Franco-German War in 1870 and carefully followed his precedent. On 31 July Grey therefore asked both France and Germany for a promise to respect Belgian neutrality. The French at once gave the promise. The Germans answered that they could not reveal their plan of campaign. This was disturbing, though not in the way that was subsequently imagined. In the years immediately before the war Belgium had been more friendly with Germany than with France or Great Britain, and the British now feared that the Germans had struck a bargain which would allow them to pass through Belgium without resistance. On 1 August however the British received what they thought was good news. The Belgians declared that they were determined to defend their neutrality against all comers.

It is commonly supposed that many people foresaw the German invasion of Belgium. Some members of the British government, for instance, later claimed that they had not committed themselves to aiding France in the conviction that a German invasion of Belgium would remove all doubts. Even Grey wrote later: 'There was little for me to do. Circumstances and events were compelling decision.' Though it is always difficult, if not impossible, to prove a negative, this seems to be wisdom after the event. No affair illustrates better Maitland's dictum: 'It is important to remember that events now long in the past were once in the future.' The full-scale invasion of Belgium was inconceivable until it happened. British and French staff officers had discussed the defence of France. They had not discussed the defence of Belgium, and the military plans which they made were totally unsuited to it. The British staff officers concealed many things from the civilian politicians. But in this case they had nothing to conceal. They did not foresee the German invasion of Belgium and made no preparations against it.

It might be supposed that the French foresaw the invasion of Belgium and concealed this possibility in the hope that it would surprise the British into involvement. This, too, is not the case. The French military experts knew, of course, that the Germans had accumulated marshalling yards at Aachen and had greatly increased the railway lines from Aachen to the Belgian frontier. But they refused to believe that reservists, called to the colours after some years in civil life, could at once be used as fighting troops. They therefore much underestimated the forces available to the German high command on the Western Front and anticipated at most a German short-cut across Luxembourg. Joffre, the French commander-in-chief, had made dispositions to deal with this and indeed hoped that it would happen – he supposed that it would increase his chance of victory. There is clear proof of French ignorance about the coming invasion of Belgium. In their desperate pleadings for British entry into the war, they used every conceivable argument, especially that of honourable commitment. It never occurred to them to argue that Belgium was in danger.

Thus, on 1 August, when the first declarations of war flashed across Europe, Great Britain still seemed to be well out of it. Almost half the Liberal cabinet were against entering the war, and Grey himself did not propose it. Churchill, the most bellicose minister, sent a message to the Conservative leaders that the government was about to break up. He wanted preparations for an immediate coalition. Bonar Law, the Conservative leader, did not care for Churchill and returned no answer. Instead he sent a letter to Asquith the following day urging support for France and Russia. In the atmosphere of the moment, this letter seemed designed to embarrass the government rather than to produce any action.

When the cabinet met on the morning of Sunday, 2 August, Lord Morley, leader of the peace party, was cheerful and confident. He said to Churchill: 'Winston, we've beaten you after all.' Morley had thought of a policy which was both honourable and yet would avoid war. The French were constantly complaining that they had moved their fleet to the Mediterranean in the confident hope that the British would protect them in the Channel. Morley proposed to do so. The Germans should be warned that Great Britain could not allow the German fleet to enter the Channel and attack French shipping or French ports. In this way, the honourable undertaking to France would be discharged. Great Britain would be secured from a naval engagement on her doorstep. The way would be open for what Morley called 'diplomatic energy and armed neutrality', as against Grey's policy of armed intervention. The cabinet accepted Morley's proposal. Later this looked like a first step towards supporting France, and its significance was therefore not grasped. At the time, it seemed a step the other way. The Germans, who had no intention of risking their fleet in the Channel, at once promised not to pass the Straits of Dover. They attached a condition: Great Britain must remain neutral.

The British did not accept this. All the same they were slipping into another honourable undertaking – this time with Germany.

At 6.30 in the evening the British cabinet met again. There were now reports, which proved true, that German troops were entering Luxembourg. British commitments to the neutrality of Luxembourg were vague and imprecise. They provided neither motive nor justification for action. But the German move raised the fear that they would also cross a corner of Belgium. What should Great Britain do then? Once more the cabinet consulted the precedent of 1870. Gladstone's government had then resolved that 'a substantial violation of Belgian neutrality would compel us to take action'. The cabinet of 2 August 1914 repeated this resolution. Again, what appeared later as a step towards war was made as a security for peace. Crossing a corner of Belgium could be presented as not a substantial violation of her neutrality, and in fact, though the British did not know this, some Belgian ministers were playing with the idea of resisting the Germans only in the territory actually invaded, while keeping the rest of the country neutral.

These subtle calculations were made futile by what happened in Brussels exactly when the British cabinet was meeting. The Belgians had mobilized on 1 August. They garrisoned their frontier against France as well as against Germany, and the people spent Sunday, 2 August, in a holiday mood, happy that, as a small neutral, they would escape the clash of the Great Powers. At 6.30 pm the German minister sent a message that he wished to see the foreign minister. He arrived at 7 pm, pale and trembling. The Belgian said: 'Are you not well?' The German replied: 'I climbed the stairs too quickly.' He then read out the German demand to march through Belgium and asked for an answer within twelve hours. The paper dropped from his hands on to the floor. The Belgian said: 'No, no, it is not possible.'

The Belgian cabinet met at 9 pm and sat until half past two the following morning. They resolved to reject the German demand and to defend their neutrality. But they imagined that the Germans would hesitate if faced with a resolute resistance, still associated with neutrality. They supposed, too, as others did during the crisis, that there was plenty of time during which diplomacy could prevail. They did not therefore appeal to the other Powers for assistance. On the contrary they ordered their troops to fire on any French soldiers crossing the frontier. The only appeal was from King Albert to King George for 'diplomatic assistance'.

The next morning, which was August Bank Holiday, the British cabinet met again. It approved the draft of the speech which Grey was to make in the House of Commons that afternoon. One embarrassing point came out. Grey had told the French, but not the Germans, of the decision taken the previous day to prevent the German fleet entering the Channel. Perhaps he had been hoping after all that the Germans would enter and so provoke a British intervention. Asquith had unwittingly spoilt Grey's manoeuvre by blurting out the story to the German ambassador during the evening. However, this was now all dead stuff. News of the German ultimatum to Belgium came in while the cabinet was meeting. Morley felt that all was lost and resigned in despair. The rest of the cabinet agreed that Grey should tack a passage about Belgium on to his existing draft. Lloyd George, who had been excited by the Bank Holiday crowds, was now as resolute as the rest.

In the afternoon Grey addressed the House of Commons. Most of his speech was a rambling defence of his past dealings with France. It was feeble and apologetic. He still made no recommendation and asked others to decide policy for him: 'Let every man look into his heart, and his own feelings, and construe the extent of his obligation for himself.' The MPs were disturbed and unhappy. Towards the end, Grey gave the news about Belgium, though still in a confused way. Opposition, though vocal, trailed away to nothing. Members departed, many of them dreaming that Belgium could be saved without war.

It almost seems that Grey shared this illusion. Churchill recounts that, as they left the House of Commons, he asked Grey: 'What happens now?' Grey replied: 'Now we shall send an ultimatum to Germany to stop the invasion of Belgium within twenty-four hours.' This sounds like a conversation made up after the event. At any rate nothing of the kind happened. The cabinet met during the evening and resolved to ask the Germans for an assurance that they would respect Belgian neutrality. There was no threat of war, no time limit. No decision actually to go to war was ever made by the British cabinet.

Grey still thought that there was no hurry – or perhaps it was another case of circumstances deciding for him. After the cabinet he had dinner and went to bed. The polite request to Germany was not sent off until 9.30 the next morning. By then it was already out of date. The first German troops had crossed the Belgian frontier at 8 am. News reports of this reached London about midday. There was still no Belgian appeal for assistance. (This reached London only at 12.50 am on 5 August, almost two hours after Great Britain had declared war on Germany.) Grey did not again consult the cabinet. He may have consulted Asquith. The king was not informed. Essentially Grey acted on his own.

At 2 pm on 4 August he dispatched an ultimatum to Germany. The Germans were again asked for an assurance that they would respect the neutrality of Belgium. A satisfactory reply must be received 'here by 12 o'clock tonight'. The request was of course refused. Goschen, the British ambassador, saw Bethmann at 7 pm. Bethmann said that England was going to war 'just for a scrap of paper'.

Did he use these very words? We shall never know, for when anyone thought of asking, both Bethmann and Goschen were dead. We do not know whether Bethmann spoke in German or in English – probably in German. We know, however, that the words were already running in Goschen's mind. A fortnight earlier there had been private theatricals at the British embassy. The play was a piece by Sardou, its title: *A Scrap of Paper*. Goschen burst into tears and asked for his passports.

In London Asquith told the House of Commons that an ultimatum had been sent. He went to his private room where his wife asked him: 'So it is all up?' He replied: 'Yes, it's all up' and also burst into tears. Yet apparently British ministers were still not sure that all was up. Asquith, Grey, Lloyd George, and others met in the cabinet room, waiting for the reply from Germany which never came. Someone had a bright idea for shortening the suspense. Germany had Central European Time, which was one hour later than Greenwich Time (then unsullied by the later invention of Summer Time). Midnight in Berlin was therefore 11 pm in London, and the British ultimatum could be treated as expiring at that hour. This did not accord with the wording of the ultimatum which had asked for an answer *here*, that is London, by midnight. Was someone afraid that the Germans might give a favourable answer after all? Was it an ingenious idea for getting off to bed? Or was it merely another example of the unreason-ing haste which characterized the entire crisis? We shall never know.

At 10.15 pm the king held a privy council at Buckingham Palace. It was attended by the first commissioner of works and two court officials. The Privy Council authorized a state of war with Germany from 11 pm. This was the formality which took Great Britain into war. With a last flash of muddle the wrong declaration of war was sent to the German ambassador. A news agency reported that Ger-many had declared war on Great Britain. A counter-declaration was at once sent to the German ambassador. The news then turned out to be false. A Foreign Office clerk raced round to the German embassy and recovered the British note which the ambassador had not opened. The clerk substituted the correct declaration which merely asserted that Germany had not replied. It was then 11.05 pm. At exactly the same time Churchill left the cabinet room for the Admiralty and dispatched the telegram to all warships: 'Commence hostilities against Germany.'

It was easy for the Royal Navy to do this in theory, though, given the shortage of German ships out of port, not so easy in practice. But what else should the British do? Every other country had had detailed war plans drawn up before the diplomacy began, and the war plans made the running. But the British resolved on war first and decided on action afterwards. The cabinet had authorized the mobilization of the expeditionary force on 3 August. They had not decided where it should go to, if anywhere. On 5 August Asquith, who was acting secretary of state for war, summoned a war council. The civilians present were Grey, Haldane, and Churchill; the soldiers, every distin-guished general Asquith could lay his hands on.

There was a rambling and uninformed discussion. Great Britain had gone to war for the sake of Belgian neutrality. How was she to ensure this? Lord Roberts, the senior general present, suggested that the expeditionary force should go to Antwerp. Churchill answered that the navy could not guarantee a safe passage east of the Straits of Dover. Sir John French, who was to command the expeditionary force, thought that the army might cross the Channel to Le Havre and then decide where to go – perhaps to Antwerp, perhaps to Amiens. Sir Douglas Haig thought that the regular soldiers should stop at home and train the mass armies of the future. Sir Henry Wilson, director of military operations, cut in impatiently. He explained that there was no choice. The expeditionary force could not help the Belgians. It could only take its allotted place on the French left wing. The marshalling yards were prepared, trucks ready, lines cleared. It was Maubeuge or nowhere.

On 6 August the cabinet resolved that the expeditionary force should go to Amiens. No one took any notice. The time-table said Maubeuge. To Maubeuge it went. In this accidental way Great Britain found herself involved as a continental Power in a continental war.

The End of the Line

On the last day of July 1914 the international expresses stopped running all over Europe. They were not to run again for six years and never in their old untrammelled glory. Troop trains ran instead. By 4 August the Great Powers of Europe, other than Italy, were at war. However, not all were at war with each other. France, Germany, Russia, and Great Britain had become involved in war because of a quarrel which was initially Austrian. Yet when the others were at war with each other, Austria-Hungary, the cause of it all, was still at war with no country except Serbia. Berchtold continued to hope that something would turn up. Even after the German mobilization, he went on talking about a diplomatic solution. When the Germans declared war on Russia, Berchtold used this as a further excuse for delay: Austria-Hungary was pledged to aid Germany only if Russia attacked Germany and not the other way round. Conrad for this part thought that every day without a declaration of war made his precious plans for mobilization easier. The Germans lost patience. They were at war for Austria-Hungary's sake, and yet she took no action even on paper.

Finally on 6 August Berchtold dispatched a declaration of war to St Petersburg, alleging quite untruly that Russia had seen fit 'to open hostilities against Germany'. There was now an awkward pause on the other side. Neither France nor Great Britain desired to go to war against Austria-Hungary, nor had they any practical means of doing so except for naval blockade in the Adriatic. Once Austria-Hungary declared war on Russia, France was technically bound to go to war by the terms of the Franco-Russian alliance. But French statesmen did not wish to invoke the alliance for the sake of left-wing opinion; and British statesmen, of course, were even less attracted to this obligation. The French therefore invented the story that Austrian troops had been sent to the Western Front, and on this pretext declared war against Austria-Hungary on 12 August. The British government added its own declaration of war at once, merely because the French had already done so. Both British and French diplomats still asserted their friendship towards Austria-Hungary. Little did they foresee that before the war ended the dismemberment of Austria-Hungary would become a principal Allied war aim. To round off the record, Austria-Hungary declared war against Belgium on 29 August, alleging, again untruthfully, that Belgium was 'lending her military cooperation to France and Great Britain'.

Luxembourg did not go to war despite Germany's violation of her territory. Romania did not go to war despite the binding terms of her alliance with Austria-Hungary and Germany. Montenegro went to war against Austria-Hungary in support of Serbia, even though Prince Nicholas knew that he would lose his throne if the Serbs won and equally, of course, if they lost. The insatiable appetite of his people for war gave him no choice. The Turks could have chosen neutrality as they did in the Second World War. Instead, with gratuitous folly and misjudgement, they committed themselves to alliance with Germany and thus provided the entente with another ancient empire to dismember. Portugal wished to honour her alliance with Great Britain. Being forbidden to do so by the British, she contented herself with not declaring neutrality. The Japanese also honoured their alliance with Great Britain, though much to their own advantage. They demanded German withdrawal from Far Eastern waters and the surrender of Germany's leased territory of Kiao-Chow. The Germans did not reply, and Japan declared war on 23 August. All other powers remained neutral, some with good intent, some for the duration of the war.

None of the cherished plans provided the quick and final victory for which they had been designed. The French plans came near to producing catastrophe – for the French, not for the Germans. The French armies were mobilized with great efficiency on the German frontier. They were then sent forward against the most heavily fortified positions in the German line. There was no attempt at strategy or tactical deployment. These were among the worst, though least known, massacres of the First World War. Ironically, the French armies were saved from total destruction by the Schlieffen plan. The development of the German threat to the French left wing finally compelled Joffre to break off his senseless attacks in Lorraine. Instead, much against his will, he won the battle of the Marne.

The German advance through Belgium and into northern France was the most perfect operation of military art as this was understood in the early twentieth century. The German armies moved with almost effortless precision. The time-tables proved accurate to the minute even when the Germans were on enemy territory. Decisive victory was not achieved. The German impetus was running down even before it encountered resolute resistance. When the German troops had to face real fighting, they had been on the march for nearly a month – often covering forty miles a day. This sort of physical exhaustion was a problem which Schlieffen had not allowed for. His marvellous plan broke down for two reasons. French armies, directed by Joffre, stood immediately in the way. French armies, directed by Galliéni, threatened the German right flank. The manoeuvre had failed. As was the rule in manoeuvres, it was then abandoned.

The British deployment on the French left wing was also beautifully conducted. The expeditionary force duly arrived at Maubeuge. Instead of settling into a quiet sector of the French line, it found itself full in the track of the German Army which was sweeping across Belgium. The British were rudely pushed aside. Then later they played their part, somewhat cautiously, in the battle of the Marne. But the British forces were now embedded in the French front. A landing in the German rear might have been more effective. Perhaps Morley's 'armed neutrality' could have had a more decisive effect, once Germans and French had fought each other to a standstill. There had, of course, been another British mobilization. The Grand Fleet assembled at Scapa Flow. No Armageddon followed. On the contrary, the periscope of a mythical German submarine led the Grand Fleet to abandon Scapa Flow and to seek refuge in the remote bays of western Ireland. For many months, Great Britain and the Channel were defended only by the shadow of Nelson's name. This proved effective.

The Great Powers had plunged into war for the sake of quick victory. They continued to pursue this illusive hope for the next four years. Afterwards men looked back and puzzled how it could have happened, as they continue to do to the present day. There was a varied array of war criminals. The Allies wished to arraign 'Kaiser Bill'. This was ironically perverse. As the record shows, William II was one of the few who made persistent and constructive attempts to avoid war. Bethmann had greater responsibility, yet came off far better. Poor Tsar Nicholas also received much condemnation, partly because he had been conveniently murdered by the Bolsheviks. Yet it seems that if the affair had been left to the crowned heads of Europe there would never have been war at all. The so-called 'military monarchs' were peaceful, well-meaning men. Unfortunately, in the twentieth century, they believed it their duty to do what their statesmen said.

Some have propounded an exactly opposite explanation. The war has been blamed on the peoples of Europe. The cheering crowds, it is said, gave the statesmen no choice and drove them into war. This, too, will not do. The crowds cheered only after the decisions had been made. There were none of the demonstrations, intended to make statesmen do something or not do something, that there were later in the 1930s and often are at the present day. In Austria-Hungary, for instance, the crowds cried 'Death to the Serbian dogs' only after war had been declared. No one in Berlin waved banners inscribed 'Stand by Austria-Hungary'. Indeed this was a sentiment which would have occurred to no German outside the diplomatic service. The German crowds cheered only when mobilization was proclaimed, and they did so because they believed that Germany was in imminent danger of a great Russian invasion.

In St Petersburg there were no banners inscribed 'Stand by Serbia'. Here, too, the crowds cheered only when Tsar Nicholas II took a solemn oath not to make peace as long as there was a single invader on Russian soil – though as a matter of fact there were none at the time. French crowds demonstrated patriotic support for President Poincaré when he returned from St Petersburg, but it would be absurd to suppose that he needed this encouragement. British crowds were the only ones which demonstrated before their country was at war. The Bank Holiday crowds would have been puzzled to say what they were cheering for. Few Englishmen cared about France. None cared about Russia, and few knew much about Belgium. Presumably English people felt that, when other countries were already at war, their own should not be left out. It would be unfair to deduce from this that the English were peculiarly bellicose. Nor did their cheers have much influence on the decisions of the government.

In every country the governments decided, almost without weighing public opinion. More narrowly, foreign ministers decided as a sort of technical exercise. The considerations which moved them were no different from those on previous occasions. It has been suggested that the balance of power had broken down. Hence the German ministers were eager for war. This is the reverse of the truth. For years past, Germany had been the strongest of the Powers, and others – Russia in 1909, France in 1905 and 1911 – had given way when faced with a German threat. In 1914 the French and, more hesitantly, the Russians believed that they were strong enough to face the threat. This may have been a mere change of sentiment or it may have been a real change of power. The actual outcome certainly showed that Germany could not win a quick victory as everyone had expected her to do during earlier crises.

These earlier crises had ended without war, partly because the issues at stake were not worth fighting about. French access to the upper Nile in 1898; French control of Morocco in 1905 and 1911; even Serbia's claim to Bosnia in 1909 were topics of remote importance. There was a topic of real importance in 1914: the assertion of Habsburg prestige against Serb nationalism. But none of the Great Powers wished to dispute this. All would have acquiesced in the Halt in Belgrade, a perfectly satisfactory diplomatic solution. Instead the crisis ran away with them.

When cut down to essentials, the sole cause for the outbreak of war in 1914 was the Schlieffen plan – product of the belief in speed and the offensive. Diplomacy functioned until the German demand that France and Russia should not mobilize. No power could have accepted such a demand in the circumstances of the age. Yet the Germans had no deliberate aim of subverting the liberties of Europe. No one had time for a deliberate aim or time to think. All were trapped by the ingenuity of their military preparations, the Germans most of all. In every country, the peoples imagined that they were being called to a defensive war, and in a sense they were right. Since every General Staff believed that attack was the only form of defence, every defensive operation appeared as an attack to someone else.

There is no mystery about the outbreak of the First World War.

The deterrent failed to deter. This was to be expected sooner or later. A deterrent may work ninety-nine times out of a hundred. On the hundredth occasion it produces catastrophe. There is a contemporary moral here for those who like to find one.

Stumbling to the Brink

This essay first appeared as a review of Zara Steiner's Britain and the Origins of the First World War *(London, Macmillan, 1978) in the* Observer, *5 February 1978.*

* * *

Though the First World War is now sixty years away, it still provides fertile ground for historical debate. Until recently we thought we had more or less settled its causes: the outbreak of war was a muddle, a mistake, and that is all there was to it.

Then came Fritz Fischer and his followers, announcing that the war was deliberately planned by the rulers of Germany, either to establish their domination of Europe or to quell social discontent at home. But what about the other European Powers? Were they innocent victims of German aggression? Or did they, too, plan to remodel Europe in line with their ambitions?

Zara Steiner is the first English historian to consider the origins of the First World War in the post-Fischer age. She is well qualified to do so. She is an outstanding authority on the workings of the Foreign Office; she has an unrivalled command of the sources and she has a gift for clear exposition. Her verdict is apparently clear. Sir Edward Grey was a wise, pacific statesman, determined to maintain the independence of France but equally anxious to conciliate Germany and win her for peaceful cooperation. There was no British design for an aggressive war against Germany and forces outside the Foreign Office and the government did not shape Grey's policy. As Steiner writes, 'Grey made the final choice and until August 1914 was the master of his own ship.'

On closer examination this verdict seems less certain. Grey's mind pivoted on the balance of power. French independence, he believed, was essential for British security and this independence was menaced by Germany. Now where did he get this idea from? Surely from the anti-German experts in the Foreign Office, much as Truman got the Cold War from the anti-Soviet experts of the State Department in 1948. As so often, German aggression was a self-fulfilling prophecy. Once others assumed it, the Germans duly responded in character.

The balance of power changed, I think, not because the Germans planned to change it but because changes followed inevitably from the increasing economic strength of Germany and the relative decline of the French. Indeed it could be plausibly argued that in the long term the balance of power was more threatened by Russia than by Germany and some projectors already foresaw a coalition of the three Western Powers against the coming Russian giant. Grey had in fact formed a picture or perhaps accepted one thrust upon him by his advisers. He may have been the master of his ship but his sailing orders were laid down by others.

There were other factors which Steiner considers in the later part of her book. The two service departments had long planned deliberately for war against Germany just as the German High Command planned for war against the Triple Entente. By 1914 the Admiralty perhaps thought that they had re-established British naval supremacy without a war. The War Office however had devised the dispatch of an expeditionary force to France and had given commitments to the French that were binding in all but name.

It is possible that Grey did not grasp the consequences of the preparations made by the War Office. In August 1914 he was genuinely surprised that his declaration of war on Germany was at once followed by the departure of the British Expeditionary Force to France. Presumably he imagined that a mere declaration of war would be effective of itself. As he complacently told the House of Commons on 3 August, 'If engaged in war we shall suffer but little more than we shall suffer if we stand aside.' Far from Grey being all-powerful, Sir Henry Wilson, the director of military operations, was more powerful than Grey.

Steiner devotes much attention to the radical wing of the Liberal Party and its attempts to check Grey's foreign policy. The critics were vocal, ingenious and deeply sincere. But in Grey they were faced with a brick wall despite his conciliatory appearance. In his own mind he never shifted from the balance of power. As he could not emphasize this argument too blatantly he fell back on evasion and even direct lies. Most governments, I suppose, cheat their own supporters more than they mislead the Opposition. None has done so more persistently than the Liberal government of Asquith and Grey. Certainly they did so from the highest motives but they cheated all the same.

Towards the end Steiner seems to recognize this. She writes:

For the most part, Grey responded to external events. This is not to deny that he and his colleagues were part of a broader political, bureaucratic and military framework which restricted the number of options when the moment for decision came. Or that their decisions were based on erroneous assumptions about the nature of war, its effects and costs.

This is not a very glowing testimonial to the rulers of a great country. Indeed it is very close to Lloyd George's verdict, 'We all muddled into war.'

Whatever Grey's aim it was not achieved. To quote Steiner again, 'Germany was beaten but Britain had clearly lost her "free hand" in fact if not in theory.' Not satisfied with this conclusion she shifts her ground on the last page:

It may well be that, for reasons which the historian can only dimly perceive, Europe was deeply ready for war . . . It may be that some profound boredom with the long years of peace and with the tedium of industrial life led men to volunteer for France and to find in that Hell a final confirmation of manhood.

As she says, it may be so. At any rate her brilliant exposition provides many ideas to argue over and some to agree with.

Back on their Pedestals

This essay was first published as a review of George H Cassar's Kitchener: Architect of Victory (*London, William Kimber, 1977*) *and John Terraine's* The Road to Passchendaele: A Study in Inevitability (*London, Leo Cooper, 1977*) *in the* Observer, *1 January 1978. Of Lord Kitchener (1850–1916), Taylor observed at the end of his brief biographical notes to* English History 1914–1945 (*Oxford, Clarendon Press, 1965*): '*promised posthumous glory after the war; received none*'.

*   *   *

There seems no end to books on the First World War. Their prevailing tone however is changing. The era of 'Oh! What a Lovely War' with its picture of the war as meaningless slaughter has been replaced by a new trend towards rehabilitation. Fallen idols are put back on their pedestals. Generals are credited with strategical insight. If any idols remain fallen, it is the politicians, with Lloyd George perhaps the most criticized. Historical revision is always welcome even when, as in this case, it can perhaps be carried too far.

Kitchener was certainly due for vindication. In his lifetime he was the undisputed British warlord, the only man on the British side who tried to run the war all on his own. His death in 1916 came when his reputation was already in decline and by the end of the war he was forgotten. The brilliant biography by Sir Philip Magnus did nothing to restore him. Professor Cassar thinks differently. For him Kitchener was the architect of victory. Kitchener was above all a great organizer. A sentence he wrote during the Boer War characterizes him: 'I must say I like having the whole thing cut-and-dried and worked out.'

After forty years spent outside England he suddenly found himself in charge of the entire British war effort. Kitchener created the new armies. He equipped them and he determined British strategy so far as anyone did. He had two clear convictions. He held from the first that Great Britain had no option but to stand firm with the French. On the other hand he did not think that a decisive breakthrough could be achieved for at least three years and until then he favoured an 'active-defensive' strategy. In this he was wise before his time. A defensive strategy did not suit the French nor did it suit the politicians at home. Kitchener was driven to accept French offensive proposals which he knew would not succeed. He was lured unwillingly into the Gallipoli campaign. In his own sad sentence, 'We have to make war as we must and not as we should like to.' The offensives in France failed. The landings at Gallipoli were pinned to the beaches.

Kitchener tried to conduct the Gallipoli campaign from afar, sending detailed instructions to Hamilton, its ineffective commander. The threat to British imperial prestige harassed him and he lost his bearings. For reasons of pride he rejected the withdrawal from Gallipoli which he knew to be unavoidable. Gallipoli ruined him as it ruined Churchill. Kitchener was pushed aside and became only, as Margot Asquith called him, 'a great poster', still admired by the public but written off by the politicians.

All the same Kitchener was the greatest military figure produced by Great Britain during the First World War. It was his misfortune to be placed in power at a time when no one could succeed. It was a further misfortune that he understood nothing of British politics and British leaders. Professor Cassar has served Kitchener well. His book is an outstanding biography, rich in material from new sources and with a firm grasp of the issues at stake. Kitchener died too soon to be the architect of victory but he had some of the qualities which would have fitted him for this task.

John Terraine has always been Haig's champion and now seeks to vindicate Haig at his most vulnerable point – the third battle of Ypres, also known as Passchendaele or the Battle of the Mud. This time Terraine uses the strategy of indirect approach. He has not written a formal history of the battle. Instead he presents raw material from which the reader can draw his own conclusions. The book is a series of quotations skilfully arranged: quotations from Haig's diaries, cabinet proceedings, memoirs of generals and politicians, statistics, private letters, a true do-it-yourself book. Of course the book is not as innocent as it seems. All histories are selective and these quotations have been selected for a purpose, even if Terraine may have tried to play fair.

Terraine traces the various threads that were spun throughout 1917 until they formed the web of Passchendaele. There was the weather, allegedly worse than usual; there were the U-boats, mistakenly supposed to be based on Ostend and Zeebrugge; there were the mutinies in the French Army which made a diversionary offensive by the British desirable; there was the failure by Lloyd George and other members of the war cabinet to understand questions of strategy.

Most of these factors have been going the rounds for a long time. Terraine implies that added together they led up to an inevitable conclusion. Passchendaele, it seems, was not deliberately willed by anyone; it was just something that had to happen.

This sounds a powerful argument but has no real meaning. 'Inevitability' is a magic word with which to mesmerize the unwary. Only death is inevitable. Short of that nothing is inevitable until it happens, and everything is inevitable once it has happened. The historian deals with past events and therefore to him all history is inevitable. But these past events were once in the future and then they were not inevitable. If things had happened differently in the early days of 1917 – if there had been less distrust between Lloyd George and Haig, if Haig had not been so blindly committed to an offensive in Flanders, if Robertson had done his duty as Chief of the Imperial General Staff and been as loyal to Lloyd George as he was to Haig – Passchendaele would not have been inevitable though something else would have been.

This is to my mind a very foolish argument which does not even serve Terraine's purpose. It is no great compliment to present Haig as like everyone else, a victim of circumstances, who did not know what he was doing. Inevitability looks a good subtitle for a book. The soldiers in the trenches sixty years ago found a simpler explanation for the Battle of the Mud: 'We're here because we're here because we're here because we're here.'

A Monument to the Revolution

This essay first appeared as a review of the 1962 reissue of John Reed's Ten Days That Shook the World (*London, Lawrence and Wishart, 1962*) *in the* Observer, *4 February 1962.*

In 1964 Alan Taylor was invited to write the introduction to the Penguin edition of Reed's book. The Communist Party of Great Britain held the copyright and objected to Alan Taylor's introduction. So Penguin published it with no introduction until the copyright expired in 1977. Then Alan Taylor's introduction was used.

*   *   *

Lenin believed that everyone should read the works of Marx and his own. These apart, only one book received his certificate: 'Unreservedly do I recommend it to the workers of the world'. This is the book, and it deserves Lenin's recommendation. John Reed's account of the Bolshevik revolution is a tremendous work, one of the most exciting and important ever written.

It is in the first place magnificent reporting. This is Petrograd to the life as it was in the gloomy autumn of 1917, with the Imperial Ballet still playing to crowded houses in one part of the city, and the Bolsheviks seizing power in another. Here are the political leaders of every complexion, confusedly wrangling, gesturing with words. Here, too, are ordinary men caught up in the turmoil, from the tsarist officer abandoned by his men to the rough sailors who have decided that this is a class war.

Moreover, Reed's book established a legend. From the moment of its publication in 1919 it became, both for the Russian Bolsheviks and for the rest of the world, the established version of what happened in November 1917. There was much going on in secret which Reed did not know. All the same, when we think of the Bolshevik revolution, we still see it as Reed saw it at the time, or as he shaped it unconsciously with literary art.

This has been an awkward book for the Communist Party to handle. For Reed, as for the rest of the world, the Bolsheviks were simply 'Lenin and Trotsky' with Trotsky usually in the foreground. Kamenev, Zinoviev, Lunacharsky make an occasional appearance. Stalin's name appears once at the end of a list of commissars. Otherwise there is not even 'the impression of a grey blur', which he made on another observer. This was no doubt how it was. But it raised difficulties when Trotsky was in exile and all the others, except for the dead Lenin, were being imprisoned or executed.

The record of publication tells its own tale. The American edition came out in 1919; it is one of the few first editions which I prize. The book appeared here in 1926, with three trivial corrections in footnotes, quaintly in favour of Kamenev. There was another edition in 1932. Then silence until the present reproduction – a sign, let us hope, that Trotsky is due for rehabilitation. It is to the credit of the communist publishers that Reed's text is given intact, as I have ascertained by checking it, sentence by sentence, with the original edition.

Reed was an American journalist of high qualifications. Though sympathetic to the Bolsheviks, he inevitably saw things from outside; missed some, and invented others which did not happen. For instance, Lenin never said that 6 November was too early and 8 November too late; 7 November was exactly right. On the contrary, Lenin had been urging an immediate rising for the previous six weeks. Reed did not unearth the real argument that Lenin wanted the rising to be in the name of the party, and Trotsky, more wisely, in the name of the Soviets. Reed also got the secret party meeting wrong. He says that ten voted against insurrection and only two (Lenin and Trotsky) in favour. In fact the figures were the other way round, with only Zinoviev and Kamenev against.

Reed also caught only a confused echo of the second meeting at which Lenin enlisted the support of the rank and file against the leaders; but at least he caught it, which is more than can be said for the communist who later corrected him in a footnote. Both meetings were largely irrelevant. Though the Bolsheviks made preparations for a rising, they did not start one. The offensive came from Kerensky and the Provisional government. The military revolutionary committee, under Trotsky's leadership, actually supposed that they were defending democratic freedom.

Later on, the truth was obscured. The Bolsheviks could not bear to admit that they had been pushed by events instead of directing them; and everyone else, too, regarded them as malign, but subtle, planners

– a misunderstanding which persists about all communist acts, as well as about the Bolshevik Revolution, to the present day. Basically Reed got this right, despite his minor errors of fact. The Bolsheviks responded to a challenge, and made a success of it.

Reed was right in a deeper sense. Outside Russia people were already depicting the Bolsheviks as monsters of wickedness, German agents, bloodthirsty terrorists who nationalized women. Reed recognized their high and courageous idealism. Wherever he encountered ordinary people, he found them on the Bolshevik side. He understood that the immediate Bolshevik object was to end the war by a peace of general reconciliation. The most dramatic scene even in this dramatic book is the moment when Lenin read the Decree on Peace:

Suddenly, by common impulse, we found ourselves on our feet, mumbling together into the smooth lifting unison of the *Internationale*. A grizzled old soldier was sobbing like a child ... 'The war is ended! The war is ended!' said a young workman near me, his face shining.

So it continues: the Decree on Land; or Lenin, according to Reed, holding up his hand for silence and saying quietly: 'We will now proceed to the building of socialism.' It was a time of fantasy, preparing great evils and great disappointments. It was a great time all the same, beginning a new epoch in human history. Reed makes this time real, vivid, personal. Like every good journalist, he had the good luck that something sensational and revealing happened whenever he moved out of his apartment. Perhaps, when it did not happen, he made it up. Even the Bolshevik Revolution can hardly have gone at this breathless pace. Still, the most momentous event of our century found a worthy chronicler.

This is a great and unique book. Reed escaped disillusionment. He became a communist, and died of typhus in 1920. He was given a Hero's Grave under the Kremlin wall. There his body is likely to remain so long as people believe in human brotherhood and idealism.

How It All Began

This essay first appeared in the New Statesman and Nation, *21 May 1955.
It was a review of* The Russian Revolution, 1917: A Personal Record *by
N N Sukhanov, translated and edited by Joel Carmichael (Oxford, Clarendon
Press, 1955). While welcoming and praising Carmichael's translation of 'this
wonderful, indispensable book' Taylor regretted that the book had been abridged
with no indication of where parts had been omitted. 'Every scholar must still
go to the original text; and copies of this are rare since the Stalinists have been
suppressing it for the last twenty years.'*

*Nikolai Nikolayevich Sukhanov (1882–1940) was a prominent member of the
executive committee of the Petrograd Soviet at the time of the 1917 February
Revolution. However, he and other independent socialists were displaced by
Menshevik and Socialist Revolutionaries. From April 1917 until 1920 (when it
was closed down) he edited the socialist-internationalist newspaper* Novaya
Zhizn (New Life). *During the 1920s he worked as an economist, including a
period at the Agrarian Institute of the Communist Academy. In 1931 at the
Menshevik show trial he was convicted of being a counter-revolutionary.*

* * *

What should we not give for a record of Christ's life by a Roman
philosopher who was himself waiting for a Messiah, who was deeply
affected by Christ's personality and whose judgement was yet never
submerged by belief? Nikolai Nikolayevich Sukhanov was a witness of
this kind during the Russian Revolution. His book is incomparably
the best and most important account of those tremendous events from
which spring most of the problems of our world.

A revolutionary socialist and an economist of distinction, Sukhanov
was wanted by the secret police but protected during the world war
by the Ministry of Agriculture which employed him – an arrangement
typical of old Russia. He was therefore one of the very few who could
watch the revolution in Petrograd from its first chaotic beginnings in
February; and he was on the margin of events to the end. At once a
Marxist and a democrat, he straddled between the parties; knew all
their leaders; and understood what they were up to. Trotsky called
him a Hamlet of the revolution: Lenin named him the Quarter-
Bolshevik. Let us say rather that he was a Bolshevik without faith, the

prototype of many later intellectuals. He agreed with the Bolshevik aims, but did not believe that they could be realized; and he would have supported the Bolsheviks' seizure of power if only he could have persuaded himself that they would be able to do anything with power when they got it. He records his own doubts and failings as frankly as he does the blunders and ruthlessness of others.

He became a member of the first Executive Committee of the Soviets and thereafter attended all the meetings at which the moderate socialists discussed how to slow down and stop the revolution, himself always dissenting. The Bolsheviks actually planned the seizure of power at his flat, though without his knowledge; and Sukhanov was constantly at Smolny during the last decisive days, again dissenting even less effectually. His book ends with the famous meeting at which Lenin announced: 'We will now proceed to the building of socialism':

Applause, hurrahs, caps flung up in the air ... But I didn't believe in the victory, the success, the 'rightfulness', or the historic mission of a Bolshevik regime. Sitting in the back seats, I watched this celebration with a heavy heart. How I longed to join in, and merge with this mass and its leaders in a single feeling! But I couldn't ...

Here is all the tragedy of the fellow-traveller. Sukhanov's life was finished in October 1917. He served the Bolshevik state loyally, though sceptically, until 1931, when he was caught up in a manufactured trial and vanished into a concentration camp, still idealist, still protesting, still bewildered.

His book describes the dilemma of the revolutionary intellectual. In February 1917 the old order collapsed. The masses could take the power whenever they chose to do so. But the democratic and socialist leaders did not believe that they could fulfil the desires of the masses – peace and bread; therefore they refused to take the power that was theirs for the asking. There was an interregnum, a nothing. Sooner or later the old order would be restored if the democrats remained helpless. The Bolsheviks alone promised to carry out the mass programme; and with this promise they carried the day. What should an honest socialist do? Work with the moderates who were refusing power and who were therefore implicitly pushing it back into the hands of tsarist generals? Or support the Bolsheviks, even though he knew that their promises could not be fulfilled? For after all Lenin did not give the Russian people peace and bread; he gave them starvation and war. Would he, one wonders, have seized power if he could have known that no revolution would follow in Germany or elsewhere and that Russia would be doomed to a generation of 'socialism in a single country'?

For Sukhanov, at any rate, the answer to these doubts was clear. He did nothing. At every crisis of the revolution he implored the crisis to stop – not to go back, not to go forward. Instead of action, he sought more information. 'I intensified my telephoning' is a characteristic theme. At another critical moment, he records that he tried to write a leader for his paper, but tore it up in despair; he could not decide what to say one way or the other. And therefore he was left worrying at every dramatic moment over trivial details. Could he find a tram to take him home? (He never succeeded in this.) Who had stolen his boots while he was asleep? The great leaders thought only of grand policy. He noticed the weariness, the stale tobacco-smoke, the smell of unwashed bodies. By October everyone was exhausted; and the Bolsheviks were the ones to pass Churchill's test – they hung on for the last quarter of an hour. Every intellectual who reads this book must hope that he would have gone with Lenin and must fear that he would have behaved like Sukhanov. Of course, we know the outcome. Thirty years of Popular Fronts have taught us that the communists never play fair. Sukhanov sensed this; but even Lenin did not then realize that he must inevitably betray every one of his collaborators who had any sincere convictions. Again, would Lenin have seized power if he had known that it must end with Stalin and the anonymous dictators?

Voice from the Dead

This essay first appeared as a review of Raphael Abramovitch's The Soviet Revolution (*London, Allen and Unwin, 1963*) *in the* New Statesman, *5 April 1963. Raphael Abramovitch (1880–1963), real name A Rein, joined the Jewish Bund in 1901 and was a member of the central committee of the Petrograd Soviet from May 1917. He left Russia for Berlin in 1920.*

Alan Taylor varied his view on whether Stalin distorted Lenin's legacy or continued it. In his autobiography he recalled seeing Lenin's body on his visit to Moscow in 1925 and commented: 'I decided then that he was a really good man, an opinion I have not changed.' As for Stalin, Alan Taylor was eager to suggest that he was an outcome of Russian communism, just as he had suggested in his writings on Germany that Hitler was an outcome of Germany's historical development and should not be used as a scapegoat for all the misdeeds of 1933–45.

*   *   *

The Russian Revolution seems now to have happened before the flood. Yet here is a leading participant, still alive and putting himself into history. Raphael Abramovitch, born in 1880, was already a prominent Menshevik when the Russian Revolution took place. He sat in the revolutionary Soviets, was among those defeated by the Bolsheviks, and left Russia in 1920. Between the wars he was active in the Second International. His book is not a work of personal reminiscence. There is very little in it of what happened to the Menshevik Abramovitch, or of what he did. The book is a mixture of detached history, political criticism and general complaint. It is designed to show that the Mensheviks were right, or at any rate that the Bolsheviks were wrong.

Mr Abramovitch begins with the assertion that defeat and demoralization in war were the 'primary source' of all the disruptive changes in Russia between February and October 1917. Important deductions follow from this. The Russian workers were not particularly revolutionary; they merely wanted to get out of the war. Nor were the Russian bourgeoisie particularly reactionary or oppressive; they had merely made a mess of the war. Here, in essence, is the Menshevik case. There was no need for a proletarian revolution, and no materials with which to make it. The February Revolution did all that was necessary, if only the war had been brought to an end; and the October Revolution was caused by those, including the Western allies, who kept Russia in the war. The Mensheviks, in fact, neither wanted a proletarian revolution, nor had faith in its success – Sukhanov makes the same point in his memoirs, though with more regret and less insistence on his own correctness. Lenin was the exact opposite. He wanted a so-called proletarian revolution (that is a revolution directed by himself), and he was convinced it would succeed. He would deliver the goods: he would establish socialism, end the war, and set the spark to revolution throughout Europe. Lenin got the Bolshevik Revolution; this was his success. He did not deliver the goods; this was his failure, and it took him prisoner.

The most valuable part of Mr Abramovitch's book is its clear demonstration of the consequences. Lenin was always authoritarian by nature – his German ancestry no doubt. He would have been less authoritarian if he had not been trapped by the failure of his high hopes. He would not relinquish power, even though he had not fulfilled his promises. Therefore he had to make his dictatorship permanent. It is the fashion nowadays, in Soviet Russia and elsewhere, to blame Stalin for all the evils of Bolshevism. Mr Abramovitch shows that Lenin devised the Soviet system as it existed under Stalin, and still exists.

There was no difference of principle between Lenin and Stalin, except that Lenin was more ingenious in manipulating Marxist phrases. Lenin was perhaps not quite so dictatorial inside the Communist Party, and maybe even a little softer to his former Menshevik comrades. But the terror, one-party rule, the abandonment of everything social democrats had stood for, were Lenin's doing. Mr Abramovitch observes that Soviet Russia was not a class state. It was the first totalitarian state, where the bureaucrats running it tyrannized over everyone, including themselves. He pushes this a bit far: there has always been a working-class twist to the dictatorship, though no doubt the Russian workers often did not notice this.

This is a good book to the death of Lenin. Its later chapters on Stalin fall away. E H Carr has given Stalin a place in history. Mr Abramovitch gives him only a place in crime. He comes near in fact to accepting what is now the communist version of events: that Stalin was mad, an ogre, a tyrant on the pattern of Ivan the Terrible. He even relies on that absurd book by 'Alexander Orlov', *The Secret History of Stalin's Crimes*, which is recommended in private by communists as the correct account of what happened in the Stalin era. 'Orlov' treats Stalinism as a personal aberration, an interpretation which suits communists. Mr Abramovitch departs from his own Marxist approach in taking this line. But if he had kept clear of the 'ogre' version of history, he would have had to strike a balance; and this he is reluctant to do. The nearest he comes to it is in arguing that, between the wars, the social democratic parties of western Europe did much better than the communists of Soviet Russia not merely in winning mass support but even in the amount of socialism they introduced.

There is no doubt that Lenin and Stalin between them landed the Russians in for a tough time. They also made Russia one of the two Great Powers in the world. Would a cosy Menshevik democracy have done this, or anything like it? Our materials for judging Soviet economic progress exist, though they are inadequate. Materials for understanding Soviet politics after 1928 hardly exist at all. For instance, was Stalin being true to his nature in conducting the purges, and fraudulent when he produced the constitution of 1936? The question can be answered only by use of the 'I say so' method, favoured by Sovietologists who, when evidence is lacking, stamp their feet as proof. I say, Stalin was a bad man; therefore he was. Mr Abramovitch is not free from this method. It can be used the other way round. Maybe Stalin was a puzzled administrator of limited ability, who found Soviet Russia in a mess as the result of Lenin's mistakes, and somehow pulled her out of it. The proof? I say so.

Politics in the First World War

The Raleigh lecture on History, given at the British Academy on 4 February 1959 and subsequently published in The Proceedings of the British Academy *(1959).*

*　　*　　*

Lord Stansgate, who had been a Liberal member of parliament during the First World War, was in the audience at the lecture. He said to me afterwards: 'I had no idea it had been like that.'

In 1920 General Groener, Ludendorff's successor and last quartermaster-general of the imperial army, wrote of the First World War: 'The German General Staff fought against the English parliament.' The phrase is quoted and, to a large extent endorsed, in *Der deutsche Reichstag im Weltkriege*, a substantial volume laid before the Reichstag committee of inquiry into the causes of Germany's defeat by Dr J V Bredt, himself a Democratic deputy. Dr Bredt argues that the Reichstag played an important and occasionally decisive part during the war. If it did not shape German policy, this was its own fault, and that of the parties; the General Staff gave way whenever it was faced by a parliamentary majority. Dr Bredt looks sadly over to the enemy side across the Channel where things, he believes, were different. The British House of Commons asserted civilian control; the German Reichstag did not. Hence the Allies won the war; hence the sentence of General Groener with which I began.

The defeated – both Reichstag and General Staff – have received much attention from historians. Indeed German politics during the First World War are one of the few fields in recent history which is in danger of being overworked. What did the British parliament and British politicians do during the First World War? The theme has been strangely neglected. Metternich's complaint against old Austria has become the guiding principle of English historians: 'administration has taken the place of government'. The machinery of public authority has been studied, from the war cabinet down to local agricultural committees. Only one writer has presented 'a political history of the war', and even he hesitated over the claim.[1] No word of mine should be taken as criticism of Lord Beaverbrook's splendid volumes. Their brilliant presentation, wealth of material and deep understanding of men's motives, stir the admiration of the professional historian, not his jealousy. But Lord Beaverbrook deals, as he says himself, with the peaks of politics, not with the general course of political events. Some of the great questions are passed over lightly, of intent. Thus of Ireland: 'The issue is dead, and it does not possess a spark of life or interest to the reader of today',[2] 'it would be unprofitable to dissect its lifeless body'.[3] Lord Beaverbrook adds in his usual disarming way: 'I am quite prepared to admit that I may be wrong in the small importance I now attach to these Irish stories.'[4] Again, conscription – the question which began the disintegration of the Liberal Party – 'was not a burning issue'. 'To trace all the ramifications of [the politicians'] beliefs would be tedious to the last degree.'[5] During the great moments of crisis as described by Lord Beaverbrook, the House of Commons provides noises off; it never occupies the centre of the scene. This, though it may well be a true picture, merits examination. This lecture may be taken as a supplement to Lord Beaverbrook's work, or, in a phrase which he has used in a different connection, 'another version of the same'.

The House of Commons, elected in December 1910, was indeed ill prepared to direct, or even to influence, the conduct of a great war. The general election had been fought, to the boredom of the electorate, on the question of the House of Lords. Thereafter the House plunged from one passionate party controversy to another. Foreign affairs were rarely discussed: less than in the parliament of 1906–10,

1. Lord Beaverbrook would have liked to call Volume I of *Politicians and the War* (London, Thornton Butterworth, 1928) 'a Political History' but was 'only too well aware that the description would be a misnomer'. Volume II (London, Lane Publications, 1932), 'does not profess to be a detailed history of the politics of the war'. In *Men and Power 1917–1918* (1956), however, he describes the two earlier volumes as 'an earnest attempt to provide an impartial political history'.

2. *Politicians and the War*, I, 50.

3. Ibid., II, 64.

4. Ibid., II, 13.

5. Ibid., I, 207, 206. But on II, 44: 'A frank discussion and vote in the cabinet would have broken the administration to pieces . . . We find here the germ of a fundamental difference of view as to the aim of the war and the methods by which it was to be conducted which completely transcended party.'

and hardly at all after February 1912. In August 1914 all these great causes of controversy were dimmed. The House of Lords had surprisingly reached a lasting settlement, or next door to it, in 1911. Irish home rule was pushed aside on the outbreak of war when the Home Rule Act, though placed on the statute book, was suspended for the duration. National Insurance had ceased to be contentious – duchesses had long been licking stamps; and Welsh disestablishment no longer stirred a flame except in the Welsh and Lord Robert Cecil. Even the longstanding argument between free trade and tariff reform appeared irrelevant when set against the background of national survival. The House was united. All members, a bare half-dozen excepted, recognized the necessity of war in August 1914. The way seemed clear for the House to become a great Council of State.

The appearance of national unity was deceptive. There were still deep cleavages in the party outlooks. The Unionists, by and large, regarded Germany as a dangerous rival, threatening either the balance of power or Great Britain's imperial interests – maybe both together. They proposed to fight a hard-headed war by ruthless methods and regarded any 'moral' advantage as a windfall. For the Liberals this 'moral' advantage was essential. Many of them had come to support the war only when Germany invaded Belgium, and even the less radical among them were relieved to escape from a 'realistic' position. Entering the war for altruistic motives, the Liberals wished to conduct it by high-minded means, and they found it harder to abandon their principles than to endure defeat in the field. There would have been raging conflict between the two parties if the profound differences of outlook had been brought into the open. The leaders of both were therefore anxious to keep it under cover. The House heard a general oration from Asquith on 6 August and then adjourned on 10 August. It met for a brief session from 25 August to 17 September, solely to finish with home rule, and this caused bitterness enough. Then it met again on 11 November. In the nine months of Liberal rule Asquith gave one war survey, on 1 March 1915 – a survey which did not mention the campaign in France, and no debate followed.[6]

6. Churchill alone dissented from this policy of silence, and twice attempted to survey the war in broad terms (on 27 November 1914 and 15 February 1915). These attempts obviously embarrassed the House, though they set a pattern for the Second World War; few members listened, and none followed Churchill's lead.

This unspoken coalition between the front benches was not new.
The habit had been growing for some time, and the scenes in the
House became increasingly artificial. The leaders met amicably at
round table conferences at Buckingham Palace, still flushed from the
passionate debates over the Parliament Bill or home rule. Even their
disputes here were to some extent staged. The very men who failed to
agree at the Palace negotiated secretly for a full coalition and were
impeded only by their back-benchers. Austen Chamberlain, embarrassed as usual by his own honesty, remarked: 'What a world we live in
and how the public would stare if they could look into our minds and
our letter bags.'[7] Hilaire Belloc exercised his satirical imagination on
this theme, but, as often happens, reality outdid the wildest flights of
fantasy. There is nothing in *Pongo and the Bull* to rival the improbable
scene in May 1915 when Bonar Law, making a morning call on Lloyd
George, was conducted through a side door to Asquith; whereupon
the two men destroyed one government and made another within a
quarter of an hour. The war in fact provided the means of stilling
party disputes which the leaders had failed to find for themselves.

There were other, less melodramatic, reasons why the House of
Commons was virtually ignored. For one thing, Kitchener, the secretary of state for war, sat in the Lords. Here he surveyed the war,
inadequately, about once a month, but he did not allow the undersecretary to follow his example in the House of Commons. It is indeed a
minor oddity of the war that, until Lloyd George became prime
minister, only the Lords discussed broad questions of strategy; and
one member, Lord Milner, openly defied the rules of security – to the
bewilderment of the Germans.[8] Generally speaking, the Liberal government practised individual enterprise in politics as rigidly as in economic affairs. Each minister was left free to conduct his own department, and Asquith, acting as the detached chairman, intervened only
when it was necessary to arbitrate between ministers. Here incidentally
is the explanation, forgotten in later years, why Grey before the war
consulted the cabinet little – and informed the House still less – on
foreign policy. That was his department, and it was his job to run it.

7. Charles Petrie, *Austen Chamberlain* (2 Vols., London, Cassell, 1939 and 1940), 1,
258.

8. Milner discussed the evacuation from Gallipoli a fortnight before it took place.
The Germans concluded that this was a ruse, to cloak preparations for a further
landing.

So, when the war began, the cabinet never approved the ultimatum to Germany; this was settled by Grey, perhaps with assistance from Asquith. The cabinet endorsed the dispatch of the expeditionary force to France only after this had begun, and their naming of an assembly point (Amiens instead of Maubeuge) was disregarded by the military authorities. The secrets of naval strategy were locked in Fisher's breast, from which they never emerged.

The prorogation on 17 September had behind it the assumption that the war would be lost or won before the House met again. By 11 November this assumption had been belied. Deadlock set in; a long war was in the offing. But this did not provoke any discussion in the House of Commons. A new factor aided the policy of silence. The First World War produced an excessive enthusiasm for secrecy, or 'security' as it came to be called. There was something to be said for keeping shipping movements and losses secret, though this was carried rather far when the sinking of the *Audacious*, which took place on 27 October 1914, was announced only on 13 November 1918. But it seems unlikely that the Germans overlooked the presence of a British army in France. 'Security' operated more against the British public than against the enemy. The authorities, military and political, had no idea how to win the war; therefore they wished to keep silence until, by some miracle as yet unforeseen, the war was won. In theory reports of proceedings in parliament were free from censorship. This meant in practice that nothing could be mentioned in parliament which might infringe the requirements of 'security'. Questions were unofficially censored before they were set down; members were kept quiet by the appeal to patriotism.

The policy of silence might have worked if everyone outside the government could really ignore the war, if 'Business as Usual', in Churchill's phrase, really made sense. Quite the contrary. Where direction was lacking, enthusiasm had to take its place. For nearly a year and a half the army was raised by voluntary recruiting, which provided three out of every four men for the greatest armies ever put into the field by this country. The public had to be kept constantly astir by recruiting meetings and, though ministers and members of parliament spoke a good deal, these meetings provided a platform for less official orators. Here Horatio Bottomley made his fame. Recovering from the discredit into which he had recently fallen, he rose before the end of the war to become the tribune of the people, respectfully consulted – not only according to his own account – by the war cabinet itself.

Silence in high places cleared the way for demagogues. Still more, it cleared the way for the masters of the press. The public wanted news and could find it only in the newspapers. Official statements told nothing, and the alternative means of communication, developed later in the twentieth century, were as yet unknown. Soon too the public wanted leadership, and again only the newspapers provided it. The 'press lords' did not snatch at influence and power; these were thrust on them by the abdication of the politicians. Northcliffe, who controlled half the circulation in London, was the most notorious of these press lords, but he was not alone. Robert Donald, editor of the *Daily Chronicle*, played almost as great a part. C P Scott and J L Garvin were to join him as kingmakers in the great crisis of 1916.[9] The politicians railed and complained without ever appreciating that the fault lay in themselves. Lloyd George alone realized the true position. Always more at home on the public platform than in the House of Commons and unfettered by traditional rules, he early recognized that public opinion must be satisfied somehow. He commented on 23 June 1916: 'The Press has performed the function which should have been performed by Parliament, and which the French Parliament has performed.'[10] Lloyd George used the press, and the press used Lloyd George. The two grew great together. Lloyd George had never cared much for the society of other politicians. Now he built up a group of advisers drawn almost entirely from the press. The chief of these were Riddell, who owned the *News of the World*; C P Scott of the *Manchester Guardian*; and Robertson Nicoll, editor of the *British Weekly*, a strong though tardy supporter of the war (like Lloyd George himself),[11] who could best interpret the feeling of the pro-war dissenters. The only politician admitted to these gatherings was Addison, a radical doctor from the East End, who had entered parliament

9. It is often implied that Max Aitken who was even more a kingmaker in December 1916 also owed his power to the press. This is not so. Aitken only became a press lord in the decisive sense later.

10. Lord Riddell, *Lord Riddell's War Diary* (London, Nicholson and Watson, 1933), 151.

11. On 1 August 1914 Lloyd George received from Nicoll a letter opposing entry into the war. He found it in the pocket of his dress-suit on 7 August and pinned it to Nicoll's pro-war leader of 5 August. Riddell, *War Diary*, 11.

in 1910 and had worked with Lloyd George on National Insurance. Through these men Lloyd George gauged public opinion more effectively than by sitting regularly in his place in the House of Commons.

Even so, feeling in parliament stirred under the surface. The back-bench Unionists resented the unofficial coalition of silence to which Bonar Law had committed them. Early in 1915 some of them set up the Unionist Business Committee under the nominal leadership of Walter Long (once Bonar Law's rival) to press – irrelevantly – for tariffs. They were drawn instead into complaints against the inadequate supply of munitions, complaints which were seconded by the former auxiliaries of the Liberal government – the Irish Nationalists and Labour. This was a startling development. The Liberals and Unionists exactly balanced after the general election of 1910, but Asquith had a stable and substantial majority thanks to the Irish and Labour. These two held the balance, but only in appearance; for, while they could certainly put the Liberals out, it would have been intolerable for them to put the Unionists in. Hence Asquith could make more demands on them than they on him, simply by evoking the ghost of a Unionist administration. Labour slipped back into being Lib–Lab; and at each stage of the home rule crisis, the Irish were pushed from one concession to another as the price for getting anything at all. In August 1914 Asquith assumed that the two parties would continue their tame acquiescence, apart of course from the few Labour men who actually opposed the war, and he concerned himself more with the Ulstermen than with the Nationalists once home rule was technically on the statute book. This was one aspect, and by no means the least, of the fatal self-confidence which brought Asquith to ruin. He took it for granted that for the Irish and Labour (as for everyone else) he was the indispensable man.

For these two parties it soon ceased to be true. The Irish Nationalists had nothing to gain by supporting Asquith now that home rule was laid aside. On the contrary they had good reason to attack the Liberal government, or rather its outstanding member Kitchener, who had depreciated the surge of Irish loyalty by refusing to authorize an Irish Brigade.[12] With Labour it was the other way round. Far from

12. The Ulster Volunteers, on the other hand, got official recognition. Hence Carson and the Ulster Unionists supported Kitchener and even Asquith, as later they supported other military leaders. Carson indeed was the vital link between Asquith and the generals, a curious and yet appropriate position.

being slighted, Labour – meaning the Labour movement and not merely the handful of Labour men in the House – was called into the seats of the mighty for the first time. The Treasury agreement of March 1915, and its ancillary agreements, made the trade unions partners in the industrial life of the country. It was hopeless thereafter to regard Labour as a mere auxiliary of the Liberal Party. Both Labour and the Irish were feeling their way to independence, though for different reasons. Both wanted the war to be won – Labour because the working people of the country were fighting it, the Irish because of Redmond's belief that a victory for freedom abroad would bring freedom for Ireland also. Neither, however, cared particularly that Asquith should win it, still less Kitchener.

Both were ready to join the Unionist revolt. On 7 May 1915 the revolt exploded. During a debate on the Defence of the Realm Act, Redmond moved the adjournment of the House – ostensibly against state purchase of the liquor trade, really as a protest against its irrelevance to the shell shortage. The Unionist Business Committee were emboldened to draft an open motion on this subject. Bonar Law tried to head the rebels off. On 13 May, just before the House rose for the Whitsuntide recess, he sent a message to the Committee urging postponement. He thought he had succeeded. But Hewins, the real inspirer of the Committee, was unappeased. Hewins had been a professor of economics and, like most academics turned politician, combined high principles and impracticality in equal measure. On 17 May Hewins warned Bonar Law that he would force a debate on munitions when the House resumed. Bonar Law at first acquiesced, then asked Hewins to hold his hand. The next day Hewins learnt that the Liberal government had resigned and that a coalition was being formed.

Bonar Law had not feared that the Unionist rebels would fail. He feared that they would succeed. Then, perhaps after a general election, 'there would have been a Conservative government which would have had to introduce conscription after terrible controversy'.[13] The Liberals would have become 'an ordinary party opposition with effects most disastrous to the country'.[14] Ostensibly the crisis was

13. Bonar Law in the House of Commons, 4 April 1917; Hansard, 5th series, xcii, 1392.

14. So Bonar Law told Redmond: D Gwynn, *The Life of John Redmond* (London, George Harrap, 1932), 467.

provoked by Fisher's resignation as first sea lord on 15 May, not by the threat of Unionist revolt. This was a stroke of luck for Bonar Law, enabling him to cloak the real danger, but the warning from Hewins gave the decisive push which sent him on his dramatic visit to Lloyd George. The first coalition was indeed made by parliamentary pressure, but it was created to thwart this pressure, not to satisfy it. The only good result of the crisis was the Ministry of Munitions with Lloyd George at its head. Otherwise the party leaders were more in control than ever. Even the semblance of a front Opposition bench vanished. The discontented Unionists were unable to appeal to public opinion; they were denied a conflict and a general election which, according to Bonar Law himself, they would have won; Liberal ministers kept the key posts; so did Kitchener, the worst offender even in the eyes of his Liberal colleagues; the Unionist recruits got the crumbs. The manoeuvre was completed, the new government formed, before parliament reassembled. The back-bench Liberals were equally dismayed. Their government – the last Liberal government in British history as it turned out – was gone without a word of explanation. Belatedly Asquith called the Liberals together and appeased them with twenty minutes of emotional explanation. 'Some of the members were moved to tears as was the prime minister himself.'[15]

The Liberals did well to weep. Despite Asquith's rigging of appointments, the Liberals were now taken prisoner in their turn by 'national unity'. Previously Bonar Law had kept the Unionists quiet so as not to embarrass the government; henceforward the Liberals had to acquiesce in unwelcome policies so as to maintain the coalition. Thus in May 1916 Bonar Law wrote to Asquith: 'I believe that it is easier for you to obtain the consent of your party to general compulsion than for me to obtain the consent of my party to its not being applied.'[16] Asquith did not understand the great issues which the conduct of the war provoked. Though resolved on victory, he supposed that the only contribution statesmen could make was to keep out of the way, while free enterprise supplied the arms with which generals would win the battles. The only dividing line he recognized was the

15. C Addison, *Four and a Half Years* (2 Vols., London, Hutchinson, 1934), I, 79.

16. Bonar Law to Asquith, May 1916; J A Spender and Cyril Asquith, *Life of Lord Oxford and Asquith* (London, Hutchinson, 1932), II, 211.

old one between tariff reform and free trade. Hence his overriding concern when making the coalition was to put free-traders at the Exchequer and the Board of Trade. Even here his calculation went wrong. McKenna, chancellor of the exchequer, betrayed his own free-trade convictions. With the financial rectitude of a born banker, McKenna introduced in September 1915 the first real war budget – a budget on which incidentally his successor Bonar Law did not improve; and this included, among other revolutionary innovations, the McKenna duties, ostensibly designed to reduce imports, which were in fact protection. Lloyd George appropriately threw a note across the cabinet table to Walter Long on 16 September: 'So the old system *goes* destroyed by its own advocates.'[17] The McKenna duties produced one of the first divisions of the war. Ten radicals voted against them on 1 October – a tiny number, yet a sign of the coming disintegration.

The dispute was, in the circumstances of war, a triviality, as the division showed. The great underlying conflict was between freedom and organization. Could the war be conducted by 'Liberal' methods – that is, by voluntary recruiting and *laissez-faire* economics? Or must there be compulsory military service, control of profits, and direction of labour and industry? When the coalition was being formed, Runciman wrote to McKenna:

If we are honoured with an invitation to come in I feel that we must first know with whom we are asked to associate ... in particular ... if they were told that we had an open mind on compulsory service or taxation.[18]

His question remained unanswered. But it was constantly pushed forward by the march of events. Of its two aspects – conscription and the control of industry – the second was the more urgent. For at least a year ahead voluntary recruiting would in fact provide more men than free enterprise could equip. But economic direction was far more difficult to apply. Not only was it more alarming in theory. It was unwelcome to both capital and labour, yet it could not work without their consent. On paper the government had all it needed with the Act setting up the Ministry of Munitions, or indeed with the Defence of the Realm Act. In practice these powers were ineffective unless industry accepted them. Lloyd George grasped this intuitively when

17. W S Hewins, *The Apologia of an Imperialist* (London, Constable, 1929), II, 52.
18. S McKenna, *Reginald McKenna* (London, Eyre and Spottiswoode, 1948), 223.

he ended the strike in South Wales by agreeing to the miners' demands instead of by invoking legal sanctions as Runciman, at the Board of Trade, wished to do. It was no doubt illogical that men safely at home should kick against lesser sacrifices than those which they expected from the soldiers and which they would willingly make were they themselves in the trenches; but it was an inescapable fact.

Ministers and members of parliament alike felt that they were contending against H G Wells's 'Invisible Man'. Members demanded the enforcement of penalties and railed against the feebleness of ministers. Ministers could not understand their own helplessness and sought to turn the flank of this baffling problem. One such attempt, strangely enough, was liquor control – restricted hours for the opening of licensed premises. The question had been initiated by Lloyd George in the last days of the Liberal government when he had proposed state purchase of the liquor trade – the first of his many attempts to find an inspiring cause that would sweep him to national leadership. Lloyd George aimed principally to recapture the allegiance of the radical dissenters – once his most solid backers – and to reconcile them no doubt to other, less welcome, war measures; he also hoped to establish his reputation as 'the man of push and go' – to borrow the phrase applied to a more forgotten figure, G W Booth – and so dispel the remaining suspicions against his pre-war radicalism. State purchase miscarried, and Lloyd George forgot it when he arrived at the Ministry of Munitions. But liquor control had the same dual purpose. Liberals (who in any case liked the idea for its own sake) could argue that working men would be industrious and productive without direction of labour, once they were sober; Unionists of the planning school welcomed liquor control as the prelude to control of everything else. At least some Unionists did. Others, though equally 'planners', opposed it, and not merely from their longstanding connection with 'The Trade'. They suspected, rightly, that it was a red herring, ostentatiously displayed to divert them from more serious quarry.

The Unionists answered by pressing for compulsory military service. No doubt many of them did so from simple impulse. They were after all simple men, and conscription was the obvious sentimental response to the situation, as Sir John Simon – one of its opponents at the time – recognized in later life. But conscription, too, was a red herring. There was little to be said in its favour from a military point of view.

Sir Auckland Geddes, director of national service, said when all was over:

With, perhaps, more knowledge than most of the working of conscription in this country, I hold the fully matured opinion that, on balance, the imposition of military conscription added little if anything to the effective sum of our war efforts.[19]

The immediate effect of conscription was to stop voluntary recruiting, which ceased on 27 January 1916 – the day when the first Military Service Act became law. Thereafter the compulsory system, far from bringing more men into the army, kept them out of it. Men in reserved occupations who were doing vital work could not be prevented from succumbing to patriotic enthusiasm so long as enlistment was voluntary. They stayed at their jobs once conscription went through. The figures prove it. There had been a great outcry in the autumn of 1915 that 650,000 single men were evading military service. When the Act was passed, it raised 43,000 recruits in its first six months of operation (about half the average number raised in a single month by the voluntary system). Its more important result was to produce 748,587 fresh claims to exemption, most of them valid.[20] This was not at all what the simple-minded enthusiasts for conscription had expected. More clearsighted Unionists were unperturbed. They were content either way. If compulsion produced millions of fresh soldiers, then their needs would overwhelm the 'free' economic system. Alternatively if it produced only claims for reservation, industrial conscription was being attained by the back door.

These considerations were appreciated on the Liberal side. The strictest Liberals opposed any hint of conscription, military or industrial. The proposal to set up even a National Register produced the first division of the war on 5 July 1915, when thirty voted in the minority. Sir John Simon resigned from the government at the end of the year, thus drawing on a stock of moral inflexibility that was not much replenished later, and 105 votes were cast against the Military Service Bill for single men on 5 January 1916 – fifty-odd Liberals

19. The words have often been quoted. I take them from Lord Simon, *Retrospect* (London, Hutchinson, 1952), 107.

20. Brigadier-General Sir James Edmonds, *Military Operations: France and Belgium 1916* (London, Macmillan, 1932), I, 152.

when the Irish are deducted. Others, including Pringle – later an assiduous 'wee free' – acquiesced, however, when they were assured that industrial conscription would not follow. McKenna and Runciman took this line inside the cabinet. On 29 December 1915 they, too, determined to resign, then thought better of it and stayed in the cabinet to thwart the economic effects of conscription, which they did with marked effect. Runciman especially remained a rigid free-trader at the Board of Trade, and his helplessness in face of shipping losses produced on 9 November 1916 what Addison described as 'the most invertebrate and hopeless of any memoranda presented to the government during the war by a responsible head of a department on a great issue'.[21] By the autumn of 1916 economic liberalism was played out. The only logical alternatives were to abandon liberalism or to abandon the war. Hence the cry for 'peace by negotiation', first faintly heard in November 1915 and raised even within the cabinet a year later. But on the whole this cry came only from those who had opposed the war all along. Most Liberals drifted in the wake of Asquith, their leader, trapped like him by the decision of August 1914. They had willed the end, but would not will the means.

This great conflict was not confined to the House of Commons or even to the press. It was voiced also by the demagogues of the recruiting platform. Uninstructed public opinion agreed with the Unionists in clamouring for military conscription. On the other hand it agreed with the Liberals in opposing any sort of economic interference or control. This was shown when independent candidates first appeared in defiance of the electoral truce. The truce remained unbroken until December 1915, except in the anomalous instance of Merthyr Boroughs, vacant by the death of Keir Hardie, where the 'official' pacifist, nominated by the ILP, was beaten by a pro-war Labour man. The first real breach came at Cleveland on 10 December 1915. Here Bottomley and his Business Government League ran a local publican on the combined ticket of compulsory military service and no liquor control. Bottomley, himself disreputable, attracted only disreputable supporters. Pemberton Billing was a more formidable and more successful campaigner. In January 1916 he almost won Mile End; on 10 March he captured East Hertfordshire from a Unionist. To the usual popular demands for a free liquor trade and

21. C Addison, *Politics from Within* (2 Vols., London, Herbert Jenkins, 1924), II, 10.

universal conscription, he made an addition of his own: 'a strong air policy'. The Zeppelin raids had begun, and Pemberton Billing, voicing the demand for reprisals, became the one and only 'Member for Air'. It seems odd that he should defeat a Unionist, but this conformed to the general rule: official Unionists always did worse at by-elections than official Liberals, and for a topsy-turvy reason. Unionist voters were contented with the coalition and therefore supported the official Liberal when they had no nominee of their own. Liberals resented the coalition and voted for the independent candidate, however eccentric, who received time and again roughly the Liberal poll of 1910.[22] The Liberals felt that they were being dragged further and further away from Liberalism; the Unionists complained only that the process was not going on fast enough. Ultimately the two complaints coincided to cause the crisis of December 1916.

Before this, there was to be a last display of Asquith's virtuosity. Asquith developed over conscription all the tactical hesitations which had bedevilled home rule, waiting for events to enforce the solution which he himself could not impose nor even foresee. He had no policy of his own, only a desire to keep the Unionists in without driving the Liberals out. First he postponed decision by the Derby scheme – presenting attestment to the Liberals as a device for evading conscription, to the Unionists as its preliminary. In January 1916 he accepted conscription for single men, again appeasing Liberals by a reminder of all the married men who would escape. The demand for general conscription continued to grow, and on 19 April Asquith expected the government to break up. He devised another elaborate compromise which satisfied neither party, and on 26 April presented this scheme to the House in the first secret session of the war. The secrecy was

22. Contested by-elections in 1916, with programme of unofficial candidate. *January*: West Newington: Independent against the Liquor Control Board. Mile End: Pemberton Billing (almost successful) against the Liquor Control Board and for air-raid reprisals. *March*: East Hertfordshire: Pemberton Billing, successful. Hyde: Independent against the Liquor Control Board and for conscription. Market Harborough: Independent for conscription. *April*: Wimbledon: Kennedy Jones, 'Do It Now'. *May*: Tewkesbury: Independent for strong War Council. *August*: Berwick: an Independent called Turnbull on whom I have no information. *September*: Mansfield: Turnbull again. *October*: North Ayrshire: 'Peace by Negotiation' candidate. Winchester: Independent was merely described as 'author and journalist'. The disappearance of pro-war independent candidates after the passing of general conscription is striking. I have not included Irish by-elections, which shed no light on British politics.

imposed in order to conceal the party rifts from the public, not to deny knowledge to the enemy. Asquith had a stroke of luck – his last. April 26 was the Tuesday after Easter. On the previous day Dublin had broken into revolt. The House, too, revolted. In a surge of patriotism, it demanded a final, comprehensive measure, and this demand grew even stronger three days later when the news arrived that Kut had surrendered to the Turks. Asquith gave a sigh of relief. He withdrew his compromise, carried universal military service and yet preserved the unity of the government.

This was a triumph of tactics, however undeserved. But it was disastrous for Asquith's prestige. Everyone knew that the solution had been imposed upon him. The House had intervened effectively for the only time in the war; it had dictated to the government instead of being led. Moreover there was a price to pay. Asquith had escaped an explosion over conscription only by raising the yet darker shadow of Ireland. Now he attempted to retrieve his reputation by 'solving' the Irish question. He crossed dramatically to Dublin. Then, as usual, he shrank from the creative effort that a 'solution' would imply. There was someone eager to take his place. Lloyd George had come near to resignation in protest against the delays over conscription and had been urged to it by Scott and Robertson Nicoll. He had been deterred by a message from the king[23] and perhaps more by his reluctance ever to carry out the threat of resignation. But his advocacy of conscription was known, and he had lost the favour of 'that crowd' – his former radical supporters. Ireland was the way to regain it and to eclipse Asquith as well. Lloyd George came nearer to solving the Irish question than anyone had ever done; secured agreement, by means however equivocal, between Carson and Redmond. The unity and confidence of the Liberal Party seemed restored; that of the Unionists endangered. Bonar Law cared much for Ulster, little for the rest of Ireland. When Hewins complained that the proposed Irish settlement would break the Conservative Party, Bonar Law replied pugnaciously: 'Perhaps the Conservative Party has to be broken.'[24]

Once more Asquith wasted this great opportunity. The approval of Bonar Law, a mere iron-merchant from Glasgow, meant nothing to him, but he started back in alarm at opposition from Lansdowne, a

23. Riddell, *War Diary*, 170.
24. Hewins, *Apologia of an Imperialist*, ii, 81.

great Whig aristocrat, though of trifling weight in the Unionist Party. The Irish settlement was abruptly jettisoned. The failure did Asquith incalculable harm. It lost him the last scrap of support from the Irish Nationalists. It shook his position inside the Liberal Party; for, though Liberals might be in two minds over conscription, most felt strongly about home rule. Addison reflected this opinion when he wrote of Asquith: 'His conduct of this business had more to do with determining the attitude of many Liberals, including myself, than any other circumstance.'[25] Asquith used a favourite manoeuvre to cover his retreat. He distracted attention from his failure over Ireland by agreeing, on 20 July, to a committee of inquiry into the campaign in Mesopotamia and threw in, for good measure, an inquiry into the Dardanelles as well. Such inquiries had in the past clearly displayed the power of the House – the inquiry into the Walcheren campaign, for example, in 1809 and, most assertive of all, the inquiry into the conduct of the Crimean War. These past inquiries had been forced on a reluctant government by the House – the Crimean inquiry brought the government down. The inquiries of 1916 were offered to the House as substitutes for real action: raking over dead campaigns instead of facing the great undecided question of economic direction. When the House accepted them, this was not a proof of its power, merely a sign that the crisis over conscription was exhausted.

For the moment the life seemed to go out of political controversy. There were no more independent candidates at by-elections, demanding a more energetic conduct of the war. Few members listened to Winston Churchill on 22 August when he preached the doctrine of full war socialism: rationing, direction of industry, industrial conscription. Still fewer applauded. Lloyd George, unexpectedly translated to the War Office by the death of Kitchener, forgot home rule as he had forgotten state purchase, and now hoped to establish his fame by the simple expedient of winning the war. He said on 22 August: 'We are pressing the enemy back ... We are pushing the enemy on the Somme ... He has lost his tide.'[26] A month later he committed himself to the knockout blow. He was to make out later that he had done this in order to anticipate Wilson's proposal for a negotiated

25. Addison, *Politics from Within*, I, 260.
26. Hansard, 5th series, LXXXV, 2556.

peace.[27] In fact he championed the knockout blow because he supposed that, as secretary of state for war, he was himself about to deliver it. He had believed what Robertson and Haig told him. Hence his annoyance with them when their prophecies proved wrong; hence, too, his brisk publicizing of this annoyance – he had to erase the memory of his own confident prophesying. In the autumn of 1916, with failure on the Somme, the inexorable question again raised its head: *laissez-faire* or controls? This time it could not be diverted by the irrelevant controversy over military conscription. Economic liberalism was on its last legs. Food, shipping, coal, manpower, all clamoured for control. Asquith talked action, did nothing.

The stage was set for a new Unionist revolt, this time against Bonar Law. The occasion seems a triviality, as Lord Beaverbrook and other writers have pointed out: the debate of 8 November over the disposal of enemy property in Nigeria. Yet even this was an appropriate symbol of the difference in outlook between idealistic Liberal and hard-headed Unionist. The Unionist rebels wanted to confine the sale of this enemy property to British subjects; the government, on Liberal principles, to dispose of it according to free-trade rules. Sixty-five Unionists voted against the government, only seventy-three for it. The moment had almost arrived at which Bonar Law must leave the government or split the party. He talked of destroying the rebels at a general election, and Beaverbrook takes this threat seriously. It was surely empty, as Bonar Law must have known. The Unionists in the country were ahead of the rebels in parliament. The rogue candidates of the spring had become official Unionist candidates by the autumn. Kennedy Jones, for example, fought Wimbledon in April with the cry, 'Do It Now'. In December he was returned unopposed as official Unionist at Hackney. A general election would not have destroyed the rebels; it would have returned them in greater force. Bonar Law could save the Unionist Party, and in particular his own leadership of it, only by destroying the Asquith government. In this sense, the division of 8 November was the decisive event of the war so far as the British House of Commons was concerned. It set the train to the mine which brought down Asquith and put Lloyd George in his place.

27. D Lloyd George, *War Memoirs* (London, Nicholson and Watson, 1933), II, 851–9.

But it was only the beginning. Bonar Law could destroy the coalition. What would be its successor? Why not a predominantly Liberal government such as had existed until May 1915? The answer could not be determined by the Unionists. It rested with the Liberals themselves and with their former associates. One striking change, though little perceived at the time, was the gradual estrangement of these satellites. The Irish Nationalists had lost all faith in Asquith after his feebleness over home rule in the summer. Moreover, despite their insistence on Irish members remaining at Westminster in full strength, they had unconsciously abandoned the Union and henceforward acted only when Irish interests were affected – especially over the extension of conscription to Ireland. But this was a negative development: eighty supporters lost to Asquith, not found by anyone else. The transformation in regard to Labour was more positive. The Labour movement grew more self-confident with each day of the war. 'Labour' supported Asquith so long as he was there, and even on 1 December Henderson called him 'the indispensable man'. Yet essentially Labour did not care about Asquith as against any other leader. They were only interested in winning the war. In December 1916 the Labour Party came of age. The moment can be precisely defined: it was the meeting of Liberal ministers on 4 December which advised Asquith not to cooperate with Lloyd George. Henderson attended the meeting, no doubt regarding himself and being regarded by others as one of Asquith's humbler followers. Then in a flash of blinding truth he declared (much to his own surprise) that Labour would support any prime minister who got on with the war, and a couple of days later he was in the war cabinet – no longer a Lib–Lab hanger-on, but spokesman of an independent Labour movement.

Still, a Unionist government, sustained only by Labour votes, would have been a shaky affair and would have brought with it the revival of party strife which Bonar Law dreaded. The position could be changed only by a Liberal split. Lloyd George himself could not provide this. He had powerful elements of the Liberal press on his side – both the *Daily Chronicle* and the *Manchester Guardian*; he had other prominent journalists backing him as the saviour of the country – Burnham, Geoffrey Dawson, Garvin, to say nothing of Northcliffe; he had even the support at this time of the military leaders from Robertson to Henry Wilson. But he had no contact with the Liberal rank and file in the House of Commons. He knew few of them and never tried to extend his personal influence. His political actions were shaped by intuition and the advice of journalists – Riddell or Robertson Nicoll – who claimed to know public opinion. At this moment knowledge of public opinion was not enough. A new government had to count votes. The counting was done with decisive results by Christopher Addison, the one man in Lloyd George's intimate circle who was also in the House of Commons. Addison had already taken a preliminary sounding during the critical days over conscription earlier in the year. On Monday, 4 December, he began canvassing the Liberal members more systematically. He soon reported that forty-nine Liberals supported Lloyd George unconditionally; by Wednesday, 6 December, he had found 126 who would support Lloyd George if he could form a government.[28] By this canvass Addison became the real maker of the Lloyd George government. The Unionist rebels forced Bonar Law into action. Max Aitken brought Lloyd George and Bonar Law together. It was Addison, and the Liberal rebels, who put Lloyd George in the first place.

The Liberal split, which in fact ended the great Liberal Party for ever, was more than a split over the conduct of the war. It revealed a deep division within the party which had been long a-growing. The Liberal leaders, associated with Asquith, were 'patricians': Asquith himself, 'last of the Romans', Crewe, Grey, Harcourt, McKenna – men of almost excessive culture and refinement. The supporters of Lloyd George were lower-class in origin, in temperament, in position. As a historian I rely more on feel than on figures, but I ran over the brief biographies which *The Times* appended to the successful candidates in the general election of 1918, and these confirmed my impression. Most of the Lloyd George Liberals were businessmen who had founded their own firms or were running a firm still with their family name. *The Times* says of one what could have been said of nearly all: 'a fine example of the self-made man'. The firms were all in wool or engineering, and no doubt doing well out of the war. None of these Liberals was a banker, merchant or financial magnate. Those who were professional men also belonged to the second eleven: solicitors, not barristers; school teachers, not schoolmasters (a term reserved by *The Times* for those who taught at public schools). Hardly any had

28. These are speculative figures. Lloyd George gives 136 in all as his supporters.

been educated at Oxford or Cambridge.[29] They were nearly all Nonconformists – usually Methodists – often the sons of Nonconformist ministers. Many of them had been keen land-taxers before the war. In short, they resembled Lloyd George in everything except his genius. Their political ability was low; all they had was impatience with the arrogance and incompetence of the Asquith group. None made a serious mark on public affairs, and Lloyd George found it hard to recruit ministers from among them. Addison was the ablest of them, a proof how second-rate they were.

Still, Addison and these second-rank Liberals made Lloyd George prime minister. Bonar Law recognized Addison's crucial importance when he fired the mine on 28 November by asking: 'One cannot go on like this, Addison, do you think?'[30] Lloyd George had often threatened to resign – over munitions, over Gallipoli, over conscription, over his restricted powers at the War Office. He had always dodged away at the last moment. No doubt it was more difficult for him to dodge on 4 December when Asquith turned against him, but the preliminary information coming in from Addison also made it unnecessary. By 6 December Lloyd George had a cast-iron guarantee in his pocket that he alone could be prime minister: the Unionist rebels ruled out Asquith, the Liberal rebels would not have Bonar Law. It must have given him considerable amusement to watch first Asquith and then Bonar Law stubbing their toes on the submerged rock of the back-benchers. For Lloyd George's government sprang much more directly from parliamentary feeling than Asquith's coalition had done. The first coalition was made against parliamentary discontent, to silence and thwart it; the second coalition owed its existence to parliamentary discontent, which dictated to Bonar Law as much as against Asquith. The second coalition was not a deal between the leaders of the two parties. Rather it was a defeat for all the leaders except Lloyd George, a defeat for the 'Three C's' as much as for the 'Squiffites', a defeat even for Bonar Law despite his tactical change of course at the last moment. The back-benchers represented a sort of unconscious plebiscite to make Lloyd George dictator for the duration of the war.

29. Even the rare exceptions to these generalizations had something exceptional about them. Gordon Hewart, though a barrister, began as a journalist and went to the Bar late. H A L Fisher, though a fellow of New College, was vice-chancellor of Sheffield University when invited to join Lloyd George's government.

30. Addison, *Four and a Half Years*, I, 269.

Lloyd George himself looked beyond party and parliament. He did not address the Unionist MPs. He never attended a meeting of his own Liberal supporters until after the armistice, and then did not know what to say to them. His only speech, on becoming prime minister, was to 'Labour' – that is, to a joint meeting of the Labour MPs and the national executive. Ramsay MacDonald surmised that Lloyd George planned to become leader of the Labour Party. A shrewd guess, but not shrewd enough. Lloyd George planned to become leader of 'the people', and Labour was merely one instrument to this end. His disregard of party came out clearly when he chose the war cabinet. When the government was being formed, Addison and Carson allotted the jobs under Bonar Law's eye – the one speaking for the coalition Liberals, the other for the Unionists. Yet neither was included in the war cabinet. Instead Lloyd George put in men of no party weight: Milner and, later, Smuts. Even Curzon counted for little with the Unionists in the House of Commons. Only Labour, the smallest party of the coalition in numbers, had a more or less official representative in the war cabinet, Arthur Henderson. Again, Lloyd George made no attempt to build up a coalition Liberal organization. Addison repeatedly complained about this.[31] He supposed that Lloyd George could not devise a party programme. This was true, but it was still truer that Lloyd George would not even try: he wanted neither a programme nor organized backing. He preferred to keep the coalition Liberals as individuals with no leaders except himself. He soon humiliated Addison and divorced him from the coalition Liberals.[32] Their other spokesmen on joint committees with the Unionists, such as the Committee on Home Rule, were Gordon Hewart and H A L Fisher, both singularly unrepresentative.

Lloyd George made no secret of his intentions when he first addressed the House as prime minister on 19 December 1916. Parliamentary government, as it had been known for the last century or so, ceased to exist. A war cabinet without departmental or party ties

31. He records these complaints in his diary on 12 April, 15 October, 21 November, 28 December 1917. In the end Lloyd George paid a penalty. He had few candidates ready for the general election of December 1918 and so was taken captive by the Unionists.

32. In June 1917 Lloyd George made out (quite falsely) that he had had to intervene in the engineers' strike and clear up the mess made by Addison, as minister of munitions. Once Addison was safely shunted to the Ministry of Reconstruction, Lloyd George put the blame for the misrepresentation on his press officer.

would run all the affairs of the country; businessmen would head the important ministries instead of politicians; and there would be 'a franker and fuller recognition of the partnership of Labour' – meaning that Lloyd George would address the TUC, not the House of Commons when he wished to speak to 'the people'. Lloyd George carried out his threats. He rarely appeared in the House of Commons, leaving its leadership to Bonar Law – the first commoner prime minister to separate the two functions. The war cabinet submitted its annual reports for 1917 and 1918 direct to the nation without even inviting debate in the House of Commons. At least one of the leading ministers, Sir Joseph Maclay, never became a member of the House. And in January 1918 Lloyd George defined British war aims in a speech to trade union leaders, not to the House of Commons. The House was not browbeaten into impotence. It acquiesced. The back-benchers had confidence that Lloyd George would win the war and, having this confidence, insisted that he be left alone.

Lloyd George had another asset, perhaps an even greater one: the Opposition. Its existence was something new: there had been no Opposition since May 1915. Asquith made out that his function was independent support for the government as Bonar Law's had been in the first nine months of the war. But there was an essential difference. Bonar Law sustained the Liberal government against his own rank and file; Asquith hoped to destroy the Lloyd George government so far as he hoped for anything. What difference of principle divided the Opposition from the government? The great issue of *laissez-faire* or controls was settled – dictated by events as much as by policy; soon not even Runciman was denouncing convoys or rationing. The obvious course was to support peace by negotiation, since Lloyd George's was pre-eminently a war government. But Asquith never touched it, despite repeated alarms that he would do so. On the contrary, Lloyd George was pinned to relentless prosecution of the war for fear that Asquith would re-emerge as the war leader if he weakened. Peace by negotiation certainly looked up in the course of 1917. It was carried to a division more than once; it was stimulated later in the year by the Lansdowne letter; it produced candidates at three by-elections, all of whom did badly.[33] None of the support came from the 'official' Opposition. They were even more hostile to it in the House than the

33. Rossendale, 13 February; Stockton on Tees, 30 March; South Aberdeen, 3 April 1917.

government benches and, in their anxiety not to be tarred with peace by negotiation, failed even to formulate war aims, abandoning this opening first to Labour and then to Lloyd George himself.

An Opposition in wartime might have been expected to claim that it could run the war better than the existing government. This claim was so grotesque in view of what had gone before that Asquith never dared to make it. In his usual fashion, he drifted, waiting for an issue to turn up; and what turned up was defence of the generals against interference by politicians. There was no principle behind this: no man had more cause than Asquith to resent the interference of generals in politics. His support of them sprang from lethargy, that fatal reluctance to lead which had brought him down. He had ruined himself as prime minister by sheltering behind Kitchener. 'If it had not been for Kitchener, Asquith might have gone right through the war',[34] according to Bonar Law. Equally he ruined his Liberal followers by backing Robertson and Haig. The best chance of discrediting the government came with the wasted victory at Cambrai – the only victory in the war for which the church bells were rung. But Asquith and his followers were saddled with their devotion to Haig and made nothing of it. The outcry in parliament came from a strange coalition of Kennedy Jones, the 'Do It Now' Unionist, Joseph King, advocate of peace by negotiation, and David Davies, a former associate of Lloyd George's. They were told that Haig had made an inquiry and that Smuts was making a further inquiry for the war cabinet. The result of these inquiries was never published, and this was perhaps as well. For they reached the complacent, though not surprising, conclusion that 'no one down to and including the corps commanders was to blame'; the fault lay with the regimental officers and the other ranks.[35] It was a conclusion worthy of Asquith himself.

The Liberal Opposition indeed stood only for the principle that Asquith was divinely appointed to go on being prime minister for ever. This principle was enough to scare even the most discontented back on to the side of Lloyd George. Asquith often seemed to be on the point of splitting the Unionists, as Lloyd George had split the Liberals. Each time the Unionists cowered into silence at the question

34. Riddell, *War Diary*, 234.
35. Captain W Miles, *Military Operations: France and Belgium 1917* (London, HMSO, 1948), III, 296.

– Asquith or Lloyd George as prime minister? For instance, many Unionists resented the apparent predominance of press lords in Lloyd George's administration. Austen Chamberlain voiced this resentment with the backing of the Unionist War Committee. To his dismay he was applauded by the Opposition Liberals and at once repudiated their support. 'They and I do not act from the same motives or pursue the same objects. I have tried from the first . . . to support the government of the day in carrying the war to a successful conclusion. When these hon. Gentlemen can say the same, and not before, shall I desire their cheers or their approval.'[36] The applause indeed so horrified Austen Chamberlain that not only did he drop his attack; within a month he joined the war cabinet and accepted the press lords as his colleagues.

The same story was repeated even more dramatically during the series of disputes between Lloyd George and the generals during the spring of 1918. The danger seemed menacing. Asquith espoused the cause of the generals; it was backed even more emphatically by Carson and the die-hard Tories. Yet essentially the danger was unreal. The die-hards would not dethrone Lloyd George, if this meant restoring Asquith. On the eve of the Maurice debate, which was expected to destroy Lloyd George, Carson attended the Unionist War Committee, and reported sadly: 'Their hate of Asquith overrides all other considerations, and they will not back him tomorrow.'[37] So it proved. Even Carson voted for the government. Only Asquith and ninety-seven Liberals went into the Opposition lobby.[38] The division was indeed an historic occasion – the only time in the war when the official Opposition promoted a vote against the government. But it was merely a political manoeuvre, not a parliamentary revolt. Far from reasserting the authority of parliament, it made Lloyd George secure as he had never been before.

Asquith's leadership of the Opposition sustained Lloyd George in the country even more than in the House. Opposition was renewed at by-elections in the autumn of 1917 after the military failures of that year, but it was opposition demanding more vigorous measures, both

36. 11 March 1918; Hansard, 5th series, CIV, 77.
37. C Repington, *The First World War* (London, Constable, 1921), II, 298.
38. The total vote against the government was 106. The others were Irish Nationalists and anti-war Labour.

military and economic, not the overthrow of Lloyd George. Ben Tillett, the only rogue candidate to repeat Pemberton Billing's success and get in, had an Asquithite as his 'official' rival at North Salford on 2 November. Tillett adroitly combined Labour and die-hard extremism. His programme: vigorous prosecution of the war; better pay for soldiers and sailors; more direct government control of the necessaries of life; anti-profiteering of food; and air-raid reprisals on a large scale. There was no grist here for Asquith's mill. Again the famous 'Black Book' which symbolized popular loss of faith in the governing classes contained the names of Mr and Mrs Asquith, so far as a non-existent book can be said to contain anything; it did not contain the name of Lloyd George. Incidentally, Darling, the judge who conducted the case, though he could hardly believe in the Black Book (since this was said to contain his own name also), obviously thought that there was something in Pemberton Billing's allegations – striking evidence of the widespread contemporary hysteria. Pemberton Billing's last fling was to demand the internment of all enemy aliens. This nearly brought victory to his candidate at Clapham on 21 June 1918; it also produced a monster petition with a million and a half signatures, backed by the lord mayor of London. The proposal was even more abhorrent to Asquith and his followers than to Lloyd George.[39]

Asquith could not reverse Lloyd George's feat and split the Unionists. Could he rival his other accomplishments? Could he win back Labour? Or reunite the Liberals? Labour ought to have given him a chance. The Labour leaders had no great trust in Lloyd George and

39. Contested by-elections during the Lloyd George Coalition. 1917. *February*: Rossendale: Peace by Negotiation. *March*: Stockton on Tees: Peace by Negotiation. *April*: South Aberdeen: one Independent Nationalist; one Peace by Negotiation. *June*: Liverpool (Abercromby division): candidate backed by 'Discharged Soldiers' Federation' against the son of the secretary of state for war. *July*: South Monmouthshire: Prohibitionist. West Dundee: Prohibitionist. *October*: East Islington: town clerk of Hertford, a 'Vigilante', backed by Pemberton Billing; a 'National' candidate backed by Page Croft. *November*: North Salford: Ben Tillett – successful.

1918. *February*: Prestwich: Cooperative candidate. *April*: Keighley: Peace by Negotiation. A woman candidate was also nominated but her papers were declared invalid. *May*: South Hereford: Farmers' Union. Wansbeck: Labour candidate, almost successful. *June*: Gravesend: one Independent Coalition; one Independent (pro-war) Labour. Clapham: Vigilante, backed by Pemberton Billing – 'intern the lot'. *July*: East Finsbury: Vigilante, backed by Pemberton Billing, 'intern the lot'; Liquor Trade Independent – 'boycott German shipping'.

no affection at all for the profiteers round him. Moreover in the summer of 1917 Henderson left the war cabinet over the affair of the Stockholm conference. This did not revive his allegiance to Asquith. He had seen too much of Asquith as head of a cabinet; besides the Liberal Opposition gave him no support when he was in trouble. Instead Henderson resolved to make Labour the second party in the state. Stockholm set in train a development which ultimately ruined all Liberals, the supporters of Lloyd George and Asquith alike. Between July 1917 and the end of the war Henderson created the modern Labour Party. Labour continued to support the war and the Labour ministers other than Henderson remained in office. At the same time Henderson formulated Labour's own foreign policy, with MacDonald's assistance, and so secured the future backing of the idealists. More important still, he enlisted Sidney Webb to transform the programme and organization of the party so as to make it national instead of a sectional interest. The Labour Party was standing on its own feet even before the war ended. At Wansbeck on 29 May 1918 a Labour candidate, with the backing of the national party, almost defeated the coalition nominee. The writing was on the wall. Labour had staked its claim to the front Opposition bench, and soon Asquith would be pushed off it.

The only remaining expedient for Asquith was to reunite the Liberal Party. This was Lloyd George's most vulnerable spot. He could not remain prime minister if he lost his Liberal supporters, and the threat was the graver because it did not necessarily imply the return of Asquith. The Unionists might achieve the dream of forming their own war government. Yet Lloyd George remained cut off from the coalition Liberals, as he had been before Addison stamped them out of the ground. They had no party organization in the country and little even in the House. The coalition Liberal whips were always vague who the whip should go to, and even in the general election of 1918 the only definition of a coalition Liberal was negative: a Liberal who had been against a negotiated peace. Where party discipline was lacking, 'influence' had to take its place. Hence the sale of honours which Lloyd George conducted on an unprecedented scale. Of course Lloyd George, having to build up a fund in two years where the traditional parties had had half a century, was keen to sell, and the coalition Liberals, having no social position and much easily won money, were eager to buy. But such transactions were the only way in which Lloyd George could hold his followers together.

Still 'influence' was not enough. The coalition Liberals could not altogether forget their radical and Nonconformist origins. Even 'George's bloody knights' of Northcliffe's deadly phrase might respond to a clear Liberal call. Lloyd George rushed into this battle whenever challenged, quite contrary to his ordinary disregard of parliament. Where Asquith had told critics to wait and see, Lloyd George never waited, and as a result his critics never saw. Asquith could not recover Liberal allegiance as the alternative war leader. But someone else might. The gravest threat came from Churchill, excluded from Lloyd George's government on Unionist insistence and now sitting with the Liberals on the front Opposition bench. On 10 May 1917 Lloyd George held a secret session, apparently to prepare the way for direction of labour and food control. He made an effective speech, but it was Churchill who dominated the House. Lloyd George did not waste a moment. He caught Churchill behind the Speaker's chair while the debate was still in progress and, says Churchill, 'assured me of his determination to have me at his side. From that day, although holding no office, I became to a large extent his colleague.'[40] Two months later Churchill became minister of munitions. The Unionists protested, from Bonar Law downwards; but they could do nothing, short of going over to Asquith. It was safer to offend them than to run the risk that the Liberals might reunite. The operation had the additional satisfaction for Lloyd George of sending Addison from Munitions to the impressive obscurity of Reconstruction: another potential rival out of the way.

The same preoccupation with Liberal feeling was shown when Lloyd George made one of his rare appearances in the House to defend the short-lived ban on sending the *Nation* abroad. This ban, though indefensible, seems a trivial matter to have brought the prime minister down to the House at a critical moment of the war. But the *Nation* was a revered Liberal paper, despite its advocacy of a negotiated peace; revered especially by the former radicals who now supported Lloyd George. In this case Lloyd George evaded danger by retreating in a cloud of words. The conscientious objectors showed his

40. Churchill, *The World Crisis, 1916–1918* (London, Thornton Butterworth, 1927), I, 255.

other method. Sympathy might have been expected from one who had been virtually a conscientious objector in a previous war. On the contrary, once Lloyd George abandoned principle, no one else was allowed to keep it, and he carried his radical supporters with him simply by imitating Bottomley or Pemberton Billing: 'I will make the path of these men a very hard one.' Bonar Law showed more sympathy to the conscientious objectors, and it was left to Lord Hugh Cecil to divide the House against their disfranchisement – losing only by 171 to 209. The minority included a number of those usually counted as coalition Liberals.

Ireland was Lloyd George's real worry rather than the generals or even the Germans. For one thing he owed his position largely to the belief of many Liberals that he would have solved the Irish question had Asquith not let him down, and he was therefore almost driven into another attempt at solution now that he was in supreme command. But what he has written about his handling of Haig and Robertson applies also to his Irish policy: 'I never believed in costly frontal attacks, either in war or in politics, if there were a way round.'[41] The way round in regard to Ireland was to invite the Irish to find a solution for themselves, and the Convention of 1917 took the Irish question out of British politics while it lasted. Even when the Convention failed, the blame could be laid on the Irish, not on Lloyd George. The rise of Sinn Fein, too, played into his hands. The Nationalists, discredited by Sinn Fein victories at by-elections, virtually seceded from the House and so finally parted from Asquith. Lloyd George could denounce Sinn Fein as subversive: 'They are organizing for separation, for secession, and for Sovereign independence ... Under no conditions can this country possibly permit anything of that kind.'[42] This absolved him from blaming Ulster in any way, which would have offended the Unionists, while the coalition Liberals abandoned the Irish cause in outraged patriotism.

The Irish question raised a final complication in the spring of 1918. The German offensive which began on 21 March marked a moment of supreme crisis. It provoked a cry for something dramatic even though irrelevant. As in 1916, the dramatic act was conscription – this time the raising of the age to fifty. The Unionists threw in the

41. Lloyd George, *War Memoirs*, IV, 2274.
42. 23 October 1917; Hansard, 5th series, XCVIII, 790.

demand that conscription be extended to Ireland. Perhaps they did this to embarrass their Liberal associates. More probably it was merely another illustration of the general rule in British history that even the most reasonable men take leave of their senses as soon as they touch the Irish question. At any rate the proposal offered Asquith positively his last opportunity: he could rally the Liberals, and even the Nationalists, against Irish conscription and for home rule. But this was the very moment when Asquith was hoping to champion the military leaders (who also, of course, favoured Irish conscription) with Carson as his ally; hence he remained silent. Lloyd George worked out an ingenious compromise by which the Irish should get home rule and conscription together. In fact, they got neither, and Lloyd George covered the muddle by detecting a German plot in Ireland – one of those far-fetched stories which a British government produces when all else fails. In June 1918 this story served to tide things over until the end of the war. The Irish question never threatened to lead the coalition Liberals back to Asquith.

The House in fact disliked discussion of great issues. It stirred uneasily when anyone, even Lloyd George himself, attempted to survey the general course of the war. It was aggressively intolerant when anti-war members raised the question of peace terms, or strayed otherwise into foreign policy. For instance, when Joseph King tried to discuss British policy towards Bolshevik Russia, Lord Robert Cecil espied strangers and secured a secret session with general approval. There was nothing secret in the topic; the House simply did not want to discuss it or indeed anything else connected with the war. This is not to say that members were idle or indifferent to public affairs. Away from high policy, they showed considerable competence and devotion. They worked hard on electoral reform, virtually without guidance from the government, and made Great Britain a genuine democracy for the first time: universal manhood suffrage, and limited women's suffrage into the bargain. They helped Fisher to revolutionize secondary education. But they would have nothing to do with the great questions of the war. They believed, rightly as it turned out, that the Opposition would be slaughtered at a general election. More important, the supporters of the coalition were determined not to reveal their own internal differences. The unavowed compact of the front benches with which the war started became an equally un-avowed compact of the back benches before the end. The back-benchers had no idea how Lloyd George would win the war; they often disapproved of his policy when they understood it. But they clung firmly to the belief that he was not one of the 'Old Gang' under whom they had groaned for the first two years of the war. This was Lloyd George's decisive asset, though also his final liability. He was enough of a 'rogue' to eclipse wilder demagogues like Pemberton Billing and Horatio Bottomley. But, not being one of the 'Old Gang', he was expendable. When the war was over, he was expended.

Lloyd George: Rise and Fall

The Leslie Stephen lecture for 1961, given on 21 April in the Senate House of Cambridge University.

* * *

On 7 December 1916 Lloyd George had a busy day. In the evening he returned to his room at the War Office with his devoted adherent, Dr Christopher Addison. The building was empty. A solitary messenger produced a cold chicken – what strange things they kept at the War Office; warmed up some soup and a bit of fish; Lloyd George unearthed a bottle of champagne. This scratch supper celebrated the triumph of 'the people'. It was Lloyd George's first meal as prime minister. Years afterwards he wrote: 'There had never before been a "ranker" raised to the premiership – certainly not one except Disraeli who had not passed through the Staff College of the old Universities.'[1] Like many of Lloyd George's best remarks, this is not strictly accurate. The Duke of Wellington did not go to a university. The rule has often been broken since. With Lloyd George's successors, the old universities have scored a draw – four all. Yet essentially Lloyd George's remark was true. No other premier has been a 'ranker' to the same extent. Even Ramsay MacDonald took on the colour of his surroundings despite his origins – perhaps too much so. Lloyd George remained the great 'rogue' of British political life in more senses than one.

Lloyd George was not marked out only by having escaped the staff college of the old universities. He was an exception among British prime ministers in almost every way – in nationality, in economic origin, in religion, in profession. He was Welsh; he was born in a poor family; he was a Nonconformist; he was a solicitor until politics absorbed him. He was the only prime minister with a native tongue other than English – perhaps I should say as well as English; the only one with a sense of national oppression or at any rate inequality. He was much poorer at the start than any future prime minister except Ramsay MacDonald, and, unlike MacDonald, he did not marry a rich wife. He was the only practising Nonconformist to become prime

1. D. Lloyd George, *War Memoirs* (London, Nicholson and Watson, 1933), I, 621.

minister other than Neville Chamberlain,[2] though his religious outlook does not seem to have been orthodox – it was a sort of pantheism of the people, combined with pleasure in the singing of Baptist hymns. He was the only solicitor to become prime minister, and this, though it seems less significant, had its influence also. Solicitors are, by definition, the 'ORs' of the legal profession. Barristers like the ringing phrase and the drama of open dispute. Solicitors prefer to settle behind the scenes.

How did this ranker attain supreme power? And how, having succeeded, did he come to lose it? These are questions of endless fascination, whether considered in terms of the individual man or as an exercise in political history. The first question – how he got there – has been much discussed. Indeed there are few political episodes which have been canvassed in greater detail. But even the incomparable dissection by Lord Beaverbrook, which will be read as long as men are interested in political tactics, leaves much unsaid. The accounts of this affair start off, as it were, with the great topic settled: Lloyd George is clearly the man who will win the war. They deal with the mechanics of how he got to the top when his reputation was made; they do not explain how so many people reached agreement on this reputation, or exactly what it rested on. The second question has been more casually treated. Lloyd George himself was perhaps bewildered that he had fallen, others bewildered that they had ever put him into a position from which to fall. Who, having fallen out of love, can explain why he was ever in, let alone how he got out of it again? These are my two themes – the rise to power, and the fall from it; two different aspects of the same baffling personality.

Lloyd George was a politician from first to last and nothing else, though he sometimes made claim to distinction as a journalist, an author and – perhaps with more justification – a nursery-gardener. He did not come late into national politics with his reputation already established elsewhere, as some other outsiders have done – Joseph Chamberlain for example. He became a member of parliament at the age of twenty-seven and achieved a record for uninterrupted represen-

2. Asquith, though of Nonconformist origin, had ceased to have any open Nonconformist allegiance by the time he became prime minister. The other non-Anglican prime ministers, of whom there have been several, were Scottish Presbyterians and therefore conformists in their own country.

tation of the same constituency which no other prime minister can equal or nearly approach. He lived only for politics. He talked politics in his leisure hours – either the politics of the moment or political reminiscence. Political history was his only serious reading. He found diversion in cheap thrillers. His favourite bedtime author was Ridgwell Cullum. He had no taste in art or music, no knowledge of contemporary literature, no interest in the affairs of the mind outside the political world. I doubt whether he understood economic principles, though he was quick to turn them to advantage.

Though Lloyd George spent his life among politicians and in parliament, he cared little for either of them. He was never intimate with established politicians of the ordinary kind, and he did not frequent the recognized social centres. His associates were men outside the conventional pattern, like himself: Churchill, the grandson of a duke, who crossed the floor to become a radical; Rufus Isaacs, son of a fruit merchant who rose to be an earl, lord chief justice, and viceroy of India; F E Smith – the smith of his own fortunes – who invented a youth of extreme poverty for himself and perhaps came to believe in it. Even with them Lloyd George was reserved. Only Churchill called him 'David'; for all others he was 'L-G'. He stood out against the growing use of Christian names: 'I am not very active in that way. I don't believe in being too familiar with people.'[3] Similarly, he took little trouble to sound parliamentary feeling outside the debating chamber. He rarely appeared in the smoking room. He knew few members by sight and, before becoming prime minister in 1916, had to entrust Christopher Addison with the task of discovering which Liberal members would support him. He relinquished the leadership of the House to Bonar Law with relief and thereafter never made a speech as prime minister without complaining that the House was distracting him from his real work. In later years, after his fall from power, he held court in his private room and did not welcome stray visitors.

Coming into the British system from outside, he had no respect for its traditions or accepted formalities. As prime minister, he failed to sustain the elaborate shadow-play which treats the monarch as something more than a figurehead. He promised peerages without first

3. Lord Riddell, *Lord Riddell's Intimate Diary of the Peace Conference and After* (London, Victor Gollancz, 1933), 287.

securing royal approval. He appointed ministers and then informed the king by telephone. He detested titles. This, no doubt, is why he distributed them so lavishly. If others were fools enough to buy, he was willing to sell. It gave added zest to his campaign against landowners that the greatest of them were dukes, and he would have derived less pleasure from humiliating Curzon, if Curzon had not been a marquis (of Lloyd George's creation) and forever parading pride of birth. Most of all, he distrusted the permanent officials. Sometimes he overrode them. He is said to have been the only minister of modern times who could defeat the obstinacy even of Treasury officials. Usually, however, he preferred to circumvent them. He carried his private secretaries with him from one department to another, much as a French politician does, culminating, when he was prime minister, in the creation of a duplicate civil service dependent on himself, the 'Garden Suburb'.[4] After the war, Philip Kerr, one of this 'suburb', was more influential in foreign affairs than Lord Curzon, the foreign secretary, just as J T Davies, Lloyd George's principal private secretary, was a more important figure than the permanent head of the Civil Service.

Lloyd George never hesitated to go behind the backs of his established advisers, listening to amateur advice and then forming his opinion with little regard to the official papers. He consulted junior officers back from France, including his own son, for arguments to use against Haig, the commander-in-chief, and Robertson, Chief of the Imperial General Staff. He got Lieutenant-Commander Kenworthy to brief him against the lords of the Admiralty. Kenworthy was smuggled into No. 10 Downing Street late at night by Northcliffe through the garden door. The most striking instance of Lloyd George's unconventional methods is the origin of the National Health Service – that revolutionary contribution to modern life. One can imagine how

4. Lloyd George introduced two other French innovations into British political life. Until 1915 British ministers were secretaries, first lords, presidents of boards. The first avowed minister was the minister of munitions, Lloyd George himself; he soon created others. Again, British ministers with nothing to do were given a sinecure. They were not ministers without portfolio – strictly speaking, no British minister has a portfolio, he has seals or a royal warrant. The first minister without portfolio, Lansdowne, was appointed in 1915 on Lloyd George's suggestion, and the list was soon full of them. Perhaps Lloyd George's casual attitude to his private finances was also learnt from France, or perhaps it was natural to a Welshman.

it would have begun in the ordinary way: a royal commission, long papers from experts, an accumulation of facts and figures. Lloyd George merely sent W J Braithwaite, a junior official in the Treasury, to find how Bismarck's system of insurance worked in Germany. Braithwaite toured Germany and then travelled overnight to the south of France. On 3 January 1911 he caught up with Lloyd George at Nice. Lloyd George, accompanied by some friends, took him to the pier; set out chairs not too near the band; ordered drinks; and said: 'Now tell us all about it.' Braithwaite discoursed for four hours. When he had finished, the Welfare State had been born. A symbol of Lloyd George indeed – the pier at Nice, the band, the hastily improvised explanation and then the gigantic results. It gives added point to the story that there is no pier at Nice; perhaps there was one then.

Lloyd George rarely showed loyalty to those who broke ranks to work with him. J T Davies was rewarded by being made a director of the Suez Canal Company. Others were less fortunate. Braithwaite created the National Health system almost single-handed under Lloyd George's inspiration. As soon as it was made, Lloyd George deposited him in the obscurity of a special commissioner of income tax. They met again only once, twenty years later. Lloyd George said: 'Hello, Braithwaite, what have you been doing all this time?' Braithwaite replied: 'My duty I hope, sir, where I was sent to do it.' Politicians who worked with Lloyd George were treated in the same way. Christopher Addison had a large share in making Lloyd George prime minister. Some years later, when Addison's lavish expenditure on housing – incurred on Lloyd George's prompting – aroused Unionist hostility, Lloyd George jettisoned him without warning and apologized to the House that loyalty to an old friend had led him to keep an incompetent minister in office. For Lloyd George no ties were sacred. Churchill stood solidly by Lloyd George during the Marconi scandal in 1913. Lloyd George did not repay the debt when Churchill ran into trouble over the expedition to the Dardanelles. He said, quite untruly: 'Churchill is the man who brought Turkey into the war against us', and let the Unionists drive Churchill from office. Lloyd George was fond of saying: 'There is no friendship at the top.' It was certainly true in his case.

Lloyd George did not rely on individuals, however eminent. He recognized no intermediaries between himself and 'the people'. His relations with the House of Commons were a mixture of uneasy mastery and distrust. His set pieces in parliament were not remarkable. His long speech introducing the People's Budget of 1909 was poorly delivered, and one listener surmised that Lloyd George himself did not understand what he was saying. It was different when he was answering criticism or silencing opposition by last-minute concessions. He met objections to the National Health scheme so skilfully, and with such moderation, that in the end most Unionists voted for it. As prime minister, he never allowed his opponents to get the issue clear and always raised some unexpected red herring which left them baffled. So, when accused of weakness towards Germany during the peace negotiations of 1919, he rode off with an irrelevant attack on Lord Northcliffe which delighted even his strongest critics. His greatest triumph came in the Maurice debate of May 1918. Asquith, who launched it, was universally described as the greatest parliamentarian, and he had a good case, but no novice was more catastrophically out-manoeuvred. Lloyd George summed up the debate afterwards: 'They have gone away saying – we have caught the little beggar out speaking the truth for once.' Whether he was speaking the truth on that occasion, no one has been able to decide from that day to this.

For Lloyd George, parliament was less important than the public meeting. He said: 'My platform is the country.' This was the time when all political leaders did a great deal of public speaking. The period opened in the 1880s, after Gladstone's Midlothian campaigns; it tailed off in the 1930s, perhaps because interest in politics declined, perhaps because of the radio. Lloyd George came just at the top of the wave. His style was all his own. Other statesmen spoke in formal terms, carefully prepared. Churchill, for instance, learnt his early speeches, word for word, by heart and read his later ones. Lloyd George spoke with his audience, not to them, and snapped up phrases as they were thrown at him. 'Ninepence for fourpence' was the result of one such interruption; making Germany pay to the uttermost farthing, the less happy result of another. Most public speakers seemed to be the contemporaries of Henry Irving or Beerbohm Tree. Lloyd George gave a music-hall turn, worthy of Harry Lauder or George Robey, the prime minister of mirth, and the great days of the music hall, roughly from 1900 to 1930, corresponded exactly with his. In 1923 Lloyd George was persuaded to use a microphone for the first time, and he accepted it ever afterwards. I suspect that it ruined his public style, as it certainly ruined the music hall.

Speechmaking was not Lloyd George's only instrument for project-ing himself on the country, perhaps not even the most important. No public man has made more use of the press. This was not new. Palmerston wrote leaders for the *Globe* and the *Morning Chronicle*, often reproducing the very words of his dispatches and rewarding the proprietor of the latter with a baronetcy. Salisbury wrote in the *Standard*, and made his ghost, Alfred Austin, Poet Laureate. Even Sir Edward Grey briefed J A Spender of the *Westminster Gazette*. Lloyd George approached the press in a different way. He was never forthcoming to reporters. On the contrary he was the first prime minister who employed a press secretary to keep them at bay and even then often complained of their misrepresentations. Lloyd George went for the man at the top – the editor and, still more, the proprietor. Why bother to make a case when the proprietor could make it more decisively simply by issuing an order? The most famous example came in 1918. Lloyd George, angered that the *Daily Chronicle* had enlisted his critic, Frederick Maurice, as military correspondent, got a group of coalition Liberals to buy the paper and turned out the editor, Robert Donald, at twenty-four hours' notice.[5] This was not his first exercise in financial influence. As early as 1900 he persuaded George Cadbury to buy the *Daily News* and to turn it overnight from a pro-war to a pro-Boer paper. Usually he used less direct means. Common sympathy with the Boers established a deep intimacy be-tween Lloyd George and C P Scott, owner-editor of the *Manchester Guardian*, an intimacy not really broken even when Scott was denounc-ing the behaviour of the Black and Tans in Ireland. Scott remained faithful even unto death: almost his last act was to swing the *Manchester Guardian* against the National government and behind Lloyd George during the financial crisis of 1931. Even more important for Lloyd George was his friendship with Sir William Robertson Nicoll, editor of the *British Weekly*, a man now forgotten, but wielding decisive power in his time. It is hardly too much to say that Robertson Nicoll was the man who first, by supporting Lloyd George, raised him up, and then, by withdrawing his support, cast him down.

Newspaper proprietors in the stricter sense were flattered by Lloyd

5. This manipulation of 'public opinion' proved useful to Lloyd George in another way. He put some of his private political fund into the *Daily Chronicle* and sold out in 1926 at a fourfold profit.

George and often ennobled by him: Riddell, owner of the *News of the World*, the first divorced person to be made a peer; Rothermere; Beaverbrook. Lloyd George had a curious on-and-off relationship with Northcliffe, the greatest of them all, intimate at one moment, hostile at the next. The two men had much in common, despite their conflicts, both sprung from the people, both impatient with conventional politicians. There was in both the same mixture of impulsiveness and calculation, though Northcliffe was the less calculating of the two. When once asked to cooperate with Northcliffe, Lloyd George replied: 'I would as soon go for a walk round Walton Heath with a grasshopper.' A good analogy; but who more like a grasshopper than Lloyd George himself? Lloyd George did not court the newspaper proprietors merely as the makers of public opinion. He genuinely believed that they understood this opinion and could interpret it. How else had they achieved their enormous circulations? Hence he canvassed their advice before taking decisive action. He supposed also that they possessed executive ability of the highest order. When he filled his administration with 'press lords', this was not only to 'buy' them; he thought that the work would be done better by them than by anyone else, and it often was. Then, by an odd twist, he discovered the same abilities in himself. After all, if the inarticulate Northcliffe and the ponderous Rothermere had journalistic genius, how much more must Lloyd George have it too. I doubt if this were the case. Though he was highly paid by American papers after he ceased to be prime minister, this was rather for his name than for the quality of his contributions. But Lloyd George believed himself suited to a great journalistic post. In 1922 it was seriously proposed that a group of wealthy friends should buy *The Times*, then being hawked around after Northcliffe's death, and set him up as editor. Lloyd George was ready, eager to resign the premiership for this purpose. No doubt he had other reasons for wishing to be rid of office. Nevertheless the affair is striking testimony that Lloyd George rated the world of journalism highly, perhaps even more highly than the world of politics. Editors of *The Times* have often believed that they were more important than prime ministers. Lloyd George was the only prime minister who apparently agreed with them.

Parliament, platform, press, one element needs to be fitted into place, maybe the key place: politics. Though Lloyd George was never a good party man, indifferent to many party doctrines and regardless of party discipline, he was first returned as a Liberal, and managed to call himself a Liberal of some sort or another throughout his political life. The peculiar circumstances of the Liberal Party gave him his opportunity and later snatched it away again.

Few writers have noticed how peculiar these circumstances were. Historians of recent times assume, perhaps rightly, that the two-party system is a permanent feature of British politics, and they go on to assume, with less justification, that the swing of the pendulum follows inevitably from this. Hence they find nothing surprising in the Liberal victory of 1906. On the contrary, it was against all the rules. When Lloyd George entered parliament in 1890, the Liberal Party seemed clearly on the way out: sustained by Gladstone's great name and then doomed to decline and disintegration. So it happened: defeat in 1895, and thereafter disruption into warring factions. This is not surprising. Historic liberalism was a *bourgeois* cause, inspired by the advance of *laissez-faire* capitalism and successful in the days of limited suffrage. It lost drive as individual enterprise diminished and it offered little which could attract a mass electorate. This was the common pattern all over Europe. The National Liberal Party in Germany, the Liberal Party in Austria, the French opportunists, the moderate Italian liberals who followed Cavour, all saw their greatness disappear. Old-fashioned British liberalism really ended in 1874, as Gladstone recognized by resigning from the leadership. The party was revived only by the freak controversies first over the Eastern question and then over home rule. But home rule could not keep it going permanently, particularly when most Liberals were not interested in it.

How, then, did British liberalism come to have its greatest success in the early twentieth century, when – on any rational calculation – it should have been dead? The answer is to be found in economic developments which also went against the rules. Individualistic capitalism had a second innings, a sort of deathbed repentance. It is rather like the Solent which, owing to the bottleneck in the Channel between Cherbourg and St Catherine's Point, has four tides a day. You are just resigning yourself to a desolate stretch of sand or pebble when the tide comes flooding in again. So it was with the British economy and for a paradoxical reason. The terms of trade, which in the later nineteenth century had been moving in favour of Great Britain, at the end of the century turned against her. As all Europe and much of the United States became industrialized, the cost of raw materials went up, so did the price of foodstuffs which everyone was importing. There was increased social discontent in Great Britain, as real wages declined – a social discontent which Lloyd George did much to exploit; there was increased hostility to the 'stomach taxes' which tariff reform involved. There was something else: a renewed demand for the products of the old British staples – coal, shipbuilding, textiles; staples which had been losing their pre-eminence. Suddenly, with the increased prosperity of producers of raw materials outside Europe, they boomed again. All three surpassed their previous records, and British exports, thanks mainly to the old staples, reached their all-time peak in 1913.

Instead of undertaking a new industrial revolution, Great Britain could prosper again in the old centres of industry in the old way. This unexpected revival brought with it a second edition of new men, self-reliant, self-made, impatiently radical, far removed from the intellectual refinement of the established Liberal leaders. They were more assertive than their predecessors of fifty years before, unawed by the prestige of the conventional system. Cobden, for instance, despaired of ever attaining real power. His lesser successors had no such doubts. Here is a significant indication. Like their predecessors, the new men were mostly dissenters, at any rate in upbringing, though – like Lloyd George – most of them did not take their religious allegiance at all precisely. They were dissenters with a difference. The nineteenth-century dissenters called themselves Nonconformists – recognition that they were a tolerated minority. Early in the twentieth century they changed their official description and became the Free Churches – assertion of equality, perhaps even of superior virtue. The dissenters swarmed into the parliament of 1906. As Halévy pointed out long ago, that parliament had more non-Anglicans in it than any since the time of Oliver Cromwell. Barebones had come again.

These new men were the making of Lloyd George. The very things which distinguished him from other Liberal leaders brought him close to the self-made businessmen. He had no university education; nor had they. He was of poor origin; so were they. Above all, he was an avowed Free Churchman, and this became the symbol of his unique position. This first picked him out from the Liberal back-benchers and made him a national figure. It started with the Boer War. The Boers were regarded, rather perversely, as champions of the small man against the encroachments of the City and monopoly finance. Moreover they were Free Churchmen, or something like it. There would have been much less pro-Boer enthusiasm in Great Britain if the Boers had been Roman Catholics. It was an added advantage to Lloyd George that most Liberal leaders supported the Boer War almost as heartily as Unionist ministers did. Still, this was a passing phase. What really made Lloyd George's standing was the controversy over the Education Bill of 1902. Here again many Liberal leaders – influenced by the Fabians and friendly to Morant, its author – favoured the Bill. Lloyd George fought it almost alone. When the political argument shifted from education to free trade, he lost his pre-eminence. He never cared much for free trade or understood the topics in dispute. Others took up the running. Asquith, always strong-est in negation, eclipsed him. Nevertheless, thanks to the earlier conflicts Lloyd George had forced his way to the front and established his claim to high office.

Lloyd George was the outstanding 'new' radical in the Liberal government of 1905. Office gave him the opportunity to show his great executive capacity – his unrivalled ability for getting things done. The things he did were all his own, things not envisaged by ordinary liberalism or by the party programme. Everyone knows the rather synthetic passions which he aroused over the People's Budget of 1909. Yet curiously he was the least involved in the subsequent controversy over the House of Lords. He knew instinctively that the people – his sort of people – were not deeply stirred by the constitu-tional intricacies which fascinated Liberal lawyers. His judgement was correct. The two general elections of 1910, and particularly the second, produced more excitement among candidates and less among the electors than perhaps any others of modern times. Lloyd George showed his real opinion of the affair by quietly devising the National Health scheme, and carrying it, when the constitutional storm was blowing its hardest. Indeed, he proposed to settle all the burning issues between the parties – dead issues in his opinion – by agreement. He tried quite sincerely to promote a coalition government; less sincerely perhaps even at the price of his own withdrawal. What he really wanted was 'a government of businessmen' – a revealing phrase – in other words of radical back-benchers.

Lloyd George had something else in common with the new men. His financial position was improving like theirs. The private finances of public men are rarely touched on by their biographers. Still, it is pretty clear that most public men have been the poorer for their life of service, particularly when they held office. Lloyd George was in debt when he became president of the Board of Trade in 1905; his position was very different when he ceased to be prime minister in 1922. He was the first prime minister since Walpole to leave office markedly richer than he entered it. This is not all mystery. Wealthy admirers entertained and endowed him. Riddell gave him a house at Walton Heath – burnt by suffragettes during the building – which he later sold at a good price; Andrew Carnegie bequeathed him an annuity of £2,000 in remote applause for his democratic achievements. But most of his success defies inquiry. Though Lloyd George became well-off, he did not acquire a country house near London until after the war. Disliking life in London, he went off, whenever he could, to a luxury hotel at Brighton or the south of France, with an accompanying flock of civil servants and political adherents, all presumably paid for by the Treasury. It did not occur to him that he was cutting himself off from 'the people' by living in this way. 'The people' whom he knew, the Free Church radicals, lived in exactly the same way.

Besides, he remained closer to the people than any other Liberal minister including John Burns. Lloyd George was the link between the Liberal government and Labour on its trade-union side. Trade unions have now become an accepted, indeed an essential, part of the social order. It is hard to think back to a time, only fifty years ago, when unions were not recognized in many leading industries, when working men were held to be 'not like us', and when it could be solemnly affirmed that miners would keep coal in the bath if they were given bathrooms. Labour was asserting its independence in the early twentieth century, and the Liberal government were repeatedly drawn into trade disputes. Their mediation was still embarrassed and aloof. A minister thought he had done well if he got masters and men – another revealing phrase – into the same room. Lloyd George interpreted mediation differently. He was out to conciliate the men, and he extracted concessions from the employers by any means that occurred to him. It is tempting to surmise that he made his Mansion House speech of 21 July 1911, stirring up the Agadir crisis, so as to frighten the railway companies with the spectre of war into settling the great railway strike much in favour of the unions some three weeks later. At any rate, in the years before the war, Lloyd George was the favourite and most successful industrial mediator among ministers. He always got a settlement which enhanced his reputation at the same time.

The outbreak of war advanced Lloyd George's position in three ways. He was essential as the spokesman of the radical Free Churches; he could display, still more, his great executive powers; he was the only minister who could handle Labour. The decision to go to war revolved round him. There would no doubt have been a majority for war in any case: the Unionists and the moderate Liberals would have supported it. But it seemed until the last moment that there might be also bitter opposition and opposition of the most dangerous kind, opposition on grounds of morality. It is a common opinion nowadays, and was a common opinion then, that wars are opposed for motives of class, that is by the working-class movement. Experience is quite other: opposition to war is effective and decisive only when sustained by moral principle, though it may be that the working class is more moral than others. This was true in regard to the Boer War; it was true over the Suez affair; even, I think, true over the proposed war of intervention against Soviet Russia in 1920. That war was prevented because it was wicked, not because Soviet Russia was 'the workers' state'. So, too, in August 1914, the Free Churches, not the Labour movement, held the key position. When Lloyd George, sustained by Robertson Nicoll, came down on the side of war, he determined that there would be national unity, though, in a longer perspective, the two men sealed the death warrant of the Free Churches as a great moral force. His action mattered not only in August 1914; he was the principal guarantor of national unity as long as the war lasted, in a position – though he did not appreciate this for some time – to dictate his own terms.

The war also gave Lloyd George the opportunity to run things in the way he liked to run them. He could improvise; he could disregard precedent. Any other man would have quailed at starting a Ministry of Munitions from scratch. Lloyd George rejoiced that, when he entered the requisitioned hotel allotted to the new ministry, it contained a table, two chairs, many mirrors – and no civil servants. Alone among Liberal ministers, he appreciated that the war could not be conducted on the basis of *laissez-faire*. Perhaps he did not altogether deserve his reputation as the man who got things done. But at least he tried to get them done, which was more than could be said for anyone else in high office.

The third, and perhaps most important, asset came to Lloyd George unforeseen and by accident. It had hardly occurred to him that he would be the chief conciliator of labour. Indeed it did not occur to him, or to anyone else, that in wartime the conciliation of labour would be even more urgent than the raising of recruits. Until August 1914 the British people played a negative part in public life. Their only duties were to pay their taxes and not to cause trouble for the governing class. Suddenly their position changed. It was not enough to keep them quiet; they had to cooperate actively. Lloyd George was the chief instrument in industrial mobilization, thanks to his previous successes with the trade unions, and this even before he became minister of munitions. On 27 March 1915 he met the leaders of the engineering unions at the Treasury: they agreed to drop restrictive practices for the duration and received in return some rather vague promise of industrial partnership. This was a date of historic importance: the moment when the trade unions ceased to be merely instruments of resistance and stepped, however half-heartedly, into a share of control. It was the most significant event in the history of British trade unions, and hence of the British working class, since the repeal of the Combination Acts, and it was all Lloyd George's doing. He has left a vivid account of the scene – the union leaders leaning casually against a chair which Queen Anne was reputed to have used when she attended the Treasury Board, and A J Balfour, appropriate representative of the governing class, regarding them with tolerant surprise. Lloyd George writes:

His ideas of government were inherited from the days when Queen Anne sat on that throne ... This scene was fundamentally different. He saw those stalwart artisans leaning against and sitting on the steps of the throne of the dead queen, and on equal terms negotiating conditions with the government of the day ... Queen Anne was indeed dead. I felt that his detached and inquiring mind was bewildered by this sudden revelation of a new power and that he must take time to assimilate the experience.[6]

Lloyd George went further along the same path after he became minister of munitions. Though, strictly speaking, engineering alone was his concern, he acted as the unofficial minister for industry, called

6. Lloyd George, *War Memoirs*, I, 177.

in whenever there were difficulties in the coalfields or the shipyards, and overriding the dogmatic follies of the minister technically responsible – Runciman, president of the Board of Trade. In this work of conciliation, Lloyd George established a partnership with Arthur Henderson – nominally president of the Board of Education, actually the representative of 'Labour' in the coalition government. Henderson always preferred to play second fiddle, and he transferred to Lloyd George the support which he had previously given to MacDonald. The two men tackled industrial unrest together – not always successfully, but better than anyone else did.

Here then were Lloyd George's unique assets, assets which grew in strength as the war proceeded. Moreover the circumstances of the war made it easier for him to exploit these assets. Not only did 'the people' count for more; their voice became unexpectedly more effective. The Asquith coalition was a pact between the two front benches, a pact to avoid dispute and to keep things quiet. The press had to provide the criticism which was silenced in parliament, and practically all the press was on Lloyd George's side. It is often held that this was due to his personal intrigues. He is supposed to have 'nobbled' the press lords. I doubt whether anyone could 'nobble' Northcliffe. I am sure that no one could 'nobble' C P Scott, J L Garvin, Robert Donald or Geoffrey Dawson. All these men passionately wanted Lloyd George as prime minister, and their united support is the most powerful evidence that he was the right man for the job. There was another factor. The back-benchers, both Unionist and Liberal, were increasingly restive at the silence which had been imposed upon them. They threatened to revolt, and this revolt brought Lloyd George to supreme power. In the crisis of December 1916, he had three kingmakers, none of them from the front bench. Max Aitken brought over Bonar Law, a back-bencher in spirit, even though he was Unionist leader; Christopher Addison mobilized the back-bench radicals; Arthur Henderson delivered the solid backing of Labour, to his own surprise. There was one striking gap: the party whips played no part at all. They were the instrument which broke in Asquith's hands.

Lloyd George was given two tasks as prime minister: a more energetic conduct of the war and a closer partnership with the people. It was because Lloyd George enjoyed the confidence of 'the people' that the Unionist leaders came over to him, even though the revolt had been directed originally as much against them as against the

front-bench Liberals. The Unionists had always been readier to make
their peace with 'democracy' from the time of Disraeli onwards. The
Liberals feared it and Asquith tried to fight the revolt entirely within
the closed circle of the governing class. The Liberal leaders had a
curious belief in their divine right to rule. Bewildered by their defeat,
they grasped at the myth that Lloyd George had intrigued himself to
the top and, by dint of repeating it, got others to believe it too. In
reality, Asquith fought to retain power as much as Lloyd George
fought to gain it, and his later complaints resemble those of an ageing
heavyweight who has been knocked out by a younger, more agile,
opponent. Nevertheless, Lloyd George paid a bitter price for victory.
In Churchill's words, he had seized power, and the governing class
never forgave him. Even the Unionist leaders who went with him
meant to discard him once the emergency was over.

Lloyd George also suffered, in the long run, from the backing
which the press gave him. Members of parliament like to regard
themselves as the sole voice of the people and see in the press a rival
power, illegitimate and irresponsible. The House of Commons has
never forgiven its defeat at the hands of John Wilkes, and there is no
more joyful scene there than when some editor appears at the bar for
public rebuke. If members of parliament had their way, press, radio
and television would not exist, or at any rate would be silent on
political questions. Press support for a politician is the kiss of death,
though of course most members canvass for it behind the scenes.
Lloyd George obviously preferred press lords to politicians – preferred
them not only as companions, but as ministers. He treated the House
with increasing casualness. His war cabinet was composed virtually
without regard to parliamentary need; one member of it, Smuts,
served for eighteen months without ever having any connection with
either House – a unique case; the first full statement of war aims was
made to a trade-union conference, not to the House of Commons.
Lloyd George often trembled for his position. He was really in no
danger so long as he had 'the people' on his side. Every stroke which
he delivered against established authority – against admirals, field-
marshals and conventional politicians – strengthened him, though he
often hesitated before delivering it.

The fatal mine against Lloyd George exploded almost unnoticed,
particularly by Lloyd George himself. This was his breach with
Arthur Henderson. Lloyd George had been quicker than any other

politician to grasp the importance of the Labour movement, but he only grasped the half of it. He regarded it as an interest just like the Free Church interest which had originally raised him up – a pressure-group with limited sectional objectives. He never understood the political side of the movement. Keir Hardie seemed to him a fine radical pro-Boer; Ramsay MacDonald a somewhat wordy Fabian who would one day become a Liberal minister. It is fair to say that most Labour leaders also did not understand the political importance of their movement until it happened. Keir Hardie hawked the Labour leadership around to Morley, Dilke and Lloyd George himself; Mac-Donald was not indifferent to Liberal offers. Nevertheless, the Labour movement made no sense without its political content. Lloyd George never appreciated that the Labour leaders whom he praised, conde-scendingly, as simple working men of sterling character were also long-standing members of the ILP or the SDF, though not all of them remained faithful to their origin. When Lloyd George put Henderson in the war cabinet, he supposed that he was enlisting a useful agent for managing the trade unions, and Henderson modestly accepted this slighting estimate.

Nevertheless, Henderson had a special position. Lloyd George's government was composed otherwise of individuals, except for Bonar Law – men who had to depend on their personal weight and achieve-ment. Henderson was the voice of Labour and therefore, when conflict arose, acted with an independence such as none other of Lloyd George's ministers dared to show. The question at issue was whether British Labour should attend the conference at Stockholm, to discuss possible peace terms with other socialist parties. Henderson answered this question according to his own judgement and the outlook of the Labour Party, not according to the decisions of the war cabinet. He was kept on the mat and driven to resign. Lloyd George attached little importance to the incident. He put another Labour man, George Barnes, into the war cabinet and thought that by doing so he had automatically made Barnes Labour leader, much as the king auto-matically made a politician leader of his party by appointing him prime minister. Nothing of the kind. Labour did not take its leader by nomination from Lloyd George, and Barnes was civilly dead so far as Labour was concerned from the moment he entered the war cabinet. Labour continued to support the war; Labour ministers, other than Henderson, remained in office. This no doubt gave Lloyd George the illusion that nothing important had happened. He was wrong. August 1917 marked the real parting of the ways between Lloyd George and 'the people'. Labour then gave notice to quit, a notice, like so many others, deferred for the duration.

Lloyd George was secure while the war lasted. He supposed that he was even more secure when the war ended. He had fulfilled his bargain: he had won the war. The general election of December 1918 turned on the simple question whether Lloyd George should go on as prime minister. No issues of policy were at stake, despite later beliefs to the contrary. The election was a plebiscite which Lloyd George won. The Unionist and Liberal parties as such had no significance. Most electors merely wanted Lloyd George as prime minister, and, though they could express this wish only by voting for candidates who accepted the 'coupon', this was a vote against party, not a vote for coalition Unionists or Liberals. Yet this moment of triumph saw also the appearance of a decisive threat against Lloyd George's position. He aimed, whether consciously or not, at becoming sole voice of the people by destroying the existing parties and reducing politics to a collection of individuals. The Labour Party provided a new representation of the people and, as well, resurrected the two-party system just when Lloyd George had got rid of it. This was Arthur Henderson's delayed revenge for his humiliation the year before – not that so nice a man ever thought in terms of revenge. Lloyd George's coalition was reduced from all the nation to two-thirds (a third being a generous estimate for the Liberal Party). There was never at any time a hope that he could pull Labour back. Thanks to Henderson it had become fully independent: independent in its programme; independent in its constituency organizations; independent in its finance, which came from the political levy of the trade unions and not, as with the other parties, from the sale of honours.

Lloyd George was not alone in failing to read the writing on the wall. Hardly anyone did so. The defeated Asquithians thought that they would soon be back in first place on the front Opposition bench. They were still strong in privy councillors, though weak in voters. The Parliamentary Labour Party was unimpressive. Its real leaders lost their seats at the general election, and it was difficult to grasp that a party of the people could be led almost as well from outside the House as from within it, though Lloyd George himself had played country against parliament. Henderson, with his usual abnegation, found the predestined leader of the Labour Party in Ramsay MacDonald. He, not Lloyd George, became the symbol, adequate or not, for the triumph of democracy. It is fascinating to watch how Lloyd George missed the meaning of all this. He actually wanted to see 200 Labour members of parliament so that he could balance more adroitly between the contending 'interests'. But where was the base from which he could operate? During the war the 'interests' could sink their differences in a common will to win; after the war this uniting principle disappeared. Lloyd George made repeated attempts to found a centre party. This was possible only if it included representatives from both extremes. There would be none from Labour. Therefore the centre party could only be another name for the Conservatives, and they preferred their own. Even the coalition Liberals recognized this and refused to be swallowed up, clinging to the rags of their radical origin – free trade and the Free Churches. Lloyd George's centre party remained a one-man band.

Lloyd George had still one asset, achievement, and he worked it to the full. His balance sheet of success after the war was remarkable, perhaps more so than during the war itself. It is possible to debate how much he contributed to victory. Lloyd George himself said that the war was won not by him, but 'by the man in the steel helmet'. What he did after the war was all his own doing. Peace with Germany. Lloyd George alone, against Clemenceau and Wilson, secured a moderate territorial settlement, which did not deprive Germany of any 'ethnic' territory; he alone arranged reparations in such a way that they could be settled in agreement with Germany as soon as the Germans wanted to agree at all. Peace with Soviet Russia. Lloyd George secured this not only against his French allies, but against the majority of his own cabinet including particularly Churchill. Peace with the trade unions. Lloyd George circumvented the challenges from the railwaymen and the miners until they ceased to be dangerous. Peace with Ireland. Lloyd George performed the miracle which had defied every British statesman for over a century, or perhaps for five centuries – the younger Pitt, Gladstone, Asquith, to go no further back: he settled the Irish question for good and all. There was hardly a problem where he did not leave success behind him. The interwar years lived on his legacy and exhausted it.

Yet it was all dust and ashes. Each success lowered his reputation instead of adding to it. What went wrong? What turned Lloyd

George from the most admired into the most hated and distrusted figure in British politics? It was partly his method. He defined this method in classic words: 'I was never in favour of costly frontal attacks, either in war or politics, if there were a way round.' He was the leader of a predominantly right-wing coalition, yet his instincts were all to the left. He did not browbeat his followers. Instead he led them with much blowing of trumpets in one direction until the moment when they discovered that he had brought them to an exactly opposite conclusion. Conciliation of Germany was prepared under a smokescreen of 'Hang the Kaiser' and 'Make Germany Pay'. The Soviet leaders were Bolshevik untouchables until the day when Lloyd George signed a trade agreement with them. The trade-union leaders were a challenge to civilization at one moment and were being offered whisky and cigars at the next. Ireland was the supreme example. Lloyd George's successful peace was preceded by the Black and Tans, one of the most atrocious episodes in British history. The Unionists were told that Lloyd George had murder by the throat and then found themselves called upon to surrender everything which they had defended for nearly forty years. Men do not like being cheated even for the most admirable cause.

Success ruined Lloyd George in another way. Confident in his own powers, he would tolerate no rival near the throne. During the war he had colleagues of equal, or almost equal, stature – Bonar Law, Milner, Balfour. He had formidable antagonists – admirals and field-marshals. He was the little man asserting the cause of the people against great odds. After the war he reigned supreme. He had no colleagues, only subordinates; men who, however distinguished, had pinned their fate to his and had no resources with which to oppose him. He established with them 'the relation of master and servant', which Churchill acknowledged even years later, when he was chancellor of the exchequer and Lloyd George a mere private member. Though Lloyd George reluctantly restored the full cabinet in place of the small war cabinet, he then disregarded it and settled policy on his own behind the scenes.

There was another terrible flaw in his position: the sale of honours. Lloyd George could plead that governments had notoriously been selling honours for the last forty years and, less directly, long before. He ran the system too hard. Not only did he sell more honours with less excuse. Lacking a party, he sold them for his own account, as the existence of the Lloyd George fund still testifies. It was one thing for him to maintain a personal dictatorship, based only on his individual gifts. The Lloyd George fund raised the threat that he would turn his disregard of party into a permanent system. Moreover, politics had to become more respectable with the advance of democracy. Corruption was an accepted necessity in the old days of a closed political nation. Appearances had to be kept up now that 'the people' had a voice in government. The integrity of Labour finance was itself a standing reproach to the older parties. Most of all, the supply of buyers was running out. It was easy to be delicate about the sale of honours when few wanted to buy them. Those who had bought honours in the past wished to elevate their position by ensuring that no one did it again, and those who still aspired to honours wished to avoid paying for them.

Some of the forces which had brought Lloyd George to power moved away from him; others lost their strength. Independent Labour removed one prop. The retreat of the businessmen from public life removed another. Some of Lloyd George's business ministers, among them the most successful, returned to their firms when the war was over; others were itching to go. Besides, Lloyd George had one great failure to set against his many successes: he could not stave off the decline of the old Liberal staples which had long been threatening. He came to power on a wave of industrial expansion which drowned financial scruples. After the war, 'the penguins of the City' enforced deflation and unemployment. The self-made businessmen who had prospered along with Lloyd George were now ruined. The coalition Liberals vanished as abruptly as they had appeared. At the end Lloyd George was forced back on his origins. In 1922 he was hastily mobilizing the Free Churches as his last line of defence. They were no longer a decisive element in British politics now that education had ceased to be a sectarian question. He who had once seemed the man of the future was by 1922 curiously old-fashioned. He looked, and spoke, like a Victorian. His public speeches, though still effective, sounded like echoes from the past. His audiences often took his point before he made it. His support in the press also dwindled. The press lords moved from him. He quarrelled with Northcliffe in 1918; with Riddell in 1922. Beaverbrook backed away when Bonar Law left the government. There remained only his private organ, the *Daily Chronicle*.

The fall of Lloyd George was provoked by his attempt to resist the Turkish advance on Constantinople – an attempt incidentally which, like most of his enterprises, was largely successful. This was the occasion, not the cause. He was brought down, as he had been raised up, by a revolt of the back-benchers. The Conservative meeting which ended the coalition was actually summoned by the leaders in order to break this incipient revolt, and the rebels thought, until the last minute, that they would be defeated. It is curious how Lloyd George repeated, in every detail, the mistakes which had destroyed Asquith. He, too, came to believe that he was 'the indispensable man', safe from all storms. He, too, came to count solely on 'the talents' at the top and disregarded the other ranks of politics – the very men in the trenches who had made him prime minister.

There was an odd outcome. The revolt of the back-benchers in 1916, which raised Lloyd George to power, destroyed the party system; their revolt of 1922, which flung him out, restored it. The rebels of 1922 acted in the name of Conservative independence. But essentially what drove them to act in this way was Labour's independence, asserted in 1918. Once Labour became a distinct party, it could be answered only by another party, not by an individual however brilliant. Lloyd George's fall dates back to the day when he kept Arthur Henderson waiting on the mat. The rise of the Labour Party, which seemed to disrupt the pattern of politics, paradoxically restored the two-party system in a new form. Class became the determining factor in party allegiance, and there was no place for Lloyd George, the man who bounced from one class to another.

Lloyd George had triumphed when men wanted a national leader, who would save the country by opportunist means without regard for party principles or party ties. It is not surprising that Lenin admired him and dedicated a book to him; for Lenin, too, became great as the opportunist saviour of his country, jettisoning party doctrines of a far more rigid kind – and jettisoning party comrades also. Crisis had been Lloyd George's opportunity. Men disliked the atmosphere of crisis after the turmoil of the Great War. Even when there was a crisis, as with the General Strike, the strikers solemnly played football against the police to demonstrate that nothing unusual was happening. Lloyd George had one more chance. In 1931 a financial crisis threatened, real and inescapable – or so men thought then; nowadays a chancellor of the exchequer who was faced only with the deficit of 1931 would think he was in luck's way. Ramsay MacDonald, himself at sea, invited Lloyd George to join the Labour government as leader of the House and in control of the Treasury. The cuckoo seemed once more on the point of entering the nest. Lloyd George could be again the saviour of his country, inaugurating a British New Deal. At the decisive moment he was temporarily knocked out of public life by a serious operation. MacDonald and Baldwin, the two men who had destroyed him, were left to face the financial crisis as best they could. Lloyd George remained a lone voice, with no political supporters except members of his family, pathetically trying to revive the Free Church interest at great cost to his private fund. By the time of the Second World War Lloyd George was too old and perhaps too jealous of others. He cast himself, if at all, in the part of a British Pétain. The former radical was now the lamenter of past days, resentful that the great National government was composed on the basis of parties, instead of disregarding them. This final protest came appropriately from him. Lloyd George's success marked the last triumph of individual enterprise. His fall showed that the days of individual enterprise were over. Combines ruled, in politics as in everything else. Nowadays even historians work in teams.

The Perfect Secretary

This first appeared as a review of Stephen Roskill's Hankey: Man of Secrets, *Volume 1: 1877–1918 (London, Collins, 1970) in the* Observer, *12 April 1970. Maurice Hankey (1877–1963) remained secretary of the cabinet until his retirement in 1938. Thereafter he was created a baron in 1939, served in Neville Chamberlain's war cabinet 1939–40 and then as a minister outside the war cabinet 1940–42.*

*   *   *

Maurice Hankey has a special place in British history: he invented the modern cabinet almost single-handed. Until his time cabinet meetings were little more than casual conversations between gentlemen. Such easy-going ways were unsuited to a world war, and Hankey brought order out of confusion. He became secretary of everything – the war committee, the war cabinet, the imperial war cabinet, the supreme war council.

Whenever statesmen met, there was Hankey, preparing the agenda, recording the conclusions and seeing that they were carried out. Nor was he content to record. Though without political standing, he put forward his own views on strategy and international affairs. His advice was highly regarded. Asquith wanted him 'to give his attention more closely to the higher policy of the war'. Lloyd George, according to Hankey, twice offered to make him a cabinet minister – first at the Admiralty and then at the War Office. His was a prime influence during the First World War and for long after it.

Hankey received warm tributes at the time and paid more to himself. He kept a full diary and published selections from it in two substantial volumes some years ago. Captain Roskill now gives the passages which Hankey suppressed and supplements them from the letters which Hankey wrote to his wife. This is a unique account of war government from the inside and will be invaluable for historians. It is also rather dull, certainly not as lively as the diary of Tom Jones, Hankey's chief assistant, published last year. Captain Roskill's book is history rather than biography, and Hankey, apart from being a very efficient secretary, appears only as a staid Surrey commuter – which is what he was.

Moreover, like secretaries the world over, Hankey saw the great men of his day at their worst. No chairman understands the business as clearly as the secretary does, and members of committees wrangle interminably before reaching the conclusions which the secretary has formulated at the outset. Hankey had a low opinion of all the statesmen. Curzon was irresolute; Milner was ineffective; Bonar Law was second-rate. Only Lloyd George was too much for him. He was bewildered by the hesitation and bad temper which Lloyd George showed before action. In the end he was also astonished at the ingenuity with which Lloyd George would rise above the difficulties. Lloyd George is the unacknowledged hero of Hankey's diary, and the back-benchers in parliament had raised Lloyd George up. Yet Hankey despised parliament:

Perhaps the greatest advantage the enemy has over us in fighting the war is the absence of parliamentary control – though I admit that in a wider sense democratic government is far the better. The trouble is that the present parliament is ignorant, irresponsible and tiresome. It is a drag instead of a ballast, as it should be. I yield to no one in my admiration of the democratic system, nor in my contempt for the present parliament, a contempt which is shared by almost every leading man I know.

Only one man, it seems, was complete master of the situation. Hankey wrote on 9 June 1917: 'It is only in the last two days ... that I have realized what a vast and encyclopaedic knowledge I have of the events of this cataclysmic war.' On this occasion Hankey did not add his favourite remark: 'Though I say it as shouldn't.'

Hankey had strong and original views on strategy. He consistently opposed the involvement of the British armies in France. Like Lloyd George, though from an earlier date, he was an 'easterner', and the expedition to the Dardanelles was largely of his inspiration. Europe, he believed, was no concern of Great Britain's. This led him to advocate also a negotiated peace, and Captain Roskill joins in the regret that this was not achieved. Here is a good topic for academic argument and research. In practice there was always an insuperable obstacle. The rulers of Germany were set on making her the dominant Power in Europe. British governments, and presumably the British people, were resolved to prevent this. They may have been mistaken and foolish in this resolve, but there was no escaping it, and hence the advocates of the knockout blow were the only realists.

This argument over strategy merged into a wider conflict with the generals, especially with those who claimed to lay down policy. Hankey, who was himself a sort of unofficial CIGS, was naturally on the civilian side. He had the lowest opinion of Kitchener and supported Lloyd George's operations against Robertson. He welcomed Lloyd George's victory in the Maurice debate, but not without misgivings and he provides new evidence implying that Lloyd George equivocated – he had asserted that there were more British troops in France at the beginning of 1918 than at the beginning of 1917 and sustained his case with figures supplied by Maurice's own department of military operations. Until now historians have wrangled solely over a correction which was later sent from Maurice's department and somehow disappeared. But Hankey states that the adjutant-general also supplied figures just before the debate, and these showed that Lloyd George had been wrong. Lloyd George held, with some justification, that these figures were irrelevant to his case against Maurice, and therefore ignored them. Hankey records: 'This knowledge embarrassed me a little.'

This was not Hankey's only grievance against Lloyd George. He complained that Lloyd George did not always initial his minutes. Lloyd George replied: 'Well, I can repudiate them and they will hang you instead of me!' There was no danger of this. Hankey received only praise. When the war ended Hankey contemplated becoming secretary to the projected League of Nations. Lord Esher told him that he must not think of leaving his present job:

If some 'Bolshevik' (he referred to Smillie) should become Prime Minister, as he agreed may well happen, he said that none the less he could not govern without a machine, and would probably be only too glad to use me. In fact, he said that I was the supreme safeguard against extreme Bolshevism.

Bob Smillie as prime minister, with Hankey as his chief adviser, would have provided interesting material for Hankey's diary. No doubt Hankey would have mastered nationalization of the coal mines as easily as he mastered the problems of war.

A Patriot for One Ireland

This essay was first published as a review of Brian Inglis's Roger Casement *(London, Hodder and Stoughton, 1973) in* The Times Literary Supplement, *11 May 1973.*

*   *   *

Roger Casement, an Irishman, was hanged at Pentonville on 3 August 1916, as a traitor to the king of England. Ellis, the hangman, thought him 'the bravest man it fell to my unhappy lot to execute'. For half a century Casement's body lay in Pentonville jail. In 1953 Churchill told de Valera that it must lie there for ever: the law on the subject was 'specific and binding'. Twelve years later Harold Wilson was more generous. On 23 February 1965 Casement's remains were returned to Ireland. They were given a state funeral at Glasnevin. President de Valera had been ill and was told that he should not attend. He insisted that he must. At least, he was told, he must keep his head covered. De Valera replied: 'Casement deserves better than that.' Uncovered, he delivered the funeral oration.

Indeed Casement deserved better than that – better than the treatment he received during his lifetime and better than that accorded to him after his death. Even biographers sympathetic to Casement have been more interested in the authenticity of his private diaries than in his public achievements or, when they dealt with these, have presented him as an isolated, impractical figure – romantic, perhaps, but futile. At long last Brian Inglis has given Casement his due. This splendid book tells the story of a troubled soul who surmounted his troubles and rose to greatness – great as a noble character and greater still as the man who raised high the flag of Irish freedom and unity.

Mr Inglis brings great advantages to his task. Like Casement, he was brought up a Protestant and a Unionist, loyal to the British Crown. Like Casement, he came to put Ireland first and to mean by Ireland the united island. He understands Casement as no previous biographer has done. For Mr Inglis, Casement matters politically. He has looked through Casement's diaries and, though acknowledging them as genuine, emphasizes their unimportance for the study of Casement's career. Connoisseurs of official secrecy will be fascinated to learn that, while the diaries are now available to scholars, the Home Office files on Casement remain closed for 100 years. This concealment is easy to understand. The diaries were used quite irrelevantly to blacken Casement's character and send him to the gallows. We are still not allowed to know which British minister or civil servant hit on this repulsive idea. However, we can make a good guess.

Casement's achievements were unexpected. He did not learn Irish patriotism at his mother's knee. He knew nothing of Wolfe Tone or of his later hero John Mitchel. He was hardly aware that there was an Irish language. He grew up in Ulster, a Protestant and a gentleman, regarding himself as a loyal British subject. He pursued an orthodox career in the British consular service. Here fate first took a hand. When stories reached Europe of the atrocities being committed in the Congo during Leopold's pursuit of Red Rubber, Casement, being the man on the spot, was sent to investigate. Casement discovered, to his own surprise, his hatred of human brutality and oppression. Casement was not alone in the Congo affair. E D Morel conducted the campaign in England and merited an equal tribute of admiration. But it was Casement's patient investigation with its deadly array of facts that made the campaign possible.

Mr Inglis tells the Congo story very much from Casement's side. The work of Leopold in the Congo has been studied in much greater detail by Belgian scholars, sometimes to the point of apology or even justification. Others will be content to echo the words of Cecil Rhodes, no mean judge, who said after meeting Leopold II: 'Satan! I tell you that man is Satan!' At Leopold's orders thousands of natives were tortured or massacred. Vast areas of the country were depopulated. Few worse crimes were witnessed in modern history. It is little excuse that Belgium acquired some grandiose buildings from her share of the profits.

Unlike Morel, Casement was not a good organizer, nor was he at this time a good speaker. He relied more on the Foreign Office than on public opinion. Here he was disappointed. In earlier days British foreign secretaries and the Foreign Office had been themselves champions of human freedom. Palmerston, for instance, wrote more dispatches on the fight against the slave trade than on any other subject and declared that he would leave public life if parliament cut off the money for the anti-slave trade patrols.

In the twentieth century the Foreign Office went sour. In its eyes Casement was a nuisance, a consul who had exceeded his functions. The British ambassador to Brussels wrote off the humanitarians as being 'always prone to sentimentalism about slavery and other local customs to which the native populations were attached'. Casement's report was emasculated and for a time withheld from publication. Lord Lansdowne, the foreign secretary, acquiesced. Better things might have been expected from Sir Edward Grey, his Liberal successor, particularly since he later described the Congo campaign as the greatest since Gladstone's against the Bulgarian atrocities. But, as Mr Inglis points out, Grey in his memoirs devoted only a few sentences to this campaign and many chapters to his devious diplomacy. Fitzmaurice, Grey's undersecretary, remarked: 'It is not our interest to be having a row with Belgium also, if perchance we are having a row with Germany.'

Casement did not have Morel's persistence. Also he needed new employment in his life in order to keep going financially. It was the Congo that first turned Casement against the British government and made him distrust British policy. In a sense the Congo also led Casement to the cause of Irish independence. He returned to Ireland while waiting for a fresh appointment and there realized that the Irish people were in much the same situation as the natives of the Congo – ruled for good or ill by others, not allowed to rule themselves. Casement changed almost overnight from a loyal British subject into a potential rebel. This was more striking than it may seem in the light of later events. We know that Ireland was to become a republic. In the first decade of the present century this view was held only by a few Fenians in the obscure Irish Republican Brotherhood. The home-rulers who dominated Irish politics regarded themselves as British. Their aim was autonomy, not independence. Casement was the first prominent figure who transformed the dreams of the IRB into a practical creed.

Casement said at the end of his life: 'The best thing was the Congo.' He himself contributed little to the final victory, when Leopold II was discredited and forced to transfer the Congo to Belgium. E D Morel received and deserved the principal credit for this. Mr Inglis might have added that the pursuit of Red Rubber with all its horrors became unnecessary once plantation rubber proved practicable and more profitable.

Casement, however, had a further encounter with the evil he had exposed in the Congo. This time the scandal was on the Putomayo in South America. Once more Casement was the man on the spot. Once more he investigated and produced a damning report. The response of British opinion was less emphatic. The same sort of campaign cannot be conducted twice, much as the Armenian massacres of the 1890s failed to provoke the stir that the Bulgarian atrocities had done twenty years earlier. E D Morel was now denouncing Grey's foreign policies. The British and American governments, though endorsing Casement's reports, were only concerned to hush up the scandal. Casement himself left South America and the British consular service.

The few years before the First World War were decisive for Casement's historical fame and for his own fate. Though knighted in 1911, he had ceased to regard himself as a British subject and had become an unequivocal Irish nationalist. He learnt to speak on the public platform. He counted as a political figure. Casement took up the almost unnoticed movement of Sinn Fein and transformed it into a practical cause. Ireland, he preached, should not seek concessions from Great Britain. She should declare her independence and act on it. Like Arthur Griffith, he pointed to the example of Hungary, with the curious personal link that his own father had saved Kossuth when threatened with extradition from Turkey.

Casement added a further point, not made by any other Irish leader. Irish independence, he believed, should be won in cooperation with Ulster, not against her. He even held that Ulster should lead the movement as she had done in previous centuries. Ulster's claim not to be incorporated in a home-rule Ireland was exactly the same as Ireland's claim not to be incorporated in the United Kingdom. Casement often declared that he and Carson were fighting for the same cause and should appear on the same platform. It was English politicians, such as F E Smith, exploiting Ireland's difficulties for their own party advantage, whom he wanted to keep out.

Ulster provided a more practical analogy. If Ulster were permitted to buy arms in Germany and to seek German support, as the Unionists did, Ireland was entitled to do the same. As an independent country, Ireland should follow an independent policy. British maritime supremacy was no concern of hers, and the British must learn to live with a neutral Ireland. Casement's policy had its forerunners in the 'Wild Geese' and later the Irish republicans who had sought French aid for Ireland's liberation.

All the same, he made a disastrous error. He thought that the Germans would take up the Irish cause for idealistic reasons, just as Masaryk counted on the support of British idealists for the liberation of the Czechs. There were enough British idealists to make Masaryk's line respectable and not a mere act of treason. There were no such idealists in Germany. When war broke out, Casement went to Germany and tried to recruit an Irish legion. The Germans, who preferred the British Empire to a free Ireland, regarded him as a nuisance. Casement became disillusioned, embittered. When reports reached him of a projected rising in Ireland, he travelled to Ireland in a German submarine in order to give warning that there would be no German aid and that, without it, a rising could not succeed.

This was the supreme irony of Casement's career. He was arrested and condemned to death for seeking to provoke rebellion when in fact he had come in order to ensure that the rising did not take place. Casement's trial makes sorry reading. He, an Irishman, was tried by an English Lord Chief Justice and an English jury. How, he asked the jury, would they like it if they had attempted a rising in England and had then been shipped off to Dublin for trial?

Casement wished to conduct his own case and simply to deny the authority over him of an English court. He was overruled. His counsel, Serjeant Sullivan, fought the case on a technicality, based on a statute of Edward III's reign. Naturally he lost. At one moment Sullivan ventured to hint that Casement had only done what F E Smith, the prosecuting attorney-general, had done before him. When pulled up by Reading, the Lord Chief Justice – pilloried by Kipling as Gehazi – Sullivan broke down and withdrew from the case.

Casement was allowed to speak only after the jury had found him guilty. Mr Inglis does the great service of printing Casement's speech in full. It merits Wilfrid Blunt's verdict: 'the finest document in patriotic literature. Finer than anything in Plutarch or elsewhere in Pagan literature.' It moved Blunt to 'anger and delight that anything so perfect should have come from the mouth of a man of our time condemned to death'. Years later, Nehru described the profound impression that the 'extraordinarily moving and eloquent' statement made on him: 'It seemed to point out exactly how a subject nation should feel.'

Casement was condemned to death. There was an outcry in the United States, though President Wilson, himself of Ulster stock, passed by on the other side. It seemed that the trial would win neutral sympathies for Casement instead of discrediting him. Now was the time to produce the 'black diaries' – private jottings of previous years which showed beyond reasonable doubt that Casement was a practising homosexual. The idea of discrediting Casement by means of the diaries seems to have originated with Ernley Blackwell, legal adviser to the Home Office. It was taken up by many others. Herbert Samuel, then home secretary, wrote: 'Had Casement not been a man of atrocious moral character, the situation would have been even more difficult.' Asquith asked Page, the American ambassador, whether he had heard about the diary. Page replied that he had seen it and had been given photographed copies of some of it. Asquith said: 'Excellent, and you need not be particular about keeping it to yourself.'

What was the relevance of the diaries even if they were genuine? None. No one had ever suspected Casement of homosexuality, and it never affected his policy or public conduct. For that matter, there were two practising homosexuals in the cabinet which determined to blacken Casement. One of them later committed suicide: the other went into exile in order to escape prosecution. Asquith, however, passed no word of condemnation on either of them. Was it worse to run after boys than to develop senile passions for young girls and to be helpless with drink on the Treasury bench? Such was the state of Asquith, and it is held not to derogate from his conduct of affairs when prime minister. The loathsome story has no interest except as illustrating the desperate measures that an imperial government will resort to when cornered.

Casement's death had quite other significance. It created the importance of Sinn Fein. The Easter Rising had been conducted by a few members of the IRB, not by Sinn Fein. Thanks to Casement, Sinn Fein got the credit for it. The independence of Ireland triumphed when Casement was hanged. He represented a second cause. He said in his last speech:

We aimed at winning the Ulster Volunteers to the cause of a United Ireland. We aimed at uniting all Irishmen in a natural and national bond of cohesion based on mutual self-respect. Our hope was a natural one and, if left to ourselves, not hard to accomplish. If external forces of destruction would but leave us alone we were sure that Nature must bring us together.

Here is Casement's message for the present day. There is no Irish problem beyond solution. The problem that has racked Ireland for centuries is the British presence in Ireland. That problem can be solved only by British withdrawal.

Distressful Country

This essay first appeared as a review of Whitehall Diary, Volume III: Ireland 1918–1925 *by Thomas Jones, edited by Keith Middlemas (Oxford, Clarendon Press, 1971) in the* Observer, *17 October 1971. Thomas Jones (1870–1955) was privy to many government secrets as assistant secretary (then deputy secretary) of the cabinet between 1916 and 1930. He was most influential during Lloyd George's premiership (1916–22). He had come to Lloyd George's notice as secretary of the National Health Insurance Commission for Wales (1912–16) and was one of Lloyd George's Welsh appointees when he became premier. Jones was a radical, having been a member of the Independent Labour Party and Fabian Society as a young man. He who had begun as an academic, being professor of economics at Queen's University, Belfast (1909–10), and ended his career as president of the University College of Wales, Aberystwyth (1945–54).*

Alan Taylor warmly praised Jones's Whitehall diaries as a source. He wrote of the first volume, published in 1969: 'No more important source on politics and politicians in the twentieth century has been published for many years.'

*　　*　　*

Tom Jones was deputy secretary to the cabinet from 1916 to 1930. He kept a diary throughout his official career, and two previous volumes have published lavish extracts from it interspersed with letters. This final instalment is the most sensational volume of the three. Diary is a misnomer for it. T J, as he was always called, took every cabinet on Irish affairs and attended many less formal meetings of cabinet ministers. The cabinet minutes which he drafted can be seen in the Public Record Office. These minutes tell only the conclusions reached. T J himself kept detailed notes, and it is these which are now published.

T J also recorded the meetings between British and Irish negotiators which produced the treaty of 1921. The reader feels that he is actually sitting in at cabinet meetings and intimate negotiations. No such revelations have been made before, and it is pretty certain that none such will be made again. T J trampled on the Official Secrets Act. Thanks to his indiscretion, Lloyd George's Irish policy can be followed in more detail than any other episode in British history.

The revelations are not only sensational historically. They are a sensation for today. For once study of the past really helps to explain the present. The story displays, with ghastly relevance, the origins of partition and of the Irish Republic. It underlines the inescapable involvement of the British government. In 1921 Lloyd George seemed to have found a solution for the Irish question. Now new troubles are upon us, and Lloyd George's solution has become merely another epoch in Ireland's distressful history. The book is not easy to read. Indeed if it were not so sensational, it would be boring. This is very much the raw material of history – rambling discussions, half-formed sentences, questions posed and never answered. The reader must work hard to grasp the broad pattern, despite welcome aid from the editor.

One thing stands out. There was a total lack of sympathy or understanding for Ireland on the part of British ministers. In their eyes Ireland was a nuisance, not a nation. Bonar Law had come to the conclusion 'that the Irish were an inferior race'. Lloyd George said: 'There is a hard side to the Irish nature. They are greedy beyond any other part of the United Kingdom.' He growled that, if Ireland received dominion status, she would escape her share of the costs of the war. A free Ireland might levy tariffs on British goods: 'That means war. We'd have to reconquer Ireland.' The Irish who were fighting for the freedom of their country were branded as 'murderers'. Yet the British government had evidence, which they refused to publish, that their own Black and Tans were murderers on a worse scale. Ignorance strengthened prejudice. For a long time Lloyd George believed that de Valera, the talker, was a moderate, and Collins, the 'gunman', an extremist.

Most of Lloyd George's cabinet went along with him. H A L Fisher was an honourable exception. He protested: 'The present situation is degrading to the moral life of the whole nation.' T J secretly supported Irish nationalism. He manoeuvred between the two sides and was the principal architect of the final settlement. The truce and the negotiations which followed it sprang on the British side from war-weariness, not from enlightenment. Macready, the general commanding in Ireland, asked: 'Does the cabinet realize what is involved? Will they go through with it? Will they begin to howl when they hear of our shooting 100 men in one week?' Negotiations were the only alternative.

Partition was the essential preliminary to negotiation. This was the instrument with which Lloyd George placated his Unionist supporters and colleagues. Once Northern Ireland received home rule, the way was clear for concession to the rest of Ireland. Lloyd George had another use for partition. Having established it in order to please the Unionists, he then hinted that he would end it in order to please the Sinn Feiners. Ending partition was the bait which persuaded Griffith and Collins to accept dominion status.

It would be wrong to say that Lloyd George was being dishonest. He was merely being adroit. The Irish question was one problem; the Ulster question was another. Lloyd George rolled them together and hoped to settle both at once. Convinced of Irish 'meanness', he really believed that the Northern Irish would abandon their separate position when they discovered that they were paying higher taxes than they would do in a reunited Ireland. When Craig, the prime minister of Northern Ireland, was unmoved by this argument, Lloyd George hit on another, and as it proved successful, device for winning over the Sinn Feiners. He offered a commission to redraw the boundary between the North and the Free State. Griffith and Collins believed that Northern Ireland would lose so much territory as to become unworkable. Lloyd George had no idea what the Boundary Commission would produce. It was enough for him that it did the trick. The agreement for a treaty between Great Britain and Ireland was signed in the early hours of 6 December 1921.

This summary makes the negotiations sound simple. T J's account must be read in full in order to recapture the confusions and misunderstandings which took place. Of all the negotiators Birkenhead comes out best: clear-headed, logical, politically courageous. Churchill was emotionally for the Irish at one moment, emotionally against them at the next. Lloyd George used Churchill and then denounced him: 'No Churchill was ever loyal. Churchill is fancying himself as a leader of a Tory revolt.'

T J goes on to tell the sequel. The civil war in Ireland destroyed any attraction the Free State might have had for Northern Ireland. The Boundary Commission was terminated at the request of both parties. Partition ceased to be an expedient and became a permanency. Lloyd George's economic calculation, though sincerely meant, proved wrong: Northern Ireland was better off with Great Britain than with the Free State. This remains an obstacle to the present day.

The greater obstacle is made clear in T J's account. British statesmen regarded Ireland as a domestic problem. None of them appreciated that Ireland was a nation. Economic considerations counted; strategic considerations counted; the feelings of the Conservative Party counted most of all. The overriding consideration of Irish freedom came at the end of the list.

Saving Lloyd George's Soul

This essay first appeared as a review of The Political Diaries of C P Scott
1911–1928, *edited by Trevor Wilson (London, Collins, 1970) in the* Observer,
14 June 1970.

*　　*　　*

During the 1920s one leader-writer on the *Manchester Guardian* would
ask another: Who is writing the long leader tonight? Answer: The old
man (C P Scott, the editor). And the subject? Saving Lloyd George's
soul again. Here is the principal theme of the diaries which Scott kept
between 1911 and 1928.

Scott was among the greatest of radical journalists. He edited the
Manchester Guardian from 1870 almost until his death in 1932. He
opposed the Boer War – 'the best thing the *Manchester Guardian* has
done in my time'. He was himself a radical MP from 1895 to 1905.
Lloyd George was then his close associate, and thereafter, although he
often differed from him, he did not waver in his belief that Lloyd
George was the most dynamic radical force in British politics.

There has been a rich flow of diaries on the politics of this period
recently – first Tom Jones's and then Hankey's. Both these men,
though outstanding, were civil servants and therefore in a sense
observers. Scott was himself a participant, seeking to influence policy
and sometimes to make it. The notes which he made were for his own
immediate guidance, not for the enlightenment of posterity. Of course
there are striking stories and some surprises, such as Lord Fisher
proposing Redmond in 1916 as British prime minister or Churchill in
1925 advising the Poles to make an alliance with Germany against
Russia. But Lloyd George is the central figure, and this book does
much to explain his magical fascination even for the clear-headed.

The diaries start with the Agadir crisis of 1911. Lloyd George
swung on an anti-German course, in order to prevent 'the formation
of a great naval base right across our trade route'. Asquith said in
contrast: 'If you ask me whether, to put it brutally, it is worth our
while to go to war about Agadir, I should say it is not.' Asquith
wanted Tangier in a division of spoils – 'one of the few desirable spots
which we do not already possess'. In August 1914 Lloyd George did

not care about the balance of power, or so he said. He told Scott he 'would have resigned rather than consent to our going to war if Germany would have agreed not to violate Belgian territory or if even so she would have agreed only to pass over the small projecting piece between Luxembourg and France'. Though Lloyd George flung himself into the war, he remained almost indifferent about Europe and told Scott in March 1915: 'It was not a question of "crushing" Germany but of defeating her. Personally he would rather crush Turkey than Germany' – a remark which illuminates his post-war policy.

Scott backed Lloyd George as the only man who could win the war. Asquith came in for Scott's sharp condemnation: 'Really Asquith gets worse as he gets older and it is time he were dead and buried politically.' In January 1916 Scott recorded an interview with Asquith: 'He struck me as anxious and nervously excited and he walked rapidly round about the room nearly all the time that I was with him, like a trapped animal. To me he seemed a beaten man.' Scott often urged Lloyd George to resign. Lloyd George threatened and then withdrew.

Even in December 1916, so Lloyd George told Scott, 'There was not the least intention of displacing Asquith and that this took place was entirely due to his having been persuaded to go back on the agreement he had made' – a statement confirmed from other sources. Lloyd George also made a good remark about Asquith's disgruntled Liberal followers: 'Their view of a government is as a sort of family concern in which they hold the shares and McKenna is General Manager.'

Scott continued to support Lloyd George until the war ended, though often with reservations. After the armistice Scott told President Wilson: 'I had good hopes of Lloyd George . . . but he was extremely elusive and in dealing with him you had to keep an extremely bright outlook.' The peace negotiations restored Scott's faith. He wrote of Lloyd George: 'He is showing more of the real quality of statesmanship than I ever thought him capable of. Liberals ought to back him steadily and quietly, so as not to rouse the Jingoes.' Disillusionment followed. Smuts stirred up Scott against the peace treaty. He wrote: 'I view it as a thoroughly bad peace – impolitic and impracticable in the case of Germany, absolutely ludicrous in the case of German Austria.' Smuts did not refer to German South West Africa.

Ireland completed the estrangement. Early in 1920 Lloyd George said to Scott: 'Don't desert me. Come and see me sometimes and correct my faults . . . Or help my better self.' Scott could see no better self during the Irish atrocities committed at Lloyd George's orders. He told Lloyd George in 1921 'that the things done under his authority were on the whole worse than those done in 1798 and that for a parallel it would be probably necessary to go back to Cromwell. He disputed that, but did not seem to mind.'

A few months later Lloyd George concluded the Irish Treaty. He said to Scott: 'We have succeeded at last in the task we have both worked at for more than thirty years.' From that moment, Scott and Lloyd George drew together once more. Scott's heart was set on a radical coalition – left-wing Liberal and moderate Labour united under Lloyd George's leadership. It was dismissed as an impossible aim. Ironically it is more or less what we have ended up with. Socialism is forgotten. We have a Whig chancellor of the exchequer, a Liberal home secretary, and a prime minister who has Lloyd George's ingenuity without his inspiration.

Trevor Wilson has done a fine job in editing these diary entries. He provides scholarly guidance without thrusting himself upon the reader. He seems, however, a little puzzled that Scott, though an idealist, was also shrewd. He therefore turned for enlightenment to Malcolm Muggeridge, who furnished him with the splendid Scott sentence: 'Truth like everything else must be economized.' This sentence which Malcolm has been hawking round for thirty years, was, I fear, a joke at Malcolm's expense. In any case it was a very sensible remark. Why should a man be an imbecile merely because he has high beliefs? Many saints have been smart operators, and C P Scott was numbered in the holy company.

Seebohm Rowntree: The Workers' Friend

This essay first appeared in the Observer, *3 September 1961, as a review of Asa Briggs's* Social Thought and Social Action: A Study of the work of Seebohm Rowntree, 1871–1954 *(London, Longmans, 1961). Alan Taylor was at Bootham between 1919 and 1924. He wrote in his autobiography of Rowntree's addresses to the boys: 'His theme was always the beneficent social reforms that Lloyd George was promoting. To me, regarding Lloyd George at that time as the Devil incarnate, this was bewildering.'*

* * *

Forty years ago, as a boy at Bootham, I knew more than most people about two subjects. One, Gothic architecture, was my own enterprise. The other was inescapable. It was Seebohm Rowntree. A month rarely passed without an address from him or one of his associates: The Problem of Poverty; Industrial Democracy; The Evils of Gambling; Welfare, not Wealth. England, we were taught, should become one jolly cocoa works. Bernard Shaw foretold this, more cynically, in *The Apple Cart.*

Seebohm Rowntree ranks high among the shapers of our contemporary society. He did not aspire to be a political leader. He exercised great influence behind the scenes in a variety of ways. He was an important, though dull, writer. His study of poverty in York, first published in 1901, was a pioneer work; all modern approaches to the subject stem from it. He was an active industrialist, for many years head of the Rowntree Cocoa Works. There he tried out his ideas, both in works management and in housing; then he preached from his own practice to conferences of managers and businessmen.

He also gave invaluable advice to Lloyd George. He helped to devise Lloyd George's land programme before the First World War. Lloyd George made him director of the Welfare Department at the Ministry of Munitions; there Rowntree brought into existence, among other things, factory canteens. Later, Rowntree was the principal inspirer of the Liberal programme of 1929, 'We Can Conquer Unemployment'. Though this did not win the election for the Liberals, it has been the unacknowledged source for much Labour and even Conservative

policy. In the 1930s Rowntree and Astor studied agriculture afresh
with lasting results. There is much else to record, as for instance
Rowntree's attempt to mediate during the coal lock-out of 1926,
which was almost successful. He carried his teaching to America; and
regarded the United States as his second home. Altogether it is a
formidable record.

Rowntree was not interested in personal fame. This biography by
Professor Briggs suits him well. It is a sound utility product, plodding
steadily forward without literary adornment and built to last. Though
it is unlikely to rank as a Book of the Year, it will be on the shelves of
students in ten years' time, which is more than can be said for most
Books of the Year. The subject has, of course, more than biographical
interest. As Professor Briggs points out, the Welfare State has been
established, in one form or another, in every advanced industrial
country. But often it has come simply as the result of working-class
pressure.

In England the enlightened middle class itself took the lead. The
workers received as a gift what elsewhere they had to fight for. The
class struggle has become an uneasy memory or not even that. The
workers have become partners in industry – at least that is what they
are told by their leaders and what they perhaps believe. Timely
concession was no doubt a British tradition. Even more important
than this was the moral approach, especially among Nonconformist
businessmen; and here, as on earlier occasions, the Society of Friends
gave the lead.

Professor Briggs would have made Rowntree's significance clearer if
he had explored the transformation which came over the Society
early in the twentieth century – a transformation largely directed by
Seebohm's brother. The Quakers moved away from the quietism
which they had practised for more than 200 years – a quietism which
had led them, for instance, to disapprove of John Bright – and went
out into the world. Though the Society did not much increase its
membership, it enormously increased its influence. Seebohm Rowntree
was a worldly Quaker of the new type.

Probably he was a bit too worldly even by the new standards. It
was fitting for Quakers to be Liberals or even to support the Labour
Party. Seebohm Rowntree was the only prominent Quaker to stick to
Lloyd George, even during his worst coalition period. Yet there was
good reason for this: Lloyd George was the one man who got things

done, and Rowntree was more interested in results than in the high principles of his associates. Rowntree had something else in common with Lloyd George: he thought he knew better than anyone else.

There is a comic undertone in the story of his mediation in the coal dispute of 1926, when he was bitterly resentful at the intrusion of other mediators, particularly the Churches' Committee, and blamed them for his failure. He wrote: 'I find it difficult to control my language when I think of those blank! blank! blank! Bishops, and the harm they have done.' Again he rarely hinted that the Cadburys were doing at Bournville everything which he did at York, and Professor Briggs, too, does not explore this subject.

But perhaps cocoa breathed good industrial relations of itself. There was in Rowntree an element of condescension as well as of goodwill and good works. 'I have always felt great sympathy with working people', not, however, to the extent of becoming one of them. Industrial partnership meant that they lived in model working-class houses, while he spent his last years in a wing of Hughenden, which he leased from the National Trust. Listening to his exhortations in Meeting those long years ago, I used to say to myself: 'This man is out to kill socialism.' So he was. The maddening thing is that he has succeeded.

Trotsky

These essays were first published as reviews of the volumes of Isaac Deutscher's life of Trotsky – The Prophet Armed: Trotsky 1879–1921, The Prophet Unarmed: Trotsky 1921–1929 *and* The Prophet Outcast: Trotsky 1929–40 (*Oxford, Clarendon Press, 1954, 1959 and 1963*) *– in the* New Statesman and Nation, *20 February 1954, the* New Statesman, *26 September 1959 and the* Observer, *27 October 1963.*

* * *

The Prophet Armed

One early morning, in October 1902, Mr and Mrs 'Richter' were still abed in their lodgings near King's Cross. There was a violet knocking at the door. Mrs Richter, opening it, called out: ' "The Pen" has arrived!' In this way Trotsky, 'the young eagle', burst – under his first pseudonym – into Lenin's life. The meeting was a symbol of their future. Lenin was orderly, quiet in speech and habit, hardly to be distinguished from his neighbours. Trotsky rode contemptuously over the conventions, knocking violently at doors and expecting them to open at the impact of his genius. He was at a loss when there was no door to force open. Lenin was to end as a sacred mummy, in the silence of death still dominating the lives of two hundred million people. Trotsky was to be murdered far from Europe and – what would seem worse to him – his very name has been erased from the history books. Mention Bronstein, and men think you are referring to a chess player. The greatest writer and perhaps the greatest leader that revolution ever produced is forgotten; and the younger generation of readers will puzzle why a book has been devoted to him.

Mr Deutscher has done a striking work of rehabilitation. *The Prophet Armed* is the story of Trotsky's triumph. It carries him through the victory of the revolution and the civil war to his highest moment, when he seemed the predestined successor of Lenin. A further volume will tell the story of his fall and of his unquenchable resistance until he was rubbed out by an ice-pick. Mr Deutscher has mastered all the printed sources and has been the first to use extensively the Trotsky archives now at Harvard. Yet it may be questioned whether he is the right man for the subject. We can perhaps get over his ponderous style, suitable enough when he is pontificating on Bolshevism in the columns of the Astor press. But, like all Marxists – even the lapsed ones – he wants always to discover profound historical forces where there was only the will of men. He writes of the early Bolsheviks: 'Lenin's party had its roots deep in Russian soil'; this of some two or three thousand men, bewitched by an academic ideal. In 1917 'the whole dynamic of Russian history was impelling Lenin and Trotsky, their party, and their country towards the revolution'; when it would be truer to say that these two wrenched 'history' (whatever that may mean) violently from its course. In the most preposterous passage of all he describes the Russian working class of 1917 (who, poor chaps, had no idea what was happening to them) as

one of history's wonders. Small in numbers, young, inexperienced, uneducated, it was rich in political passion, generosity, idealism, and rare heroic qualities . . . With its semi-illiterate thoughts it embraced the idea of the republic of the philosophers.

The reader must put up with this hocus-pocus for the sake of the gigantic individual who overshadows it.

Trotsky himself used to claim that history was on his side. When he came to the Congress of Soviets fresh from the conquest of power, he called to the protesting Mensheviks: 'You have played out your role. Go where you belong: to the dustheap of history.' Yet no man ever chose his role in greater isolation or followed a course of more determined individualism. Trotsky carried to its peak the era of individual greatness which had begun with the French Revolution. His was a more powerful voice than Danton's, self-educated, self-made, self-advised. One could say of him as of Napoleon: 'his presence on the battlefield was worth ten divisions'. It is ironic that Trotsky, the greatest of revolutionary socialists, should have owed his success to liberal enterprise and capitalist freedom. The age of the individual was finished when men were eclipsed by machines – and nowhere more decisively than by the machine of the great political party. In the First World War genius still counted. Lloyd George, Clemenceau, Trotsky, were each in their separate ways the saviours of their countries. It is no accident that the careers of all three ended in barren failure when the war was over. The leaders of the Second World War needed bureaucracies and party organizations. Even

Winston Churchill had to become leader of the Conservative Party; and only backward countries, Yugoslavia or France, could produce heroes – a Tito or a de Gaulle. Trotsky came just in time. Now he could never rise from provincial obscurity.

Trotsky had no background of Marxist training or of party experience. Mr Deutscher writes: 'He diligently studied Marxism, which in this its golden age gave the adept a solid mental equipment.' In reality Trotsky learnt from Marxism only that capitalism was doomed – a fact which he knew instinctively already. His own writings that have survived never dealt with economic developments; they were concerned always with political strategy, owing more to Clausewitz than to Marx. He never adapted himself to the needs of practical work in a party. When he first came to London in 1902 it was as a detached individual; and he stood outside the conflict between Bolshevik and Menshevik. Though himself a revolutionary, he opposed Lenin's exclusiveness; and always hoped to close the breach between the two socialist currents. Even after the revolution of 1905, when his actions had outstripped Bolshevik theory, he kept up a tolerant association with the Mensheviks; and the outbreak of the First World War found him more solitary than ever. He joined the Bolshevik Party only in the summer of 1917, some two months before he was to carry it to supreme power. The exact date is unknown; and the possession of a party card meant nothing to him. His position in the world did not depend on the accuracy of a filing-cabinet.

In the slovenly decay of imperial Russia Trotsky's voice could fill a continent. When the revolution of 1905 broke out, he was an unknown youth of twenty-five. At St Petersburg, knowing nobody, representing nobody, he forced himself on to the Soviet; and before it ended he was its dominating figure. At the final meeting he even ruled out of order the police officer who had come to arrest the members: 'Please do not interfere with the speaker. If you wish to take the floor, you must give your name.' In those days words were more powerful than armies. It was the same on a more gigantic scale in 1917. The Bolsheviks did not carry Trotsky to power; he carried them. Lenin made the party resolve on insurrection, but he was still in hiding when it broke out and at first could not believe in its success. The seizure of power in October was Trotsky's work; and Lenin acknowledged this immediately afterwards, with supreme generosity, when he proposed that Trotsky be put at the head of the new revolutionary government.

One may even ask – what did Lenin and the Bolsheviks do during the civil war? They held on clumsily to the reins of civil power in Moscow. It was Trotsky who created the armies; chose the officers; determined the strategy; and inspired the soldiers. Every interference by the Soviet government was a mistake; and the greatest mistake was the campaign against Poland, which Trotsky opposed. The achievement was not only one of organization. It was the impact of a fiery personality, the sparks from which flew round the world.

The man of action in Trotsky was always second to the man of words, even at the greatest moments of decision. He was never happy over a victory until he had written about it; and in later years literary triumph seemed almost to atone with him for the bitterness of defeat. Bernard Shaw said that, as a political pamphleteer, he 'surpassed Junius and Burke'; what is even more to the point, he is the only Marxist who has possessed literary genius. Time and again the force of this genius posed problems that were still unperceived by others and even pointed to solutions that were unwelcome to Trotsky himself. Immediately after the revolution of 1905, when he was still in prison, he discovered the central dilemma which a victorious Russian Revolution would face and which indeed the Soviet Union still faces. How was revolutionary Russia to maintain itself in a hostile world? Backwardness made revolution easy, but survival difficult. Trotsky gave already the answer to which he adhered all his life: permanent revolution. The Russian Revolution must touch off revolutions elsewhere. 'The working class of Russia will become the initiator of the liquidation of capitalism on a global scale.' It was in this belief that Trotsky led the revolution of 1917, defied the German Empire at Brest-Litovsk, and composed the most ringing phrases in the foundation manifesto of the Communist International. But what if the more advanced proletariat failed to respond? It was useless to maintain for long Trotsky's earliest answer: 'luckily for mankind, this is impossible'.

The impossible is what men get from events – and often at its most unwelcome. Trotsky foresaw even in 1905 the conflict that would follow between workers and peasants, if they were ever cooped up together in isolation. Once more he fell back on pious hope. The working class would remain by its very nature enlightened, progressive, tolerant. Somehow 'proletarian dictatorship' would escape the evils which other forms of dictatorship had always produced. Did

Trotsky ever believe this? It seems unlikely. In the early days of doctrinal dispute he always preached toleration, despite his own sharp and wounding phrases. Lenin had an easier time of it. Both men understood the virtue of intellectual freedom. But for Lenin it was one of the many bourgeois virtues that he was prepared to discard – confident that communism would resurrect it in a higher form. In just the same way he was ready to write off the greatest artistic achievements of the past. The very wonder of them was an embarrassment in the present. Trotsky could never bring himself to renounce European civilization. He recognized Russia's backwardness and resented being associated with it – an attitude possible for a Jew, but repugnant even to Lenin. As the net of intolerance drew tighter, as the European revolutions failed and the Russian masses became increasingly discontented, Trotsky grew more explosive.

His response was characteristic. At one bound he reached totalitarianism in its most ruthless form. His own gifts betrayed him. A dictator lurks in every forceful writer. Power over words leads easily to a longing for power over men. Trotsky could never resist a challenge. He wrote *The Defence of Terrorism* at the height of his labours during the civil war; and he justified the conquest of Georgia against the social semocrats of western Europe, though he had himself opposed it. Now in 1921 he preached the militarization of labour and permanent dictatorship of the Communist Party. Lenin restrained him. But the weapons which Trotsky forged then were soon to be turned against him by Stalin. He was to purge his betrayal of freedom by many years of resistance and exile. The glories of his revolutionary triumph pale before the nobility of his later defeats. The spirit of man was irrepressible in him. Colonel Robins, the American Red Cross representative at Petrograd, pronounced history's verdict: 'A four-kind son-of-a-bitch, but the greatest Jew since Jesus Christ.'

Without Lenin

In 1921 Trotsky was second only to Lenin in Soviet Russia. As commissar for war, he had just brought the civil war to a victorious conclusion; he was incomparably the greatest orator and most brilliant writer in the Communist Party; the two names 'Lenin and Trotsky' were synonymous throughout the world with the Bolshevik Revolution. Three years later Lenin was dead. Five years after that, Trotsky left Russia for ever, a disregarded and helpless exile, surviving in Soviet eyes only as a counter-revolutionary conspirator. This is as dramatic a story as any in history; and Mr Deutscher has made the most of it. Drawing on the Trotsky archives at Harvard, he has told the story more accurately and with fuller detail than ever before. His book is compulsory reading for anyone interested in the history of Soviet Russia and of international communism. It will be highly and deservedly praised. It has some grave faults. Like all commentators on Soviet Russia, Mr Deutscher goes in for a great deal of verbiage to cover up the shortage of solid information. Much of the book is written from 'inner consciousness', not from the facts. Stalin, in particular, has intentions attributed to him which make sense, but do not rest on solid evidence. More than this, there is a deep equivocation in Mr Deutscher's approach. Emotionally, one might say, he wants Trotsky to win; and he cannot help hinting that Trotsky will win posthumously at some time in the future. Yet, when he looks objectively at the circumstances of the 1920s, he also cannot help admitting that Trotsky's ideas were impossibly romantic. The tone of the book is constantly changing gear; and the reader, like Mr Deutscher, ends by being bewildered. Ought he to let his emotions run away with him and admire Trotsky's heroic stand? Or ought he to sympathize with puzzle-headed Stalin, doing his best for the revolution in difficult circumstances?

Towards the end of the book Mr Deutscher quotes a remark by Krupskaya which, he says, she probably learnt from Lenin: Trotsky was inclined to underrate the apathy of the masses. This sentence tells the whole story. Trotsky wanted the Russian people, or if not the people at any rate the Communist Party, to go on living at the fever-heat of the first revolutionary years. But the fever was over. Men wanted a quiet life. They were no longer moved by great speeches, no longer fired by appeals to revolutionary idealism. Trotsky early denounced the control which the bureaucracy had established over the party. What he never recognized was that the bureaucracy represented the general will. Time and again Trotsky tried to fire party meetings; and when this failed be tried to fire the masses by the old method of speeches at the street corners. There was no response, only an embarrassed and uneasy silence. Besides, what did Trotsky want? He demanded democracy within the party, an endless freedom of discussion dominated by his own fiery words; yet he was as firm as any of his antagonists that there must be no democracy outside the party. As Mr Deutscher says, the Bolshevik Party had to become monolithic if it was to survive; yet by becoming monolithic it ceased to be Bolshevik – at any rate in Trotsky's sense. Mr Deutscher cannot bring himself to admit that Lenin, despite a deathbed repentance, created the monolithic party and that Stalin fulfilled Lenin's testament except, of course, in one personal particular.

Trotsky could never merge himself in the party and lead it from inside. He triumphed during his historic partnership with Lenin. On his own, he became more and more the assertive unique individual, watching his increasing isolation with a sardonic pleasure. The passionate disputes described in this book were really marginal to the decisions taken in these years. Here Trotsky seems at the centre; but if one compares the story as told by Mr Carr in his most recent volumes, it appears that he contributed little to the actual working-out of policy. Lenin himself accepted Trotsky as a true Bolshevik. The others did not. For them he was always an outsider who had come late to the party without ever being absorbed in it. Sometimes they combined against him; sometimes they sought to use him. They never accepted him, nor he them. Trotsky carried to excess the weakness of the intellectual in politics. He was ruthless in stating principles; he was soft and indifferent in questions of personality. Mr Deutscher shows how time and again Trotsky was in sight of victory; he always let the chance slip once his theoretical correctness was admitted. In 1923, for instance, assisted by promptings from Lenin's sickbed, he humiliated Stalin; then – much to Lenin's annoyance – casually left Stalin in office. At the end of 1929 he was actually preparing to support Stalin's new course, the second revolution. Here is a paradox indeed: it was the threat of support, not of opposition, which made Stalin send Trotsky into exile. On the other hand, Trotsky could never resist speaking his mind. He insisted quite correctly that, given the failure of revolution elsewhere, there must be 'primitive socialist accumulation' in Russia: the peasants and even the industrial workers must be ruthlessly exploited in order to build up heavy industry. This is the course which Stalin inaugurated in 1929 and which Soviet Russia has followed to the present day. But Stalin and his successors never explained clearly what they were doing, and perhaps did not even realize it themselves. Trotsky understood ideas; he did not understand men. He was a heroic and noble character; his mind brilliantly penetrating even when he was wrong. Yet he made no mark on Soviet history from the moment that Lenin's hand was withdrawn. The epic time was over; and Stalin triumphed over Trotsky as Baldwin triumphed over Lloyd George.

The Old Pretender

The writings of Henry James, according to Philip Guedalla, can be divided into three parts: James I, James II and James the Old Pretender. The life of Trotsky fell into three similar periods, and Mr Deutscher has rightly devoted a volume to each.

The first Trotsky was a triumphant leader: principal director of the Bolshevik Revolution in November 1917, maker of the Red Army, victor in the civil wars, co-founder with Lenin of the Third International, and author of its original manifesto. Trotsky II was the centre of opposition in Russia, advocate of world revolution, yet fumbling at the same time towards revolutionary construction within Russia.

In 1929 Trotsky was expelled from Russia, and therewith from history. As he put it himself, 'my past now cuts me off from chances of action'. He was virtually interned, first in Turkey, then in France and Norway; and though finally finding a home with more freedom in Mexico, he could be only a commentator on events, not a maker of them. He had no contacts inside Russia and few followers in Europe. What he said and did, though still full of interest, mattered to no one except to Trotsky himself; and the arguments among the handful of Trotskyites were of no more significance than the personal wrangles at any other exiled court.

Though only in his fifties, he felt old; anticipated an early death, was known by his intimates as the Old Man, and quoted Lenin: 'the worst vice is to be more than fifty-five years old'. He had outlived his age. When he was assassinated on 20 August 1940, men were surprised to learn that he had not died many years before.

This is a sad story in a minor key. Mr Deutscher tells it with sympathy and understanding. He tells it, too, with a full command of sources. At the direction of Trotsky's widow, he has been allowed to use the secret Trotsky archives at Harvard, which were originally to remain closed until 1980. We can thus follow every detail of Trotsky's harassed life: his discouragements and renewed vitality, his family affections, and the relations with his followers.

As a personal portrait of a great man this is a very good and moving book. Unlike Lenin, Trotsky could not merge himself in the revolution. He was deeply human. He loved his wife, and she sustained him ungrudgingly. His last dying act was to return her kiss, an appropriately romantic end. Trotsky had also strong feeling for his children, and a tragic part of his fate was to involve them in it. The countless miseries of exile would have made any other man despair. Trotsky's spirit rose above circumstances. His wit and gaiety were rarely dimmed. His energy found new outlets till the last moment. In Mexico, when all else failed, he became an enthusiastic collector of cacti. He went on writing even when he found no readers. Maybe these last years were a record of futility. With Trotsky, it was better to fight to no purpose than to lay down the sword.

Mr Deutscher is reluctant to admit the emptiness of the story. He himself took part in the faction fights among the Trotskyites. Moreover, he has written a life of Stalin, and is anxious to give Trotsky weight as Stalin's great opponent. Mr Deutscher even comes near to implying that the great purge was an operation against Trotsky. Stalin had many anxieties. It is difficult to believe that Trotsky's return as master of the Kremlin was among them.

Mr Deutscher backs away from the great question which Trotsky came near to facing at the end of his life: was there any sense in 'the revolution' at all? The question had been looming ever since 1917. Marxism was, in origin, a democratic creed. The masses, it taught, would move towards revolution. The duty of communists was to lead that revolution, not to make it. Lenin and Trotsky claimed to be doing this in 1917, and Mr Deutscher has endorsed this claim in his previous books. In fact, while the first Russian Revolution of 1917 came from below, the second was made from above; and the Bolsheviks have been stuck with the consequences from that day to this. Trotsky, not Stalin, defended terrorism in 1920; and when Stalin used terror, Trotsky could object only because it was being applied against himself.

Trotsky, in exile, asserted that the revolution had been betrayed.

He could not admit that, in the democratic sense, it had never taken place, and he had even to defend Soviet Russia as an essentially working-class state, which had fallen into the wrong hands almost by mistake. At the end of his life he came nearer to reality. Suppose, he asked, that the workers did not want to rule either in Russia or elsewhere? Suppose that the Second World War ended without the proletarian revolutions in advanced capitalist countries which he was prophesying? Then 'nothing else would remain but to recognize openly that the socialist programme, based on the internal contradictions of capitalist society, had petered out as a Utopia'. Mankind would be offered a future of 'bureaucratic collectivism', not the happy anarchism of William Morris.

Even now, Trotsky found an outlet for his fighting spirit. If his gloomy expectations were fulfilled, 'it is self-evident that a new minimum programme would be required – to defend the interests of the slaves of the totalitarian bureaucratic system'. Mr Deutscher walks warily round this flash of insight, and still whistles for democratic, proletarian revolutions at some time in the future. Trotsky himself closed his eyes again and declared in his last testament: 'My faith in the communist future of mankind is not less ardent, indeed it is firmer, today than it was in the days of my youth.'

Trotsky was too great a man to be consistent. He sacrificed freedom to an illusion; never quite admitted the illusion; and yet knew that freedom for all was the one thing that mattered. Though his activities in exile affected human destinies not one whit, they were an honour to the human spirit. Life at St Helena turned the great Napoleon into a petty, tawdry figure. Trotsky's years of exile were the noblest period of his life.

The Great Antagonists

This essay was first published as a review of Ian Grey's Stalin: Man of History *(London, Weidenfeld, 1979) and Ronald Segal's* The Tragedy of Leon Trotsky *(London, Hutchinson, 1979) in the* Observer, *7 October 1979.*

* * *

Stalin and Trotsky rank among the greatest rivals in history. Their rivalry was far more than personal, though even that was intense. It was a rivalry over the future of Russia, almost indeed over the future of mankind.

No two men had more conflicting ideas about human nature and human society. Trotsky was a romantic, voicing the enthusiasm of the nineteenth-century revolutionaries. His supreme weapon was oratory and literature, so much so that he proposed to return to writing immediately after conducting the Bolshevik seizure of power in 1917.

Stalin had not the slightest touch of romance in his composition. His supreme weapon was organization and intrigue. For him all morality was a sham; power was all. Not power for its own sake, though he came to love power. Stalin wanted power to achieve his aim of creating Great Russia. Trotsky preached permanent revolution until universal communism was established. Stalin cared only for socialism in a single country. Trotsky was a missionary for humanity. Stalin was a new Peter the Great.

It is a great stroke of luck that substantial books on both men should appear at the same time. Both books are works of careful scholarship though without any startling new revelations. Both are sympathetic to their subject as any good biography should be. Each presents a version of events so different from the other that it is difficult to believe that their respective subjects were living at the same time or even on the same planet.

Ian Grey has behind him a long record as a writer on Russian history. For him Stalin was set on continuing the work of the great tsars from Ivan the Terrible to Peter the Great. Grey narrates. He makes no moral judgements, except to remark in an almost offhand way that Stalin was transformed by the Bolshevik ethic that all means were justified by the ends into an inhuman tyrant.

Ronald Segal comes with a background of works on literature and of campaigning against racial discrimination, first in South Africa and then all over the world. He is concerned about the human being in Trotsky and it is significant that he devotes almost as much attention to Trotsky's works of literature as to the policies and acts that made Trotsky world famous. Segal is, I think, right in seeing Trotsky as a writer who strayed into politics, not as a professional politician obsessed with power. He was always 'The Pen', his first pseudonym. Here indeed is the explanation of Trotsky's failure in the great contest over the leadership of Soviet Russia.

Trotsky was interested in the victory of ideas, not of himself. Time and again he refused to assert his personal dominance or to employ political manoeuvres. Stalin also had his ideas and indeed held rigorously that all the other Bolsheviks were wrong as he showed by eliminating them sooner or later. Trotsky was wholeheartedly devoted to international revolution even though events showed it to be impractical. Stalin despised socialists and communists outside Russia. His sole concern was to make Russia a great industrial power within a decade where other countries had needed centuries.

There is another fascinating point that emerges from both books. Lenin, the supreme figure of the Bolshevik Revolution, had something of both men in his composition. He admired Trotsky's oratory and literary gifts which he could not emulate. But he also feared Trotsky's tendency to put ideas before party loyalty. Stalin was for Lenin the almost perfect Bolshevik, except when he dismissed Lenin's conflicts over philosophy as 'a storm in a teacup'. In the long run Lenin came to resent Stalin's ruthlessness, yet because of his own Marxist ethic could not contend against it.

Lenin had personal conflicts with Stalin and ideological conflicts with Trotsky. As a result he could not decide between them and died leaving only a confused testament which gave no clear guidance. Trotsky failed to grasp the opportunity if it ever existed. Stalin took his opportunity with both hands.

The conflict between the two men determined the course of European history in the twentieth century. Stalin's success marked the end of international socialism. It secured the victory of Russia in the Second World War and the subsequent balance of terror between the two world powers, Soviet Russia and the United States. We live with his heritage to the present day. As an individual Stalin had little of interest to show. He was the greatest of administrators and perhaps the greatest of warlords. Yet he remained a dim figure, sometimes savage, sometimes captivating – as Sukhanov called him, 'a grey blur'. Trotsky directed the Bolshevik Revolution and as a war leader won the civil war and the wars of revolution. Thereafter he left no mark on events except perhaps to accelerate Stalin's dictatorship. The last decade of his life was spent in impotent exile while his brilliant writings were disregarded.

For the practical historian who judges only by results Stalin appears as a supreme realist who changed the face of the world; Trotsky as a man of words who left only marginal jottings on the historical record. Yet even the most hard-headed historian has twinges of human feeling. Then Stalin appears as totally commonplace in both character and ideas; Trotsky, to quote an early American observer, as 'a four-kind son-of-a-bitch, but the greatest Jew since Jesus Christ'.

The two new books present the conflict between the two men in all its variety – conflict of personality, conflict of policies, conflicts over the basic truths of human nature. They illuminate the history of Russia and of mankind in the twentieth century. Most of all perhaps they reveal the conflict that rages in the mind of the historian throughout his life. Who is for realism? Who is for inspiration? Such is the fearsome choice.

Mussolini: The Cardboard Lion

This essay first appeared as a review of Denis Mack Smith's Mussolini
(London, Weidenfeld and Nicolson, 1982) in the Observer, *28 February 1982.
In writing of Mussolini six years earlier Alan Taylor had observed*:

Mussolini had one considerable gift: he was a forceful genius, and all his
genius went into words. Fascism itself was a work of propaganda, not a
serious programme.

*   *   *

Though there was little to admire in Mussolini he was certainly a
man out of the ordinary. He was totally without principles or scruples.
His so-called policies were a chaos of contradictory brags and boasts.
The weapons that carried him to power were the bludgeon and the
castor-oil bottle.

He early laid down the guiding line that the masses needed not to
understand but to *believe*: 'If only we can give them faith that
mountains can be moved, they will accept the illusion that mountains
are moveable, and thus an illusion may become reality.' One clear-
sighted observer called Mussolini 'a lion of cardboard'. Most observers
saw only the lion.

When Mussolini began his career he at least did not deceive
himself. But as time passed and Italians increasingly succumbed to his
deceptions, he became a victim of his own frauds. Soon after the
Fascist seizure of power he told a reporter that the Fascist revolution
was 'incomparably bigger, more complex and bloodier than the
Russian Revolution of 1917; anything that Lenin could do, he could
do better'. At one moment his revolution was 'a restoration, a revival
of order, a continuation and not a violation of past Italian traditions'.
Later however it became 'a profound political, moral, social revolution
that in all probability will leave nothing or almost nothing of the past
still in existence'.

In fact fascism was little more than terrorist rule by corrupt
gangsters. Mussolini was not corrupt himself but he did nothing
except to rage impotently. There has never been a dictator who
threatened more and achieved less. He claimed to be reconstructing

Italy. But the only mark he has left on it is the destruction of the heart of the Roman Forum.

Mussolini was a great showman whose technique improved as the real situation deteriorated. Every change of policy became a battle – 'the battle of the lira', 'the battle of the Pontine Marshes'. Whenever Mussolini's name was mentioned in the sham Chamber, the sham deputies rose to their feet, gave the so-called Roman salute and cried, 'Hail the Duce'. Mussolini often hailed himself and in his latter days burst into *Giovinezza*, the Fascist marching song, whereupon all the deputies rose to their feet. He also discovered in himself a superior version of Napoleon and even, when things were going badly for himself, compared his fate with that of Jesus Christ.

Yet it was not merely the Fascists who applauded him. Five former liberal prime ministers voted steadfastly for him, as did some distinguished liberal academics including the economist Einaudi and the physicist Fermi. Perhaps they were wise in their day and generation. Mussolini's open critics such as Matteotti and Amendola were murdered.

It is often said that Mussolini was the agent of a declining capitalism. Denis Mack Smith does not discuss this point at any length and there is indeed not much to discuss. The industrialists at first welcomed the restoration of order but they backed away from Mussolini soon enough. Mack Smith's detailed narrative shows that Mussolini, despite all his boasting, understood how to exploit events rather than how to create them. I had always supposed that Mussolini's assault on Abyssinia in 1935 was carefully timed to make the most of the European situation before Germany became strong enough to be a threat to Italy. Nothing of the kind. Mussolini had been preparing the Abyssinian war for years past. It just happened to break out when the European situation was changing fast.

Even so Mussolini did not altogether abandon old plans when caught up in new ones. At the height of the Second World War, when Italy was approaching ruin, Mussolini was still pushing on with the fortification of the Alpine frontier against Germany. Even in 1945 Mussolini had a vague hope that Churchill would welcome him as an associate. By then he had lost all contact with reality, but in a sense he lived with his dreams from the beginning.

Mack Smith has given us a full picture of Mussolini from his beginnings as the blacksmith's son to his end as a discredited and hunted dictator. The most striking feature of Mussolini's personality to my mind was how he grew more solitary as he grew older until at the end he had no companion at all except his faithful mistress, Clara Petacci. In his early days, no doubt, he had some socialist comrades. Later he had Fascist associates but few of them influenced him and their only conversation was to exchange gangster stories. Usually he sat alone hour after hour, sometimes rehearsing his rhetorical gestures or pulling faces at himself, sometimes playing the violin, and often reading cuttings from the European press. After all, he had once been a successful newspaper editor himself and he was still writing newspaper articles in 1944 – very good ones they are too, with even the title they were later collected under showing a spark of the old fire: *The Year of the Stick and the Carrot.*

Mussolini's brother Arnaldo ran his press propaganda for him and was probably the only human being he acknowledged except Clara Petacci. But Arnaldo died in 1931 and thereafter Mussolini more and more lost touch with reality. He had always inflated his resources. When he seized power he claimed to have 300,000 blackshirts behind him; the correct number was under 30,000 and the police could easily have dispersed them. Later, when the Second World War began, he claimed to possess an army of 150 divisions, some of them armoured. The correct figure was ten divisions, none of them armoured.

By 1940 Mussolini had 300,000 men to send to North Africa. He alleged that the British had the same. In fact the correct British figure was 35,000 – a force strong enough, however, to destroy the entire Italian Army. Mussolini never ceased to summon imaginary legions. Even in 1945 when he was virtually a prisoner at Salo he proposed to march to the rescue of Hitler on the Eastern Front. I suspect that right at the end he dreamt of becoming the leader of the Italian resistance and so of starting his run of pretences all over again.

Mack Smith is a scholar of high rank. Here he gives us all the facts and also all the drama of Mussolini's life except for the very end. Here, having got Mussolini into the hands of the partisans, he merely writes, 'Many different stories have been told by presumed eyewitnesses of what happened next.' Surely Mussolini should have been allowed a sensational final exit.

It is difficult not to be sorry for Mussolini, a pretentious scoundrel, caught up by reality. The truly contemptible figures were those of high culture and morality who were taken in by him, in Italy and elsewhere. I prefer Mussolini, commending his speeches as having resolved all the problems of modern society: 'there is nothing left to discover, no question left unanswered'.

The Baldwin Years

This was one of a series of BBC Television lectures entitled 'The Twenties' which were broadcast between 3 February and 17 March 1962. 'The Baldwin Years' was broadcast at 10.43 pm on the evening of 10 March and it was first published in the Listener *on the same date. The series stemmed from Alan Taylor's work on* English History 1914–1945 (*Oxford, Clarendon Press, 1965*).

*   *   *

It was a golden age. I use that phrase not as a term of praise but in a technical sense: the Baldwin years were the last years of the gold standard. Baldwin had a first run in 1923 for a few months; he became prime minister again in 1924, and remained in office until 1929; and the Baldwin years were the short period when people had the feeling that the war was really over. Problems were solved: you can mark it by the return to the gold standard in April 1925, or on the international side by the Treaty of Locarno which at the end of 1925 seemed to mark the end of the war and to imply that Europe was stable. There was, for these few years, something like a relaxation – a return to the old, or going on to the new. Baldwin was more than merely prime minister: he marked the Baldwin years. There was in him some special characteristic which gives the shape and the feel of this strange, maybe short-lived, time when men said: 'The war is over; we've saved what is the best of the old, and we've got on to something more progressive as well.'

Baldwin, although he presented himself as an old-fashioned English country gentleman, was in reality much more representative. Like the restored gold standard, like the general feeling that standards – not only gold standards, but standards of morality and of conventional behaviour – had been restored, Baldwin was a bit of a sham: or, if not a sham, shall we say an actor? To outward appearance Baldwin was a staid, solid English gentleman. Firm in his movements, one associates him always with a bowler hat, with a clean-cut, resolute appearance, rather slow, but at the same time penetrating in his look; one felt there the movement of honesty. He was known for his taste for country life; whether correctly or not, it was supposed that he kept pigs, and one associated him with this strange thing that people who keep pigs do with pigs, scratching their backs. Not only this, but it was supposed that he had been a country gentleman for generations. It was all a wonderful façade: he was not a country gentlemen at all, he was an iron-master. Baldwins were a well-established iron and steel firm. Baldwin had taken it over, not with great success, from his own father. His country life was something he had picked up. He himself once said, towards the end of his life, how rarely he had seen spring in Worcestershire, and he implied that this was because he had been prime minister; but he did not see much of spring in Worcestershire even when he was not prime minister.

Again, despite this idea of the wonderful, straightforward, simple English gentleman, with, one would imagine, forebears of impeccable country atmosphere and also – perhaps? – of impeccable stupidity, Baldwin was really an intellectual in disguise. Kipling, no mean writer, was his first cousin. His paternal grandfather was George Macdonald, a writer of highly imaginative and, I think, rather detestable fairy stories. In Baldwin there was a dreamer. The Baldwin age, which he helped to conjure up, was partly a return to a romantic time which had hardly existed.

More than this: not only in regard to a romantic picture of an English countryside but even in his picture of English industry, Baldwin created a sort of fantasy which would have done credit to the imagination of his cousin, Rudyard Kipling. In one of his striking speeches, in 1925, he described how when he was a young man the steelworks his father owned had been run in a paternalistic way, how he himself knew most of the workers by their Christian names, how indeed you would feel there was hardly a difference between master and man, except that the master had slightly different functions. The idea that the master drew considerably more money from the steelworks than the men is something which in those dear, paternalistic days hardly existed: the young Mr Baldwin had turned up and had clocked in at six o'clock in the morning, along with the men; had done, not perhaps quite the same hard work, but equally responsible work; they were all a happy family together, and he said how this had changed, and the great monopolies had taken over, and that he would like to bring into this new, more thrusting, aggressive world some of the atmosphere of the old days.

But if you had gone back to the steel industry of the early twentieth century, when Baldwin claimed to be growing up in it, you would have found it very tough. It was a time in which men were pushed into joining unions by the knowledge that they would be hit on the head by a steel bar if they did not join. There was a real class war at work when Baldwin built up this picture that the class war had been something which did not exist at all, and which now he didn't want to exist again: this was a fantasy.

But what is true about the Baldwin age is that some of these fantasies, not all, became real. If one looks back, therefore, to the England of the later 1920s, the period when Baldwin was prime minister, when there was something like a pattern of life of a particular kind, one can see, not the sort of revival of old standards which Baldwin claimed that there was, but the fact that other – in many ways more tolerant – standards were growing up. They were given the blessing that they were part of English traditional life, which they were not at all. Perhaps the biggest transformation of our society in the last fifty years has been this: for whatever reason, whether wisely or not, the trade union movement, and particularly the heads of the trade union movement, have changed their position, and, instead of being merely instruments of resistance, have accepted their responsible place in society and particularly in industrial organization.

The trade union leader of the late nineteenth century thought of the boss – or rather it was his duty to think of the boss – as an enemy. It was his job simply to fight the boss in order to get more wages for the members of his unions, and he fought with gloom because the boss was the stronger. The change started during the First World War when it was essential to get men at work in the factories, but it went on thereafter, even at times when there seemed great industrial strife – during the General Strike, for instance – and developed in the period after the General Strike. The trade union leader came forward and said: 'What I want for my men is security.' And while the trade union leader still went on fighting the boss, in the sense that he wanted more wages, he also cooperated with him, because he recognized that increased productivity and an efficient working industry were as much in the interests of his members as in the interests of the employer.

One can date this very well from the strange, forgotten Mond–Turner Conferences, which took place in 1927–28. Sir Alfred Mond, subsequently Lord Melchett, was a great industrial leader, head of

Imperial Chemicals. (By the way, Ben Turner was knighted: this was another thing that happened in the Baldwin age; for the first time, the trade union leaders began to be knighted. We are so used to this now that we are surprised, of course, if any trade union leader is not knighted.) Ben Turner was not the important one. The big trade union leader of this time and the counterpart, almost, of Baldwin as the essential figure of the age, was Ernest Bevin. It was Bevin who played the real, vital part in the Mond–Turner conversations. These conversations were the first decisive recognition that the employer and the trade union leader were both concerned to improve relations in industry and to increase productivity as a cooperative venture. Yet Ernest Bevin was a good and firm fighter for the interests of his own members as well.

This is a characteristic feature of the Baldwin years, and Baldwin provided for it the extra element of approval. Beyond this, there are some other strange things about Baldwin. To outward appearance he seemed sane, solid, level-headed. Yet there was in him the character of a dreamer. He used to sit on the Treasury bench sniffing the order paper; and when he was not doing this he was cracking his fingers and pulling faces. I have often thought that people ought to have raised a cry: 'Is there a doctor in the House?' This apparently level-headed, sane man was most peculiar in his behaviour and, beyond this, Baldwin was really a remarkable actor; he was, incidentally, the first politician who made a mark on radio: the old hams, Lloyd George, Ramsay MacDonald, were no good when they were faced with a microphone. They tried to play the old rhetorical tricks that they had played when they were addressing great public meetings. Baldwin, here again, was the man of the new type, who gave the impression that he was the simple, straightforward, honest Stanley Baldwin: he did this, of course, by supreme artistry. It is said that the first time he gave a political address at the microphone, as the green light went on he struck a match and lit his pipe. I have my doubts about this – I have heard a record of the broadcast, and it doesn't sound as though he is talking with clenched teeth, which is what people do if they are smoking a pipe; but it may be that he struck a match, lit a pipe, and then put it down, and that this was part of the effect. At any rate, how characteristic that this man, who looked so simple and so unassuming, could do something which is far more difficult than talking in an ordinary straightforward human way, where people can see you. Baldwin was an artist in presenting himself, and an artist in presenting this very new England, as it was in many ways, as though it was the old one: indeed, in smuggling into the established old order a whole lot of flexible new ideas.

There is, however, more to it than this. In every period there is a cleavage of generations: the sons are impatient with their fathers, and rightly. But in the twenties the cleavage was probably greater than it has ever been. The war made a special sort of cleavage: the older generation were the people who had grown up before the war and whom, in a strange way, the war had not affected. In the Baldwin government of 1924–29, for instance, Winston Churchill was the only man who had served in the trenches, and that only for a very short time and in rather exceptional circumstances. All the rest – including Baldwin himself – had been too old for the war, and though they had suffered, no doubt – it cost them a lot of money, many of them had lost sons and relatives – it had come when the whole of their life and pattern of behaviour had been fixed, and things that happened as a result of the war were tiresome but had not changed the way they looked at life. Then there had come the specifically war generation, sometimes described as the lost generation. A great many of them were killed, and those who managed to survive were sapped by the terrible years they had gone through, as one finds if one looks at their writing and many of their judgements.

But by the second half of the 1920s, the Baldwin years, there was growing up a generation which had not been affected by the war. In order to serve in the war at all you had to be born not later than the year 1900, which technically is not the twentieth century; for those born in the twentieth century the war was something that happened in their young years, but not all that terribly disturbing, and the recovery from the war is what marked them – the belief not only in war to end war, in a better world, a home for heroes, but the feeling that, after all, things had pulled round, and that the catastrophes of war which they could remember elder brothers experiencing had come to an end. If one looked round the world of the mid-1920s one could not help saying that there had been an astonishing recovery and that on the basis of this there was a possibility of limitless progress.

It is difficult now, with the experiences of the thirty or forty years in between, to recapture this element of easy Utopianism. Things were never quite as easy as they were before the war, but in the mid-twenties there was a relaxation. The gold standard was a tremendous symbol; it made people feel 'this is the real pound that we used to know'; there was this solid foundation – but a solid foundation on which to advance. The younger generation felt that they were getting it both ways. They had escaped the war, the damages of the war had been overcome, and at the same time the new vision which the war had brought was presented to them without the conflicts and troubles which the elder generations had gone through.

The twenties, and particularly this later period of the twenties, was in this way the beginning of our modern world, almost of our contemporary world, in which the old standards, other than gold, were not merely shaken but disregarded; and the cleavage between the older generation and the younger was not merely one of impatience on the part of the younger generation but of resignation: 'this is how the old feel, but really we are not concerned with it any more'. Consider on the one side the respectable, conventional values which were being turned out not only by Baldwin but by the so-called representatives of culture, and turn to contemporary literature. They used to have rebels before the First World War who were supposed to be wonderfully radical enlightened people, like H G Wells or Bernard Shaw, but in the 1920s these were dear fuddy-duddy old men: Bernard Shaw was still trundling around in his homespun suit, claiming that he was a rebel, yet one had only got to pick up any of his writings to see how utterly drab and respectable he was. The real creative things that were happening in the twenties were things in which all these old, conventional, traditional standards had been jettisoned. But many of them had got going already before the war: one of the great revolutionary books – and terribly conservative books – of the 1920s, *Ulysses* by James Joyce, was actually started in 1912, and its revolutionary impact, in the long run, has probably been more powerful than the impact of the First World War itself.

The whole younger generation, and the whole atmosphere of the time, no longer bothered about the old standards. If you pick up again the conventional representatives – Baldwin, any typical headmaster, the sort of opinions you would get in the first leading article in *The Times* – here you would find an assertion that England was still a Christian country, still conforming to the standards of morality which had been laid down in the nineteenth century. But then if you turn to ordinary standards of behaviour, perhaps the most significant thing of the twenties is that it marked the triumph of the one- or two-child family. When people look back to the twenties the significant figure which represented what was happening at the time was Dr Marie Stopes. Marie Stopes was, I would say, for the twentieth century, the greatest, most sincere, and most effective propagandist of contraception. The great difference between her and the fate of her predecessors, such as Annie Besant, to say nothing of Carlile, was that she was not prosecuted. In the nineteenth century, when people talked like this – and these are really respectable standards – they were prosecuted and sent to prison. Dr Marie Stopes was not prosecuted: she had meetings at the Albert Hall, and – even greater distinction, perhaps – she was invited to speak at the Oxford Union. She was the admired friend of Professor Samuel Alexander, the greatest philosopher of the time. Therefore this outward appearance of simply continuing the old age was an appearance: by the younger generation these standards had been rejected. The great belief of the 1920s was in integrity: you could almost put it that it did not matter what you did as long as you believed in what you were doing; it would be wrong to abandon standards which you yourself accepted, but it was not wrong to abandon standards which other people accepted. This was a doctrine of emancipation but it was also a doctrine of loyalty and of maintaining something new.

Growing up in the twenties there was already a spirit of readiness to create, in terms of one's own beliefs and not of patterns which were imposed from outside. It may be said that much of this seems irrelevant to what was really happening in the 1920s; that Great Britain was not keeping up in the race; that there were never less than 1,000,000 unemployed from 1921 right up to 1939. And only once, in the year 1928, did the number of the unemployed sink below 10 per cent. All this is true, but we get the picture wrong when we look back at the twenties through the later experience of the 1930s. Unemployment was an evil in the twenties, but it did not yet seem to have become the dominant evil. In the twenties men felt so much more the world opening up: the conquest of the air, on the most practical basis the world opening up, or rather England opening up. It is in the 1920s that the motor car really mattered; it was then that people began to move out from the centre of towns to the suburbs and beyond. The atmosphere of emancipation, of movement, counted far more: and therefore the Baldwin age, though short-lived, was an age of genuine hope and confidence, however misplaced, about the future.

Man Behind the Scenes

This essay first appeared as a review of Memoirs of a Conservative: J C C
Davidson's Memoirs and Papers 1910–1937, *edited by Robert Rhodes
James (London, Weidenfeld and Nicolson, 1969), in the* Observer, *31 August
1969. John Colin Campbell Davidson (1889–1970) was Conservative M P for
Hemel Hempstead from 1920 until 1937, when he was created a viscount and
succeeded as M P by his wife (1937–59). He served outside of the cabinet as
chancellor of the Duchy of Lancaster 1923–24 and 1931–37 and as junior
minister at the Admiralty 1924–26, essentially as Baldwin's protégé. He was
also chairman of the Conservative Party 1926–30.*

*　　*　　*

Political leaders, if they are wise, have always enlisted a confidential
agent – some loyal follower of good judgement who would give advice
and information without pushing himself forward. J C C Davidson
(now Lord Davidson) was an outstanding example. He was the man
behind Bonar Law, though Beaverbrook disputed the position. He
was the man without a rival behind Baldwin. Indeed he became
Baldwin's closest intimate, and he and Mrs Davidson provided Baldwin with a second home. For more than twenty years he knew all the
secrets of politics. Every historian must be grateful that Lord Davidson
has now revealed at any rate some of them.

His memoirs, though invaluable, need to be used with care: Davidson did not keep a diary. He began to write his memoirs only some
thirty years later. Then he fell ill and added further recollections in a
series of tape-recorded conversations with Mr John Barnes. Finally
Mr Rhodes James shaped the material, along with many contemporary
letters, into the present admirable book.

The story has thus gone through a number of hands and has also
been influenced by the passage of time. Sometimes, one feels, Lord
Davidson gave a particular answer because Mr Barnes asked a particular
question. Sometimes Lord Davidson remembered what he had read in
someone else's book rather than what he had himself experienced. No
man can recall past events without being affected by what has happened
in between. Despite this, the book is a unique contribution to knowledge
of political events.

*

Davidson liked decency and respectability in politics. He disliked the rackety ways of Lloyd George and his associates. Bonar Law set him a problem. Law himself was modest and honourable. Yet, lamentably, he took Lloyd George's side against Asquith. Davidson comments mournfully:

That Asquith was out-manoeuvred there is no doubt whatever, but that the country under prosecution of the war also benefited, there is also no question. Yet, it was a sad chapter in the history of British politics, and that is really all that can be said about it.

Lloyd George himself once defined the issue. Davidson records:

Lloyd George suddenly turned round and said, 'Bonar, I think that you know you are different from most of us, because you are a man who would act on principle; if you thought a thing was right you would do it.' Bonar replied, 'Well, I think it's my Covenanting blood.' And then Lloyd George grinned across at Bonar and said, 'Bonar, you know, I can conceive of circumstances arising in which I might be compelled to act on principle myself – but you can't say that of F E or Winston, can you?'

Not surprisingly, Davidson did not like Beaverbrook, whom Law called 'my most intimate friend'. Davidson records: 'I never slept a night under Lord Beaverbrook's roof. I dined, I lunched there, but I never slept there. I didn't like the house or the way it was run.' Davidson did not win the battle over Law with Beaverbook. His triumph came in the days of Baldwin, particularly when he helped to emasculate Beaverbrook's campaign for empire free trade.

Davidson was one of those who helped to make Law prime minister. His part in making Baldwin prime minister was even more decisive. Law was reluctant to name his successor. Davidson drafted a memorandum for George V which stressed the claims of Baldwin. He insists that this was his independent opinion, but it is difficult to believe that the king, or his secretary Lord Stamfordham, did not take it as Law's view also – as indeed it was. Davidson adds that Beaverbook was backing Curzon – not because he liked Curzon, but because he knew that the coalition Conservatives would join Curzon and would not join Baldwin. This information is new and surprising. Beaverbrook, according to his own account, was far too distressed about Law's illness to worry about his successor.

At any rate, Baldwin became prime minister, and Davidson served him faithfully. It was Davidson who prepared and directed the organization which broke the General Strike. Contrary to the received opinion, it was Davidson also, not Churchill, who controlled the *British Gazette*. He records:

Birkenhead, who had been quite calm in the prior negotiations, was absolutely mad, and so was Winston, who had it firmly in his mind that anybody who was out of work was a Bolshevik; he was most extraordinary, and never have I listened to such poppycock and rot . . .

Winston, after a great fight, agreed to be blue-pencilled and the blue pencil was seldom idle . . . He is the sort of man whom, if I wanted a mountain to be moved, I should send for at once. I think, however, that I should not consult him after he had moved the mountain if I wanted to know where to put it.

Davidson was rewarded by becoming chairman of the Conservative Party. He discovered to his embarrassment that he had to handle the recommendations for honours. Many prominent men offered money to the party fund in exchange for some honour, and Davidson, according to his records, returned the cheques. Was this really all? Were the politically ambitious entirely mistaken in supposing that money and honours somehow went together? Or did Davidson keep a record only if he returned the cheque? We shall never know. Lloyd George provided the shameless and yet sensible justification for the practice that it was better to sell honours than to sell policies, as happened in America or as the Labour Party sold its policies to the trade unions. One piece of information tells how the party funds were used. Lord Birkenhead persisted in writing for the newspapers when he was a cabinet minister. The cabinet objected, and Davidson bought Birkenhead out of journalism with £5,000 a year from the party funds.

Most of the revelations are of course less sensational. Baldwin is always the central figure. Davidson wrote: 'He really is a most extraordinary man.' Baldwin once left £100 at a home for retarded girls and with it this note:

from one who once saw S. Mary's Home, and having been feble-minded from the cradle regarded it with simpathy and under-standing.

Passing thro' this vally of shaddoes as a useless 'Fantum' himself he desires to be the humble means of bringing a ray of light to kindrid infortunates.

Baldwin defined his guiding principle: 'When in doubt, choose the path you like least.' Perhaps this is why this lover of the English countryside spent all his summers at Aix-les-Bains.

In 1945 Churchill asked Davidson: 'What was it that enabled SB to win elections while I always lose them?' Davidson replied that SB had three rules:

One. He never imputed evil or dishonourable motives to his political opponents. *Two*. He believed in understatement rather than overstatement. *Three*. He managed to convey the impression that honest chaps though the Opposition might be they lacked tradition and experience in dealing with the larger problems of life at home and abroad, and with a sob in his voice suggested that in these anxious times it might be wise for the country to give the government he led another turn.

Very crudely put, but I think essentially true . . .

Davidson followed these rules himself, and his memoirs are a last service which he has performed for his beloved master.

Leo Amery

Leopold Charles Maurice Stennett Amery (1873–1955) was a leading Conservative on the imperialist wing of the party. He served as a junior minister (1919–22) in Lloyd George's post-war coalition government. After many of the Conservative leaders followed Lloyd George out of office, Amery entered the cabinet as first lord of the admiralty under Bonar Law and Baldwin, 1922–24, and then was secretary of state for the colonies and dominion affairs, 1924–29. He returned to office under Churchill as secretary of state for India and Burma, 1940–45. These essays first appeared as reviews of his memoirs, My Political Life, Volume I: England before the Storm 1896–1914, Volume II: 1914–1929 *and* Volume III: The Unforgiving Years 1929–1940 *(London, Hutchinson, 1953, 1953 and 1955), in the* New Statesman and Nation, *23 May 1953, 21 November 1953 and 13 August 1955.*

*　　*　　*

Tory Fabian

A photograph at the beginning of this book shows the young Amery of twenty-two. Apart from a few lines in the face, it could be the Mr Amery at eighty who has written his autobiography. He has not changed either in appearance or in outlook. The controversies of the Boer War, of tariff reform, or of the Irish question are still contemporary to him. He often reproduces passages from books or even newspaper leaders, written fifty years ago, and remarks: 'they still have a lesson for today'. His taste is for quotations from Bunyan and Cromwell; but the best motto for the book could be found in the words spoken by Metternich to Guizot on the steps of the British Museum: 'Error has never approached my spirit.' Or, as he himself says: 'My heroes remain heroes and my villains remain villains.'

Mr Amery is that unusual thing – a politician with a purely intellectual approach. Though he has always been a member of the Conservative, or, more accurately, of the Unionist Party, he has never sympathized with the irrational loyalties and sentiments which make up Toryism. For him, politics are a matter of rational, though often violent, argument. His most decisive weapon has always been a letter to *The Times*; and he used his massive *History of the Boer War* to prove the case for imperial unity and military reform. Things were to be achieved by a small group of men, meeting as a dining-club and working out a policy – exactly the tactics which the Webbs applied in a different sphere. The villains of whom he speaks are the soft-hearted politicians who ran away from his logic and tried to muddle into some compromise – Balfour or Asquith. His heroes reduce themselves to one: Joseph Chamberlain, his last words to Amery: 'if I . . . were the . . . House of Lords . . . I would *fight*'. Fighting is indeed the only thing if you want a clear-cut solution. So Mr Amery wanted to fight the Boers in order to show the supremacy of imperial power. So he wanted the Unionist Party to commit itself to thoroughgoing Protection. So, in the Irish question, he wanted the Lords to die in the last ditch against the Parliament Bill, and Ulster to raise the standard of rebellion against home rule.

There is much to be said for this approach. Questions can only be really settled if they are fought through to the end. There would be no problem in South Africa now, if imperial supremacy had been ruthlessly maintained. Resistance by the House of Lords would have brought either a reformed second chamber or, at the very least, a House much improved by the addition of some two hundred Liberal peers. Rebellion in Ulster might have led to a new start in Ireland on a more realistic basis. But all these things cut against the spirit of moderation and compromise which underlies British politics. We may feel impatient when Mr Attlee declares that the Labour Party will work African Federation once it is the law of the land. It would be more glorious to announce that the Labour Party would seek to wreck it. But is it not a wiser and better course than Bonar Law praising civil war against home rule, which was equally the law of the land? Mr Amery quotes with approval a letter from Leo Maxse: 'I am sorry we have no Kruger in our party today.' Extreme was to answer extreme, an English Kruger to outdo the Boer. If Mr Amery were still capable of doubt, he might meditate the words which Chesterton addressed to Walter Long:

> Walter, be wise! avoid the wild and new!
> The Constitution is the game for you.

In South Africa, at any rate, Mr Amery got his conflict of extremes. Now he does not like the results; and he has to fall back on the old British remedy of pious wishes:

One can only hope that what South Africa is undergoing is a belated backwash and echo of old controversies and that the normal course of a broader and more generous national life will presently reassert itself.

Though this is a pugnacious book, exciting and well-written, it lacks historical perspective. The reader is not taken back into a vanished era; he is invited to fight the old battles over again. The autobiography is overlaid with argument; and the characters in it never come alive except as the vehicle for ideas. Nowhere is there a real answer to the question: why did the men of the Edwardian epoch allow the wisdom and advantage of centuries to run away through their fingers? The problem cannot be determined by rational debate; and it is not surprising that Mr Amery, the intellectual politician, has spent most of his life in baffled frustration. Now, in old age, he seeks once more to argue us into wisdom. Yet this wisdom of imperial cooperation which he advocates itself rests on irrational sentiment. Though politics is the art of the possible, things do not become possible merely by proving that they are correct.

More of Mr Amery

Mr Amery is cursed with a facile pen. He has been on the fringe of politics for fifty years, and sometimes near the centre. He has had enough interesting experiences to fill a volume; but he insists on writing three, and these will tax the reader's patience. It is difficult to get up much interest in yet another account of Grey's speech to the House of Commons on the outbreak of the First World War; and though Mr Amery's tour of the dominions was no doubt of great interest to him, it is of none to us, especially when it is extended by long quotations from his after-dinner speeches. Yet these are a testimony to Mr Amery's vitality, not only then but now. Unlike many old men, he does not live in the past. He is concerned only with the present; and his political autobiography is designed to advocate an imperial tariff union as much as to contribute to the historical record. In a changing world, Mr Amery has remained unchanged. He has never doubted that he was right. He has aspired to make events; and the aspiration is still with him.

The more detached reader will be interested rather in the question:

why did this able, courageous man make so little impact on events? Why did he remain always slightly below the first rank in politics? The answer is perhaps to be found in these pages. His speeches were always a little too long, always a little too clear and assertive. Mr Amery had no patience with compromise, no time for waverer. He pressed always for resolute action. During the First World War, he tried to push Lloyd George into supreme power, long before that master of political tactics judged that the time was ripe. Every leading statesman received from Mr Amery long letters of advice, full of promptings to the logical course that is so seldom possible in a democracy. He advocated a small war cabinet and a unified command – two essentials for winning the war that were achieved much later than he wished. After the war, he tried to get from the coalition something more constructive than anti-socialism. When he failed, he took the lead in overthrowing Lloyd George, only to discover that with Baldwin he had saddled himself with a statesman much more procrastinating.

He makes here an interesting contribution to history. It has always been a puzzle why Baldwin suddenly decided to fight an election on the issue of protection in the autumn of 1923. Mr Amery shows that Baldwin was alarmed by the news that Lloyd George was returning from the United States with a programme of imperial preference. Baldwin determined to get in first: his motive was to dish Lloyd George, not to save the empire, and he lost interest in protection once his object had been achieved. Again, Baldwin's motive in making the National government of 1931 was to keep out Lloyd George; and he was of course seconded by Neville Chamberlain, who never got over the humiliation of Lloyd George's verdict in 1917, 'when I saw that pinhead, I said to myself he won't be any use'. Mr Amery also refuses to be overawed by Churchill's later fame. In the twenties he was, Mr Amery insists, a Victorian free-trader; and his policy at the Treasury prepared the way for the great economic crisis. It can indeed be plausibly argued that for Sir Winston, empire has always been a matter of military grandeur rather than of economic cooperation.

Mr Amery, on the other hand, returned from his tour of the dominions in 1928 resolved to repeat more successfully the campaign of Joseph Chamberlain. It came to nothing; and this, too, can be explained from his book. Mr Amery has always moved, as Milner did, in too narrow a circle. All Souls has been his ruin. He remarks complacently that the cabinet of 1922 contained three fellows of All Souls. This is less impressive when it turns out that the other two were Curzon and Lord Halifax. Mr Amery has always supposed that the country was with him, if he could capture the common-room at All Souls and a few undergraduate clubs; as, during the First World War, he tried to win the war by establishing a private dining circle. He spoke assiduously at elections; but the English people were always remote from him. A man of his ability and integrity ought to have been a socialist; and his schemes for developing the empire will be achieved by a Labour government, if they are ever achieved at all. Privilege and planning go ill together; and neither All Souls nor *The Times* are good training for one who would lead in a democracy.

Churchill and Myself

Advancing age has no terrors for Mr Amery. It has neither checked his ready pen nor dimmed his controversial zest. Here he comes with a third volume of his autobiography and briskly contemplating the writing of a fourth. His self-confidence is superb. He is always expecting to be offered the highest office and to save the most critical situation; yet, when this does not happen, he is never discouraged but bustles off to organize yet another 'strong committee' or to attend yet another dinner with other influential persons.

He has no doubt who were the two most important figures in England between 1929 and 1940: they were 'Churchill and myself'. In 1936 'apart from Churchill, I was obviously the person most qualified to undertake the coordination of defence'. In the autumn of 1939 'I felt myself better qualified, both by study and by experience, for the business of waging war than anyone in active politics except Churchill'. In May 1940, according to Hore-Belisha, Lord Beaverbrook 'took the view . . . that I should be prime minister as the man who had really turned out the government and as best qualified all round'. Mr Amery adds: 'I discouraged the idea, not because I lacked confidence in myself, for, like Churchill, "I thought I knew a good deal about it all."'

The present volume is a further assertion of Mr Amery's equality. Since Churchill has combined autobiography and history, he will do the same. His own experiences and contemporary records are therefore submerged in a narrative drawn from published sources. The spate of historical evidence has become a curse; for every autobiographer now tells us what was happening in the world instead of what he knew at the time. Sir Winston Churchill can be forgiven anything; but Mr Amery could have reduced this volume a great deal if he had not been eager to bend the bow of Ulysses. Most of the story is in a very minor key. Mr Amery was excluded from the National government, at first no doubt as too rigid a protectionist, and later because his fiery spirit consorted ill with MacDonald, Baldwin and their adherents. Hence he could only criticize, or more occasionally support, from outside. The funniest chapter in the volume describes his unofficial appearance at the Ottawa conference and the terror of the British ministers when faced with a thoroughgoing imperialist.

Mr Amery took an independent line on two great issues of foreign policy: of all Tories he was the most eager to appease Mussolini and the most reluctant to appease Hitler. He still finds much to admire in fascism and clings to the fantastic notion that the Italian alliance would have been enough to turn the scale against Hitler. More broadly he regarded the League of Nations as an instrument for conciliation, which was certainly the Conservative view in the 1920s; and he is right in saying that Churchill alone interpreted the League as a fighting alliance to defend the existing territorial settlement. The Labour Party, after all, combined advocacy of sanctions and of disarmament almost till the end. Mr Amery was one of the few Tories who frankly opposed sanctions in the Abyssinian affair of 1935, and he has some discreditable things to tell of the Conservative leaders who paid lip-service to the League. Hoare, for instance, argued 'that we might get out by the failure of others to support us or, alternatively, that Mussolini might find his difficulties too great for him . . . We were committed to the current and perhaps there might not be a Niagara!' Neville Chamberlain held 'that we were bound to try out the League of Nations for political reasons at home . . . If things became too serious the French would run out first, and we could show that we had done our best.' Yet Mr Amery was surprised when, after Munich, Attlee refused to listen to talk of a coalition: 'nothing would induce them to look at anything of the sort so long as Chamberlain was prime minister'. Mr Amery commented sadly: 'I fear there is no real leadership in him, or, indeed in any of his crowd, except possibly in Morrison.'

On Germany Mr Amery took the opposite line – the first, or at any rate the second of the resisters. Yet his reasoning had not changed: Germany was a danger to the British Empire, Italy was not. Churchill developed high principles in these years; Mr Amery remained the pugnacious imperialist he had always been. Hence it was something more than a manoeuvre of 'the inner circle' which prevented his becoming prime minister in May 1940. Despite all his practical experience, Mr Amery has kept too much of the academic in political life. He has been too intellectual, too consistent, to capture the popular imagination; and he has relied too much on dining-clubs. Yet he will have a place in history, and it will be a high one. 'Speak for England!' was one of the greatest ejaculations in the history of parliament (not recorded in Hansard by the way); and his speech of 7 May 1940 deserved Lloyd George's compliment 'that in fifty years he had heard few speeches to match it in sustained power and none with so dramatic a climax'. That speech brought down the Chamberlain government and ended a disgraceful era in British politics. The man who made it does right to be vain.

Too Good for This World

This essay first appeared as a review of Robert A Dowse's Left in the Centre: The Independent Labour Party 1893–1940 *(London, Longmans, 1966) in the* Observer, *14 August 1966.*

Alan Taylor grew up in a house where discussion of radical politics was a norm. Both his parents had been advocates of Lloyd George radicalism before the First World War, supporters of conscientious objectors during it, and became members of the Independent Labour Party (ILP) at the end of it. Taylor joined the ILP at the age of fifteen. He later recalled: 'I went with my parents to the ILP meetings every Sunday evening as I had once gone to chapel with my mother.'

Alan Taylor became sceptical about the ILP by the 1930s, not least when it broke away from the Labour Party. The mid-1930s was a period when, with Hitler in power in Germany, he also broke with the anti-war sentiments of his upbringing. This essay and the next one, 'A Wasted Life', show not only his critical powers as a historian, but the disillusion of one who had believed in the ultimate success of the ILP brand of socialism.

*   *   *

The decline of political parties seems to be a favourite topic for historical study, perhaps a reflection of the death-wish which is said to have overcome the British people. The other week there was Trevor Wilson analysing the decline of the Liberal Party, and now Mr Dowse does the same for the ILP.

The theme is a bit different, of course. The Liberals had an 'up', or more than one, before they went down. The ILP was threatened with decline almost as soon as it started and can hardly claim to have got beyond being a sect. Its story has little more importance than that of one of the short-lived heresies chronicled by Gibbon. It is a fascinating story all the same: a particularly clear version of a political group that had everything right with it except the ability to win support.

The policy and principles of the ILP were perfect. Take any political question of the time from India to family allowances or from the First World War to women's suffrage, and the ILP alone was right without reserve. Its leaders from Keir Hardie to Maxton were men of the purest idealism, and Ramsay MacDonald might be included in the same list. The members of the ILP were the political saints of the twentieth century, and the world would be a much better place if their lead had been followed.

And yet it was all no good. Far from winning a parliamentary majority, the ILP never managed even to establish a preponderant influence within the Labour Party. When it finally insisted that its policy should be taken seriously it merely pronounced sentence of death upon itself.

Mr Dowse goes competently and devoutly over the subject. There is a great deal of the detailed information which is supposed to be useful to historians. Mr Dowse also develops such curious aspects of the story as the Two-and-a-Half International, a characteristic ILP invention, and the way in which Clifford Allen persuaded wealthy Quakers to subsidize revolutionary, though idealistic, socialism.

Unfortunately the book is rather dull, with the facts left to keep afloat as best they can. Moreover Mr Dowse's general attitude, or explanation, is, to my mind, perverse. He holds firmly that the decline of the ILP was 'a consequence of structural factors which left little room for manoeuvre'. There is an implication that if these structural factors had been different – if, say, the National Administrative Council of the ILP had had more power over the districts – all would have been well.

Such technical obsessions are common among social scientists. Similarly one could argue that democracy would have survived in Germany if some clause of the Weimar constitution had been different, or that we should not be troubled by the Trinity if Arius had known how to rig the Council of Nicea.

There is, however, a different and more likely explanation: the righteous never win. The Fifth Monarchy men, for instance, were not poor fighters or even poor political tacticians. They were ruined by being too good. Europe produced many saints of the ILP kind in the early twentieth century – Kurt Eisner in Bavaria, Michael Karolyi in Hungary – and they too were all ruined by their goodness. The saint becomes effective only when he sells out, as MacDonald was accused of doing. The ILP did not sell out, and therefore it ran out of money both literally and in a metaphorical sense.

However, the ILP is dead but not forgotten. Its spirit reappears with every new manifestation of the Left. The present Parliamentary Labour Party is full of ILP figures. Unlike their prototypes, most of them will sell out. Some few will remain true to their principles and for them, as for the ILP, Gresham's Law will apply: bad money drives out good. Down with Keir Hardie and up with Horatio Bottomley. Down with Lansbury and up with Bevin. Down with – who? But clearly up with Harold Wilson. It is lucky for the ILPers that they are in their graves. Better far to decline than to see what Labour's triumph has brought us to.

A Wasted Life

This essay first appeared as a review of John McNair's James Maxton: The Beloved Rebel (*London, Allen and Unwin, 1955*) *in the* Observer, *15 May 1955.*

*   *   *

There is nothing more tragic than to miss the conductor's beat in the orchestra of life, to go on playing old tunes in art or politics when the ear of the public can be caught only by new ones. It is moving and noble to cling to a dying cause, but it is also futile, and we can only lament the waste of human material.

James Maxton was a figure of this kind, a Jacobite of the twentieth century. He had every quality save one – the gift of knowing how to succeed. Passionate sincerity; unstinted devotion; personal charm which made him irresistible to men of the most divergent classes and political outlook; a power of oratory in parliament and on the platform which made him the equal of Gladstone – the catalogue of his virtues is endless.

Yet his record of achievement is barren. Worse than barren, it is destructive. When he stormed into politics, the Independent Labour Party was a great and creative force, inspiring the policy of the Labour Party, even deciding (to its subsequent regret) who should be the first Labour prime minister. When he died, the ILP, thanks to his leadership, had dwindled to a diminutive sect. Indeed, if it had not been for the endowments obtained by Clifford Allen, whom Maxton drove out of the party, it would probably have vanished altogether.

Maxton's failure was more than the failure of a man. It was the failure of a movement – the movement of romantic revolutionary socialism. Keir Hardie, Maxton's predecessor, could combine romance and reality. He made great romantic speeches on the platform; but, more than any other man, he also carried through the hard practical work of creating the Labour Party. The mantle of Keir Hardie was divided on his death between Ramsay MacDonald and James Maxton; and both were ruined by the legacy. The times demanded action; they could only make speeches. In the first age of democracy the masses welcomed the prospect of a socialist Utopia. In the harder

age which followed the First World War they demanded concrete
results. Revolutionary socialism turned into the Bolshevik dictatorship;
parliamentary socialism achieved the practical gains of the Welfare
State. There was no third way between Lenin and Arthur Henderson.
Maxton sought this way all his life. His audiences grew ever larger,
his personal popularity ever greater. But his followers diminished; and
at the end the ILP group in parliament was an insignificant remnant.
By a hideous irony, Maxton, the revolutionary socialist, will be
remembered in history for his speech in praise of Neville Chamberlain
after the capitulation of Munich.

It would be a hard, perhaps an impossible, task to write an honest
book about Maxton – a book that would pay full tribute to his
wonderful qualities and yet reveal the causes of his complete failure.
Mr McNair has not attempted it. His admirable book is a straight
essay in hero-worship. Maxton can do nothing wrong; and no one else
can do anything right. There is a stridency of tone, an exaggeration of
Maxton's influence, which unconsciously goes some way to explain
what went wrong. The triumphs of the platform are accepted as
sufficient in themselves. Time and again we are told of the great
meetings where resolutions were passed; we are left to find out for
ourselves that nothing happened afterwards. Strikes were proclaimed;
no strikes followed. Thousands pledged themselves to down tools
against war; then they returned to the armament factories. Bewitched
by Maxton's personality, we murmur as we close the book: 'They
were all out of step except our Jimmy.' Yet it is difficult to believe
that this will really be the verdict of history on British politics in the
first half of the twentieth century.

Ernest Bevin

These essays first appeared as reviews of Alan Bullock's The Life and Times of Ernest Bevin, Volume I: Trade Union Leader 1881–1940. Volume II: Minister of Labour and National Service 1940–1945 (*London, Heinemann, 1960 and 1967*) *in* Encounter, *October 1960, and the* Observer, *16 April 1967.*

*　　*　　*

Nobody's Uncle

Alan Bullock is a biographer in the Victorian manner: solid, accurate, exhaustive. There is no showing-off by the author, and no amateur psychoanalysis. The record is left to speak for itself, and if the result is sometimes pedestrian, that is how it was for Bevin. Though Bullock admires Bevin as much as he detested his previous theme, Hitler, this difference of feeling has not produced any difference of treatment. Bevin, like Hitler, is presented from 'outside', as a public figure. 'Life' and 'Times' merge into each other after the first few pages. Alan Bullock stands 'outside' Bevin in another sense. He is not a trade unionist or even a member of the Labour movement. This detachment has its advantages. No living writer could have presented a fairer or more informative account of Bevin's life. But detachment has its own disadvantages. Bullock, being on the outside, has failed to realize how much Bevin was on the outside too. The reader is made to feel – from the subtitle on – that Bevin was a characteristic labour leader of the early twentieth century. In fact he was unique for good and ill, a strange, solitary character, self-made in career and, still more, in ideas.

Bevin was a man without roots or background. Father unknown; left to fend for himself at the age of eight; never acquiring a craft or skill. He remained all his life a casual labourer, ready to turn his hand to anything and without much belief in the trained expert. An engine-driver or a maker of precision-tools would never have challenged the bankers as ruthlessly as Bevin did at the time of the Macmillan Commission. He would have been taken in by them and assumed that, as experts, they knew what they were talking about.

Bevin, the casual labourer, always knew better than the experts, and often with justification. But there were many things he did not know. He knew little or nothing of industrial England. Bristol, where he grew up, was an isolated pocket of urbanism in a rural sea, and even as a town it was a backwater in Bevin's time. In a curious way, Bevin did not know anything about the Industrial Revolution. The transport and general workers whom he organized could all have existed just as well without it, except for the bus-drivers who depended on the internal combustion engine. Bevin dealt with docks and transport undertakings, with hotels and restaurants. He never dealt with factories or engineering shops. Alan Bullock quotes Bevin's favourite saying: 'I like to create.' This was the one thing he never did. The members of his unions were moving things about, not creating them. Even when Bevin drew up schemes for European cooperation, they were the dreams of a trader, not of a creator. There was something lacking in a labour leader who knew little of industry and nothing of the north of England.

It is easy to see what Bevin lacked. He lacked comradeship, the unconscious solidarity which the Labour movement represented. Of course there was plenty of spite and intrigue in the Labour movement, as I daresay there is even in the Church of Rome or the Communist Party. The pull of comradeship was strong all the same. That is why the open breach with MacDonald was such a misery and a torment in 1931. But not for Bevin. He always treated the Labour movement as his personal property. The members of his union were for him 'my people'. He did great things for them, but in the feudal way that a duke might look after his retainers. 'Loyalty' was the great cause which Bevin preached; it is a feudal word. If anyone was disloyal – that is, went against Bevin – then no consideration of comradeship could save him. Ben Tillett was no doubt a tippling old bore when Bevin drove him out of the presidency of the union. All the same, no other labour leader would have been so merciless. Lansbury and Bevin had worked together for years on the board of the *Daily Herald*. Did this deter Bevin when he marched up to denounce Lansbury for hawking his conscience round the Labour movement? It did not. The delegates to the conference voted for Bevin and against Lansbury; but there was not one who, in his heart, would not have liked to be Lansbury and none who wanted to be Bevin.

Bevin was solitary in another, even more significant way. He played politics by ear and with total disregard of ordinary patterns. He often displayed a dislike of intellectuals. This made him popular with the English upper classes who also dislike intellectuals, and I suspect that Alan Bullock gets some pleasure from the way in which Bevin slammed the impractical theorists. Yet Bevin was not really, to borrow his own phrase, a guileless practical man. He was a rival intellectual, playing the same game but with rules of his own. His mind ran over with cockeyed ideas; and his rambling talk, if taken down, could have gone alongside Hitler's *Table Talk* as an intellectual curiosity. Bevin could never have had a two-volume *Life* or won the admiration of the Foreign Office if he had stuck to trade union organization. It was his chaos of dynamic ideas which made him count in British politics. He saw things which his more humdrum colleagues missed. Often he saw aright. He appreciated earlier and more clearly than others the futility of a non-revolutionary General Strike; though it is fair to add that he saw through the General Strike more quickly because he had believed in it more passionately. This was a typical intellectual's change of front which would not have disgraced Crossman: all for the General Strike one day, dead against it the next. Bevin transformed the emphasis of trade union action from strikes to negotiation, and no man used the new method to better effect. It is hardly an exaggeration to say that Bevin laid the foundations of the Welfare State. But, lacking a theory or any general conception, he left the Labour movement in the bewilderment over the Welfare State which still bedevils it. He prided himself on never reading a book. Perhaps he was lucky to escape Marx; but if he had read William Morris, or even Ruskin, we should not now be in such confusion.

Bevin had also the intellectual's consuming interest in foreign affairs. He became the appointed negotiator for the trade unions – labour's foreign secretary – as early as the Councils of Action in 1920. Again he played by ear, and he played alone. Once more it was exchange of goods, access to raw materials, which interested him. These were the obsessions of a transport man, and they produced strange results. Intellectuals said many silly things between the wars. Did any intellectual say anything sillier than this: 'The old Austro-Hungarian Empire was economically perhaps the soundest thing that existed in Europe'? The empire was a device by which Magyar landlords and German capitalists exploited oppressed populations, yet

Bevin took it as his example in 1937. He was always dreaming of vast free-trade areas, sometimes for the Commonwealth, sometimes for Europe, without any thought how they contradicted each other. He once wrote to Cole: 'Really, old man, look how you have boxed the compass.' In fact, Cole erred, if at all, from rigidity of principle; it was Bevin who boxed the compass at a moment's notice, and, when he changed, everyone had to follow him.

Bevin's obsession with trade also made him exaggerate the efficacy of economic sanctions, just as he treated the League of Nations as the Transport and General Workers' Union on a larger scale. His denunciation of Lansbury at the Labour Party conference of 1935 was the highlight of Bevin's pre-war career. Lansbury's pacifism has been dismissed as impractical. Was Bevin's line any better? This sane, practical man committed himself to the extraordinary proposition that Baldwin's government could be relied on to support the League of Nations against Mussolini. Lansbury seems a monument of common-sense in comparison to this. Bevin battered down opposition. He won; he did not persuade. Men feared him; some admired him. But few felt for him the affection that they felt for Arthur Henderson – a man of equally impeccable working-class origin, who rose as high but by less ruthless methods. Bevin had many great qualities. He had one great defect: nobody called him Uncle.

The Tiger Who Walked Alone

Ernest Bevin was a big man with a strong personality and a mighty voice. Beaverbrook called him, rightly, 'a powerful beast'. He probably ranks first among British trade union leaders of the twentieth century. His contribution to the Second World War was magnificent and decisive. Without Bevin as minister of labour there would not have been a contented working class. After the war, he was a forceful foreign secretary, though opinions differ about his achievements.

All the same, three large volumes of biography make a heavy call on our interest or admiration, particularly when Alan Bullock, the biographer, rivals the ponderous style of his subject. The first volume, on Bevin's career as a trade union leader, was perhaps justified. Four hundred pages on Bevin the wartime minister of labour are not designed to stir eager curiosity.

The length could be excused if Bevin had left a large number of private papers, full of revelations. There is virtually nothing of this kind – merely notes for a few speeches and two or three cantankerous letters. Some wartime leaders, notably Churchill and Eden, were allowed to use the official records. Alan Bullock has been barred by the fifty-year, soon to be the thirty-year, rule. The bulk of his material comes from parliamentary debates, Bevin's speeches, newspaper articles, and the volumes in the official *Civil History of the Second World War*.

The analysis of Bevin's policy and achievements is, of course, competently done, but there is nothing new in it, at any rate nothing new for the student who has worked through the official histories. Occasionally Alan Bullock claims too much for Bevin. He seems to forget that the final word on manpower lay with Sir John Anderson, who conducted the manpower budget; perhaps Bevin forgot it himself.

Of course Bevin became a minister in order to do a vital job and Alan Bullock is right to lay most emphasis on this. Though Bevin told a startled Labour conference: 'I am here as one of your nominees in the war cabinet,' he was, in fact, Churchill's nominee and no one else's. He said to one of his friends: 'You know, Harry, I'm a turn-up in a million,' and he cared little about either the Labour Party or individual colleagues. When the Parliamentary Labour Party voted against the government in order to demand firmer action on the Beveridge Report, Bevin not only voted with the government, as other Labour ministers did. He turned up at the party meeting the next day and insisted that, as he had broken standing orders, he must be expelled. Though the party did not oblige him, Bevin ignored it for the next eighteen months. His idea of party democracy was that, once anything had been carried by the block-vote of his union, everyone must conform implicitly.

As man and minister, Bevin had two sides. He was, without dispute, a marvellous boss. He knew how to get the best from those round him, and they repaid him with deep affection. He said characteristically to one subordinate: 'Anything you make a mistake about, I will get you out of, and anything you do well I will take the credit for.' Only the first part of the remark was true.

Bevin showed a different spirit towards colleagues, whether of his own party or not. He trampled on opposition and rejected proffers of reconciliation. Thus Citrine tried to remove a misunderstanding. Bevin replied: 'I respect other people's positions and opinions but I expect mine to be respected also: and that is all.' He girded constantly against Morrison and said: 'Don't you believe a word the little b—— says.' He snubbed Morrison's attempt to discuss post-war policy and answered only: 'When the leader puts a policy before all of us we shall have to give it our serious consideration.' He was furious when Morrison released Sir Oswald Mosley from detention. This showed, Bevin declared, that Morrison was not to be trusted. He spoke openly of resigning from the government and was only talked out of it by Brendan Bracken of all people.

Bevin's greatest dispute was with Beaverbrook, a dispute which raged for nearly two years. There was a clash of principle and method. Beaverbrook improvised; Bevin advanced by slow, methodical stages. There was still more a clash of personality. Beaverbrook despised and neglected committees. Bevin arranged that the Production Executive should meet in Beaverbrook's own room. Beaverbrook retaliated by continuing to work at his desk during the meetings.

Here again the hand of friendship was refused. Beaverbrook wrote: 'How I would like to give support in complete agreement with you and your policy.' Bevin replied: 'I have no policy or platform except that of the government as a whole, arrived at through the war cabinet.' In the summer of 1942, according to Bevin's own account, which no doubt grew in the telling, Beaverbrook, then out of the government, told Bevin that Churchill was on the way out and offered to help make Bevin prime minister instead. Bevin indignantly went off to Churchill, who refused to believe him. Bevin complained of Churchill's relationship with Beaverbrook: 'He's like a man who's married a whore: he knows she's a whore but he loves her just the same.'

Despite his parade of loyalty, Bevin usually spoke of 'my policy' and described the working class as 'my people'. Any workers who opposed him were liable to be dismissed as Trotskyites – a charge which even Alan Bullock finds difficult to sustain. Beaverbrook once described himself as 'the cat that walks alone'. Bevin was a tiger who walked alone, and woe betide any who came near him. He was an elemental force, invaluable in wartime. But it is not surprising that other members of the Labour Party fell out with him. Bevin often bullied for a good cause: he was a bully all the same.

A Socialist Saint

This essay was first published as a review of Ross Terrill's R H Tawney *and His Times: Socialism as Fellowship (London, Deutsch, 1974) in the* Observer, *18 August 1974.*

*   *   *

R H Tawney was the sort of socialist who could happen only in England. Other writers presented socialism in terms of economic change or administrative improvement. Tawney's concern was with morality. For him socialism was a religion, and he was bewildered when his close friend William Temple resigned from the Labour Party on becoming a bishop. Tawney was in his modest way a twentieth-century saint. Of all intellectuals he was the most acceptable to the interwar Labour movement. He wrote one Labour programme – 'Labour and the Nation' – singlehanded. Crossman said of his most famous book: '*The Acquisitive Society* is my socialist bible,' and Gaitskell said at his memorial service: 'I think he was the best man I have ever known.'

Ross Terrill has written a book about Tawney's ideas rather than about his life. This was the right choice. To outward appearance Tawney's private life was much like that of any other professor of history. He wrote some outstanding works of history. He gave many lectures. He was assiduous in the Workers' Educational Association.

But Tawney was a professor with a difference. He lived up to his own principle of social equality. Despite the 'effortless superiority' (Asquith's phrase) that came from education at Rugby and Balliol, he was always on the side of the common man. In his own words: 'In the interminable case of *Dubb* v. *Superior Persons and Co.*, whether Christians, Capitalists or Communists, I am an unrepentant Dubbite.' When serving on the Somme during the First World War, his closest friend was a bricklayer – 'the man whom of all others I would choose to have beside me at a pinch'.

Thereafter he usually wore a tattered sergeant's jacket. At the London School of Economics, where he taught, he spoke scathingly of the snobbery which dominated Oxford. He never became an MA, because that degree was acquired merely by paying money. When

Ramsay MacDonald offered him a peerage, he replied contemptuously: 'Thank you for your letter. What harm have I ever done to the Labour Party? Yours sincerely, R H Tawney.' The only practical lesson that can be drawn from his voluminous writings is that members of the Labour Party should refuse all political honours. Tawney's concern was with equality – not so much equality of reward as equality of esteem. He wrote:

If men are to respect each other for what they are, they must cease to respect each other for what they own. They must abolish, in short, the reverence for riches, which is the *lues Anglicana*, the hereditary disease of the English nation. And human nature being what it is, in order to abolish the reverence for riches, they must make impossible the existence of a class which is important merely because it is rich.

The revolution Tawney wanted was a change of heart, exactly as did George Lansbury, who was also a saint in his way. Capitalism and the power of private wealth would simply disappear when men came to see that they were essentially immoral. This was the doctrine which he hammered out in book after book.

It was an admirable doctrine. Yet it is difficult not to feel that Tawney, despite his goodness and social simplicity, did not escape effortless superiority himself. It was all very well to be on the side of Henry Dubb – 'common, courageous, good-hearted, patient, proletarian fool'. Would the real Henry Dubb, if he had read any of Tawney's books (which he did not), have relished either the name or the description? For that matter would Tawney have liked to be addressed as Henry Dubb?

Though on Henry Dubb's side, Tawney was himself a Superior Person. His writings were addressed exclusively to the Superior Persons whom he claimed to despise. His books were sophisticated and allusive, the products of a classical education and beyond my comprehension, let alone that of Henry Dubb. Of the 354 articles by Tawney which Terrill lists, most appeared in the *Manchester Guardian* – a journal for Superior Persons – and not a single one in any newspaper read by Henry Dubb. It was no accident that Tawney's two admirers, Crossman and Gaitskell, were the products of that superior educational emporium, Winchester College. Tawney's socialism was essentially for public-school men. Tawney never contemplated the problem of power. No man saw more clearly the political monopoly possessed by the governing classes, yet all he could contribute to ending this was to reiterate that it was morally wrong. The revolution was to come simply by the rich and powerful reading Tawney's works and seeing the error of their ways. Events do not work out like this in real life. The rich and powerful are now trembling in their shoes not because their wickedness has been borne in on them, but because the trade unions are stronger than they used to be. At this terrible prospect the governing classes have forgotten the lessons of democracy they learnt at Balliol and are howling for a strong man or the rule of the army.

The curious thing is that as a historian – a topic relatively neglected in Terrill's book – Tawney emphasized the triumph of power over morality. Tawney was a very distinguished economic historian. Of the three Labour academics in the interwar years (Cole, Laski and Tawney) he was the only one to be elected a Fellow of the British Academy – a correct estimate of their respective merits. Many good judges rank Tawney's historical books among the greatest works on English history written this century. Their common theme is the social revolution of the sixteenth century when the village communities with their open fields were broken up and the land of England seized by a few rich men – the version of history that Cobbett had presented less professionally a century before. Cecils, Russells, Cavendishes and the other great families founded their fortunes on robbery and the ruthless use of power. If Tawney had gone on to study economic history in the nineteenth century, he would have concluded, as Marx did, that the great capitalist families made their fortunes in the same way.

What lessons did Tawney draw from this history as applied to the present day? Only that the heirs of these thieves and brigands would eagerly relinquish their spoils at the first breath of moral rebuke. I prefer the slogan I learnt in my socialist youth: 'The rich will do anything for the workers except get off their backs.'

Perhaps Tawney himself had doubts. Towards the end of his life he was trying to persuade a colleague to think well of the work of a young Marxist historian (presumably Christopher Hill). The colleague, an anti-communist, kept saying: 'But he's a communist, you know, he's a communist.' Tawney answered reflectively: 'Now is that a good thing or a bad thing?' R H Tawney was a great and good man, though I do not think that what he said was of much use to Henry Dubb.

Bolshevik Soul in a Fabian Muzzle

This essay was first published as a review of Margaret Cole's The Life of G D H Cole (*London, Macmillan, 1971*) *in the* New Statesman, *1 October 1971.*

*   *   *

Cole told his wife that *as a person* he was of no interest whatsoever: all that mattered was in his published writings which people could read if they chose. The remark was much in character. Cole had no interest in himself and very little in others. As Dame Margaret remarks in regard to his children: 'He accepted them as they came and was a kind father to them, but I doubt whether he would have felt any deprivation if he had had none.' Nevertheless Dame Margaret has done well to write his biography. Cole's books do not tell all about him. His very impersonality made him a most unusual person. Moreover he played a considerable part in Labour politics even if somewhat on the fringe. He was the outstanding Fabian of the post-Webb generation. He was, I think, the only Left figure never tinged with communism and yet equally free from anti-communism. He was the most successful socialist propagandist of his time in intellectual circles. No man was more worthy of remembrance.

Wives rarely make good biographers of their husbands. Dame Margaret Cole is the exception. She was associated with Cole's political activities almost from the first and presents them with some of his own clarity. Occasionally she slips too much from biography into general history and sometimes she exaggerates the importance of what were really coterie affairs. Broadly speaking she holds the balance right. She is equally admirable on the personal side of the story: frank as only a wife can be, devoted and yet without illusions. Cole was often prim, even priggish, and might easily have turned into a figure of fun. He was redeemed by an innocent sincerity which Dame Margaret has fully recaptured.

The extraordinary thing about Cole was that, though a left-wing socialist and an atheist, there was nothing of the rebel about him. His life, apart from the one point of his political beliefs, was one of complete orthodoxy. He had a traditionally classical education and bestowed the same education on his children. He liked the elegance of college life, particularly the table silver. His house at Hendon had large grounds, a tennis court and a badminton court. His interest in sex was minimal. He took Margaret Postgate out for country walks. One day, sitting beside her on a log, he put his arm round her and said: 'I suppose this has got to happen.' Thereafter he claimed that he had been forced into matrimony. When later he developed diabetes and was told that his enjoyment of sex would diminish, he replied: 'Thank goodness.' One of his secretaries reported: 'Womanizer was his last word in condemnation of any man.' Mostly he regarded women as a nuisance, fit only for domestic tasks. The young Margaret Cole used to boast she could not boil an egg. She had to learn this and other arts in order to care for her husband. He could not even make his own bed.

Cole was by no means a dull man despite his detachment. He was good company in an aloof intellectual way. He wrote detective stories and light verse, including an operetta on the General Strike. He often developed affection for his favourite pupils and was at one time deeply 'in love' with Hugh Gaitskell − an attachment not without embarrassment for Gaitskell whose tastes were quite other. Cole got great pleasure from country walking − hence his admiration for William Cobbett, a man whose temperament was the reverse of his own. But it had to be tame country such as the Cotswolds with hills that were 'green to the top'. He never went to the industrial regions of England if he could avoid it and, though he sometimes went abroad to look at buildings, was always glad to be back in Hendon or Oxford. He spoke excellent French, but never bothered to learn German, let alone Russian, and tolerated foreigners only when they were socialists. Indeed, if written solely in personal terms, the life of Douglas Cole would present an impeccably donnish figure.

All this was changed by a single episode when Cole was young. He read *News from Nowhere*. He experienced a total conversion. From that moment he believed in the socialist Utopia which Morris had described and dedicated his life to it. He rejected utterly the society in which he had grown up and was as rigorous against Establishment as he had previously been rigorously for it. For Cole there was no halfway house. He insisted that he was an atheist, not an agnostic − *I know* that there is no god. He attended college chapel until he was twenty-one. Then he informed the master of Balliol that he had conformed out of respect for his parents' wishes and did not propose to attend chapel any longer. The master forbade him ever to appear in chapel again. Cole was the only fellow of an Oxford college who, when presiding at dinner, never mumbled the most innocuous words of grace. He stood tight-lipped for fifteen seconds (not two minutes as John Sparrow alleges) and then sat down. On every other point of college procedure he was sternly orthodox. His attitude was shown in the education he sought in vain for his children: a traditional curriculum combined with positive atheism. Cole took the logical view that, since the upholders of existing society attached importance to religious ritual, he should be equally firm against it. What he disliked in God, apart from His non-existence, was that He was on the side of the capitalist system.

Cole's rejection of capitalism was total. Though comfortably off, he refused to invest his surplus money or even to take interest from his bank. When I remarked to him that he was making a present of the interest to the bank, he replied: 'Better that my banker should commit mortal sin than that I should.' Christopher Hill, as an undergraduate, was delighted to hear Cole say at a meeting: 'Of course, I should *prefer* the whole system smashed.' Cole did not merely detest capitalism. He also believed that a new and perfect society could be achieved and thought a good deal about this in practical terms. Economic reorganization was not enough for him. He wanted a fundamental revolution in men's minds and in their behaviour to each other. Socialism without democracy was worthless in his eyes, and by democracy he did not mean a resort to the ballot box every five years, but working democracy every day. In the early part of his career he preached guild socialism, and many of his books were concerned with workers' control. In one of his last speeches he urged fellow-socialists not to think that 'socialists can afford to give up being *levellers*'. He regarded *News from Nowhere* as a concrete description of the future society.

There was a paradox, even a contradiction, in Cole's political life. Though revolutionary in outlook, he was practical and reformist when it came to action. Maurice Reckitt described Cole best as having 'a Bolshevik soul in a Fabian muzzle'. During the First World War he acted as expert adviser to the trade unions and esteemed Arthur Henderson above all other Labour leaders. He was assiduous on committees of investigation and research. He founded the Labour

Research Department, the New Fabian Research Bureau, the Society for Socialist Inquiry and Propaganda and, at the end of his life, the International Society for Socialist Studies. He believed in the working-class movement. Translated into practical terms, this meant yet another group of two or three hundred middle-class intellectuals most of whom had never spoken to a working man in their lives. There was also a personal contradiction in his public behaviour. In private Cole was cool, rational and at worst slightly disdainful. Once on a committee he became ruthless and impatient. Beatrice Webb describes how, when defeated at a Fabian meeting, Cole said: 'I withdraw the word "Fools". I substitute "Bloody fools",' and flounced out of the room. He often resigned in anger and then returned some months later without a word of apology. Despite his democratic principles, Cole never shook off the belief that there was in the world one Just Man.

This was not true when Cole moved from politics to education. Here he was infinitely modest and cooperative. The Cole Group which he ran in Oxford for many years was enormously influential and produced many leading figures in the present Labour Party. Cole did not tell the young men what to think. For most of the time he sat silent, encouraging them to think for themselves. He was an inspiration, not a director, a true educator, drawing his pupils out. Only Harold Laski rivalled Cole as a socialist educator, and Laski was incidentally the only human being whom Cole personally disliked. This was a curious lapse into jealousy, though the clash of personalities was also obvious enough. Cole thought that Laski was flamboyant and romantic. Certainly Cole was neither. He disliked the excitement of big public meetings, though he sometimes addressed them, and once teased me by saying: 'All you like in politics is fighting.' In a more affectionate way Cole also disapproved of Kingsley Martin and accepted Beatrice Webb's description of him as a flibberty-gibbet. Henceforth Martin signed his letters to Cole: 'Flibber T. Gibbet.' Kingsley won that round.

Cole's books showed him at his best. There were over a hundred of them, all models of exposition and simplification. Cole was not, I think, an original scholar, and most of his books are now out of date except for his marvellous edition of *Rural Rides*. But this was what Cole intended. He served the cause of socialism with unquestioning devotion, even though nearly half his life was harassed by diabetes.

His last words, when his strength finally ebbed, were in character: 'I'm sorry to be a nuisance.' Douglas Cole came as near to complete integrity as any man of his time. I venerated him

Intellectual in Politics

This essay was first published as a review of Kingsley Martin's Harold Laski *(London, Gollancz, 1953) in the* New Statesman and Nation, *17 January 1953.*

*　　*　　*

Evidently when I wrote this review I still suffered like Harold Laski from Hope.

There are few men of whom one can truthfully say that the world would have been a different place without them. Harold Laski was one of those few. His was the most important influence in remaking English social democracy and giving it its present form. He deserved a biography which should be more than a personal tribute; and he has got it. Kingsley Martin has written a book which is a serious contribution to our political history and, what is more difficult still, presents his dead friend without fear or favour. Anyone who sets out to expose Laski's failings can save himself the trouble; Kingsley Martin treats them fairly with a detachment which Laski himself would have wished. There are some faults which may disturb the historian. Events are occasionally run together. For instance, the fall of Lloyd George and the creation of the first Labour government are both made to happen in 1921. More seriously, there is a lack of proportion. After all, Kingsley Martin is a professional journalist, despite his training as a historian; the present and future interest him more than the dead past. Hence, the last ten years of Laski's life occupy nearly half the book. Yet these were an epilogue and in many ways an unsatisfactory one. The most interesting decade of Laski's life was the twenties, the years of his intellectual growth; and the most important was the thirties, the decade of the Left Book Club and the Popular Front. This criticism does not alter the fact that Kingsley Martin has written a very good biography, at once moving and instructive.

Though Laski was to play an important part in the English Labour movement, he came to it in an unusual way. He was a Jew, not a Nonconformist, by origin; in spirit, sometimes the nearest thing we have had to a continental intellectual, sometimes an American liberal, but never a straight English radical. He learnt his socialism from French writers of the eighteenth century and his politics from American lawyers; he learnt nothing from Cobbett or William Morris. He knew little at first hand of the English working class. He was born in a rich Manchester family; after Oxford, he spent his formative years in Canada and at Harvard; and he returned to the London School of Economics. Even at Oxford, as Kingsley Martin points out, it was Cole and G N Clark, not Laski, who were prominent in the famous tram strike; and when he came to write about trade unions, his interest in them was that of an academic lawyer. He wanted to show their similarity with the medieval Church and other 'corporate personalities', not to present them as the fighting organizations of the English people. He thought it more important to manipulate politicians than to stir emotion. I remember how he once shocked me by his admiration for Disraeli and his dislike of Gladstone. Yet, by a strange twist of fate, his greatest success was to come when he emulated 'the People's William'.

This was certainly not Laski's intention. When he came to the London School of Economics, he had two ambitions. He wished to be a great political thinker; and he wished to exercise a decisive influence behind the scenes of political life. He did not achieve either ambition. . Kingsley Martin says very fairly: 'academically Harold did not fulfil the promise of . . . his early books'. At first Laski tried to develop a theory of pluralism, which he had learnt from Maitland and Gierke; it was a trail that led nowhere, and *The Grammar of Politics* now lies neglected on the shelves. Later he turned himself deliberately into a Marxist, and made more than one attempt to survey English and American history from a Marxist outlook. But though he knew a great deal of political philosophy, he lacked both detailed historical knowledge and the historian's temperament. I do not think that any professional historian could take Laski's writings on English history seriously; and though Norman MacKenzie (who has contributed the American chapters to this biography) does his best for *The American Democracy*, the verdict of scholars has not been in its favour. In private conversation Laski had the amiable weakness of inventing facts to support his argument; and in his writings, too, he inclined to believe that the facts would conform to the ideas, if only these were brilliant enough.

In much the same way, he thought that he could change the facts of the present by rational persuasion of a few individuals. He wrote constantly to Baldwin; he advised MacDonald on the composition of the first Labour cabinet – or so he imagined; even during the Second World War he tried to turn Winston Churchill into a socialist by correspondence. Though he often talked in terms of class war, he really assumed that the English governing classes could be cajoled and argued into abdicating. He did not understand their skill, their tenacity or, above all, their ruthlessness; and he was hurt and surprised when they bit the hand that stroked them. It bewildered Laski when the director of the London School of Economics, himself a 'liberal' pundit, objected to his writing for the *Daily Herald*; and the ban successfully imposed on Laski was certainly an odd demonstration of academic freedom, when one considers the political activities in which heads of college have subsequently engaged. But did Laski really suppose that Sir William Beveridge would weigh *The Times* and the *Daily Herald* in the same liberal scales? The failure of the libel action, in which he attempted to vindicate himself from the charge of preaching 'bloody revolution', broke Laski's heart. Certainly the campaign against Laski by the Beaverbrook–Churchill combination showed few scruples. But was it reasonable for an advanced socialist to expect sympathetic consideration of his views from a special jury and a High Court judge? The answer to mudslinging is to sling better mud back. He who goes to equity must go with clean hands; he who challenges the ruling classes needs quite other equipment.

Laski got this unexpectedly. It was not his reasoning power, his assiduity, or his social contacts that made him an important figure; it was the following that he came to command. He built this first within the London School of Economics. Though his was not an original mind, he was an inspired and inspiring lecturer; even more, he was a devoted teacher. He gave himself to his pupils without reserve; and he gave himself to them all, brilliant and mediocre alike, as Norman McKenzie describes in his moving account of Laski as a teacher at Cambridge during the war years. The influential academic figures of the past – a Jowett or a Lowes Dickinson – worked through a few distinguished pupils; Laski created a heaven which went much wider. The Labour government of 1945, for instance, had many of Cole's pupils among its members; none, I think, of Laski's. His influence operated in the junior ranks of the Labour movement and in India, Burma and West Africa. Kingsley Martin observes rightly that the most enthusiastic education officers in the army during the war would often turn out to have been trained by Laski. High academics never took Laski seriously as a thinker but he had exactly the right form for the new audience of 'mass-intellectuals'.

It was this audience that gave Laski his unique position. The intellectuals of previous generations were a closed, limited body. Bentham changed English history by capturing a few dozen disciples. In the twentieth century the number of those who made reason the master of their lives became much larger. The intellectuals ceased to be a small academic class; instead, their outlook was to be found indiscriminately in all walks of life. Here was the natural market for the Left Book Club; here was the wider audience waiting for Laski's guidance and inspiration. There was a decisive political consequence. Owing to the peculiar constitution of the Labour Party, the mass-intellectuals found their expression in the constituency parties, and there was a growing cleavage of outlook between these and the trade unions. The constituency parties needed their own representative and this need often sought strange outlets, from Oswald Mosley to Aneurin Bevan. Laski alone filled the role perfectly. He was not merely the spokesman of the mass-intellectuals, he was their personification. What use should he make of his power? This was a new problem, and Laski did not solve it. He might have remained a thinker and writer, inspiring others; he might have become a practical politician, fighting every detail. Laski tried to combine the two roles. Though he became chairman of the Labour Party, he would not contest a parliamentary seat. Kingsley Martin passes a verdict that must be quoted in full:

No man, however disinterested or clever, can accomplish by letter, conversation and private memorandum, the feat of changing the policy of a great party, since that is based not on the wishes or opinions of individuals, but on the interests of classes and groups. A man who wishes to lead a revolutionary movement, or even less ambitiously to redirect a party's policy, must change the balance of power within the party, must make it to the interest of its leaders to change their minds, or of their followers to change their leaders. That involves working with other men in a team, taking the knocks and rewards of party politics and inevitably to some extent losing the type of respect and influence which is paid to the scholar and teacher.

Laski realized this towards the end of his life, when he refused to stand again for the Labour Party executive.

Yet perhaps his influence could not have been so great if he had shrunk from stark, practical responsibilities. Laski had something to contribute to the intellectual atmosphere of the time which only he could give. He strove with the problem which confronts every reasoning man – how to be both a liberal and a Marxist. No one who believes in liberty can ever work sincerely with communists or trust them; yet no one who has socialism in his bones can ever condemn communism without reserve. This is the dilemma of our times; all Laski's later writings and all his political activity revolved round it. Sometimes he got the emphasis wrong, as in the days of the Popular Front. But essentially he was right. The answer to communism is not anti-communism; it is a democratic socialism, equally convinced of its principles, but more tolerant in applying them. How much easier the situation in Europe would be today if the Labour government had followed Laski's advice in 1945 and put itself at the head of European social democracy. How much more peaceful and secure the Middle East would be if this country had welcomed Jewish social democracy instead of following the barren anti-Semitism of Ernest Bevin and the Foreign Office. Laski knew, none better, the difficulties of his policy; he did not need any disillusioned communist, returned from Utopia, to tell him the evils of Moscow rule. But he still believed that the world could be saved; and he tried to save it. In the last article he ever wrote, which was published after his death, he argued against Bertrand Russell's division of the world into two irreconcilable power blocs: 'Lord Russell builds his policy upon despair. I build my policy upon hope.' This was a noble legacy. If today in this country there is still no communist movement of any size, if all socialists can still be at home in the Labour Party, we owe it more to Harold Laski than to any other single man.

The Road to Great Turnstile

First published in the New Statesman, *14 January 1966, as a review of* Father Figures *by Kingsley Martin (London, Hutchinson, 1966), the first and as it proved the only volume of his autobiography.*

*   *   *

How to succeed without trying is a rare art. There is one still rarer, a speciality of intellectuals: How to succeed while persistently trying to fail. Rousseau is the acknowledged master of this art. He was perhaps the most influential writer of modern times, and his autobiography is a record of follies, mishaps and discomfitures. Kingsley Martin is a latter-day Rousseau. He has had unique success as editor of a weekly periodical. He increased the circulation of the *New Statesman* fivefold, he actually made the paper pay; his influence and importance were acknowledged all over the world. Yet, according to his own account, he stumbled into greatness unawares. He shamelessly parades his failings and mistakes. Thus, at Cambridge, 'I spoke at the Union, but was so nervous that I usually had to run to the lavatory instead of speaking.' When in America, he wrote home: 'I am not really an able person in any important way. And yet I am not content to be second. I wish I could cease to be jealous and ambitious, and yet if I did I should cease to do any work at all.'

He extracts comedy even from the hardships of the First World War, when he served in the Friends' Ambulance Unit:

I was told to empty a large bin of lime into small receptacles. Although warned, I rendered myself useless for several days by completely skinning my arms to the elbow. Then they sent me to clean out the gutters of the roof. I forgot that it was made of glass, and people washing many feet below were surprised when the roof fell in and I with it.

Fortunately Kingsley Martin, unlike Rousseau, has a sense of humour. Rousseau took his woes seriously. Martin laughs at them and even, I suspect, piles them on. He remarks when describing his friendship with Lowes Dickinson: 'Our talk was gloomy in the extreme – but we were very merry just the same.' He remained merry in a world where everything was going wrong and where he himself always expected the worst. He remained merry despite his own setbacks. Besides, his mysterious gift for success came into play, like a natural law. Though he stepped unerringly on every banana-skin in sight, he bounced up, after each fall, higher than before. When hoping for a fellowship at Cambridge, he was invited to dinner at Peterhouse and arrived home too late to change.

I just ate something in my rooms and thought no more about it. Next day I learnt that the whole high table had waited dinner for me until eight o'clock. My name was something worse than mud . . . I expect, looking back, I lost a good chance of staying in Cambridge and becoming a professor.

Perhaps a little exaggerated, but certainly a setback.

However, failure at Cambridge carried him to the LSE, which suited him much better; 'a wonderful home of free discussion, happily mixed race, and genuine learning. It seemed my natural home'. Then another fall. Martin wrote a little book about the General Strike and criticized the Samuel Commission. Beveridge, director of LSE, had served on the commission and had largely written its report. 'A young member of his staff criticizing his Royal Commission with such disrespect was really too much.' Martin was refused 'normal promotion'. Down again, and 'in the midst of this row', he was invited to succeed C E Montague as principal leader-writer on the *Manchester Guardian* at £1,000 a year – 'an extraordinary offer'. He wrote his own terms – £800 a year, but three months away from Manchester. Failure once more followed success. 'Within a month or two of my arrival I realized that things had gone wrong. The Scotts had decided that I was both incompetent and dangerously left-wing.'

In 1930 he was back in London, unemployed and prowling round for a job. Arnold Bennett summoned him to the Savoy and asked: 'What are your . . . p-p-politics?' Martin answered, 'rather too timidly', that he would call himself a socialist. 'I should hope so,' said Bennett, and with this Martin was in as editor of the *New Statesman*. The paper was in poor shape after the erratic latter days of Clifford Sharp. It soon received a shot in the arm. Keynes, in his turn, summoned Martin and asked: 'Are you going to stand for the necessary interference with free trade and *laissez-faire*?' The answer proving satisfactory, Keynes handed over the *Nation*, of which he had grown tired. Not long after, events threw in the *Weekend Review* also. The amalgamated paper had a bit of everything: intellectual Fabianism

from the *New Statesman*, emotional radicalism from the *Nation*, gaiety
and satire from the *Weekend Review*. Martin himself was both serious
and frivolous. 'I suppose my prime attitude was a dissenter's. A
dissenter sees that the world is bad and expresses his moral indignation.' A few sentences later: 'Editing the paper was fun. We constantly
laughed at ourselves.' He fought for the impossible without expecting
to win. After a lifetime of gloom, however, he ends up cheerful: 'In
1965, I am not sure that the primitives will always conquer.'

  Characteristically, in this last sentence, as often elsewhere, Martin
has wandered beyond his brief. The present volume is intended as a
first instalment, ending when Martin reached the editorial chair. Old
students of Critic's Diary do not need to be told that the autobiographer provides a bit of everything, from anecdotes about personalities
to dabblings in psychology. Schooldays, for instance, send Martin off
on his old hobby-horse of flagellation. The deepest theme is indicated
in the title. Martin was not only a dissenter. He was the son of a
dissenter, with an equally fine record. Basil Martin was a Congrega-
tional minister who moved away from Christianity, became a Unitar-
ian, and finally 'believed more and more in less and less'. His
windows were broken during the Boer War, his furniture seized
during passive resistance against the Education Act of 1902. Kingsley
Martin loved his father. Not surprisingly, he managed to turn this
into a grievance:

All boys in adolescence must break with their parents. My trouble was that
my father gave me no chance at all to quarrel with him ... His causes
became my causes, his revolt was mine ... I was much retarded because I
did not work out these dissenting positions for myself, but freewheeled, as it
were, with the momentum that I had gained from my father's lonely struggle
against Calvinism.

This is the voice of Kingsley Martin, amateur psychologist, inventing
explanations long afterwards. It is wrongheaded, like most psychology.
I had much the same relationship with my father and have derived
nothing but strength from his example. Father–son hostility is a great
waste of time. It becomes an obsession, as it did with Samuel Butler,
and it prevents a dissenter from getting on with his real job which is
to kick against the world. Martin was lucky in his father, and he knew
it. Perhaps he got a bit stuck in the relationship. As the title of his
book indicates, he sought father substitutes, until he became a father

figure himself in the editorial chair. He writes with deep affection of the older men whom he venerated: Lowes Dickinson in particular, but even – until disappointed – Beveridge and C P Scott. There are also plenty of contemporaries in the book, but they are written up from outside, adorned with anecdotes in a lively journalistic way. The young Martin seems to have had few friends of his own age. He gives the impression at Cambridge of being always on a bicycle – the machine of a solitary 'flibberty-gibbet', Beatrice Webb's word for him. He remained a solitary flibberty-gibbet throughout life.

There were other reasons for this detachment. Martin, despite his disclaimers, has always been a professional. He meant to be a professional historian – a fate he escaped fortunately for history and still more fortunately for himself. He became a professional journalist, he ended as a highly professional editor. He may boast that it was all done without hands. This only makes his professionalism the greater. The professional in any walk of life has no time for intimate social contacts. Moreover, in a typically intellectual way, Martin never knew much of what was going on around him. He was born in Hereford. He grew up in Finchley. What do they know of England who only Hereford and Finchley know? Instead, Martin knew a great deal about the rest of the world. The *Manchester Guardian* always set him to write leaders on Kenya. When the *New Statesman* made a profit, 'I forgot to get my salary doubled. Instead, I had a good conscience travelling round the world at the paper's expense.' He thinks he is unworldly. In fact, he has worldly wisdom of a superior kind:

The secret is never to spend as much as you earn and always to have something in hand. It's fatal to invest money . . . When the crash comes you lose the lot. You might have had fun with it.

Kingsley Martin has had fun. He provided fun for the readers of his paper. He now provides it for the readers of his autobiography. At the Day of Judgement, he will be asked, like Matthew Arnold: 'Why cannot you be wholly serious?' This will make him laugh more than ever.

Bewitched by Power

This essay first appeared as a review of R H S Crossman's The Charm of Politics *(London, Hamish Hamilton, 1958) in the* Manchester Guardian, *21 November 1958. Richard Howard Stafford Crossman (1907–74) went on to be a cabinet minister (1964–70) under Harold Wilson and to continue to aspire to write a major work on modern British politics (for which purpose he kept detailed diaries). Crossman had been an Oxford city councillor, being elected in 1935 and leading a Labour group of six. In his autobiography Alan Taylor wrote of the first year after he returned to Oxford to teach at Magdalen College from October 1938:*

We made hardly any acquaintances outside Magdalen: only Dick Crossman whom I first encountered making an enormous bonfire for his stepchildren on Guy Fawkes' Day. With his overpowering though fickle enthusiasm he urged me to become an Oxford city councillor as he was. A year later he had forgotten about Oxford and its city council for ever.

* * *

Mr Crossman is the Burke of our day. He has given up to party what was meant for mankind. He has a wonderful gift of exposition, picking out the essential facts in a situation and drawing general conclusions. He writes with inexhaustible zest, every sentence tingling with life. He will bite at new ideas and worry them, as a dog does a bone. Anyone who has seen him in action at a summer school must recognize that he is an inspired teacher; and his occasional writings are proof that he could have produced a great textbook of politics. But he has been tempted into what is mistakenly called practical life. He serves devotedly on the national executive of the Labour Party; devises schemes by which we shall all be well off in 2008; and dreams of the time when he will be an undersecretary. Yet there are nearly 300 Labour MPs, to say nothing of another 300 Labour candidates, all cut from the same cloth; and only one Crossman. His admirers must content themselves with this collection of essays, splendid reading indeed, but not the great book that he ought to have written. Why has he made Burke's fatal choice?

The answer is to be found in the revealing title which Mr Crossman has given to his new book. 'Charm' does not mean that he finds politics delightful. It is 'charm' in the magical sense; he is enthralled by them. He makes the point himself when he describes Warden Fisher of New College, reliving the great days when he sat in cabinet with Lloyd George; and one can see the young Crossman resolving to succeed on the battlefield where Fisher had failed. Yet the 'chirruping Dons' to whom he refers could have warned Crossman that he too would fail, as all intellectuals fail in practical politics. Burke, John Stuart Mill, Fisher – it is the same story. Though they are 'charmed' by politics, they cannot resist, too, the fascination of an idea; and, like Crossman, they can never decide which is the mistress, which the wife. What are the 'politics' by which Crossman is charmed? Are they politics as understood by Aristotle, Rousseau, or Harold Laski – the deep unconscious tides of ideas and concepts? Or are 'politics' the counting of votes and the manoeuvres of parliamentary committees? Both are important, both real; but it is fatal to mix them up. The great 'politician' in the practical sense does not know what he is doing; this is the source of his strength. Of course, he knows how to win men or to work the machine; but he does not check his acts by referring to the book of general principles. Crossman, like most academics, cannot resist lifting the lid all the time to look at the works; and any cook can tell him what happens to a cake if you keep opening the oven door.

Crossman has seen the works. He has discovered the secret of politics. This secret is power. True, the essential part of it is that it must be unconscious power. Would F D Roosevelt, would even Hitler, have succeeded if he had said to the people, 'I am an opportunist. All I want is power, I don't care for what.' The true art of politics is to have ideals and to believe in them, but not too much. The politician uses ideals; he is not used by them. To academic minds this seems hypocrisy; and from Machiavelli onwards intellectuals have tried to explain the conjuring trick. Crossman is in this tradition – a marvellous explainer of tricks, but a fumbler when it comes to pulling rabbits out of a hat. When Mme de Staël deserted the intellectual Benjamin Constant for a young guards officer, Constant complained that his successful rival had no conversation. Mme de Staël replied: 'Speech does not happen to be his language.' General ideas are not the language of politicians, at any rate not of those politicians who win the game.

St Mugg of Manchester

This obituary of Malcolm Thomas Muggeridge (1903–90) appeared in the Guardian, *15 November 1990. Muggeridge outlived Alan Taylor by two months.*

* * *

Malcolm Muggeridge and I became friends when we were in Manchester more than fifty years ago: he as a leader writer on the *Manchester Guardian*, I as a lecturer at the university. The Muggeridges had the ground floor of a converted Didsbury house; my wife and I had a flat in the attic. It was very much a communal life. Thereafter our ways parted, but the deep affection Malcolm and I felt for each other never dimmed. He wrote not long ago that though we had never agreed about anything, we had never quarrelled: a rare tribute for Malcolm to pay.

I can best characterize Malcolm Muggeridge by taking the title of one of his books, *In a Valley of This Restless Mind*. I have never known a man so restless, physically and in his thinking. He could not write a leader or a chapter in a book without jumping up half a dozen times to pace around the room or rush out for a walk along the bank of the Mersey.

His life was the same on a larger scale. Malcolm never stayed in one job or even in one town for long. When I first knew him he was still under thirty. Yet he had already managed to fit in three years at Cambridge, then a spell teaching English at a Christian university in Travancore, and after that three years teaching at Cairo University. Malcolm liked India and did not like Egypt, from which he escaped to the *Manchester Guardian*. [Arthur Ransome, then the *Guardian*'s correspondent in Egypt, recommended him to C P Scott, and he joined the paper as a leader writer in 1930.]

In outlook Malcolm was a birthright Fabian, accustomed from his earliest years to Fabian summer schools with their sandals and home-spun tweeds (though his father combined managing a shirt-making business in Croydon with Labour politics). His Fabianism was rein-forced by marriage to Kitty Dobbs, the ravishing niece of Beatrice Webb.

Fabianism suited well the *Manchester Guardian* of the time. Difficulties came with the financial crisis of 1931. Crozier and Wadsworth, the two senior figures on the paper, were for supporting the National government. Malcolm was for opposing it, and he triumphed when Ted Scott, the editor, returned from holiday.

I remember the victor's mien that Malcolm brought back with him from the editorial office. He had a vision of leading the *Manchester Guardian* on some great campaign of liberation. Some months later the vision turned to dust when Ted Scott was drowned in Lake Windermere. Crozier, Ted's successor, set the *Guardian* on a staider course.

Malcolm soon developed a new enthusiasm: the Soviet Union. He sought a Utopia and like others at the time was convinced that he would find it in Moscow. I warned him that he would be disappointed. He would not listen: 'The only danger is that I shall be unworthy. Soviet Russia will be too good for me.' Off he went, leaving his worldly possessions, and incidentally his family, behind him.

Malcolm arrived in Moscow when the Stalinist tyranny and the great famine which Stalin induced were just beginning. Within a couple of weeks Malcolm was disillusioned. Not only did he lose his faith in communism, he also turned sharply against all the left-wing ideas which he had acquired in his youth. This was the greatest crisis of his younger life. Many years were to pass before he discovered a faith again. Until then he gave the appearance of being an embittered cynic. This was not really true: Malcolm was a cynic who got great fun out of it.

Once escaped from Moscow, he had to put his life together again. Once more it was astonishing how much he fitted in during the six years before the war: a stretch on the *Evening Standard*, a year or so as assistant editor of the *Calcutta Statesman*, and then back to reviewing novels for the *Daily Telegraph*.

He also wrote some novels himself. *Winter in Moscow* was an account half fancy, half fact of that terrible time: the best account, I think, ever written. *Picture Palace* displayed Malcolm's idealistic lack of common-sense. The book was a very funny and reasonably fair picture of life on the *Manchester Guardian* when Malcolm was there. Unfortunately it contained highly libellous portraits of leading figures on the paper, easily identifiable. The book had to be withdrawn and has never been published.

It was much the same with a biography of Samuel Butler, author of

Erewhon, which Jonathan Cape commissioned. Cape hoped to revive Butler's flagging sales. Malcolm saw in Butler a hero of his youth, and produced a version so scathing that Butler must have sunk into even deeper obscurity. Yet all I can now remember of these disappointments and setbacks is the gaiety they provoked.

The world changed again for Malcolm when the Second World War broke out. Once more he had found a cause. 'This war,' he told me, 'will be a crusade against evil things.' Of course among the evil things Malcolm included the Soviet Union, and there was not much of the crusade left for him when Soviet Russia became our ally. However, if Malcolm did not find a crusade for long, he found entertainment when he became an intelligence officer in MI6. This culminated in the remarkable arrangement whereby he directed British intelligence on the east coast of Africa and Graham Greene directed it on the west; which illustrates the Muggeridge law that real life always surpasses in fantasy the wildest products of the imagination.

Malcolm finished the war as an intelligence officer in Paris where he performed the incomparable service of getting P G Wodehouse out of France to the security of Switzerland.

After the war Malcolm became among the first – in words – of the cold warriors. Discerning in the Labour government unwitting tools of Moscow, he even spoke for Conservative candidates at by-elections. His more serious task was to put his journalistic career together again. He was by now a first-rate and very experienced leader writer. Over the years he was sometimes in Fleet Street, sometimes in Washington, sometimes in New York. He liked all three places. Perhaps it would be more correct to say that he liked least of the three the one where he happened to be at the moment.

The climax of this period was reached when Malcolm became editor of *Punch*. This was then a prestigious appointment, and for this reason he disliked it from the first. 'How absurd' was his favourite phrase, and he now applied it to himself. Besides he liked writing; he did not like administration, particularly the routine which goes with the work of an editor. He regarded the readers of *Punch* as being as absurd as himself, not an endearing characteristic to them.

Malcolm left *Punch* with great relief. Once more there was a change in his life. He withdrew increasingly from London and enjoyed his country house in Robertsbridge, Sussex. Here he could walk out into the fields whenever he wanted. He could write what he wanted, and still got great enjoyment from this.

Television was a great emancipation for him as it became for some others, including myself. It even took him back to India thirty years later. No more Raj; no more sahibs; no more viceroy. With what enjoyment Malcolm seated himself on the throne of the deserted vice-regal palace at Simla. As a television debater I thought him less good, being inclined to repeat the same idea over and over again. I did not regard him as a formidable television antagonist. Perhaps I was disarmed by my abiding love for him.

Malcolm's puritanism suited him as he grew older. It was really a flashback to his early Fabianism where teetotalism and vegetarianism had prevailed. Malcolm had never liked good cooking and dismissed vintage wine as 'merely alcohol, dear boy'. This had not prevented him from drinking to excess in his younger days.

The greatest change in him was his discovery of God and Jesus Christ. All religion is to me a buzzing in the ears, and I cannot explain or even describe what happened to Malcolm. All I know is that he was utterly sincere.

Sometimes he had full faith in a future life. Sometimes he believed only in 'that of God that makes for righteousness'. Sometimes he gave the impression of wishing that his faith went deeper. Certainly religious faith enriched his later years without making him in any way sanctimonious. I suspect he understood little of theology and perhaps cared little also. [In 1982, Muggeridge surprised his friends by being received into the Roman Catholic Church, after bringing Mother Teresa to the attention of the world through the medium of television. He wrote an account of this sea-change, after years of atheism, in *Conversion: A Spiritual Journey* (1988).]

The one fixed point in Malcolm's life was his marriage with Kitty Dobbs, a marvellous woman as beautiful in old age as in youth. They often quarrelled, as was inevitable with Malcolm's restlessness. But they always came together again. On one occasion Kitty ended a quarrel which had lasted three weeks by saying: 'You had better stick to me. You'll never find anyone who loves you so much.' This was true. Malcolm and Kitty were as much in love at the end of their lives as they had been when they married.

Thus Spake Hitler

This essay was first published as a review of F H Hinsley's Hitler's Strategy *(Cambridge, Cambridge University Press, 1951) and* Hitlers Tischgespräche im Führerhauptquartier 1941–42, *edited by Henry Picker (Bonn, Athenaum, 1951) in* The Times Literary Supplement, *4 January 1952.*

*   *   *

Though Hitler finished as a charred corpse soaked in petrol, he achieved his deepest wish: he staked out his claim in history and eclipsed his rivals. The other dictators of our time – Mussolini, Stalin, even Lenin – seem commonplace in comparison; industrious politicians with a different set of tricks. Hitler had a depth and elaboration of evil all his own, as though something primitive had emerged from the bowels of the earth. At the same time, there was a superb cunning, which enabled him to exploit others. Perhaps there has never been a man who understood power better or who turned it to baser uses. It is loathsome to read of his actions, most loathsome to read his own utterances; yet, with all the disgust, it is impossible not to feel also that here was a piece of human nature on a gigantic scale. No doubt Hitler personified the ignorance, brutality, and greed of millions of his countrymen. He became more than life-size. The millions made their weight felt in all Hitler's words and acts.

Hitler lived on two planes more than most men. He was a man of action, rising to supreme power in Germany and thereafter almost a world-conqueror. He was also what for want of a better word must be called a 'thinker'. The great problem is to find a link between the two. Hitler, though evil, was great in action. He knew when to wait, when to act; his intuition simplified everything and cut to the heart of the situation. At the end of his career he made gross miscalculations which ruined him; but they were the miscalculations of a gambler who knew that he was playing for the highest stakes. But when he philosophized, he was opaque. His thought moved in a fog of his own making, a mixture of prejudices and misconceptions. The men round him were often playing a part, pretending to believe for the sake of their own advantage. Hitler had unquestioning faith in the rubbish that filled his mind. How could a man so ignorant, so enslaved by stupid dogmas, have achieved such practical success?

A new book gives a picture of Hitler at the height of his power. Martin Bormann, Hitler's most devoted sycophant, was anxious not to lose any of his master's words; and he arranged for a shorthand writer to attend at mealtimes in headquarters. Dr Picker performed this duty from 21 March until 2 August 1942; and, as well, he drew on the scantier notes of his predecessor who had begun his task in the previous July. Hitler had overcome the difficulties of the first Russian winter; Stalingrad and the entry of the United States into the war were still before him. He imagined himself within sight of decisive victory and could talk of his plans for making an Aryan world. He had always been given to monologue, and success made him pontificate more than ever. No one interrupted, hardly anyone spoke once Hitler had been launched on some theme; and the massive tedium is made worse by the fact that the shorthand writer laid down his pencil whenever Hitler ran dry. After all, the poor chap had somehow to eat his dinner with one hand, while scribbling with the other. These interminable mealtime harangues in the bunkers, or in Hitler's special trains, can be paralleled only by Coleridge table-talking, as immortalized by Sir Max Beerbohm. But at least Coleridge's hearers could nod; the participants at Hitler's headquarters had to sit bolt upright and maintain an intelligent interest. It must have been among the graver perils of high office to have to listen to this relentless bore. Yet a leading German historian has edited Dr Picker's notes with scholarly gravity. Each fragment is numbered and given a title; and there is a weighty introduction, combining praise and blame. Certainly Professor Ritter condemns Hitler for thinking himself a superman; but only a great statesman would deserve to have his opinions reproduced so fully, and it is likely that more Germans will read this book for Hitler's inspiration than for Professor Ritter's criticism.

The table-talk is a revelation of Hitler rather as he wished to appear than as he was. He was talking before an audience of some twenty people, half of them professional soldiers, and no doubt his eye never wandered far from the shorthand-writer. Though he spoke little of himself, neither he nor his listeners had any doubt that he was 'one of Germany's greatest sons'. He made no attempt to hide his origins or to erase them. He was the man from the gutter; and he explained on one occasion that he had become a non-smoker in Vienna because

he could not afford both cigarettes and bread. The audience was not
suited to the reminiscences of early days in the party, which he
favoured when he was with his old comrades. Once he gave a
detailed account of his coming to power, emphasizing its legality and
placing the responsibility on Hindenburg and Papen. All the same,
this seizure of power was never far from his thoughts. It was the time
when he had known how to wait and to let his rivals destroy each
other. Now he was waiting for a similar miracle, by which the
enemy coalition would somehow be dissolved. He hated both Russia
and America, and despised them. His dream was that the English
governing classes would somehow come to their senses and make
peace with him. 'If Hoare comes to power he only needs to release
the Fascists.' He had hopes even of Mr Churchill. 'Better a hundred
times Churchill than Cripps'; and he blamed the German diplomatists for not managing to arrange a love affair with one of Mr
Churchill's daughters – this, he imagined, would have reversed British
policy.

These were mere asides. More often Hitler would philosophize in
the common German way. There is nothing here to sustain the
view that he was a close student of Nietzsche; it would be nearer
the truth to say that he translated Wagner into political terms. His
hostility to Christianity was vulgar claptrap; it was a religion for
women and weaklings. The Gods and the laws of nature, which he
often invoked, were merely a cloak for his principle that the stronger
were always right; this principle, though he did not know it, was
soon to operate against himself. He praised the Oberammergau passion play as a wonderful demonstration of the Jewish danger: 'Pon-
tius Pilate appears as a Roman so superior racially and intellectually
that he stands out as a rock in the midst of the Near Eastern scum
and swarm.' Hitler was confident that he himself belonged to Olym-
pus, if there was one: 'the most enlightened spirits of all times will
be found there'. And with the present period of struggle, 'we are
moving towards a sunny, really tolerant outlook: man shall be in
the position to develop the faculties given to him by God'.

But only one sort of men shall be in this sunny position: Germanic
men. The striking revelation of these disquisitions is that Hitler
believed implicitly his own racial theory. This was not merely anti-
Semitism, though he held, for instance, that a single Jewish ancestor
would still reveal effects even though he was as far off as the sixteenth

century. But all his judgements were based on blood and breeding. Thus he thought that the population of northern France had been made tougher by the intermixture of German blood during the occupation of the First World War; and he said of the Grand Mufti: 'He gives the impression of a man among whose ancestors there was more than one Aryan and who perhaps springs from the best Roman blood.' For he held, of course, that the ancient Greeks and Romans were of Teutonic stock; hence the true Germans were to be found among the monuments of antiquity, not in the primitive forests. His illusion did not, however, extend to the modern Italians. Mussolini was the only man among them, and even here his approval sprang from the fact that, when they met, they were always in agreement. Only the Scandinavians and the Dutch were to be included in the new German Empire (the Swiss would be used as hotel-keepers); and to make this empire attractive to them Berlin was to change its name to 'Germania'.

This imperial theme was Hitler's favourite; he returned to it again and again. The only human element in it was his intention to develop Linz into a great city and to endow it with the artistic plunder of Europe; this would humble Vienna and punish the Viennese for their early neglect of him. But for the most part his plans were far more grandiose: to turn Europe into a German Valhalla, built of concrete instead of stage props. Concrete fascinated him; it expressed what he imagined his character to be. Cities of concrete, inhabited by hard Aryan men, and bound together by concrete roads. Such was his vision of the future. He had already attained this ideal. These talks were delivered in a concrete cellar, far in the Russian plains; and his dreams turned always to the empire that he had conquered. Most empire-builders claim to benefit the 'colonial' peoples whom they have subdued; or at the very least intend to exploit them. Hitler was concerned only with 'German soil'. It was not enough to turn the Russians into slaves; they must disappear. He stormed against the idiocy of denying them the means of birth control; at the same time they should be encouraged in their superstition against inoculation. The German conquerors were to live in their fortified towns, isolated from the Russians and above all never interbreeding with them. The Russians were to become ignorant, diseased, rotten, and finally to perish. As to the lesser Slav peoples, the process of extermination could already be begun with them. Such was the German cultural mission, the defence of European civilization against the barbarism of the East.

Yet, absurdly enough, Hitler had little confidence in these Germans whose imperial greatness he was creating. He railed against the methods of German bureaucracy and often envied Stalin, 'a man of real genius'. Some of his hearers must have shivered to themselves as Hitler described how he would deal with a 'mutiny' in the Reich: 'Execute all leading men of opposition outlook, and especially those of political Catholicism, at once; shoot all the inmates of the concentration camps within three days; shoot all criminal elements, whether free or in prison, within three days.' This would involve 'some hundred thousands of men' and would make other measures superfluous. This, and not the sunny tolerance of moral outlook, was the reality in Hitler's future. His 'Germania' was imaginary. He feared and hated the actual Germans only a little less than he hated the inferior races. The only Germans he cared for were the men of the SS, and they were to breed for the future as well as to fight for it. Though he was 'one of Germany's greatest sons', he dared not, as he confessed, drive unguarded through the streets of any German town; it did not even occur to him to regret that he could not walk there. Choosing terror, he had condemned himself to a life of fear. Hitler was beyond good and evil only in the sense that any criminal or gangster is beyond good and evil. He believed that with power he could do anything; and the Germans who supported him shared this belief. Though he was wrong, they were wrong also; and most wrong now, if they suppose they can shoulder all their faults and crimes on to Hitler's shoulders.

Hitler's Seizure of Power

This was first published as 'The Seizure of Power', a chapter in the book published by the International Council for Philosophy and Humanistic Studies entitled The Third Reich (*London, Weidenfeld and Nicolson, 1955*).

*　　*　　*

National socialism was based on fraud; and no fraud was greater than the legend that a seizure of power by Hitler took place on 30 January 1933. Certainly this day, on which Hitler became chancellor, was the most important moment in his life and a turning point in German history. But there was no seizure of power. That had been tried by Hitler at Munich in November 1923. It had failed; and he was determined never to repeat the attempt. There was an alternative path to power which he sometimes contemplated: that the Nazi Party should actually win a majority of the popular vote and thus install Hitler as chancellor by strict democratic choice. But this alternative, too, proved beyond him. The Nazis never received more than 37 per cent of votes at a free election for the Reichstag. The third path, and that which Hitler followed, was the way of intrigue; he would become chancellor as the leader of a minority and would then use the power of the state to establish his dictatorship. The answer to the question how Hitler came to power is therefore to be found more in the actions of those German politicians who were not national socialists than in those of Hitler himself. He waited; they decided.

The Weimar Republic always suffered from a multiplicity of parties. No single party ever possessed a majority in the Reichstag and every German government after 1918 rested on a coalition. This would have mattered less if there had been at least a majority in favour of the republic; but this, too, was lacking after the first elections in 1919. The middle-class liberal parties faded and disappeared. Only the social democrats remained a genuine Weimar party. The nationalists welcomed anything that weakened the republic; the communists welcomed anything that discredited the social democrats. The Roman Catholic centre party certainly took part in republican governments along with the social democrats; but it had no republican principles. It was a sectarian party, ready to work with any system that would

protect Roman Catholic interests; and in the last days of the republic
it stretched out its hand to the forces of destruction, just as in the last
days of the empire it had turned to the republicans. Every party
contributed to the fall of the Weimar Republic – the social democrats
from timidity, the others with conscious ill-will. But none contributed
with such cynicism as the Centre – indifferent to the republic or even
to Germany, so long as the Roman Catholic schools enjoyed their
favoured position.

The failure to establish strong stable governments brought unexpected power to the president. The makers of the constitution in 1919
had intended to give him the position of monarch in a parliamentary
state: choosing the chancellor, but without independent authority in
himself. The chancellor was to be the heir of Bismarck, the true
wielder of power. But the short-lived chancellors never held this
position. They were little more than parliamentary managers for the
president. Even Ebert drew on his reserve of authority. Hindenburg,
who became president in 1925, possessed it in greater measure and
believed that his duty was to use it. Moreover, as the military leader
of the world war, Hindenburg both commanded the allegiance of the
army and voiced its demands. The army was the one stable point of
order in an unstable society. It is a mistake to suggest, as some have
done, that the army chiefs were bent on overthrowing the republic.
They would have attempted this only if the republican politicians had
accepted permanently and sincerely the disarmament imposed upon
Germany by the Treaty of Versailles; and none did so. The generals
were willing to work with the republic if it provided stable government. But this it failed to do; and the generals were obsessed with
anxiety lest Germany's limited army, the Reichswehr, be called upon
to intervene in civil strife. They did not make this civil strife, nor even
welcome it. They were insistent that a civil solution should be found
for it. That solution, they supposed, could only be strong government;
and, since this was beyond the republic, it must come in some other
form. They were indifferent whether this form should be a presidial
government (i.e., one resting on the authority of the president),
monarchy, or dictatorship. Their overriding concern was to keep the
army out of politics.

There was another impulse making for strong government between
1929 and 1933. These were the years of the Great Depression, which
– starting in the United States – carried unemployment and financial

collapse across the world. Keynesian economics were unknown, at least among public men; and it was universally supposed that, when men lacked the money to buy goods, the answer to the crisis was to deprive them even of the little money that they had. When, in the autumn of 1931, the British National government unwillingly abandoned the gold standard, and so stumbled on the path to recovery, a former Labour minister exclaimed plaintively: 'No one told us we could do this!' His ignorance was universally shared. The only solution proposed was the reduction of wages and unemployment benefit; and for this a strong government was needed. Moreover, in times of bewilderment and distress men demand authority for its own sake. They have no idea what should be done, but they long for a commanding voice which will resolve their doubts. Here again it is a mistake to suppose that Germany's economic leaders were consciously set on overthrowing the republic or destroying the trade unions. They would have accepted a republican leader if one had appeared with unquestioned authority and self-confidence, just as Franklin D Roosevelt was accepted by the business leaders of the USA. But they demanded strong government from somebody; and they were rightly convinced that the republic could not provide it.

This, then, was the background of Hitler's rise to power. Far from his hammering at a door which was long kept closed against him, he was constantly being invited to enter by those within; and he held back in order to increase his market value. Everyone assumed that he would end up as chancellor sooner or later. The real problem in German history is why so few of the educated, civilized classes recognized Hitler as the embodiment of evil. University professors; army officers; businessmen and bankers – these had a background of culture, and even of respect for law. Yet virtually none of them exclaimed: 'This is anti-Christ.' Later, they were to make out that Hitler had deceived them and that the bestial nature of national socialism could not have been foreseen. This is not true. The real character of national socialism was exposed by many foreign, and even by some German, observers long before Hitler came to power. It could be judged from Hitler's writings and his speeches; it was displayed in every street brawl that the Nazi brownshirts organized. Hitler did not deceive the responsible classes in Germany: they deceived themselves. Their self-deception had a simple cause: they were engaged in fighting the wrong battle and in saving Germany from the wrong enemy. Hitler's hostility to communism was his strongest asset. The Bolshevik peril in Germany had once perhaps been real: therefore anyone who was anti-communist seemed to be on the side of civilization, and the communists themselves fed this illusion by treating Hitler as their only serious enemy. 'Better Hitler than communism' was the phrase which opened the way for Hitler first within Germany and then on a wider scale in Europe.

Further, the directors of German policy were obsessed with the struggle against the Treaty of Versailles. They regarded the disarmament clauses as a personal humiliation; and they genuinely believed, though without justification, that reparations were the cause of Germany's economic difficulties. They could not repudiate wholeheartedly a movement which raged against the Versailles system. Rather they welcomed it as an ally. Every advance of national socialism strengthened the argument that Germany should receive concessions in foreign affairs – otherwise the national socialists would get stronger still. And the argument was not without force. Can any English or French observer honestly maintain that reparations would have been ended or the Rhineland evacuated without the mounting shadow of Hitler? Even apart from questions of foreign policy, respectable Germans – especially army officers – were bound to look with favour on a movement equipped with uniforms and acting under military discipline. More than one general remarked: 'It would be a shame to have to fire on these splendid young men in their brown shirts.' Experience in other countries has repeatedly shown that the only answer to a Fascist party, with an organized private army, is to suppress it by force of law. The Red Peril and the system of Versailles made it impossible to give this answer in Germany.

Even so, the lack of alarm among civilized Germans remains a strange puzzle. The explanation may perhaps be found in the taste which so many of them had for political intrigue. A country with a long constitutional history develops a political class. The politicians look after government. The generals and bankers and professors mind their own business. This has always been true in England; and it was largely true in the third French republic, despite an occasional political general. In Germany men were always coming in from outside; a political class never had a chance to develop. Even Bismarck was a gifted amateur, who knew nothing of politics until he started at the top. Of his successors as imperial chancellor, one was a general, one a diplomatist, one a civil servant. In the reign of William II generals like Waldersee and Ludendorff pushed into politics on one side; and businessmen like Ballin or Rathenau pushed in on the other. The practice was maintained in the Weimar Republic. There was no true statesman in Germany after the death of Stresemann in 1929. Her fate was in the hands of amateurs, who mistook intrigue for political activity. Hindenburg, the president, was a retired professional soldier, a field-marshal over eighty years old. Bruening, who became chancellor in 1930, was half scholar, half army captain, but never strictly a party leader. Papen, his successor, was a dashing cavalryman of great wealth, with no political standing. Schleicher, the most influential of all, lived for intrigue and nothing else: claiming to represent army opinion with the president and the president's authority to the army, but in fact playing off one against the other. All four thought that they were a great deal cleverer than Hitler and that they would take him prisoner in no time. They never feared Hitler or took precautions against him. Indeed, the fact that he was a politician and the leader of a political party made them despise him, as they despised the other politicians. The Austrian generals of the old regime made much the same mistake when they came up against Bonaparte.

Intrigue took the place of politics when Bruening became chancellor in March 1930. The previous republican governments claimed to rest on a majority of the Reichstag, even though the claim was not always justified. Bruening did not attempt to construct a parliamentary cabinet. He relied on the authority of the president and ordered the Reichstag to vote for him, much as Bismarck had done in his great days. The Reichstag had not always responded to Bismarck's commands; it was even less likely to be overawed by Bruening. In July 1930 his measures were defeated; and the Reichstag was dissolved. Political theorists in other countries with a multiplicity of parties often lament that the executive cannot threaten parliament with dissolution. The German example shows that the remedy can be worse than the disease. General elections may provide a solution when they are contested by two strong parties. But the voter cannot be expected to solve the riddle that has baffled his leaders. A dissolution could have only one effect in the existing circumstances. The voters were told by Bruening, the chancellor, that all the parties were equally factious and difficult. Many voters therefore turned to the political leader who said exactly the same. And this leader was Hitler. The National

Socialist Party had been an insignificant group in the previous Reichstag. It was inflated and artificially fostered by the repeated electoral
campaigns of the two years that followed. How otherwise could the
voters respond to Bruening's demand and return a Reichstag of a
different character? If there had been no 'Bruening experiment', and
hence no general election in September 1930; if Germany had strug-
gled on with weak coalition governments throughout the Great Depression, the National Socialist Party would never have won at the polls
and Hitler would never have triumphed.

The election of September 1930 brought great gains to the national
socialists; and only slightly smaller gains to the communists. It lessened
Bruening's chance of achieving a parliamentary majority. Even now
there was plenty of time for the forces of order and decency to unite
against national socialist barbarism. But Hitler's victory elated the
political jugglers, instead of frightening them. They imagined that
they could use the threat of national socialism against the other
parties in the Reichstag without ever being endangered themselves;
and they even hoped that Hitler would be obliging enough to act as
their agent. Bruening depended on the authority of President Hindenburg; but the president's term ran out in 1932. At the beginning of
the year Bruening proposed a bargain to Hitler: Hindenburg's term
should be prolonged for one or two years; then Bruening would
resign, and the way would be clear for Hitler. Bruening's calculation
was clear. Hitler was to perform a service now in exchange for a
reward that might never have to be paid. Hitler's answer was equally
clear: Bruening must be dismissed and a new Reichstag elected (with,
no doubt, a larger Nazi representation); then he would support a
prolongation of Hindenburg's term. In other words, he must have his
price before he would perform his service. The negotiations broke
down. A presidential election was held, with Hitler as candidate of
the Nazis and the nationalists, Hindenburg – absurdly enough – as
the candidate of the Left, including the social democrats. Hindenburg
was elected. The voters had rejected national socialism; but they had
not supported anything, except a figurehead of eighty-five. The problem of finding a strong government, based on a Reichstag majority,
remained.

Bruening did not recognize this problem. He proposed to remain in
office and to continue to govern with the support of the president and
the Reichswehr. But this programme was rejected by the generals

and, above all, by Schleicher, their political spokesman; they were determined not to be drawn into the conflict of parties. Bruening and Groener, his minister of defence, thought that they could now act against Hitler. On 14 April 1932 the Nazi armed forces were dissolved by decree. On 12 May Schleicher told Groener that the Reichswehr had no confidence in him; and the following day he resigned. A fortnight later, on 30 May, Bruening also resigned, on Hindenburg's order. The old man had been persuaded that Bruening was the sole obstacle to a deal with Hitler and so to a government with a democratic majority. The instrument chosen for this deal was Franz von Papen, a wealthy aristocrat of no sense, though much courage. Schleicher said of him: 'People sometimes say that Herr von Papen is frivolous. But that is what we need.' And Papen characterized himself when he asked an economist for a programme: 'I know nothing of economics, but I'll do whatever you suggest. I'm a gentleman-rider; and I'll jump, I'll jump.'

Papen, like Bruening, was a member of the Centre Party, though, unlike Bruening, he carried no weight in it. Schleicher did not understand this. He supposed that the Centre would support Papen and, with Hitler supporting him as well, the 'functioning Reichstag' would be made. This scheme at once broke down. The Centre insisted that Hitler must take real responsibility, not exercise influence behind the scenes; failing this, they opposed Papen's government. Hitler, on his side, demanded power; and he, too, continued in opposition when this was refused. Papen's was perhaps the weakest government that has ever ruled a great country – a cabinet of elderly 'barons' and no support at all in the Reichstag. This did not worry Papen. He was content to wait until Hitler came to heel. And Hitler also waited until Papen's difficulties swept him away. Both gambled on Germany's distress – the one a vain intriguer, the other the greatest demagogue of modern times. In June, Papen dissolved the Reichstag, not with any hope of getting support for himself, but solely as a demonstration to Hitler that he could wear him down. The Nazi election funds would not last for ever; and, besides, the voters might turn elsewhere if Hitler failed to achieve anything.

The election of 31 July gave Hitler his greatest success: 37.3 per cent of the votes cast. But he was still far from an independent majority, and the Nazi rate of increase was slowing down. In fact, as the next election showed, the tide had already turned. The bargaining of May was renewed. Hitler demanded full power; himself as chancellor, other Nazis in all the key posts. It is true that he was prepared to include also some non-Nazis and asked only 'as much power as Mussolini got in 1922'. Papen and Schleicher were not well grounded in current history. They only knew that Mussolini was dictator of Italy, and forgot the slow process by which he had reached that position. In any case, the analogy was revealing enough: however Hitler began, he, too, would end as dictator, and they were only prepared to employ him as their parliamentary agent. They offered Hitler the post of vice-chancellor, safely under Papen's control. On 13 August Hitler was summoned to appear before Hindenburg. The president rated him for the violence and illegality of the Nazi Party. 'He was ready to accept Hitler in a coalition government . . . but he could not take responsibility for giving exclusive power to Hitler alone.' Hitler tried to repeat that he wanted 'only as much as Mussolini'. The fatal analogy roused Hindenburg's anger.

The interview of 13 August was the sharpest setback that national socialism ever received. Until then its prestige and the votes cast for it had been growing steadily. Hitler had spoken openly of the seizure of power and of the 'St Bartholomew's night' that would follow. Now it was clearly established that the so-called national revolution could take place only with the permission of the president. And that permission had been refused. Papen's gamble seemed to be working. Many of the lesser Nazis lost heart. Some worried over their security as deputies; a few over the future of the party. Hitler's great triumph lay in the iron control which he managed to maintain over his party during the next few months. If it had once begun to crumble, he would have been left isolated in a very short time. It is in this sense that Hitler was brought to power by his gifts for leadership. The National Socialist Party was never strong enough to force Hitler into power but he never needed to look over his shoulder. The other politicians worried about their followers and their voters; and worry breaks a politician's nerve sooner or later. Hitler always assumed that his control of the party was unshakeable – rather as Napoleon always assumed that he would win a battle, and therefore never wasted men in securing a line of retreat.

But for the moment it was Papen who went over to the offensive. On 12 September the Reichstag was again dissolved; and Germany was involved in yet another general election, in order to wear down the national socialists. The results, which came in on 6 November, seemed to confirm Papen's calculation. The Nazis lost two million votes; their share of the total fell to 33 per cent and their deputies from 230 to 196. It was less encouraging that most of these votes were transferred to the communists, who increased their representation to 100. Still, Papen hoped to repeat his manoeuvre of August under more favourable conditions: Hitler should be offered office without power, under strict control, in order to save himself from further decline. On 16 November Hitler again refused. Papen swung over to his alternative line: he would show that no one was capable of producing a parliamentary majority, and would then transform his temporary dictatorship into a permanent one. Instead of again dissolving the Reichstag, he would govern without it. On 17 November Papen resigned, ostensibly to give Hitler his chance. The step was meant as a pretence; for Hitler could obviously not produce a Reichstag majority. He came again to Hindenburg, this time in a rather more friendly atmosphere. But the deadlock remained. Hindenburg would make Hitler chancellor if he could offer 'a secure workable majority in the Reichstag with a coherent programme'. Hitler demanded to be made chancellor on the same terms as Papen – governing, that is, on the president's authority. Hindenburg refused. With Hitler as chancellor, the cabinet would not be a presidential government, but a party dictatorship. The future was to prove him right.

Papen seemed to have played his cards correctly. He could now resume office without being open to the reproach of barring the way against a majority cabinet. On 1 December he went to Hindenburg with his plan: he would prorogue the Reichstag, proclaim a state of emergency, and govern by decree. If there was opposition from Nazis or communists, he would crush it by force. But this was the very proposal for involving the Reichswehr in civil strife which the generals had always rejected. Schleicher opposed Papen's scheme, both as Hindenburg's military adviser and as spokesman of the army. Besides, he claimed, he could succeed where Bruening and Papen had failed: he could provide a parliamentary majority. He had been negotiating with Nazi leaders, such as Gregor Strasser, who were dissatisfied with Hitler's rigid line; and he believed, as well, that he could win the support of the trade unions. The social democrats, the Centre, and the dissident Nazis would give him a workable coalition. Hindenburg preferred Papen to Schleicher; and he authorized him to form a government.

But Schleicher soon carried the day. On 2 December the new cabinet met. Schleicher produced a report from Major Ott of the General Staff, which asserted that the Reichswehr could not do what Papen wanted. The Poles might seize the chance of internal disturbance in Germany to attack her eastern frontier; and 'defence of the frontiers and the maintenance of order against both Nazis and communists was beyond the strength of the forces at the disposal of the federal and state governments'. The Reichswehr was, no doubt, a limited force; yet it had managed to maintain internal order in 1920 and 1923, when the chance of Polish intervention had been much greater. There is little doubt that even now the Reichswehr would have been prepared to act if it had been against the communists alone. But the Nazis, whatever their violence, were a 'national' element. This was the underlying sentiment of Ott's memorandum. Papen was still ready to face the risk, but his colleagues were reluctant, and Hindenburg still more so. He said to Papen: 'I am too old and have been through too much to accept the responsibility for a civil war. Our only hope is to let Schleicher try his luck.' Schleicher became chancellor the same day.

His luck turned out to be a poor resource. He offered to make Strasser vice-chancellor; and Strasser was willing to accept. But he could not carry the Nazi Party with him. Hitler forbade any bargaining with Schleicher; and Strasser lost his nerve. On 8 December he went off to Italy for a holiday. Hitler reasserted his domination over the party and determined once more to 'throw the whole party into the struggle'. Strasser's abortive revolt and failure actually strengthened Hitler's appeal to the propertied classes; for he could claim to have shaken off the extreme, socialist wing of his party. Nazi finances were in a bad state. Even Goebbels had a feeling of 'dark hopelessness'. But Hitler's resolution was as strong as ever; and this time he was justified. Schleicher's feeble attempts at coalition had broken down. What is more, Papen – though out of office – continued to live next door to Hindenburg and to busy himself in political intrigue. He would have been more than human if he had not wanted his revenge on Schleicher; and while the latter had failed with Strasser, himself hoped to succeed with Hitler. On a more elevated plane, he could make out to be still pursuing the bargain with Hitler which had been everyone's object for the last two years. Papen and Hitler met, more or less secretly, on 4 January 1933. Papen, according to his own account, merely urged – in the most disinterested way – that Hitler should become vice-chancellor in Schleicher's government. Schroeder, the Cologne banker in whose house the meeting was held, gives a different and more likely story. Hitler insisted on becoming chancellor, though with Papen and his friends as ministers; in particular he did not ask for control of either the army or foreign affairs. Papen thought that he had performed the miracle: he had taken Hitler prisoner, figurehead of a respectable non-Nazi cabinet. Wealthy Germans drew the same conclusion. Subscriptions began to flow into the Nazi funds. Goebbels noted: 'The financial situation has improved very suddenly.'

Schleicher did not realize that the position had changed. Once in office he thought, like Bruening and Papen before him, that he had only to issue orders for the crisis to disappear. It soon ceased to worry him that his political combinations collapsed. Gregor Strasser turned out to be a broken reed: he could not carry a single national socialist with him. The social democrats and the trade unions were not won over. Like everyone else, they seem to have come round to the view that office was the best means of taming Hitler; and they still imagined that they could resist him if he attempted anything illegal. On the other hand, the extreme Right, though they distrusted Hitler, were alienated by the steps Schleicher had taken to conciliate the social democrats. The Reichstag was due to meet on 31 January. Its first subject for discussion was the *Osthilfe* – the subsidies to landowners in eastern Germany, which had involved many scandals reaching even to Hindenburg himself. On 28 January Schleicher had to confess to Hindenburg that he could not control the Reichstag; and he asked, as his two predecessors had done, for a decree dissolving it. This was the very policy of governing Germany by force which Schleicher had rejected when it had been put forward by Papen in December. Hindenburg liked Papen and by now disliked Schleicher. He refused the decree of dissolution. Schleicher then claimed that he could produce a parliamentary majority by negotiating with the national socialists. But this was exactly what he had failed to do during the last six weeks. Moreover, Hindenburg knew, as Schleicher did not, that Papen could do it more successfully. Schleicher was dismissed; and Papen was entrusted with the formation of a new government.

A single pattern ran through all the negotiations from the fall of

Bruening, or even before, to the accession of Hitler. The president
and his confidential advisers worked persistently for a coalition government, in which Hitler would provide the votes and would yet be held
in check by his associates. There was never any attempt to build a
coalition government which would exclude Hitler or the National
Socialist Party; and the delay came from Hitler, not from the side of
the respectable classes. Now Hitler agreed to come in. It is impossible
to say what led him to compromise. Perhaps he recognized that the
Nazi tide was ebbing; perhaps he felt that the old order was now
sufficiently weakened and would crumble of itself; perhaps the position
of chancellor, even under Papen's control, made the difference. More
probably, his decision sprang from his unconscious sense of timing,
just as a great general might find it difficult to explain why he flung
in his reserves at the critical moment.

On 30 January Hitler became chancellor. This was far from a
seizure of power. Indeed, the forces of the old order imagined that
they had seized Hitler. Though he was chancellor, there were only
three Nazis in a cabinet of eleven; the two key posts of foreign
minister and minister of defence were in the hands of non-political
agents of the president; and Hitler could not see Hindenburg except
in the presence of Papen, who was vice-chancellor. No arrangement
could have been neater or more cynical. Yet it broke down within the
first few days. What Hitler appreciated and his conservative associates
did not was that, while the Nazi Party was not strong enough to seize
power when the forces of the state were hostile, it was strong enough
to do so once these forces were neutral or on its side. Papen remarks
regretfully that 'existing institutions and parties gave up without a
fight'. What else could they do? They might have resisted the Nazis if
the police and the courts were there to maintain order. They could no
longer do so when the police were under Nazi control and when,
therefore, the defence of democracy took on a revolutionary character.
Again, Hitler had been crippled by the fact that he did not possess a
majority in the Reichstag; this had driven him to accept Papen's
terms. But once in office he could argue that a further general election
would give him a majority; and, since this had been the object of all
the negotiations, his demand for a dissolution could not be refused.
This time Hitler supposed that he could indeed deliver the parliamentary majority which had hitherto evaded everybody. Once the national socialists dominated the Reichstag, he could shake off Papen

and the other elderly gentlemen who controlled him, and establish a Nazi dictatorship by law.

Hitler's calculation did not succeed. The election campaign was conducted with every weapon of Nazi terror; and the burning of the Reichstag building on 27 February enabled Hitler to declare the Communist Party illegal. Nevertheless on 6 March the national socialists secured only 43.9 per cent of the votes. Even with the cooperation of the right-wing nationalists they had only a bare majority – enough to control the Reichstag from day to day, but not enough to carry through any fundamental change in the constitution. Hitler, however, was set on an enabling law which would give him all the powers of a dictator. If the so-called democratic parties had held together, Hitler would have been driven to illegal action – or would have remained powerless. The communists had been driven underground. The social democrats, though feeble in action, held nobly to their principles and voted against the enabling law, despite the threats of terror against them. The decision rested on the Centre, with its 102 votes. The leaders of the Centre were men of personal courage. But their party cared little for democracy; it was concerned only to secure the position of the Roman Catholic schools. It had a long tradition of doing this by intriguing with successive parties and governments; it had long lost the tradition of resistance which had once enabled it to defeat Bismarck. The Centre leaders were fobbed off with promises from Hitler in which they only half-believed; and on 23 March the Centre votes were cast in favour of the enabling law. These votes alone gave Hitler's dictatorship its legal character.

One barrier remained: Hindenburg's veto, and Hitler's promise that he would do nothing to override it. But Hitler, who had wooed millions of voters, did not find it difficult to cajole an old man, never mentally acute and now senile. Papen soon found that he was not needed when Hitler had his interviews with the president. He went on dreaming that some day Hindenburg would reassert his independence and that the Nazis would be overthrown – again under Papen's direction. He waited patiently, as he had waited before. And fifteen months later he thought that his chance had come. On 17 June 1934 Papen delivered at Marburg the only public speech against the Nazi dictatorship ever made in Germany after Hitler's seizure of power. Even now his line was equivocal. His appeal was to Hitler to behave better, rather than to Hindenburg and the generals to overthrow him.

In any case, Hitler was soon able to outbid Papen's feeble gesture. He, too, had his difficulties with the Nazi extremists – the leaders of the brownshirts who wanted to carry through a real social revolution now that their party was in power. He broke them in the bloodbath of 30 June. This seemed a guarantee to the generals that there would be no demagogic interference with the army. Hitler was already promising them rearmament on a great scale. Why, then, should they resist him for the sake of democracy or the constitution? This would be the very interference in politics which they had always rejected.

On 2 August 1934 Hindenburg died. The army leaders were content that Hitler should take his place. Within an hour of Hindenburg's death, the office of president was merged with that of chancellor; and Hitler became undisputed head of the state. He kept his bargain with the army. For three and a half years it remained autonomous, standing outside politics and repudiating all responsibility for the Nazi terror. Early in 1938 Hitler overthrew this balance. He was now moving towards an aggressive war in Europe; and he could tolerate no independent authority. The army leaders were discredited by a series of personal scandals, some of them without foundation. Hitler dismissed those who stood out against him; made himself head of the armed forces, the Wehrmacht; and at the same time put his agent, Ribbentrop, in the Foreign Office in place of Neurath. By February 1938 the seizure of power was complete. It had taken Hitler four years to destroy legality in Germany by legal means.

If we look back over this wretched story, we see a man bent on success on the one side, and a group of politicians without ideas or principles on the other. Hitler was resolved to gain power. He did not know how he would do it, and he tried many means which failed; but he had an unbreakable purpose. The others were only concerned to strike a bargain with him. If there had been a strong democratic sentiment in Germany, Hitler would never have come to power – or even to prominence. He would have failed even if the weak democratic parties had held together. He had two great weapons. He could promise the generals a great army if they let him in; he could threaten civil disturbance if they kept him out. The promise was more potent than the threat. One can blame all parties in turn. The communists started the habit of violence and disrupted the working-class front. The social democrats had lost all ability to act and faith in their strength. The Centre would bargain with anybody, even with Hitler.

But the greatest responsibility lay with those who let Hitler in and established him as chancellor. Hitler recognized it himself. In 1938 Papen, then German ambassador at Vienna, accompanied Schuschnigg to the fateful interview at Berchtesgaden which ended Austrian independence. In the course of the argument, Hitler turned to Papen and said: 'By making me chancellor, Herr von Papen, you made possible the national socialist revolution in Germany. I shall never forget it.' And Papen answered with soldierly pride: 'Certainly, my Führer.'

Brummagem Statesmanship

This essay first appeared as a review of Ian Colvin's The Chamberlain Cabinet *(London, Victor Gollancz, 1971) in the* Observer, *10 January 1971.*

* * *

In the dark days of 1940 Neville Chamberlain and his pre-war colleagues were arraigned as Guilty Men. This verdict was endorsed after the war by historians such as Sir Lewis Namier. The Chamberlain government, it was said, were negligent in rearming. They appeased Hitler from a mixture of fear and ignorance. They wilfully rejected alliance with Soviet Russia. The verdict went particularly against Chamberlain himself, who made no secret of his determination to pursue his own foreign policy.

Latterly this view has been challenged, mostly by historians who had enjoyed privileged access to the closed archives. We were told that, if only we knew everything, we should judge differently. The Chamberlain government armed Great Britain effectively. They practised appeasement solely in order to buy time. A Soviet alliance was never on offer.

Now the archives are open, and we shall soon know everything or very nearly. Mr Colvin has got ahead of professional historians. He has summarized the proceedings of Chamberlain's cabinet and reinforces them with the papers submitted by the chiefs-of-staff and other professional advisers. He seems to have enjoyed further advantages. He writes in his foreword: 'I am grateful to the Cabinet Office for arranging for me to see certain papers not yet on the public shelves under the Lord Chancellor's discretionary exclusion.' There is no explanation why a journalist was granted a privilege which is denied to other researchers. At all events his book contains the richest revelations yet made from the British side about the origins of the Second World War.

The results are devastating. Vindications for Chamberlain crumble into dust. He resisted conscription, cut down plans for increased rearmament, and seconded the Treasury argument that armaments must be subordinated to financial stability. He believed sincerely that appeasement would succeed. Lord Swinton said to him after the

Munich conference: 'I will support you, Prime Minister, provided that you are clear that you have been buying time for rearmament.' Chamberlain pulled out the paper he had signed with Hitler and replied: 'But don't you see, I have brought back peace.' Similarly he told the cabinet: 'We must aim at establishing relations with the dictator Powers which will lead to a settlement in Europe and a sense of security.' He hoped 'that one day we shall be able to secure limitations of armaments, though it is too soon to say when this will prove possible'.

Chamberlain is supposed to have changed his line after Hitler occupied Prague. This is not so. He made some gestures of strength, but these were intended to bring Hitler back to the conference table, not as serious preparations for war. There was to be another Munich, heralded this time by a visit of Marshal Goering to London. The negotiations with Soviet Russia were for Chamberlain always a sham, designed only to quieten British public opinion. Thus he refused the Soviet request for agreement against making a separate peace and, when the Soviet government proposed a three-Power pact, declared: 'The conclusion of such a pact would unite Germany as nothing else could do.'

Chamberlain ran his own foreign policy. He rarely consulted the cabinet. At most, he informed them what he had decided. Ministers who got in his way were either moved to less important offices or dismissed from the cabinet altogether. Inconvenient papers were concealed from the cabinet, which never heard for example the reports of opposition to Hitler inside Germany. During the Munich crisis Chamberlain conducted policy with the assistance of three senior ministers – Halifax, Simon and Hoare – thus bypassing both the cabinet and its Foreign Affairs Committee, and these three were summoned merely to confirm decisions which Chamberlain had already made. Everyone knows that Chamberlain ignored Sir Robert Vansittart, who was supposed to be chief diplomatic adviser. He also ignored the chiefs-of-staff whenever they gave advice which was unwelcome to him. For instance they reported that the possibility of war with Russia would be 'a great deterrent' to Germany and added: 'If for fear of making an alliance with Russia we drove that country into the German camp, we should have made a mistake of vital and far-reaching importance.' Chamberlain took no notice.

Other ministers come out equally badly, Halifax among them. One does not. Sir Samuel Hoare is often regarded as the ringleader in appeasement, and he was the 'fall guy' when Churchill formed his National government. It now appears that Hoare was a persistent champion of the Soviet alliance. For instance, 'We should be wise to reinsure by doing everything in our power to bring in Russia on our side.' Perhaps this explains why Chamberlain let him go so easily in May 1940. There are other curious points. Chamberlain's cabinet is often praised for preparing the fighter aircraft which won the Battle of Britain. But they did this only because fighters were cheaper to build than bombers. Again, it is alleged that Hitler went to war in 1939 because the German lead could not be maintained. Exactly the same argument was used on the British side. Sir John Simon, chancellor of the exchequer, asserted that British resources, still great in 1939, would be run down by a prolonged period of rearmament. Oliver Stanley, president of the Board of Trade, pointed the moral:

There would therefore come a moment which, on a balance of our financial strength and our strength in armaments, was the best time for war to break out ... It might be desirable to consider whether at such a period Great Britain should apply strong pressure to Germany to relax the international tension.

Hence, if it be argued that Hitler wanted a war for economic reasons, the same could be said for the British. Probably the argument is wrong in both cases.

Historians may arrive at more cautious conclusions when they explore the archives more thoroughly. Mr Colvin has made only a preliminary survey. He is after all a committed writer. He states in his conclusion: 'The inference is strong that Austria should have been the storm signal and Czechoslovakia the *casus belli*.' Moreover he was himself a participant in events. His was the news which launched a thousand ships, or at any rate the guarantee to Poland. On 28 March 1939 he brought back reports, which appear to have been unfounded, of German troop movements against Poland, and these reports hurried Chamberlain into the Polish guarantee with all its consequences. Mr Colvin says that Chamberlain was not only unwilling to run the risk of war, but also unwilling to run the risk of risks. It would be truer to say that Chamberlain aimed at peace and was ready for its sake to run the risk of entering a war inadequately prepared. So it proved. Chamberlain was dogmatic, unimaginative, perhaps vain. He lacked the flexibility of a great statesman and saw only the weakness in his own hand, never in his opponent's. His aims were high, his failure absolute. Lloyd George described him correctly: 'A good lord mayor of Birmingham in a lean year.'

Reaching for Russia

This essay first appeared as a review of Barry Leach's German Strategy Against Russia 1939–1941 (*Oxford, Clarendon Press, 1973*) *and Barton Whaley's* Codeword Barbarossa (*Cambridge, Mass., MIT Press, 1973*) *in the* Observer, *26 August 1973.*

* * *

The German invasion of Russia was the greatest decision of the Second World War, perhaps the greatest international decision of the twentieth century. Most of the consequences of the Second World War were taking shape before it started. The United States was already the greatest power in the world. Europe was relatively in decline, and the British Empire was in decline also. But Soviet Russia was still an enigma wrapped in a mystery. Was she on the point of collapse – her economic system in confusion, her political dictatorship tottering? Or was she on the way to becoming a world power? The Great Patriotic War, as the Russians call it, gave the answer. When Hitler ordered the invasion of Russia, he said that this would change the face of history. And so it did, though not in the way that Hitler intended.

We cannot have too many books on this great decision, particularly when they are as good as the present one by Professor Leach. After the war the German generals built up a version that the failure in Russia was all the fault of Hitler and that they would have succeeded if he had not interfered. General Halder, the chief of the General Staff, was particularly assiduous in demonstrating that Hitler disregarded the sound rules of strategy, and Hitler was in no position to answer back. Indeed, Hitler conveniently shouldered all the blame for both the war and Germany's defeat. Professor Leach, writing with a scholar's detachment, has explored the German strategical records in detail and returns a very different verdict: thanks to Hitler, Germany nearly won the war and, thanks to the German generals, she lost it.

The decision to invade Russia had many causes, beginning with Hitler's obsessions in regard to *Lebensraum* and the destruction of communism. It was also strategically the obvious thing to do. Germany had a large army, virtually no navy, and an inadequate air force. Great Britain, though technically in the war, represented no immediate danger to Germany and yet could not be defeated. If Germany conquered Russia, she would be impregnable. Hitler argued that Great Britain would give in once Russia was defeated. But he also said that 'if Great Britain were defeated, he would no longer be able to rouse the German people against Russia'. In short, the invasion of Russia was Hitler's prized objective all along.

There was also his conviction that Russia was 'ripe for dissolution'. The German generals shared this conviction. They, not Hitler, made the detailed preparations for the campaign and did so with extraordinary levity. Professor Leach writes:

The most remarkable features of the German army leaders' role in the planning for the East were not their willingness and optimism, but their inefficiency and errors.

When the British and Americans prepared for D-day, they began planning two years beforehand. They surveyed every detail of the coast and the land beyond it; they devised solutions for every difficulty; they knew exactly what they were going to do. The German generals acted in complete ignorance. They knew nothing of the forces opposed to them. They assumed that the Russian campaign would be even easier than that in France. The German forces would roll forward unimpeded over easy country, plentifully stocked with oil. They made no allowance for Russia's size or her backwardness. There was no large-scale mobilization. The German armies, even on their own estimates, were no stronger than the Russian. There were few reserves. The planning staff reported that 'one month's combat supplies' would be enough, and Hitler cut down German production by 40 per cent in the autumn of 1941 after the war had started.

The German generals were intoxicated by their success in France. Serious planning seemed to be unnecessary. The 'battles of the frontiers' would last a month. The Russian armies would collapse. The rest would be a matter of mopping up. There was a deep equivocation in Barbarossa itself – the nearest the Germans came to a strategic plan. Hitler intended the German armies in the centre to pin down the bulk of the Russian forces while the northern armies took Leningrad and the southern ones overran the Ukraine. The German generals proposed to go straight for Moscow. When action started, the Germans operated all three offensives at once. A month later it was clear that the attack had failed by blitzkrieg standards. The battles of the frontiers had been fought and won. But Russia had not disintegrated. Instead Russian resistance was stiffening. The German armies stood still for three whole weeks – three precious weeks lost in the best campaigning weather. Unperceived by all, it was the beginning of Germany's defeat.

On 23 August Hitler intervened. For the first time he overrode his generals and commanded that the offensive be resumed in the south. This brought great victories. But when the central armies resumed their advance in October, they could make little progress. On 2 December a German advance guard saw the towers of the Kremlin gleaming far away in the setting sun. On 5 December the Russians went over to the offensive. The blitzkrieg was over. The Great Patriotic War had begun.

A few days later Hitler said to Jodl, his closest military adviser: 'We have lost this war.' Keitel, Hitler's other henchman, said at Nuremberg: 'Hitler talked as if the Russian campaign were a sure thing ... But now that I look back I am sure it was just a desperate gamble.' Thanks to Professor Leach we can now see that it was a gamble into which the German generals plunged even more rashly than did Hitler himself. In the six months between June and December 1941 it was decided once and for all that Russia would become a world power of the first rank.

Mr Whaley's book is an exercise in intelligence. Between June 1940 and 22 June 1941, when the Germans invaded Russia, there were eighty-four security leaks which indicated that the attack was coming. Stalin refused to believe them. Why? At first Mr Whaley accepted the Wohlstetter model, based on Pearl Harbor. This states that it is difficult to hear the true signals because of the surrounding noise (i.e., other messages). Later he rejected this in favour of 'deception'. The Germans led Stalin to believe something else. One part of this is undoubted. Sea Lion – the preparations for invading England – was certainly kept going as a deceptive operation, though as much at the expense of Grand Admiral Raeder as of Stalin. Mr Whaley also insists that Stalin was led to expect an ultimatum, not an attack. This, though ingenious, is more speculative. Mrs Wohlstetter could study the American deductions before Pearl Harbor as well as the Japanese signals. We have little internal evidence for the Russian deductions before Barbarossa. As in most human affairs, wishful thinking was probably more important than mistaken deductions. Right or wrong, the book makes a fascinating detective story.

Bombing Germany

Published in the New Statesman, *6 October 1961, as a review of* History of the Second World War. The Strategic Air Offensive against Germany 1939–1945, *4 Vols* (*HMSO, 1961*), *by Sir Charles Webster and Noble Frankland.*

*   *   *

This volume has a special interest. It is one of the few works of official history in which the authors held their own against objections by the service chiefs.

The bombing of Germany by British aeroplanes began on 15 May 1940. It continued, though not without interruption, until the end of April 1945. No part of war policy stirred more argument then and since. Some held that the war could be won by bombing alone. Sir Arthur Harris, commander-in-chief of Bomber Command, wrote in 1942: 'Victory, speedy and complete, awaits the side which first employs air power as it should be employed.' Others, equally extreme, believed that the bomber offensive was an immoral waste of effort. The full account in the official history, now published, will start the argument afresh. The volumes are a model of scholarly accuracy and impartiality, a bit cumbersome and long-winded, but never failing to tell the truth as far as it can be ascertained. They are a great achievement, and it is sad that Sir Charles Webster has not lived to receive the praise which is his due.

Many will use these volumes as an opportunity to denounce those in charge of British policy from Sir Winston Churchill to Sir Arthur Harris. Others will extol British courage and achievement. In my view, the historian is not concerned to fight past battles over again, still less to fight them differently. His duty is to explain. We can safely assume that all leaders in wartime make mistakes; we can also assume that the mistakes were honest mistakes and that there were good reasons for making them. Criticism after the event places one piece on the board differently without appreciating that this affects every other piece. For instance, the bomber offensive did not knock Germany out in 1943. Nevertheless, it prevented the Germans from putting a far greater air strength on the Eastern Front and so helped the Soviet victories. What indeed would have happened to Soviet determination without it? The present authors conclude cautiously and wisely:

Strategic bombing . . . made a contribution to the war which was decisive. Those who claim that Bomber Command's contribution to the war was less are factually in error. Those who claim that its contribution under different circumstances might have been yet more effective disagree with one another and often overlook basic facts.

The basic fact is that Bomber Command operated in the unknown and that it had to proceed by trial and error. It started the war with the wrong strategy and inadequately prepared for that. Its pre-war plan was for precise bombing by daylight of selected targets. This proved impossible, as the Luftwaffe was also to discover. Sir Charles Portal, chief of the Air Staff, refused to believe that a long-range fighter could be invented. He was wrong, as the Americans showed in 1944; and this was one of the great mistakes of the war. But it was supported in this country by all informed opinion. Night bombing seemed to be the only alternative. This, too, was supported by informed opinion for mistaken reasons. It was held that the morale of the German people was weaker than that of the British. This turned out to be quite untrue. The Germans sustained much greater blows than the British had done without any shaking of morale until the very end. It was also held that German industry was already fully stretched and that relatively small losses would bring Germany to her knees. This was a catastrophic error. Germany's economic mobilization was on a small scale and had made few inroads on civilian production, which declined much less than in Great Britain. Air attack actually stimulated her war production, which reached its peak in July 1944 when independent strategic bombing was already over. One can argue that the production would have been still greater without the air attacks; one can equally well argue that the increase would not have taken place without the stimulus from air attacks.

What seems broadly true is that strategic bombing demanded more economic effort from Great Britain than it inflicted economic damage on Germany. But even this is not a decisive argument. Strategic bombing, when it started, sprang from the motive that there was nothing to which British resources could be more usefully devoted. This was unanswerable. Churchill endorsed it. He never believed, as is sometimes alleged, that bombing could win the war; he believed rightly that it was the best contribution which Great Britain could make towards winning the war in the circumstances of the time. The claim of Sir Arthur Harris that bombing alone could win the war was never tested by events for he was never given either the free hand or the resources which he laid down as necessary.

There was a narrower issue in dispute – that between area bombing which Harris favoured and the bombing of precise targets, which Harris dismissed as 'panaceas'. We can see in retrospect that Harris was right, though not always for the right reasons. Area bombing was the only operation of which the hastily trained crews of Bomber Command were capable. Precision bombing would have demanded a long period of training, during which no bombing would have taken place and supplies to Bomber Command would have been cut down in favour of competing needs. Bomber Command, in fact, had to bomb in order to justify itself; and area bombing was its only possibility. Moreover some of the 'panaceas' were inaccessible; others were not the 'panaceas' which they were alleged to be. For instance, Bomber Command was repeatedly urged to attack the ball-bearing factory at Schweinfurt, a difficult operation. It ultimately did so with disappointing results. The Germans discovered to their surprise, and still more to that of the Ministry of Economic Warfare, that they had enough ball-bearings in stock to keep them going until new production was started.

Still, the strongest argument for area bombing was that Sir Arthur Harris believed in it. He had brought new inspiration to Bomber Command after the failures of 1941. He alone understood the operational needs and difficulties of his command. Nor was it irrelevant that he had personal access to Churchill and strong support from Cherwell. A commander who claims to know how to win the war when others are doubting will always do much to carry the day.

The situation changed once the Allied armies landed in France. The German night fighters lost the guidance of their advanced radar stations. Bomber Command could undertake precision bombing against German oil supplies and did so with tremendous effect. This, of course, does not prove that it could have been done successfully while western Europe was under German occupation. Strategic bombing had been intended to make an Allied invasion unnecessary; instead it helped to make it successful. As with most past controversies, careful study of the record does not enable us to decide for one side or the other. It only enables us to understand what they were arguing about and why they argued as they did.

Can we draw any moral or guidance for the future? Fortunately not about strategic bombing in the strict sense. Strategic bombing, as practised in the last war, is now as obsolete as bows and arrows. A new war, if it comes, will undoubtedly be much more devastating, probably much faster, at any rate quite different. But, though weapons change, men remain the same. The lasting interest of this story is in the human sphere – how decisions were shaped, not how they were carried out. As technical power increased, confusion of counsels increased also. There was never a single strategic direction of Bomber Command. Sir Arthur Harris often determined strategy. Sir Charles Portal gave instructions for operations. Lord Cherwell influenced strategy as well as providing scientific assistance – or sometimes, as in the case of 'Window' (the device of dropping tinfoil to interfere with German radar), retarding it. The Ministry of Economic Warfare tried to determine bombing policy. The Admiralty wanted Bomber Command diverted to the war against the U-boats and often got its way. For a short period in 1944, Sir Arthur Tedder was put in supreme charge in order to prepare for the invasion. Things were done to impress public opinion or were sometimes prevented by it. Other things were done to impress the Americans or to prove them wrong. The prime minister intervened with ideas of his own.

In all this turmoil one almost forgets the crews of Bomber Command who ultimately had to carry out the conclusions of these conflicting authorities: 59,000 lost their lives. If the past be any guide, all the expectations of all the experts who are now preparing for war will turn out to be wrong and the experts will go on being wrong while the war is being fought. In the end, no doubt, someone will win. Clemenceau said that war was too serious a business to be left to soldiers. Nowadays it is too serious a business to be left to anybody.

Boom and Bombs

This essay was first published as a review of Andrew Boyle's Trenchard (*London, Collins, 1962*) *in the* New Statesman, *30 March 1962.*

*   *   *

Trenchard was the first chief of the Air Staff and held the post longer than any of his successors. He is rightly named 'father of the Royal Air Force', though he disliked the phrase. He was also a remarkable character on his own account. Harold Macmillan, generously coining a blurb for a rival publisher, has called him 'a great man: great in stature, great in courage and great in achievement'. He was big rather than great. In physique he was outsize and made himself bigger by his powerful voice. His generation knew him as 'Boom'. He was a man of few words, but these few were penetrating. His brief speeches should be printed in capital letters. On paper, he was crisp, clear and effective. He was the man to send when disorder threatened. He quelled a mutiny at Southampton in 1919 among the troops returning from France. He restored duty and discipline in the Metropolitan Police after a bad period in the thirties. He deserves the excellent biography which Andrew Boyle has written. It is a bit long and a bit too laudatory. But it is easy to read, clear on the issues and brings a good deal of new information – some from Trenchard's papers, more from his vivid conversation in old age.

The important thing in Trenchard's life was his creation of the Royal Air Force. Thanks to him, it became an independent force, instead of being divided between the two existing services, the army and the navy. This was a remarkable achievement, particularly against such a formidable opponent as Beatty, the first sea lord. What inspired Trenchard was more important still. He believed that the principal function of the RAF was to drop bombs. Of course, he recognized that it had other functions also: patrol work for the navy, and direct combat in cooperation with the army at the front – a task which he himself directed for much of the First World War as commander of the Royal Flying Corps. Independent bombing was the new and most important task. The next war, he believed, would be won by dropping bombs, not by land fighting. He applied this doctrine in practice and made the RAF predominantly a bomber force. The doctrine had vital consequences. It shaped British policy before the Second World War and British strategy during much of the war itself. In Trenchard's view there was no defence against bombing; there was only the 'deterrent' of a superior bomber force. Baldwin was repeating Trenchard's doctrine when he said: 'the bomber will always get through'. Hence British policy had to be cautious, or even craven, so long as the German bombers were thought to be more formidable than the RAF. On the other hand, the excessive confidence of Bomber Command also sprang from Trenchard's doctrine. He was responsible, in the last resort, for the strategical air offensive which has recently been scrupulously examined in an official history.

Trenchard's biography shows how this doctrine originated. It sprang from dogma, not from experience. During the First World War the RFC, forerunner of the RAF, worked with the army, observing enemy movements, fighting German aeroplanes. Trenchard was in command, not as a particularly skilled pilot, still less as a technician, but simply because he knew how to command. He was a competent regimental officer of high character, devoted to Haig, whom he resembled. Late in 1917 Rothermere was made first secretary for air – perhaps as a manoeuvre by Lloyd George to keep Rothermere's brother Northcliffe quiet. Trenchard was recalled from France to become chief of the Air Staff; and, according to him, for an odd reason. Rothermere said that he and Northcliffe were about to launch a press campaign against Haig, and needed Trenchard as cover. Trenchard, being loyal to Haig, at first refused the job; then, most strangely, accepted. He soon quarrelled with Rothermere, though over another question. He insisted on sending all available aeroplanes to France. Rothermere was playing up to public opinion which had been frightened by German air raids and wanted to keep most of the aeroplanes in England. Trenchard was dismissed, and Lloyd George, regarding him as an ally of Haig's, approved. Meanwhile Trenchard's old post, commanding the RFC, had been filled. He was hastily put in charge of a new independent bombing force at Nancy. This again was a gesture to satisfy British public opinion, which was clamouring for 'retaliation'. Few bombs were dropped on Germany, and to little effect. Trenchard talked big rather than acted; and his talk convinced him, if not others. He, previously the advocate and practitioner of air power as a wing of the army, now became the champion of the independent bomb.

This new faith grew stronger when he returned as chief of the Air Staff after the war. He fought for his own independent position and that of the RAF. He needed a decisive argument. He found it in Iraq. In 1922 warning pamphlets and a few incendiary bombs subdued a tribal rising at a cost of £10,000, where a military expedition would have cost £500,000. This trivial affair made a decisive mark on British history. The RAF won its independence. It became the cornerstone of British power in the Middle East. The lesson of the Iraqi villages was applied to the cities of Europe. They, too, could be bombed into subjection, much as Trenchard cowed the mutinous troops at Southampton with his booming voice. The bomber aeroplane was the strategical equivalent of a fist banged on the table. Boom and Bomb became one. In the middle twenties Trenchard was planning to bomb France – an unlikely enemy, but a possible rival. When Germany appeared as a real danger, bombing was again offered as the only answer.

Mr Boyle praises Trenchard as the man who prepared victory in the Battle of Britain. This is not so. The Battle of Britain was won by Fighter Command and radar. Trenchard had despised the one and knew nothing of the other. What Trenchard prepared was the strategical air offensive of 1940–41, which was a total failure, and, more remotely, the air offensive of 1942–44, which, though more successful, did more damage to this country than to the Germans. Like Haig, his hero, Trenchard was an extremely resolute and dogged commander, whose weapons did not come up to expectations and whose plans did not correspond to the facts. He was a strategical player who called above his paper. It is all dead stuff now, at any rate in Trenchard's terms. The conventional bomb and the conventional aeroplane have had their day as weapons of war. Still, it makes an odd story. Trenchard would not have hit on independent bombing if he had not become involved in an obscure intrigue of Northcliffe and Lloyd George, and if the tribes of Iraq had not been troublesome. Coventry, Hamburg and Dresden all paid for it. Maybe our strategy now is based entirely on cool, rational calculation. But it is just possible that there are still some in high places who think that Boom and Bomb are the same thing.

Strong Silent Man

This essay first appeared as a review of Denis Richards's Portal of Hungerford *(London, Heinemann, 1978) in the* Observer, *12 March 1978. Sir Charles Portal* (later Viscount Portal of Hungerford, 1893–1971) *was chief of Air Staff 1940–46.*

* * *

Sir Charles Portal, known to his intimates as Peter Portal and later Viscount Portal of Hungerford, was chief of the Air Staff from the autumn of 1940 until the end of the war, a far longer stretch of service than any of his colleagues on the Chiefs of Staff's Committee. His reputation was high. Churchill called him 'the accepted star of the air force' and said of him 'Portal has everything.' Ismay, when asked who had been the greatest commander on our side, replied, 'Not difficult to answer: Peter Portal – *quite easily.*' Eisenhower went even further: 'Greatest of all the British war leaders – greater even than Churchill.'

Portal's greatness is difficult to recapture. He was a lone wolf who kept few personal records. One colleague said of him, 'There is a human side to Portal, but you won't see it in the office.' He took his solitary lunch at the Travellers' Club and said to another close colleague: 'Don't talk to me when you see me at the club, will you – or I shall have to talk to the other members.' His contribution to the war has to be reconstructed largely from the official records, a task that Denis Richards has performed admirably.

At the Chiefs of Staff's Committee and later with the combined chiefs-of-staff, Portal had little to say, but what he had to say was decisive. Unlike Brooke, he did not lose his temper. Unlike Pound, he did not fall asleep. He remained silent during the long wrangles and then at the end produced a skilful compromise that reconciled all differences.

It is not surprising that Eisenhower admired him. Though Portal naturally put the claims of the air force first, he was one of the few leaders who recognized that the defeat of Germany must be a combined operation. He sustained both Harris who believed in independent bombing and Tedder who advocated army–air force cooperation. He even managed to be on good terms with Beaverbrook which the other air marshals did not. He was not afraid to stand up to Churchill, though in the most conciliatory way, and often induced Churchill to withdraw some fiery minute, substituting instead a 'Do as you wish.' When Churchill criticized the bombing of Dresden, Portal quietly showed that Churchill had urged the further bombing of German cities and Churchill for once cancelled his minute of complaint.

Maybe Portal lacked sympathy with the navy and did not fully appreciate the Battle of the Atlantic. Thus he wrote of the Naval Staff, 'They were *entirely* defensive in their thinking, being haunted by the thought that if sea communications were severed we *must* lose the war.' Evidently Portal did not realize that the successful passage of a convoy was a greater offensive victory than unsuccessful bomber raids on Germany.

Portal had the prime responsibility for air strategy. He had been brought up in the Trenchard school and Trenchard was a whole-hearted believer in offensive bombing, insisting as early as the Norwegian campaign that if this had been operated '*it probably would have ended the war by now*', a fantastic idea. Portal was slow to realize that the early bomber attacks on Germany were not achieving significant results, but, as he explained to Churchill, they were what the RAF had been designed for. After the fall of France, Kitchener's Law operated, 'We have to make war as we must and not as we should like to.' Great Britain had to bomb Germany as a demonstration that she was still in the war and Portal did his best to put a good face on it. He gradually retreated from the position that independent bombing would win the war unaided and argued instead that it was the essential preliminary to a landing in northern France. He did not espouse Lindemann's idea of sapping German morale by 'terror-bombing'. As he told the boys of Winchester College after the war:

The loss of life, which amounted to some 600,000 killed, was purely incidental and in as much as it involved children and women who were taking no part in the war we all deplored the necessity for doing it.

Here Portal was being a little less than frank. Towards the end of the war he tried to divert 'Bomber' Harris from independent to precision bombing. He did not succeed and perhaps doubted whether Harris even at this late date was altogether wrong.

British bombing strategy is still a contested issue. Denis Richards devotes three chapters to it when his narrative material runs out.

These chapters are implicitly a sustained attack on the official history of the strategical bomber offensive by Sir Charles Webster and Noble Frankland. The two official historians reached the conclusion that until 1943 the offensive was ineffective, probably inflicting more damage on the British than on the German economy. Thereafter, they admitted, the results were greater though not enough to win the war on their own. Richards, a long-time champion of the bomber offensive, disputes these conclusions, incidentally revealing that both Portal and Harris refused to provide any information for the two official historians.

It is really time this controversy was ended. With the bomber offensive the British did the best they could. Their expectations were at first grossly inflated. But it can be argued that the bomber offensive compelled the Germans to produce fighters instead of bombers and so weakened Germany's offensive air strength against both Great Britain and Russia. Towards the end the RAF managed both to continue the bomber offensive and to sustain the land forces in France.

Portal's great achievement was to keep on good terms with all the contending parties except, of course, the Germans. He was a conciliator with a hard core and this enabled him to make a decisive contribution to British victory in the Second World War. His reticence was his strength. However, it makes his biography as placid, though also as persuasive, as his own arguments. In any case Portal did not worry much about his reputation. He preferred fishing.

The Cross of Lorraine

This essay first appeared as a review of François Kersaudy's Churchill and de Gaulle *(London, Collins, 1981) in the* Observer, 27 September 1981.

*   *   *

One day during the war Eden remarked to General de Gaulle, 'Do you know, you have given me more trouble than all the other exiled governments put together?' To which de Gaulle replied, 'Naturally, France is a Great Power.' These few words set the stage for the relations between de Gaulle and Churchill throughout the Second World War. Churchill was the acknowledged leader of a great empire. De Gaulle was an almost unknown figure with comparatively few followers. Yet from the first de Gaulle insisted that he spoke for the real France as against the Vichy government. Often indeed he spoke of himself as 'France'. Roosevelt, who detested him, alleged that he had claimed to be Joan of Arc, Louis XIV, Napoleon and Clemenceau rolled into one, and in the end the claim proved to be very near the truth.

The two men, Churchill and de Gaulle, had much in common. Both were devoted patriots. Both had been disregarded before the war. And both were determined to get their way. Both were now set on victory. There were two profound differences. Churchill had achieved power, de Gaulle had not. Moreover Churchill had many years of political experience and knew how to compromise, particularly with an ally such as Roosevelt who was stronger than he was. De Gaulle, had never experienced responsibility, rejected all compromise and, having defied both Hitler and Vichy, was now prepared to defy both Great Britain and the United States. Both men had the grandeur which comes from being steeped in history. They resembled prehistoric monsters and the conflict between the two dinosaurs had its comic side, except for those involved in it.

François Kersaudy has told the story with inimitable skill and careful scholarship. He has explored the memoirs of the two men with the satisfactory conclusion that both memoirs are highly unreliable in detail though deeply true to the spirit of the combatants. Kersaudy has laboured intensively over the archives of the British cabinet and

Foreign Office. He has even made the surprising discovery that an anonymous onslaught on de Gaulle in the *Observer* of 13 June 1943 was written by Churchill himself. There is enough of general narrative to enable the reader to understand what the two heroes were quarrelling about. But essentially this is a story of two personalities, not a record of events. If the two men had disputed less, this would not have changed the face of history but it would have deprived a succeeding generation of much innocent enjoyment.

Churchill had helped to discover de Gaulle as expressing the spirit of unconquerable France. Despite his repeated outbursts of rage against de Gaulle he could never forget that in similar circumstances he would have taken the same line of unyielding devotion to his national cause. But Churchill had also to wage war and if he called on de Gaulle to make sacrifices this was because he had had to make many himself. De Gaulle was not by conviction pro-British as Churchill was by conviction pro-French. Indeed de Gaulle often spoke as though he was still living in the days of the Fashoda crisis.

Unable to defend France from the Germans, he was all the more determined to defend her and her empire from the British. When the United States took the British line, this made de Gaulle all the more resolute against them both. De Gaulle championed the French cause in Syria, in St Pierre and Miquelon, in Northern Africa and finally in France itself. After D-Day he denounced the 'counterfeit money' that the Allies were circulating in Normandy and his first act on arriving there was to install a French commissionner in Bayeux against express instructions.

De Gaulle's defiance provoked Churchill beyond endurance. He wanted to arrest de Gaulle or to cut off his supplies. The letters and records reproduced in this book provide an anthology of vivid abuse. De Gaulle appears as 'that hateful man' and 'a bitter foe'. 'He was one of those Frenchmen who hated Britain and might even be prepared to join with the Germans in attacking Britain sometime.' Eden did his best to restrain Churchill and was throughout a good friend to de Gaulle. Even the war cabinet rebelled and challenged some of Churchill's orders.

In the end peace would be patched up. A meeting would be arranged. Attendants listened to the distant rumble of thunder on the other side of the door. Finally the door was opened. The two would be sitting side by side on a sofa. Each had made a great concession:

Churchill was speaking in French and de Gaulle was smoking a cigar. During one of their disputes, Churchill said of de Gaulle, 'He's selfish, he's arrogant, he thinks he's the centre of the universe ... he ... You're right, he's a great man.' And on Churchill's death de Gaulle wrote to Queen Elizabeth, 'In the great drama he was the greatest of all.' For once both men were right.

Pen Pals at War

This essay first appeared as a review of Joseph P Lash's Roosevelt and Churchill 1939–1941: The Partnership that Saved the West (*London, Deutsch, 1977*) *in the* Observer, *22 May 1977*.

*   *   *

The morning after the Japanese attack on Pearl Harbor Churchill had a discussion with his chiefs-of-staff. One of them advocated a continuation of the same cautious approach to America that had seemed politic when her intervention was in doubt. Churchill answered with a wicked glint in his eye, 'Oh! That is the way we talked to her while we were wooing her; now that she is in the harem, we talk to her quite differently.'

Perhaps an apocryphal story. But it characterized the relations between the two countries and in particular the correspondence between Churchill and Roosevelt. Churchill was set on getting the United States into the war. Roosevelt was determined not to be involved until the appropriate moment, depending partly on American opinion and partly on the development of American armaments.

At a casual glance the correspondence appears to be an intimate exchange between two old friends. In fact they had never met before August 1941. Roosevelt had once set eyes on Churchill in 1917; Churchill had been unaware of Roosevelt's presence. Moreover Churchill had often attacked the New Deal in his journalistic days, and Wilkie used some devastating sentences of Churchill's during the election campaign of 1940. Even then Churchill did not disavow them, minuting, 'It is all too true. Less said soonest mended. Do nothing.'

The letters were official documents despite their casual tone. The Foreign Office scrutinized and censored Churchill's letters, though Churchill sometimes printed the censored version when he wrote his war memoirs. Roosevelt's letters were all written by his confidential advisers and he merely added a friendly phrase towards the end. The two pen friends were in fact adroit statesmen, each trying to out-manoeuvre the other. This was a competition Roosevelt won. He was the most skilful; he also of course held the stronger hand.

The letters provide the frame for Joseph Lash's book. But he often strays far from his ostensible brief. Lash is a journalist of long experience and was also acquainted personally with Roosevelt from New Deal days. For him Roosevelt was the supreme manipulator, using devious means for a righteous cause. Lash even admits that Roosevelt provided precedents for the way in which President L B Johnson involved America in the Vietnam War with, however, the difference that involvement in the world war was right and that in Vietnam wrong. Like other admirers of Roosevelt he thinks that Roosevelt always knew where he was going though he went there in a roundabout way. I doubt this. Roosevelt seems to have believed for a long time that Germany would be defeated, or at any rate tamed, without direct American involvement. It was not only American opinion that had to be converted; he had to be converted himself. As Felix Frankfurter remarked, 'Presidents sometimes don't tell themselves things.'

However, there is the theme: the two great statesmen drawing ever closer and cooperating to save democracy. Lash sees Roosevelt from the inside with a wealth of anecdotes, most of them by no means new. Churchill is seen from outside largely with the aid of British records that have not been used before. Curiously, therefore, though the book is much more about Roosevelt than about Churchill, what it has to tell about Churchill is fresher and more interesting. Indeed at one level the book is interesting throughout. It is written with high journalistic skill of narration. The material is marshalled so powerfully that it sounds as though it had never been used before.

At another level the appeal of the book flags. Like so many American works on recent history it is very long, sparing the reader no detail and no anecdote. After all, the two men have been around as historical figures for a long time. Everything Roosevelt did has been raked over again and again. We know all about his hesitations and evasions. We know how rapidly he adapted himself to new situations, jettisoning overnight policies he had previously advocated. Churchill's record has been less subject to revision though it is crying out for the attention of scholars. But he too was by no means as straightforward as he appeared. Above all both men made mistakes and Lash seems unaware of these.

All the same this is a very good book, or would be if it were half the length. Both men come alive with a slight hint of halo hovering over them. So too do the men around Roosevelt, from Stimson to Hopkins. The British statesmen and diplomats are mostly lay figures, which perhaps in the Churchill system they were.

Churchill and Roosevelt with all their faults were truly great men. Their intimacy was more assumed than real. Both put the interests of their own country first and both were naturally set on remaining in office. Over lend-lease Roosevelt was more concerned with reducing British economic independence than Lash appreciates. Churchill was concerned to preserve British strength, though less effectively. Nevertheless, their overriding interest was to defeat Nazi Germany, and they achieved their aim.

Roosevelt made the United States the greatest power in the world; Churchill at any rate secured that Great Britain emerged victorious from the greatest of all wars. Defeat of Germany was indeed a righteous cause, and these two men did more than any others to accomplish it. Their story is well worth telling again however often it has been told before.

The War of the British Succession

First published in the Observer, *5 March 1978, as a review of* Allies of a Kind: The United States, Britain, and the War against Japan, 1941–1945 *by Christopher Thorne (London, Hamish Hamilton, 1978) and* Imperialism at Bay: The United States and the Decolonisation of the British Empire 1941–1945 *by William Roger Louis (Oxford, Clarendon Press, 1977).*

* * *

I am inclined to patent my new name for the Second World War in Asia.

During the Second World War and for a generation after it Germany occupied the centre of the stage; Japan seemed remote and almost irrelevant except of course to those engaged in the war against her.

With the passage of time perspectives have changed. The war against Germany now appears as, let us hope, the last episode in the long struggle for the mastery of Europe which had occupied most of modern history. The Far Eastern war had deeper consequences: within a short time it ended the white domination of Asia which had characterized the previous two hundred years.

This was totally unexpected. The British fought to restore the empire they had lost at the end of 1941; the Americans, though by no means anxious to restore the British Empire, assumed that it would be replaced by their own predominance, suitably cloaked in idealistic phrases. Both were disappointed. Japan, though defeated in battle, won a moral victory. Asia for the Asians ended the age of imperialism.

This is a tremendous theme and here at last are two magnificent books devoted to it. Christopher Thorne's is a staggering achievement. Its 700 pages survey not only Anglo-American relations and the war against Japan. They also illuminate the problems of China, India, South-East Asia and Australasia. Thorne's research ranges over the continents. He is a master of diplomacy as well as of war and also, what is perhaps even more important for a historian, a master of personalities. All the participants from Roosevelt and Churchill downwards come alive. Churchill's outlook is summarized in a single phrase: 'Why be apologetic about Anglo-Saxon superiority? We are superior.'

Roosevelt was at his most devious in his patronage of both Britain and China. He could have said with Pearl Buck, 'If the American way of life is to prevail in the world, it must prevail in Asia.' Revealing, too, was the remark of the American chiefs-of-staff that, if Puerto Rico were ever to be given its freedom, its inhabitants would first have to 'voluntarily and under no duress acknowledge the facts' and grant the United States unshakeable defence rights there.

The British had comparatively little military strength to spare for the Far East: only 10 per cent of the British servicemen who died in the war died there. But their ambitions were none the less limitless. As Churchill said, 'All, all shall be restored.' The Americans regarded the British as tiresome and somewhat ineffective allies. If the British were to act at all, it should be with the aim of reopening land communications with China, on whom the Americans set exaggerated hopes in both the military and political spheres. The British, judging China more realistically, strove for an offensive towards Burma and South-East Asia, which they did not achieve until the war was almost over.

The Far Eastern war was a racial war by implication and often in practice. Thus Roosevelt, though anxious to end British rule in India – perhaps even by 'reform on the Soviet line' – also thought that the Indians needed an infusion of Nordic blood. As Thorne remarks, 'The saviour of the East, it seems, was to be neither a Gandhi nor a Curzon, but Siegfried with a sitar.'

Both the British and the Americans thought that they alone understood the Asiatics and that their partners did not. Their partnership was often strained. The British broke one of the main American diplomatic codes, though they ended their eavesdropping once America was in the war. Roosevelt remarked, 'I do not mean to be unkind or rude to the British, but in 1841, when you acquired Hong Kong, you did not acquire it by purchase.' To which Oliver Stanley, the British colonial secretary, replied, 'Let me see, Mr President, that was about the time of the Mexican War, wasn't it?'

Often the records quoted by Thorne give the impression that the British and Americans were more concerned to thwart each other than to get on with the war against Japan. Or rather they ran both struggles at the same time. In the last resort they were forced together and became 'allies of a kind'. There were ties of common interest and common ideals, but there was also much misunderstanding and some hostility.

Roger Louis presents the same relationship, as limited to the Anglo-American debate on the future of colonial possessions after the war. As this debate was conducted between diplomats or academics it had fewer of the open brawls that marked the arguments between the respective chiefs-of-staff or the somewhat irresponsible pronouncements of President Roosevelt. The British prided themselves on their record of colonial administration and insisted that they could maintain it, even in the mandated territories, without international supervision. The Americans preached trusteeship which would replace imperialism by international control.

There followed a curious twist. The Americans, though anxious to eliminate all other empires, wished to acquire one for themselves. Their eyes were set on the Pacific Islands which they proposed to transform into a ring of strategic bases directed against Japan.

The arguments went on throughout the war. In the end they proved irrelevant. At the San Francisco conference the British, faced with Australian as well as American pressure, succumbed to the principle of trusteeship for their mandated territories and later dismembered their entire empire for reasons quite unconnected with American promptings. As for the Americans, they duly secured strategic control of the Pacific Islands but, as Japan ceased to be a danger, the islands proved to be so many white sea-elephants; nor did the islands help the Americans much when they tried to assert their supremacy on the mainland of Asia and in Vietnam.

As often happens in war the British and Americans were trying to provide against past dangers and did not foresee the future problems with which they would be faced. In the eyes of both British and Americans the Far Eastern war was the war of the British Succession. As things worked out there was no successor except the peoples of Asia themselves.

To Our Everlasting Shame

This essay first appeared as a review of Martin Gilbert's Auschwitz and the Allies (*London, Michael Joseph/Rainbird, 1981*) *in the* Observer, *11 October 1981. At the time he was writing the review Alan Taylor wrote to the author*:

The conduct of the Foreign Office, or most of its members, stirs me to such indignation and contempt that I hesitate to review the book for fear of losing all control. However, to hold the balance of my conscience clear I must add that by now I have as much sympathy with the Palestinians as with the Jews.

* * *

Auschwitz is now a name of horror without parallel. This was the worst of the murder camps which the Nazis set up in eastern Europe. Yet curiously it attracted least attention until a late stage in the war. Martin Gilbert has set out to explore this contradiction. Why did Auschwitz remain relatively unknown for so long? Gilbert provides a variety of answers. First was lack of information: until 1944 hardly anyone escaped from Auschwitz to tell the tale. Second was its double character: unlike the other camps which were centres of murder only, Auschwitz was partly murder camp and partly munitions factory. Even those who worked in the factories often did not know what went on in the gas chambers across the way.

The most powerful factor was psychological. What went on at Auschwitz passed all belief. Once labelled incredible the murders could be dismissed from contemplation. Those who had to determine policy in Great Britain and to some extent in the United States were not sympathetic to the Jews in the first place and were made even less so by what they called 'typical Jewish exaggeration'.

Two years ago Bernard Wasserstein produced an admirable book on Britain and the Jews of Europe that centred primarily on the problem of whether Jews should be admitted to Palestine during the Second World War, with the firm answer from British bureaucrats: No. Gilbert covers some of the same ground but he approaches the problem at an earlier stage: not so much what to do with the Jews when they should escape from Europe but how to get them out and end or mitigate the German policy of mass murder.

Much of this involves an examination of British records, particularly from the Foreign Office. These provide an anthology of hard-heartedness. 'HMG do not recognize a distinct Jewish nationality . . . This is a major fallacy . . . Once we open the door to adult male Jews to be taken out of enemy territory, a quite unmanageable flood may result . . . There are signs of increasing anti-Semitism in Britain itself.' The Jews were accused of inventing or at least exaggerating the atrocity stories with 'the main object of filling Palestine with Jews'. Eden's private secretary recorded: 'Unfortunately AE is immovable on the subject of Palestine. He loves Arabs and hates Jews.' This applied to most of the British cabinet ministers with the solitary exception of Winston Churchill, who repeatedly voiced his sympathy with the Jews and was as repeatedly overruled when he proposed any practical action.

Gilbert devotes less attention to the American record which was however equally discreditable. Unlike Great Britain the United States had plenty of room and, even more important, plenty of food and other resources. Roosevelt in his usual way spoke out in favour of the Jews and systematically avoided any action to benefit them. After all he had to win anti-Semitic as well as Jewish votes and money. The routine American answer became that the only way of saving the Jews was to win the war. Carried further, this became the answer that any attempt to aid the Jews would retard the winning of the war and therefore actually injure them.

When Auschwitz had been in action for nearly two years, information about the mass murders at last reached the West and there was a desperate search for ways of ending the slaughter. The Jewish leaders pleaded for Allied statements to Germany warning of stern penalties for the atrocities when the war was over. The Allies were generous in words and little more. Gilbert explores in detail the negotiations between Eichmann, the murder chief, and Joel Brand, a self-appointed Jewish spokesman. There was high talk of exchanging Jews for lorries, cocoa and supplies of war the Germans needed. Gilbert seems to think that something might have been achieved if the Allied leaders had supported Brand. I think the negotiations were fraudulent from beginning to end.

The question of bombing Auschwitz was more important. The Jewish leaders pleaded that Auschwitz and the railways leading to it should be bombed. The official answer was always that Auschwitz was too far away, that innocent Jews as well as evil Nazis would be killed and that the accurate bombing of such distant railways was impossible. Gilbert is able to show from maps in the Churchill papers that the Allied aircraft which brought aid to Warsaw in August 1944 actually flew over Auschwitz on their way. In this case again the failure to act on behalf of the Jews was a lack of will, not of resources: the Foreign Office even concealed the necessary maps from the Air Ministry.

Gilbert uses a sentence by a member of the Foreign Office, already used by Wasserstein: 'In my opinion a disproportionate amount of the time of this Office is wasted on dealing with these wailing Jews.' Another member of the Foreign Office answered that the Jews 'have been given cause to wail by their sufferings under the Nazi regime'.

A colleague recently criticized me for describing the Second World War as 'a good war'. After reading this record of Nazi achievements I am more than ever convinced of the truth of the verdict.

The Cold War

This essay first appeared in the New Statesman, *24 June 1966. The books referred to were Douglas Clark's* Three Days to Catastrophe *(London, Hammond, 1966) on the proposed Anglo-French expedition to Finland, Arnold Rogow's* Victim of Duty *(London, Hart-Davis, 1966) on James Forrestal, Haakon Chevalier's* Oppenheimer *(London, Deutsch, 1966), Martin Herz's* Beginnings of the Cold War *(Bloomington, Indiana University Press, 1966) and Gar Alperovitz's* Atomic Diplomacy: Hiroshima and Potsdam *(London, Secker and Warburg, 1966).*

*   *   *

Many years ago – almost beyond the memory of living man – Sir Norman Angell, still happily active, exposed the great illusion that war was a profitable venture. He had, however, an illusion of his own, one perhaps inevitably shared by practically all writers on human affairs: the belief that men would be convinced by rational demonstration. The inaccuracy of this belief was displayed almost immediately by the outbreak of the First World War, and there has been comparatively little to justify it since. If men are now a little shaken in their enthusiasm for war, after two experiences of mass destruction, they have clung obstinately to a substitute, which has provided most of the features of war except actual fighting. For twenty-one years European relations have been shaped by the Cold War, and now that it is threatening to thaw, a new version is sustained in the Far East. Yet any justification for the Cold War has been grotesquely thin all along. Time and again, it seemed, a little sanity could have ended it. But, of course, sanity and the Cold War do not live well together. Ignorance, prejudice and obstinacy have from the start been more effective counsellors.

The Cold War has been the greatest obstacle to rational thinking in my lifetime. On most other topics, a rational approach has been tolerated and sometimes welcomed. When I contemplate such various questions as colonial policy, sex relations or medical treatment, I am astonished at the advances which have been made and at the enlightenment shown. On the Cold War, attitudes have remained everywhere rigid and irrational. The few who tried to remain sane got the feeling that they must be the madmen. In time they shouted with the crowd. Otherwise they were either ostracized or lapsed into despair. Take, for instance, a now-forgotten episode of folly: the projected Anglo-French expedition to aid Finland against Soviet Russia in the winter of 1939–40. Could anything have been crazier than to take on Soviet Russia when we were already at war with Germany? It is not surprising that respectable historians have steered clear of the affair and have left its dissection to a gifted amateur [Clark]. Yet at the time all the leading politicians clamoured for intervention, and their names are still held in honour. Among the few opponents, Beaverbrook is usually dismissed as a man of no political judgement. D N Pritt opposed it: he was expelled from the Labour Party for his wisdom and never readmitted. What is this mania which bites people when they contemplate either communism or Soviet Russia?

The Russians are extremely tiresome and communists even more so. Communists would like to be all the wicked things their opponents say they are. They would like to be subversive, unscrupulous and ruthless. In fact, they are only unsuccessful. Social revolution was a nineteenth-century habit which came to an end in 1918. The last fifty years have been one of the most unrevolutionary ages in history so far as Europe is concerned, and even outside Europe revolutions have sprung more from the desire for national independence than from deep social causes. It is only possible to get into a fright about the communists by reading what they say they are going to do instead of considering what they have done. James Forrestal, the first American secretary of defence, was a good example [see Rogow]. He played a large part in inventing the Cold War. He drove himself mad by reading the works of Marx and Lenin, and ended up by throwing himself from a high window. Professor Rogow tries to discover private reasons for Forrestal's mental state – difficult relations with his father, social ambitions and so on. Most people have these troubles or some of them and yet keep going. It was the Red Spectre which pushed Forrestal over the edge.

Robert Oppenheimer was another victim of the Cold War [see Chevalier]. He was largely responsible for the atomic bomb, for which I do not thank him, and after some qualms went on to produce the hydrogen bomb, for which I thank him even less. He was framed as a fellow-traveller and fell on evil days. It was not quite as simple as that. There really was an approach to Oppenheimer through his friend Chevalier by a known communist. Oppenheimer tried to cover his friend by making out that the approaches had been made to others. Ultimately he was found out – and serve him right: those who try to play both with communists and the American government should know they are in for trouble. Chevalier now covers up for himself by presenting the episode as a good deal more harmless than it was. Of course, it was silly for a communist to suppose that he could get atomic secrets from Oppenheimer. Communists are often silly, though this is no justification for the Cold War.

The Russians, as a Great Power, are also not much help to those who would like to present their policy sensibly. It is impossible to treat Soviet policy except by guesswork, and sensational guesses are always more welcome than prosaic ones. Since the Russians refuse to open their archives, they can be credited with grandiose and malevolent plans for dominating the world. A record of a sort can be pieced together from the events of the last fifty years, and this record runs all one way. The Soviet government want to be left alone, though they also want to be treated with normal respect. Their motives are fear, suspicion and pride. All the rest is dreaming. Their suspicion and fear are not unjustified. Nothing perhaps is more extraordinary in modern European history than the persistent refusal, which goes back long before the Bolshevik Revolution, to treat Russia as an equal. In the nineteenth century it produced the follies of the Crimean War and of Disraeli's Jingoism. In the twentieth it produced, among other things, the Second World War. Only alliance with Soviet Russia could have prevented that war, and the Russians won it for us.

It was obvious throughout the war that, if Germany were defeated, Russia would be the dominant power in eastern Europe. This was inescapable. Indeed the war only made sense on the basis: better Russia than Germany. Western opinion and, still more, Western policy closed their eyes to this obvious fact. Martin Herz, of the American Foreign Service, has just produced a little book which is presumably intended to explain the Cold War, though it reads more like another shot in it. He is not altogether one-sided. He shows how the American government dangled a reconstruction loan before the Russians (mainly for fear of large-scale unemployment in America) and then pulled it away again. But his main theme is Russian aggressiveness in Poland. The Russians insisted on keeping the territory which they had acquired from Poland in 1939 – not surprisingly, since nearly everyone, including Churchill, thought that their claim was morally justified. More than this, the Russians wanted a friendly government in Poland and, as Stalin said of all eastern European countries, 'a freely elected government in any of these countries would be anti-Soviet, and that we cannot allow'. The British had applied similar logic in Greece. The British and Americans applied it everywhere in western Europe by taking precautions against the communists. When the Russians followed their example, this was paraded, and still is, as justification for the Cold War.

Yet even in this gloomy subject there is an occasional rustle of common sense. The Americans have always been fiercer in the Cold War than we have. But they have also produced more critics and have been more generous, of course, with evidence. The detailed records of the Potsdam conference destroy the accepted legend completely. They show, perhaps almost too emphatically, that the Cold War was deliberately started by Truman and his advisers. Gar Alperovitz is first in the field to make this clear. He tries maybe to prove a bit too much. He nibbles at the thesis, propounded long ago by Patrick Blackett, that the atomic bombs were dropped on Japan solely as a demonstration against the Russians. I do not think that this can be sustained, and indeed Alperovitz does not try to sustain it with any firm evidence. He has to fall back on 'seems to have been', 'might explain' (twice), 'would accord with' (also twice), 'would tie in with'. In other words, he is guessing. There is solid evidence the other way. Most American military experts still thought that Japan could not be conquered without heavy fighting; the scientists wanted to show that the money spent on the bomb had not been wasted; most decisive of all, the emperor of Japan did not abandon his constitutional reserve and insist on peace until the bombs had been dropped. The bombs were used to give him the final push.

These arguments about Japan are irrelevant to Alperovitz's main theme. Given that the bombs were going to be dropped, for whatever reason, awareness of this was bound to affect American policy towards Soviet Russia. Roosevelt's death had already brought a change. Roosevelt was a man of world vision and also a shrewd political tactician. He put off final settlements with Russia until after the war, in the belief that they could then be used to generate further goodwill. Truman saw things differently. He had an anti-Soviet past and anti-Soviet advisers – James Byrnes, his secretary of state, backed Barry

Goldwater in the 1964 presidential election. Truman also had the impatient ignorance of a little man with anyone who failed to acknowledge American power. Russian insistence on equality made him want a showdown at once. Then he retreated and even acquired briefly the reputation of continuing Roosevelt's policy. The retreat was in fact tactical: postponement of confrontation until the bomb went off. Potsdam was supposed to be the showdown. But it came too soon. Stalin still thought that he was strong enough to get his way. Truman thought that he would soon hold the whip hand. Therefore he worked to evade decision and to keep the door open for a conflict on more favourable terms. Thus the Cold War was provoked by design. It was intended to be shortlived. Truman and his cronies calculated that Soviet Russia would run away once the bomb had gone off. They underrated Soviet obstinacy, as Hitler had done before them. They also misjudged what the bomb could do. It could destroy: it could not liberate nor even, except at the height of world war, terrify. All that Truman achieved was to rivet the Cold War into Soviet policy as much as into his own.

There were other contributory factors later: desire by the ageing Churchill to have another round as great war leader, and the need of the British, as of other Europeans, for some excuse to get dollars. But the basic decision was made at Potsdam and soon afterwards. The Americans intended to terrify the Russians. When the Russians refused to be terrified, the Americans had to make out that they themselves were terrified in order to push up the alarms. Now even American scholars, unless hired by the State Department, conclude that the alarms of 1945 were overdone. Will this belated flash of sense make any difference? I doubt it. The Cold War is built into all our political and military thinking and into nearly all our academic thinking. Sanity has no result except to bring trouble for its propounder. The only hope is that boredom may succeed where reason has failed.

The Cold War Spreads

This essay was the last in a series of ten half-hour television lectures entitled 'World War'. These were broadcast by London Rediffusion late on Wednesday evenings between 29 June and 14 September 1966.

*   *   *

When the Cold War started it was not expected that it would last a lifetime, certainly not in the West. There was perhaps the same sort of exaggeration about Russian weakness as years before there had been about Germany's economic weakness. It was expected that, in a comparatively short space of time, Soviet influence and dominance in Europe could be rolled back. The transformation, the freezing of the Cold War, began when Soviet scientists also discovered nuclear power and were able to make atomic bombs. With this the expectation of any quick destruction of Soviet communism was put aside. It now appears roughly true that the Soviet nuclear power was on a much smaller scale than America's simply because it existed only enough to maintain the balance. But here again there was a new balance in the world, a balance which was completed when the Russians discovered hydrogen bombs as well. From the middle of the 1950s instead of a Cold War it was really a frozen frontier. Nothing in Europe is more striking than the fact that, except as a phrase, the Cold War faded out on both sides. After all, Cold War implied that there was a deliberate policy to inflict damage on the other. On the one side it was believed, though quite wrongly in my opinion, that the Russians were planning to spread communism in western Germany. On the Russian side, it was believed, with rather more justice, that the Americans hoped, perhaps even intended, to push Russia out of Europe behind her own frontiers.

From the middle of the 1950s, both these anxieties diminished. In fact one can fix almost an exact point in 1956. This was the Hungarian rising. It began as a genuine movement for greater freedom in Hungary, led largely by people who were communist or half-communist but who resented the purely mechanical dictatorship to which they had been subjected. The Russians themselves – this is a most extraordinary moment I think in European history – contemplated accepting a sort of libertarian communism, if you can imagine such a thing could exist. But the Russians intervened when they came to believe that this movement in Hungary was swinging away and would bring to power parties which had existed before the war. They feared that Hungary, instead of being neutralist, would break right out of the Soviet system of defence and perhaps even go over to the other side. So the Russians crushed the Hungarian rising and restored a communist government. Though one must say it was a communist government which has proved itself a good deal less tyrannical than its predecessor. If there had really been an intention to turn the Cold War into a hot war, this was the moment of greatest opportunity. The whole of eastern Europe was in considerable discontent. Yet when willingness to turn towards the West was strongest, no such move took place. Here was the clear indication that the Cold War was not really a war any longer, that the two sides had accepted a division of Europe, a division which they tended to talk about as though it was a division of the world, assuming that Europe was all the world. There was a continuation of security and defence which by this time had become much more habit than anything else. It's very difficult to believe that at any time after 1956 there was any serious chance of attack by one side or the other. The thing had really settled down. When we look at Europe, the most important legacy of the Cold War – I speak of it in the past because I think as a serious factor in policy it isn't there at all any more – was not the shaking out of European countries into those which were Russian satellites and those which were America's satellites or, to speak more politely, associates. This was an inevitable pattern. On the whole, the west European countries had similar sorts of institutions and economic arrangements to the United States, and, in any case, were increasingly able to stand on their own feet economically, if not from a military point of view. Similarly these east European countries had very often been associated with Russia or even Russian protection. The extension of Russia into Europe which people treated as though it was very new, was in fact very old. Russian influence in 1956 or even in 1966 was a good deal less extensive than it was in 1815 or at any time between 1815 almost and 1870, despite little upsets. So there was really nothing very surprising about this.

What was surprising and new in Europe was the division of Germany – something which had been totally unexpected. The one unstable element I think in the Cold War earlier on had been the assumption made by both sides that Germany would remain a united country or that the line of division of a military occupation was a freak which couldn't last. Instead, it was to last more than twenty years and to give every indication of almost the deepest legacy in Europe for with it the most considerable of European powers ceased to exist from the point of view of power politics. The Germans exist. In western Germany they are highly prosperous, in eastern Germany I gather a good deal less so. German national consciousness exists. Nobody has the slightest doubt that there are people called Germans and that indeed one can point to Germany quite clearly on the map. But in the sense of a Great Power the Germany which had risen to greatness in the late nineteenth century, which had conducted two great wars and had been, in a sense, the centre of two great wars in the twentieth century, this Germany was eliminated and as long as the partition remained, it would continue to be eliminated. In one way, you can say that the Cold War, far from leading to war, had its own built-in security for peace. After all, the country which caused two world wars in the twentieth century was Germany. When Germany doesn't exist as a Great Power, there's really nobody to cause world wars. World wars can happen by mistake maybe, but the sort of impulse of militarism, of confidence in victory, the desire in the Second World War to avenge the defeat of the First, all this was got out of the way. And at very little cost, so far as the rest of Europe was concerned. Neither side seriously desired to end this happy, though unexpected result.

At any rate, the Europe which came out of the Cold War was divided into a highly prosperous, increasingly flourishing western zone and on the other side a Europe which was becoming a bit more industrialized than it had been before and, at the same time, dependent on Russia not only for its security but for its industrial development.

There's one other curious thing about the Cold War – the emergence of genuine neutrals. Of course, there have always been some neutrals. There was Sweden and Switzerland in the Second World War. By a strange series of circumstances, Austria was to emerge after the Second World War in the same position. But the strangest of all was Yugoslavia, the only country in Europe where the communist government was established by its own efforts and not by the intervention of Russia. The other communist governments in Europe obviously owed their position to Soviet influence and backing and, to some extent, simply the Soviet Army. However, the Yugoslav communists had established their own communist government after the war as a result of their partisan warfare against Germany. Perhaps because of this, or perhaps because Yugoslavs are difficult people, or perhaps because of their geographical position, Yugoslavia then developed a particular form of national communism. Yugoslavia was in fact the most striking illustration of the way in which national independence can override communist principles and the clearest denial of the idea that the extension of communism necessarily meant the extension of Soviet power. On the contrary, Yugoslavia was one of the strongest forces – I don't say in resisting Russia – but in its independence of Russia. When, in 1948, the break came between Stalin and Tito, when Stalin denounced Tito as another Trotsky, and nothing can be worse than that in communist phraseology, some people thought that the Russians would invade Yugoslavia. Others said, perhaps more cynically, that Yugoslavia isn't worth bothering about. It is a very striking thing that this small country was left alone, was allowed to go on defying Soviet Russia. In the end – after Stalin's death – it was the next Soviet leader, Khrushchev, who actually went and apologized and tried to put things right, though even now the reconciliation is by no means complete.

This national communism was really only a preliminary warning of a much larger break in the communist world. This break, which came in the Far East, transformed the entire structure of world power. When it happened, you would have thought that it would have brought with it a relaxation of the Cold War. This was the victory of the Chinese communists. At the end of the war, in 1945, when Japan withdrew completely, China was left a nominally independent country under the rule of a feeble nationalist government headed by Chiang Kai-shek and very much patronized by the United States. Chiang Kai-shek's government had received enormous financial support from the United States and was to receive even more after the war was over. It was a government which had suffered a great battering during and, indeed, long before the war, and it had never displayed much capacity for uniting China. Indeed, some of its members displayed a capacity only for pocketing the American funds and thus growing enormously rich without much benefiting the people of China. The communist movement in China had conducted a great deal of the national war against Japan. It was an entirely independent movement. Far from deriving any backing from Russia, it had been on constant terms of coldness, neutrality, even hostility towards communist Russia. Indeed, it would be an attractive task to write an account of the Cold War between the Chinese communists and Moscow, which goes back as far as 1927. Chinese communism was a movement which did not look to Moscow for a lead or inspiration, and very often not even for material aid. At the end of the war in 1945, it was quite clear that Stalin hadn't the slightest idea that the Chinese communists were going to win. Perhaps he had no desire that they should win. At any rate, their victory, which was complete in 1949, owed nothing whatsoever to Russian support, nor indeed was it designed in any way to extend Russian influence or power. During 1949, Chiang Kai-shek's forces were driven entirely from the mainland and it was only owing to the protection of the American fleet that he was able to establish himself and his exiled government in the island of Formosa.

One of the most disastrous decisions of modern history was taken by the Americans when, in resentment at seeing the fall of their satellite, they refused to make their peace with reality. There had been this long battle, a sort of tug-of-war inside the American government for years past. Some of the Chinese experts in America had been foretelling the victory of communism and had been urging that the communists were likely to provide the best and most enlightened government for China. Their only reward was to be penalized and to be driven out of all influence. The overlap – and I think this is an important factor – between Europe and the Far East was again unfortunate. This was the time when the Cold War in Europe seemed to be reaching its most intense point. The affair of Berlin had only just been ended. The discovery that the Russians had got the atomic secret had just been made. For a variety of reasons there was a building anti-communist panic in the United States. This tension was suddenly reinforced in the Far East when it seemed that the same enemy, the same terrible menace which was supposed to be threatening Europe had appeared. Once American policy had decided to reject the Chinese communists and to deny that they represented China, to treat them as though they didn't exist, once this decision had been made it became increasingly difficult to retreat from it. Any recognition of communist China would be a confession that the whole of American policy over a generation had been based on a complete miscalculation.

This was reinforced in 1950 by the Korean War – another war which started by mistake. The Americans were on the point of leaving Korea when the North Koreans invaded South Korea. The Americans then felt that this was too great a challenge for them, so they intervened in order to push the North Koreans back. They advanced practically to the frontiers of China. Then the Chinese intervened and they were pushed back again. In my opinion, the Korean War, which was supposed to demonstrate the virtues of collective security and the United Nations, was a terrible illustration of the evil of trying to make peace by waging war. The only thing which the Korean War accomplished – it didn't move the division between North and South Korea one single bit – was that roughly four million Koreans were killed in the name of some principle called the United Nations, or resisting aggression, or whatever it may be. When people are killed, they are dead and it isn't much consolation that they've been killed for the sake of some principle. When they get killed in their millions, it's no good saying to them: 'Well, we're resisting communism or spreading communism.' They're dead. That's what happened to the Koreans, as under similar circumstances was to happen later in Vietnam, again with no sort of calculation. The issues of the Cold War in the Far East were at once sharper and simpler than they had been in Europe.

It would be wrong, I think, to say that there was the same tension of power. After all, in Europe, the power stakes were considerable. It really mattered which of the great world powers controlled Europe. If the whole of this area was under the control of one or the other, the world balance would change. The prizes in Asia were considerably less although it would be wrong to say that they didn't matter at all. They matter only, I think, because they lead elsewhere. If we look at the areas of Far Eastern conflict as they existed and have continued to exist between China and the United States, the prizes really lie outside the areas of conflict. The conflicts themselves were in Korea, then in a sense between Formosa, with its sham nationalist government, and communist China, and later on, up to the present day, in South Vietnam. From a point of view purely of its own resources, it doesn't matter in the slightest who has Vietnam. There are prizes in the Far East. There is the prize of Indonesia, for which the Japanese had contended earlier. You might say that Japan is a prize, but it is not likely that Japan could easily be absorbed into a Chinese communist empire or that the Chinese would want to do so. The Chinese claim that they were conducting a straight operation of defence in order to maintain their own national area and not to have American interference. The Americans claim that they were holding a line against an elaborate Chinese attack.

Now, even more than the false alarm about Russia, the alarm about China was from first to last a false alarm. China certainly exists, has existed for many centuries as a compact and confident civilization of its own. Within its own area, China is very formidable. Yet the likelihood of Chinese military expansion in the near future is almost out of the question. Why were the Americans there? Why should they have taken so seriously this Cold War in China when no great prizes were at stake? I think the answer – and it tells us a great deal about the Cold War as it has existed all over the world – was a combination of several things. There was obstinacy. The Americans had indeed made great sacrifices in the past to achieve a Far Eastern settlement as they wanted it. They resented it when somebody else achieved it. Besides obstinacy, there was misunderstanding, and a basic refusal to recognize that in any world of Great Powers, unless one world power is going to dominate the lot, then there has to be what's called tolerance or give and take. If we look at the Cold War, I think the lesson we have to draw is that the greatest Power cannot afford to be intolerant, cannot afford to insist upon its own way. Because if it does, it will get either Cold War or ultimately war.

Christ Stopped at Potsdam

This essay was first published as a review of Daniel Yergin's Shattered Peace: The Origins of the Cold War and the National Security State *(New York, Houghton Mifflin, 1978) in the* New Statesman, *13 January 1978.*

* * *

In September 1945 Senator Claude Pepper called at the Kremlin. Stalin remarked to him that the 'Grand Alliance' had been created by the single circumstance of a common enemy. Stalin went on:

That tie no longer exists and we shall have to find a new basis for our close relations in the future. That will not be easy but Christ said, 'Seek and ye shall find'.

Stalin's biblical injunction came too late. It had been followed at Yalta with outstanding success. At Potsdam the Americans began to abandon it and from Potsdam the path ran with occasional interruptions to the Berlin blockade, which marked the confirmation and also the limitations of the Cold War.

This interpretation is not new, but Daniel Yergin draws on more sources than any previous writer. In his view US policy was shaped by two rival axioms concerning the USSR. The Riga axioms were held by nearly all US diplomats before the Second World War. These axioms were simple: Soviet Russia was dedicated to world revolution and would promote it by military force. The Yalta axioms were held by Roosevelt and a few associates: the USSR was a world power concerned with security and the USA could do business with it. Roosevelt's death took the drive out of the Yalta axioms and the end of the war seemed to make them less necessary. Moreover Truman, unlike Roosevelt, liked quick, clear-cut solutions. Henry Wallace remarked, 'Truman's decisiveness is admirable. The only question is as to whether he has information behind his decisiveness to enable his decisions to stand up.'

Truman certainly received plenty of information. It ran all one way: a revival of the Riga axioms. It was expressed by George Kennan in his 'Long Dispatch', the longest document in the records of the State Department. It culminated in document NSC-68, drafted in 1950.

The Kremlin is inescapably militant. It is inescapably militant because it possesses and is possessed by a worldwide revolutionary movement, because it is the inheritor of Russian imperialism and because it is a totalitarian dictatorship.

The USSR's 'fundamental design' necessitated the destruction of the USA and thus the USA was 'mortally challenged' by the USSR. These axioms were dogma and rested on no evidence. Indeed all the evidence runs the other way. In the immediate post-war years Stalin deliberately thwarted the advance of the communist parties in France and Italy. His concern in the USSR's border states was security, not the advance of communism. His supposedly aggressive designs, as in Iran or at the Straits, also sprang from security and he abandoned them when they were resisted. Throughout these years, the USSR was a frightened power desperately on the defensive. Apart from security, Stalin's other main aim was to gather reparations from Germany, an aim which curiously led him to champion German unity when the Western Allies had already abandoned it.

These objections are irrelevant. US policy was pursuing a dogma rather than responding to events. Byrnes remarked at Potsdam:

Someone made an awful mistake in bringing about a situation where Russia was permitted to come out of a war with the power she will have ... The German people under a democracy would have been a far superior ally than Russia.

Truman was not yet convinced: 'I like Stalin. Stalin is as near Tom Pendergast [the Missouri political boss] as any man I know. He is very fond of classical music.'

But when Byrnes, as secretary of state, switched round and actually negotiated with the Russians, Truman lost patience. 'Unless Russia is faced with an iron fist and strong language another war is in the making ... I'm tired of babying the Soviets.' By 1946 the Americans had lost interest in bargaining and conducted negotiations publicly in order to appeal to 'world opinion', or in more practical terms to whip up US anti-communism. Yergin rather neglects this aspect and writes as though US policy was made only by diplomats. Surely there was a wider pressure from those who disliked the USSR's socialism. The concrete needs of US imperialism should be added. The conflict over Iran, for instance, had nothing to do with stemming communism or even with checking Soviet power. The Americans were after Iran's oil and were more concerned to exclude the British, now their humble client, than to thwart their Soviet enemy.

At this stage the Riga axioms took on a more positive form. Originally they had merely followed the negative line of disregarding the USSR. Now they demanded positive action in the name of national security. Any step taken by Russia beyond its borders in the name of Soviet 'security' would by definition clash with what became known as American 'national security'. As Kennan postulated, 'We must make the Russians understand that they must confine their security demands to our concept of security demands.' Another 'expert' pronounced: 'The basic objective of the USSR appears to be a limitless expansion of Soviet communism accompanied by a considerable territorial expansion of Russian imperialism.' Yet throughout the period, and indeed to the present day, there has been no expansion of Soviet communism and no territorial expansion of Russian imperialism. As against this, American expansion has not been far from limitless, as witness Greece and Turkey, or where it has been limited this came from military defeat, as in Vietnam, and not from modesty.

Nuclear power was a complicating factor. At first it gave the Americans an illusion of complete superiority. Then they discovered that it could not be used as a bargaining weapon. And in the end it has restrained the Americans more than it has restrained the USSR or any lesser power. As Yergin points out, the Americans were frightened by their own success. Moreover the armed forces justified their ever-increasing demands by inflated and often deliberately false estimates of Soviet strength and then were terrified by their own estimates. Here is another factor that Yergin hardly considers. Expenditure on armaments stimulated the US economy and continues to do so. If peace broke out, the USA would be in desperate straits. Fortunately for American capitalism, imaginary fears once started can rarely be dispelled: they are absorbed into the system and run on happily of themselves.

The immediate post-war period moved gradually to a climax in 1947 and 1948. The first catalysis was the economic crisis in western Europe. The Marshall Plan aimed both to stabilize Western capitalism and to draw a clear line against any communist advance. For the first time the iron curtain became official US policy. Capitalism was duly saved; communism was duly checked in the West. But there was a corollary. The Soviets also consolidated their security in eastern Europe. Non-communist Hungary and a little later non-communist Czechoslovakia were victims of the Marshall Plan. When the State Department considered censuring the USSR at the Security Council, one official objected, 'The Soviets might level counter charges against us as concerning MacArthur's actions in Japan.' No appeal was made to the Security Council.

The decisive step came in 1948 when the USA and Britain set up a separate state in western Germany. Most of the troubles in the four-power control commission had come from France. But France had to be swept into the new policy and Soviet Russia got all the blame for obstruction. In fact the USSR needed German unity in order to exact reparations from the western zones – no doubt one reason why the USA and Britain abandoned unity. The Russians inaugurated the blockade of Berlin in defence of German unity, believing that it would force the Western powers to the conference table. Instead the Anglo-Americans successfully ran the airlift. War seemed near but faced with nuclear war or nothing the USA chose no war. Yergin reveals a curious fact in a footnote – the B-29s, sent to England and pointedly known as 'atomic bombers', had not been modified to carry atomic bombs. Probably the Russians knew this all along. The Berlin blockade duly ended at the conference table, though German unity fortunately was not preserved.

There has been no serious danger of war in Europe since 1948. The Americans have fought what would once have been called colonial wars. There was a false alarm in 1962 over Cuba when the Americans got the appearance of victory and the Soviets got what they wanted – the independence of Cuba. Now both Eastern and Western blocs are losing their rigidity. Nuclear weapons are no longer the monopoly of the two superpowers. The rise of communist China has upset the calculations of both the USA and the USSR. The phrases of the Cold War are used now more by academic pundits than by diplomats. Détente is talked about and even occasionally practised. The two superpowers have not changed their characters. But maybe they are coming to recognize that bargaining is a better way of advancing their own security. As Yergin concludes,

This means a return to the Yalta axioms as the basic mode of dealing with the Soviet world, and perhaps a vindication for Franklin Roosevelt and his aims and methods.

Yergin may err on the optimistic side, but there seems just a chance that Christ did not stop at Potsdam after all.

Churchill: The Statesman

This first appeared in the collection of essays published in the USA as Churchill Revised: A Critical Assessment (*New York, Dial Press, 1969*) *and in Britain as* Churchill: Four Faces and the Man (*London, Allen Lane, 1969*). *The other contributors were Robert Rhodes James, J H Plumb, Basil Liddell Hart and Anthony Storr.*

Alan Taylor admired Churchill as war leader, though he was critical of many major aspects of Churchill's policies. Shortly after he had written this essay Alan Taylor commented to Paul Addison on Churchill's use of the war cabinet:

Churchill used it much at first when he still feared unpopularity. Later he called it in aid or used it to document his proceedings. It was not consulted on, e.g., immediate support for Russia on 22 June 1941, no Second Front in 1942, the Aegean foray of 1943, the partition of Europe with Stalin, nor of course the atom bomb. Certainly it was brought in on political matters from the Beveridge Report or 18B [Defence Regulation 18B, brought in in November 1939, was used in May 1940 to intern Mosley and other British Fascists] to Indian independence. Its function was to be a buffer against political criticism or occasionally Allied complaints. Over Oran [when the British attacked the French fleet on 3 July 1942], incidentally the full cabinet was consulted – a good illustration of the buffer principle.

He added:

... Churchill used the constitutional procedure, i.e. Chiefs-of-Staff's Committee, Defence Committee (Operations), war cabinet, only at the beginning. Later he settled things with the chiefs-of-staff and the Defence Committee (Operations) hardly ever met. In other words Churchill came virtually to run strategy and largely relations with the Big Two [Roosevelt and Stalin] with more or less unofficial advisers – certainly not after serious consultation with his colleagues. This is quite different from Lloyd George in the First World War. Perhaps the elder Pitt is the only parallel.

* * *

Winston Churchill was the subject of much criticism and unpopularity in the course of his long political career. He was dismissed as an adventurer and accused of irresponsibility. Yet he claimed to be a far-sighted statesman of wide views, surveying every problem in detachment, and in time this claim seemed justified by the record. From the beginning, Churchill was a statesman rather than a politician. Most men enter political life at a modest level and grow into statesmanship as they advance. Churchill entered politics at the top. His father had been chancellor of the exchequer and was largely responsible for giving the Conservative Party a more democratic character. Churchill himself at once moved in the society of cabinet ministers or of those who were soon to become cabinet ministers. He became a minister when he was thirty-one and entered the cabinet when he was thirty-three. He was never a back-bencher in the conventional sense, still less an obedient member of a political party. Essentially he stood alone: neither Tory nor Liberal, aristocrat nor democrat, simply Winston Churchill the statesman. He could be praised as wise, or abused as wrongheaded, but there was no mistaking him.

Churchill was mainly self-educated, and the theme of his education was statesmanship. He read Gibbon, Macaulay and other great historians, partly in order to emulate their methods, but more to discover how the lessons of the past could be applied to the present. His biographer has described how he worked through old volumes of the *Annual Register*, reading the accounts of parliamentary debates and noting what he himself would have said on each topic. Later he did much the same in practice. He rarely came to a political dispute with a background of personal experience. His mind was usually virgin soil, and he studied each problem afresh almost in an academic way. He was never content until he had produced a formidable state paper, surveying every aspect of the problem, and his speeches were also exercises in statecraft. He published his first volume of speeches before he was thirty, and by the end of his life eighteen volumes of his speeches stood on the shelves, a record equalled by no other political figure.

His practical knowledge was limited. He had served as a young officer in India and as a war correspondent in the Sudan and South Africa. He often visited the United States. He knew nothing of England beyond the society of political London and the great aristocratic houses. The life of ordinary Englishmen was beyond his ken, until he studied it from outside as the head of some government department. He approached social problems with extreme benevolence, but always with an air of gracious giving. He wished to remove poverty and injustice, not to achieve any fundamental change, and claimed rightly to be at heart a conservative even in his most radical days. His deepest devotion was to England, as she had matured through the ages, and, though it would be unfair to call him a Little Englander, he was never an imperialist in the ordinary sense. Perhaps Great Englander would be the right term. In his view the British Empire was another form of the benevolence which he sought to practise at home in social affairs. Far from being a source of profit to be exploited, Churchill's empire was simply the white man's burden – a responsibility imposed by conscience on a Great Power. Similarly, he did not regard the dominions as equals, and he saw the Commonwealth (a word he detested) as a family of children, loyally sustaining the venerable mother to whom they owed so much.

Despite the seeming rationality with which his state papers were composed, Churchill was strongly swayed by emotions – usually generous, sometimes the reverse. He responded eagerly to the call of patriotism in the drum-and-trumpet spirit, which coloured his writing of history. He appreciated both the romance of war and its horrors. He believed in concessions from strength, not from weakness. When he was powerful, his benevolence brimmed over. When challenged – either at home or by foreign enemies – he sought total victory first and advocated conciliation only when victory had been won. This was the attitude he adopted in two world wars, in the Boer War, and in the Irish troubles also. He had the same attitude towards the British workers: social reforms if they were well behaved and stern action against them if they dared to strike. He characterized his outlook in an inscription which he devised for a war memorial after the First World War: 'In war, Resolution. In defeat, Defiance. In victory, Magnanimity. In peace, Goodwill.' The inscription was not used, but Churchill set it on the title-page of the six volumes which he wrote after the Second World War.

Churchill was always anxious to learn from expert authorities. In his early days as a minister, he consulted Sidney and Beatrice Webb on social reform. During both world wars, he turned to scientists as few modern statesmen have done. Tanks were inspired by him in the First World War, and innumerable inventions, culminating in the atomic bomb, were promoted by him in the Second. If he had an intellectual weakness, it was an inability to understand economics. He remained at heart a believer in *laissez-faire* and free trade. He could understand social reform, but not socialism. His deeper weakness was impatience, particularly in his earlier years. When he was set on a course, he wanted results at once and was angered by the dead weight of habit. He expected everyone to move at the same rate as himself and, knowing his inner consistency, was not worried by the charges of inconsistency which his impulses towards new enthusiasms often provoked. To others, therefore, he often seemed irresponsible, a reputation which clung to him, not altogether undeservedly, all his life. He combined to the end mature wisdom and boyish zest, a mixture which did not always work out for the best.

The beginnings of Churchill's political career at once showed his unusual qualities. He entered parliament during the Boer War, with the special distinction of having escaped from Boer captivity. He was something of a war hero. Yet, far from breathing fire, he urged that the defeated Boers be treated with generosity – much to the annoyance of the Conservatives who had elected him. Next, though a former officer in the army, he went on to criticize the army estimates and declared that the Royal Navy was Great Britain's sure defence. This was the attitude of an isolationist, even of a Little Englander, not of an imperialist, and he swung still further away from imperialism when he championed free trade against Joseph Chamberlain's campaign for tariff reform. In 1903 he abandoned the Conservatives and became not merely a Liberal, but a radical, the close associate of Lloyd George. There was an intellectual consistency in this development, but it was characteristic of Churchill that he had carried it to extremes.

It was also characteristic of Churchill that his radicalism was self-made. It owed little to the teachings of others, except perhaps for some echoes from his dead father, who had called himself a Tory Democrat. The mainspring of Churchill's radicalism was generosity: a dislike of tariff reform as selfish, and a warm-hearted desire to benefit the poor and distressed. At the Colonial Office, he played a large part in granting responsible government to the Boers and therewith established a friendship with Smuts which lasted for half a century. He imagined that, with this gesture, all bitterness left from the Boer War was dispelled. Later developments were to show that the defeated neither forgave nor forgot so easily.

In 1908 he entered the cabinet, as a protagonist of social reform. Though he complained that Lloyd George had stolen all the plums, in fact he found plenty to do. In particular the Labour Exchanges which he promoted were a substantial step in aid for the unemployed. But the difference between Churchill's radicalism and the deeper radicalism of Lloyd George was already showing. Churchill was merely lessening the edge of economic harshness; Lloyd George aimed at a Welfare State which would transform society. The difference was shown even more clearly during an outbreak of large-scale strikes during 1911 and 1912. Lloyd George became the principal conciliator in the Liberal government and repeatedly made the employers give way. Churchill went into battle against the strikers, reinforcing law and order with the use of troops, and insisting that no concessions should be made until the strikers returned to work. By 1912 Churchill's earlier radical reputation was dispelled so far as the industrial workers were concerned, and it was never fully restored later, despite his national leadership during the Second World War. Anyone who is puzzled over Churchill's electoral defeat in 1945 will find much of the explanation in the industrial disputes more than thirty years before.

Churchill's dealings with the advocates of votes for women showed the same combination of generosity and anger on a smaller scale. Churchill supported women's franchise with some enthusiasm, so long as he supplied the enthusiasm. But when the militant suffragettes began their campaign of violence and direct action, Churchill was their principal target, and he responded by defying them. Admittedly, there was a peculiarly feminine logic in a movement which directed its main onslaught against the supporters of women's suffrage, not against its opponents. But Churchill's combativeness was easily aroused. As usual, he was ready to make concessions only from strength. Threats – and he received many from the suffragettes – were to him a reason for making no concessions at all. Once provoked, he provoked others in return, and his wiser impulses were eclipsed by his pugnacity.

It was in his attitude towards Germany that the radical Churchill showed the greatest fluctuations. Churchill was not anti-German in feeling or policy, as some Englishmen were becoming at this time. Confident in the overwhelming strength of the Royal Navy, he wanted to keep clear of foreign entanglements and regarded all countries, including Germany, with the same aloof benevolence. When the alarm of German naval building was raised in 1909, Churchill was Lloyd George's chief ally in refusing to be scared. He opposed the alarm on two grounds. First, he asserted that the Germans were as pacific as other nations. Second, he claimed, on the basis of technical advice, that Great Britain could always outbuild any foreign rival. Churchill sang a different tune when he himself took charge of the Royal Navy at the end of 1911. Then he became the advocate of a great shipbuilding programme and by 1914 was himself locked in conflict with Lloyd George. Again he could claim to be consistent. He had always been determined that the Royal Navy should remain supreme and, once convinced that the Germans were challenging this supremacy, he defied them. This consistency was less convincing to his former radical allies. Yet Churchill still held that the naval race was simply due to mutual misunderstanding and believed in 1914 that it could be ended if he had a friendly personal talk with Tirpitz, the head of the German Navy.

One other problem sent Churchill into battle in the years just before the First World War. This was Ireland. Churchill was not an eager home-ruler by background. Indeed his father had been almost the first to evoke the resistance of Ulster. But when Ulster sought to prevent home rule and threatened to rebel against the British government, Churchill again took up the challenge. He prepared to send ships to Belfast in the hope of overawing Ulster and he also perhaps encouraged the sending of troops. The Unionists accused him of planning a 'pogrom', a charge still disputed by historians. The truth will never be fully known, but it seemed at any rate that Churchill was again answering threats from others by threats and strength of his own.

All these questions were eclipsed by the outbreak of war. Churchill flung himself into combat, whatever his reserves had been before war came. When the generals failed to help the Belgians at Antwerp, Churchill went there himself at the head of a few thousand marines and even asked to be given military command. His sortie was unsuccessful. His impulsiveness had been demonstrated once again. A greater demonstration was to come, the central episode, as it proved, of Churchill's earlier career. Despite a new-found devotion to the French as allies, Churchill doubted whether the war could be won on the Western Front, once deadlock had been reached after the battle of the Marne. Where other ministers were barren of strategical ideas, Churchill did not hesitate to give a lead. He sought a back door into Germany and found it at the Dardanelles. An expedition to force the Straits and take Constantinople had every appeal for Churchill. It would rest on British sea power; it was an idea both unexpected and highly ingenious; if successful, it would bring victory without great casualties. The Dardanelles affair showed Churchill at his best and worst. He pressed it relentlessly on the admirals and his ministerial colleagues. He stood forth with the courage and determination of a true leader. Though others acquiesced and some even welcomed the campaign, Churchill never denied that he was its chief originator, nor would it have gone on so long without his persistence. When it failed, he complained that others had not matched his drive and intensity.

Some of the failure must be attributed to Churchill himself. It was a rush job from first to last. Once Churchill took up the idea, he exaggerated both the ease with which it could be carried through and the rewards which it would bring. There was no inquiry into the means available. Churchill merely assumed that battleships could force the Straits unaided. When this failed, he assumed that there was a powerful army available for Gallipoli and assumed also that this inhospitable peninsula presented no formidable military obstacles. Beyond this, he assumed also that the fall of Constantinople would inflict a mortal blow on Germany. All these assumptions were wrong. The navy failed. The army failed. Even if they had succeeded, it is difficult to see what they would have accomplished. Churchill in fact embarked on a rash gamble and then brushed aside the difficulties without consideration. As always with Churchill, when he wanted something, he was convinced that he could have it, and he convinced others also. Those who succumbed to his promptings bore their share of responsibility, but it is not surprising that they shifted the blame on to Churchill once the campaign failed. He on his side did not shrink from responsibility. If anything, he grasped at it impatiently and too readily.

Failure at Gallipoli ruined Churchill for the duration of the First World War and saddled him with a reputation for hasty, though brilliant, improvisations. He left office and served on the Western Front. When he again became a minister, it was as one of Lloyd George's subordinates, not as a leader of policy and an inspirer of strategy. Only when the war ended did he rise again to the rank of statesman. Though he had acquiesced in Lloyd George's policy of the 'knockout blow', he was among the first to preach reconciliation with Germany as soon as she had been defeated. He was eager to send food for the hungry German people. He opposed the idea of collecting reparations for many years to come. He urged that Germany be admitted without delay into the League of Nations. With him, generosity followed hard on victory. As usual, also, he underrated the speed with which most men could change from one mood to the other.

It was, however, a different question which brought Churchill once more into prominence and notoriety. In the past, he had been friendly towards Russia, believing, as his father had done, that she should control Constantinople and the Straits. During the war he responded warmly to the somewhat tattered romance of Holy Russia and her tsar. He was the more indignant when the Bolshevik Revolution overthrew these traditions. Again he had a romantic vision, this time one of horror and repugnance. He was convinced that the Bolsheviks aimed at the destruction of European civilization and imagined that somewhere millions of patriotic loyal Russians were longing for release. He sent military aid to the White counter-revolutionaries and favoured intervention on the largest scale. What really provoked him in the Bolsheviks was their rejection of the values in which he believed. They dared to repudiate the legacy of past centuries. Therefore, they must be crushed by force. Once roused, he attributed to the Bolsheviks the most evil and far-reaching designs. He soon extended the same attitude to events at home and saw in every industrial dispute the hidden hand of Moscow. With Churchill there was never a halfway house and, since the Bolsheviks were clearly not friendly, he treated them as implacable enemies.

Churchill still showed many radical impulses and strokes of generosity. He sympathized for instance with the anxiety of the soldiers to return home and imposed haste in demobilization on a lethargic War Office. He advocated a 'capital levy' to diminish the fortunes made by profiteering during the war. In 1921, he worked closely with Lloyd George in reaching an agreement with Sinn Fein and himself established a warm friendship with Michael Collins – another example of how with Churchill yesterday's enemy became the friend of today. More often, however, his radicalism was overshadowed by a pugnacious determination to maintain the greatness of the British Empire. He intervened constantly in foreign affairs, much to the annoyance of Lord Curzon, the foreign secretary, and he cared little for Lloyd George's strivings for general appeasement, particularly when these were extended even to Soviet Russia.

He set up a new sphere of influence for Great Britain and himself in the Middle East. This originated partly in the accident which made him colonial secretary, responsible particularly for Palestine and Meso-potamia. It also had deeper roots. Imperial power extending from Gibraltar to the Persian Gulf was another version of the policy which had produced the attempt on the Dardanelles. It rested on the Royal Navy and on a great military base in Egypt, and it implied an indifference to European affairs, which Churchill had often felt. The war against Germany had been for him an almost irrelevant distrac-tion; a war to be fought and then forgotten. Imperial greatness was the enduring reality. Churchill's efforts established Great Britain as the predominant power in the Middle East, at any rate until the end of the Second World War. In Palestine, he was more nearly successful in reconciling Jews and Arabs than any other British statesman proved to be. Sustained by T E Lawrence, he won the friendship of the Arab rulers in Iraq and Transjordan. He sought reconciliation with the new national Turkey, led by Kemal Pasha – another former enemy whom he wished to turn into a friend. Churchill's old desire to give Constantinople to Russia was now forgotten. The Turks became in his eyes the guardians of civilization against the Bolsheviks.

The Turkish problem ended with a curiously Churchillian twist. Lloyd George wished to support the Greeks against the Turks. Church-ill opposed this policy to the utmost of his endeavour. In 1922 the Greek Army was routed. The victorious Turks advanced to the Straits and threatened the British garrison there. Lloyd George was ready to fight, and the prospect of fighting captivated Churchill also, even in a war which he thought mistaken. Or maybe the Turks, by threatening instead of pleading, temporarily forfeited, like others, their claim on his generosity. At any rate, in this Chanak crisis, as it was called, Churchill once more became a warmonger in appearance. The British people were weary of war. They refused to support Lloyd George. The Conservative Party turned against him, and he fell from power for ever. Churchill fell with him.

Thus ended the first epoch of Churchill's life as a statesman. He had held high office, with a two-year interruption, from 1905 to 1922, a record surpassed only by Lloyd George himself. He had been home secretary, first lord of the admiralty, minister of munitions, secretary for war, and colonial secretary. He had been second only to Lloyd George in inaugurating social welfare. He had reformed the prisons. He had prepared the Royal Navy for its victories in the war. He had initiated a brilliant, though unsuccessful, stroke of strategy at the Dardanelles. He had established a new British Empire in the Middle East. These were only his more official achievements. He had also contributed to the pacification of Ireland. He had set out broad principles of foreign policy, particularly in regard to Germany and Soviet Russia. If a statesman be judged by the breadth of his interests and by the weight of his public utterances, Churchill should have stood in the front rank. Instead, his reputation was low. In 1922 only Lloyd George was more distrusted as a statesman, and Churchill's defeat at the general election was almost universally applauded by men of all parties.

For Churchill, despite his great qualities, lacked one gift essential to a statesman: he did not know how to put himself across. He had no intimate political friends except Birkenhead, Lloyd George, and perhaps Beaverbrook – men as erratic and as much distrusted as himself. He never understood how his readiness to give a lead and to pronounce on every subject irritated his colleagues. Curzon, for instance, complained of his trespassing into foreign affairs. Both Asquith and Lloyd George remarked that Churchill behaved as though he were prime minister. Bonar Law put it more bluntly. When asked whether he would rather have Churchill for or against him, he replied: 'Against, every time.' Again, Churchill never considered party or the need to conciliate his supporters. He regarded party as an instrument for putting him into office, not as an association which he should serve. He had left the Conservatives for the Liberals and was soon to become a Conservative again. Essentially he was always an Independent Constitutionalist, the description which he gave himself between 1922 and 1924.

He had no doubt of his own consistency. He was always ambitious to serve the greatness of the British Empire and to promote the principles of democracy and ordered freedom. The consistency was less obvious to others. He had been friendly to the workers and hostile to the trade unions; against great naval expenditure and then for it; friendly to Germany, hostile to her, and then friendly again; hostile to Turkey, and then friendly. He had denounced the House of Lords and was soon to champion its remaining privileges. He had supported votes for women and was soon to oppose a further extension of female suffrage. By 1922 anti-Bolshevism was the only cause to which he seemed indissolubly wedded, and even this did not last for ever. His record was blotted by impulsive acts of folly or bad temper: Tonypandy, where he was accused of sending troops against strikers; Sidney Street, where he directed an attack on a probably mythical anarchist; Antwerp; and worst of all, Gallipoli. The blame was often undeserved: certainly at Tonypandy, where he actually held the troops back; perhaps at Gallipoli. But the record stuck. He had become, in the popular view, a man who could never resist a fight. This was true. Churchill had almost an excess of courage. Certainly he had more courage than calculation. Also, he was easily roused by opposition. In Beaverbrook's words: 'Churchill on the top of the wave has in him the stuff of which tyrants are made.'

Here again, Churchill never understood the effect which he had on others. Though he fought with passionate intensity, it was always with good feeling, often almost in fun. When he argued persistently, he expected others to answer with equal persistence. Thus he blamed Asquith and Kitchener for acquiescing in the Gallipoli expedition if they did not really believe in it. Then as later he did not allow for the fact that men might agree with him merely in order to end the argument. Similarly, when Churchill knocked a man down, this was a preliminary to picking him up and treating him with generosity. The Boers, the Germans, the Irish, the trade unions were expected to forget in the twinkling of an eye the violence which Churchill had levelled against them. Hardship and failure were gradually to impose on Churchill greater patience and moderation. At heart he never learned wisdom, at any rate not the wisdom of the serpent.

Churchill was left high and dry by Lloyd George's fall and his own. His attempt to rattle the anti-Bolshevik drum produced little response. He had no principle tying him to the Liberal Party except free trade and therefore easily returned to the Conservatives in 1924 when they renounced protection. He was now the humble suitor of Stanley Baldwin, the man who had overthrown the Lloyd George government. Churchill became chancellor of the exchequer. He did not distinguish himself in the conduct of Great Britain's financial affairs. His most substantial step was to carry through the return to the gold standard at the pre-war parity in 1925. This is often held to have had a disastrous effect on Great Britain's economic position, though perhaps its influence has been exaggerated. Churchill did not grasp the economic arguments one way or the other. What determined him was again a romantic devotion to British greatness. The pound would once more 'look the dollar in the face'; the days of Queen Victoria would be restored. Apart from this stroke, Churchill's conduct of finance produced many ingenious and somewhat irresponsible expedients – a series, one might say, of minor, though in this case relatively harmless, Gallipolis.

Churchill did not, however, confine himself to budgets and the details of finance. Once more, he ranged over every field as though he were prime minister. In foreign affairs he had again become an isolationist. Now that the war was won, Great Britain, he believed, should wash her hands of European affairs and rest secure on the Royal Navy. He made permanent the instruction to the service chiefs that they need not plan for a major war in the next ten years. He was thus mainly responsible for the extensive British disarmament which he was later to denounce bitterly. He opposed the guarantee of the Franco-German frontier which Austen Chamberlain gave by the treaty of Locarno. Churchill sympathized, in benevolent detachment, with the aggrieved and discontented countries – so long as they did not challenge British interests. He admired Mussolini, both as a patriot and as the supposed saviour of Italy from Bolshevism. A little later, he declared his hope that, if the British people were ever defeated in war, they would find a revivalist leader of the stature of Hitler. He dismissed the League of Nations as a useless and undesirable barrier against national independence and patriotic wars. In short, his foreign outlook was a compound of romantic enthusiasms, far removed from the general disillusionment of the post-war period.

In home affairs Churchill was equally romantic and equally combative. The question of the coal industry overshadowed all others. As the industry declined, the owners tried to save themselves by demanding lower wages and longer hours. The mineworkers resisted. Churchill sympathized with the miners. He believed that they had been badly treated both by successive governments and by the owners. But once the miners fought back, Churchill's sympathy was forfeit, and still more so when the other unions prepared a general strike in their support. The General Strike itself appeared to Churchill as his finest hour. Where Baldwin sought conciliation and compromise, Churchill strove to transform the General Strike into civil war. He referred to the workers as 'the enemy', brought armed troops into the streets of London, and wished to make the unions illegal. It was the old pattern: a romantic charge into battle against the imaginary enemy of Bolshevism. Fortunately, neither Baldwin nor the trade union leaders were inclined to mount the barricades. The General Strike passed over without grave social disturbance, and Baldwin did his best to restore good feeling. Churchill for his part had completed the estrangement between himself and the industrial workers, who were after all a substantial part of the British people.

Throughout the five years of the Conservative government, from 1924 to 1929, there was a running undercurrent of conflict between Baldwin and Churchill. Baldwin wanted to win over the working class and to make the Labour Party fully at home in the constitutional courses as a preliminary to crushing them. Churchill wanted to treat Labour as an irreconcilable enemy. Again, it was a question of fight first and conciliate, perhaps, afterwards. As in other matters, the British people were in no mood for a fight. The one cause which might have injected some passion into politics was protection. But Churchill was debarred from using this weapon against Baldwin by his own belief in free trade. He sought some other topic which might shatter the complacent calm of the Baldwin era.

He believed that he had found this topic of controversy in India. All parties were committed to a policy of gradual concession towards India which would culminate in the grant of dominion status. The only dispute, it seemed, was over the rate at which to go. Churchill himself had been for conciliation so long as it was a matter of generosity, resting on strength. When the Indian nationalists, led by Gandhi, began to practise non-violent resistance and actually to defy the British Raj, Churchill took up the challenge. He remembered the India of his youth and looked with romantic admiration on the Indian princes. India became Churchill's obsession. On this issue, he broke with Baldwin, abandoned his high position in the Conservative Party, and went into solitary opposition. This was a period of grave crisis. The world was ravaged by the Great Depression. There were nearly three million unemployed in Great Britain. In 1931 a National government was formed to save the pound and instead was forced to abandon the gold standard. Abroad, the security established after the First World War crumbled. Hitler and the Nazis were marching to victory in Germany. Meanwhile, Churchill, who had often shown himself a statesman of great wisdom, could only reiterate his devotion to the Indian princes and his opposition to all constitutional concession. This was romantic loyalty perhaps of a Jacobite kind, but not one likely to win a response from the British people.

It has puzzled later observers that Churchill was disregarded when dangers and difficulties accumulated for Great Britain. Baldwin and Ramsay MacDonald, the two leaders of the day, have been blamed for their sloth and blindness, and the British people have been blamed as well. These charges have some justification. But the fault lay also with Churchill himself. He lost all hold on British opinion by his intemperate opposition over India. The British people would not respond to the romantic call of imperial glory. Rightly or wrongly, they were committed to the cause of constitutional concession, and Churchill's resistance seemed to them irrelevant obscurantism. He was the more diminished because on the great economic questions of the moment he had nothing to say. He remained silent during the interminable debates over unemployment, protection, and economic recovery. This was in striking contrast to Lloyd George, who, although equally isolated, produced a rich stock of creative ideas.

Churchill was drawn back to foreign affairs almost as a side issue, an interruption in his Indian campaign. Soon after the First World War, he laid down the principle: 'The redress of the grievances of the vanquished should precede the disarmament of the victors.' Hence, he had urged this redress during the 1920s. Instead the Disarmament Conference opened in 1932, with Germany still aggrieved. In practical terms, France was being asked to disarm and to accept a permanent inferiority as against Germany. The British government continued to press this policy on France, even when Hitler came to power with the avowed aim of making Germany again the greatest power in Europe. Once more, Churchill stood almost alone in opposing disarmament and all that went with it. In particular, he sounded the alarm at the increase of the German Air Force and called for a large increase in the Royal Air Force, just as he had advocated a great increase of the Royal Navy before 1914.

Churchill was again on an unpopular path. His alarm at the German Air Force had some foundation, though his actual figures were exaggerated – as the similar figures about the German Navy had been exaggerated before 1914. Then British public opinion had been ready to maintain naval supremacy at all costs. Now public opinion tended to regard great armaments – even their own – as a cause of war. Churchill imagined that both British and French would respond to the call of greatness as they had done in the past. As always, it was difficult for him to grasp that others, apart from a few despised figures, were not as courageous and combative as himself. In the eyes of most people, Churchill's outlook seemed to be purely negative: a mere maintenance of the armed supremacy which had followed the First World War. The moral climate of the time had turned, however mistakenly, against the old ideas of the balance of power and imperial greatness. If Germany had to be opposed, it had to be in the name of supposedly higher causes.

These causes existed. The one which had most appeal to men of moderate opinion was the League of Nations and its offspring, collective security. States, it was believed, should settle their disputes peacefully through the League of Nations, and the pacific countries should somehow stand together against aggression. Churchill, too, supported collective resistance to the aggressor, but not when it was presented in the Wilsonian phrases of the League of Nations. Hence he remained aloof when the Japanese invaded Manchuria. In 1935 the League was put to its great test. Italy attacked Abyssinia, and the League attempted to assert collective security by imposing economic sanctions against the aggressor, who happened conveniently to be also Fascist. Churchill was less concerned about democracy abroad and, in the last resort, preferred fascism to Bolshevism. He remained silent throughout the Abyssinian crisis from a reluctance to commit himself one way or the other. He admired Mussolini; he wanted to enlist Mussolini's aid against Hitler; he disliked the paraphernalia of the League of Nations.

The British government seemed to betray the League by endorsing the Hoare–Laval plan, which gave Mussolini most of what he wanted. British opinion was roused. There was perhaps a brief chance of overthrowing Baldwin. Churchill was not there to take it. The crisis passed. Mussolini marched on to triumph. The prestige of the League was irremediably destroyed.

A new opportunity offered in March 1936 when Hitler reoccupied the Rhineland. This time, Churchill took it. He had never felt for Hitler the sympathy which he felt for Mussolini. He was now indignant that Hitler, as he supposed, was daring to threaten British security in the air; and if others were indignant with Hitler for other reasons – such as that he had destroyed the trade unions or persecuted the socialists and the Jews – he was prepared to share these indignations also. Now faced with terrible dangers, he was even prepared to espouse belatedly the principles of collective security. Arms and the Covenant became his cry. He seemed to be at last in tune with a broad current of public opinion. He was recapturing popularity and support such as he had not enjoyed for many years. Churchill won this position only to throw it away by a new gesture of romantic enthusiasm, and the great issues of foreign policy were temporarily dwarfed in Churchill's mind by the marital troubles of King Edward VIII.

There was little element of statesmanship in Churchill's championing of the king's cause. If, as has been suggested, he calculated that Baldwin could be defeated on this question, he showed himself lacking in statecraft or at any rate in political judgement. British opinion, so far as it can be assessed, was decisively against the king. Even now, when standards have changed, it is difficult to understand how anyone could expect Edward VIII to plan marriage with a woman who was still married to someone else and yet retain his throne. Churchill was beyond all such calculations. Though he had no long-standing ties with the king or personal obligations, he could not resist the appeal of romantic loyalty. Churchill flung himself into battle on the king's side and continued to fight even when the king himself had given up the day as lost. There are some occasions when the wise course for a statesman is to remain silent. This was not in Churchill's nature. In December 1936 when Edward VIII abdicated, Baldwin was triumphant. Churchill was again solitary and discredited.

Churchill did not recover easily from this failure. During 1937 he believed that opportunity had passed him by. He believed also that the period of danger was almost over. British rearmament was now beginning to develop, though more slowly than Churchill wanted. Once Great Britain had restored equality, or something near it, in the air, she would be again secure and could once more offer Germany concessions from strength – the policy which Churchill had always advocated. For Churchill, too, favoured appeasement, once it did not spring from weakness. He, too, believed that there was no irremediable cause of war and that war, if it came, would be, as he in fact called it, 'unnecessary'. There was a further reason for Churchill's relative silence. The overriding issue in foreign affairs between 1936 and 1938 was the civil war in Spain, where the left-wing republican government was contending with a nationalist rebellion, led by Franco and massively supported by two Fascist powers, Italy and Germany.

Here was the great conflict between democracy and fascism, or so it seemed to many idealists in Great Britain. Churchill could not take sides. Emotionally he sympathized with the nationalists against the Reds. On the other hand, he did not want to see an extension of German power. He accepted the policy of non-intervention put forward by the British government and continued to support it when it was openly disregarded by the Fascist Powers. He even implied, against the facts, that Soviet Russia was cheating more grossly on the republican side. Only in 1939, when all was over, did he belatedly acknowledge that the republic, with all its faults, had been the cause of freedom. Franco's victory did not in fact have the evil consequences predicted for it, at any rate so far as British interests were concerned. Nevertheless, Churchill had failed to become the champion of democracy against fascism, as many British people wanted.

All this was eclipsed when Hitler began his march to European domination in 1938, first with the annexation of Austria and then with the virtual destruction of Czechoslovakia. Earlier Churchill had concentrated on rearmament. Now he began to propound policy. He assumed that Great Britain, with an overwhelmingly powerful navy and an increasing air force, was herself secure. Therefore she should take the lead in setting up a coalition against the aggressor. Behind this assertion was a series of assumptions which were less clearly stated. Great Britain's contribution, apart from the moral example, would be naval blockade and perhaps aerial bombardment of Germany. She would not be expected to provide a large land-army, the great mistake, in Churchill's eyes, of the First World War. Churchill's central assumption was that others were eagerly waiting to be led. France, Russia, and all the states of east-central Europe would merge their armed forces in a great coalition as soon as they were invited to do so. As a final assumption, Churchill was sure that this coalition would be easily victorious against Germany or, more probably, would deter her without fighting at all. Once this supremacy was acknowledged, concessions to Germany would follow, and she would be welcomed back into the happy European family.

Churchill was again believing what he wanted to believe, and not on the basis of much knowledge. There were some elements in France which favoured resistance, though they were to show themselves singularly ineffective, and the French Army was no more than a defensive weapon, despite its glamorous appearance. Soviet Russia, once the centre of international revolution, had become, in Churchill's opinion, both peaceful and cooperative, simply because it was necessary for the Grand Alliance that she should be so. Many others in England held a similar view about Russia, people who not long before had been denounced by Churchill as the dupes or agents of communist tyranny. Now he forgot 'the baboonery of Bolshevism' in his anxiety for Russian aid.

There was abundant evidence that the rulers of Soviet Russia were alert to the danger from Germany, but this did not make them eager to bring the danger down on their own heads, still less to engage in war for the sake of the distrusted capitalist Powers, Great Britain and France. As to the lesser states who were to be enlisted, their behaviour was witness enough that each hoped to pass the burden on to his neighbour. Churchill sometimes recognized this and spoke sternly of refusing to aid those who on their side refused to cooperate. Since the aid was offered for reasons of practical strategy, and not from altruism, the threat was empty. Churchill seems also to have believed that every associate, however small, brought an addition of strength. The experience of the First World War had already shown that small states were usually a burden, not an asset, and the experience of the second war was to confirm this, though the burden was often inevitable.

The essence of Churchill's policy was a defensive alliance of the contented powers. He reinforced it with an appeal to the great ideals of freedom and justice, thus assuming against the evidence that all the non-aggressive powers enjoyed something like the blessings of the British Constitution. The democracy which he professed was in practice not much more than a preservation of things as they were, and freedom meant similarly the preservation of sovereign independence by each state. Churchill had no vision of a new Europe, still less of a new world. He wanted to get back to the old one. Even Germany was not to be weakened or destroyed. Once the German people had tamed their dictator or shaken him off, they would settle down in happy harmony with the Western Powers, and Europe, thus consolidated, would be again secure from the interference of Soviet Russia.

The strategy which Churchill advocated from the summer of 1938 until the outbreak of war, and indeed after it, was equally traditional.

Great Britain had followed it, much to her advantage, throughout the long wars against Bourbon France and Napoleon. The continental powers, with their large armies, had done most of the fighting on land, while Great Britain, controlling the seas, provided economic aid and moral encouragement. This policy had been abandoned during the First World War, when Great Britain had built up an army of continental size and had borne, for a time, the main brunt of land warfare. Churchill had opposed this course, as Gallipoli bore witness, and he did not propose to repeat it now. Even in 1939 he was insisting that a large army was unnecessary and that compulsory military service, which he came to favour, should be adopted in order to impress Great Britain's foreign friends, rather than for any practical purpose.

The Grand Alliance which Churchill envisaged was confined to Europe and was indeed a specifically anti-German combination. He continued to hope that Italy would somehow return to her friends of the First World War, and he was even more confident that Great Britain would remain neutral in the Far East, benevolently sympathizing with both China and Japan. On the other hand, he attached ever-increasing importance to close relations between Great Britain and the United States and himself addressed direct appeals to American opinion. He did not at this time seek an alliance with the United States, perhaps recognizing that it was impossible in the prevailing mood of isolationism. In any case, he thought it unnecessary. He was convinced that the peaceful European countries would more than hold their own against Hitler, particularly if they could draw freely on the United States for raw materials and munitions. The Americans need not fear that they would be involved. They had only to look on the good cause with a friendly eye.

Churchill stressed, indeed exaggerated, Germany's preparations for war and believed mistakenly that everything there was being sacrificed for the sake of armaments. This led him into an equal exaggeration on the other side. Believing as he did that life in Germany was being conducted under almost intolerable strain, he expected that the increased demands of actual war would cause the Nazi system to break down of itself. This misjudgement was shared by many qualified observers. Paradoxically it was the main cause of Churchill's strength. His confidence that victory, though perhaps not easy, was certain in time inspired others, and appeasement seemed to be unnecessary as well as dishonourable. Churchill's arguments mattered less than the tone in which he said them, and his voice ultimately made him, in British eyes, the architect of victory. He was less successful in spreading the same confidence to potential allies across the Channel.

Statesmen have not only to devise a policy. They must also consider how to carry it out. Most of those who wished to oppose Nazi Germany were equally opposed to the Conservative or so-called National government in Great Britain. They imagined that a change of policy could be brought about only by some sort of left-wing upheaval. Churchill had no sympathy with this view. His aim was to win over the Conservative members of parliament, and even the Conservative ministers, not to destroy them. Since the Conservatives had an overwhelming majority in the House of Commons, this was no doubt tactically wise. But it was more than a matter of tactics. Churchill was as much a Conservative as those in power, indeed more so. He wanted to save old England, not to lead a left-wing revolution. The danger from Hitler united Churchill and his like with the Left, just as it created later an alliance with Soviet Russia. But Churchill intended, once Hitler was defeated, that everything should be put back as it was before, at home and abroad.

The outbreak of war in September 1939 brought Churchill back to office at last, as first lord of the admiralty. He became, without demur, the colleague of men whose policy he had denounced. He did not ask them to repudiate that policy: events had done it for him. In any case, as always with Churchill, bygones were bygones. Once a situation changed, he forgot or put aside what had gone before. As a minister, Churchill was welcomed as a symbol of energy rather than of policy. He was expected to provide the dynamism which war needed and which Chamberlain's government clearly lacked. His pugnacity, previously unwelcome, now sounded a popular note, and he became the living pledge that the war would not be merely the continuation of peace by other means. Though he tried to be on his best behaviour after the disappointments of previous years, his nature was too strong for him. He could not resist ranging over all the problems of government, and Neville Chamberlain, too, soon found himself complaining that Churchill behaved as though he were already prime minister.

Much of Churchill's promptings concerned simply a more energetic conduct of the war, abroad and at home. There were also two independent contributions to policy, both anticipating what was to come. Neville Chamberlain regarded the two world powers, Soviet Russia and the United States, with cool dislike. Churchill prepared to win them over. He opened a private correspondence with President Roosevelt and established, at any rate in his own opinion, a close personal friendship. Here again was his old belief that international relations could be shaped by individual sentiments and human affection. This belief was widely shared by Englishmen so far as America was concerned. Churchill stood more alone in his attitude towards Soviet Russia. The Nazi–Soviet pact and Russia's subsequent neutrality provoked a general revival of anti-Bolshevism, which extended even into the Labour Party. Churchill, the original anti-Bolshevik, was now less affected by it. Though he deplored that Soviet Russia was not an ally, he insisted that she still represented a balance against Hitler and foresaw the time when Germany and Russia would be enemies. He even applauded the occupation of Poland's eastern lands by the Red armies, as barring Hitler's road to the east. When Churchill wanted something, he assumed that he could have it; and from the beginning of the Second World War, he assumed that he could ultimately have alliances with Russia and America, even though he did not know how to get them.

Churchill showed the same restraint and concentration when Russia attacked Finland. Most Allied leaders wished to aid Finland, even at the risk of war with Russia – a war which some of them would have welcomed. Churchill had no sympathy with this lunatic project. On the other hand, he could not resist the attraction of a smart stroke, a way round on the Gallipoli model. According to his ingenious plan, the Allied troops, dispatched to aid Finland, would not reach their objective, but would instead wreck the sources of German iron ore in northern Sweden and Norway. It was perhaps fortunate that the Finns made peace with Russia before this idea could be tested against events. The abortive project left a legacy in the shape of a continuing Allied interest in the extreme north, and Churchill welcomed the German invasion of Norway on 8 April. He believed that the Germans were now exposed to British sea power and made prophecies of success more extravagant than any given by Neville Chamberlain. The prophecies were belied. Sea power was ineffective without control of the air. Failure to appreciate this illustrated yet again the curious contradiction in Churchill's nature as a strategist. He had repeatedly emphasized the importance of air power, more so perhaps than any other civilian statesman. Yet when it came to action, he could not resist the call of tradition and romance, and imagined that the Royal Navy could still assert the old supremacy unaided. The mistake of the Norwegian campaign was to be repeated in the Mediterranean, and still more disastrously at Singapore.

The failure in Norway at last provoked revolt among Conservative members of the House of Commons, and on 10 May Churchill found himself prime minister at the head of a real National government. He attained supreme power without intrigue – at any rate on his own part. Moreover, the new government was as little changed as possible from the old one. There was no proscription of the appeasers and not much reward for their opponents, and the Conservatives still held most of the principal posts, with Chamberlain himself in second place. This was the sort of National government which Churchill had always projected, and, though the Left might grumble, any less Conservative government would have had difficulty in commanding the support of administrators and businessmen, a consideration over-looked by those who wanted to make some sort of Popular Front revolution. There were shifts of political balance later in the war, usually towards the Left, but Churchill had ensured his essential principle at the start: there were to be no political or social changes beyond what the needs of war dictated.

Churchill was supported by men of all parties, and he held supreme power so long as he enjoyed the national confidence. All his life had been an unconscious preparation for this hour, and his qualities as a statesman must be judged principally from the way in which he discharged his trust during the Second World War. On the vital point of strategic control, he did better than Lloyd George in the First World War and probably better than any national leader except Stalin in the Second. By making himself minister of defence, he established his authority over the chiefs-of-staff and thus secured unity of strategic direction, or something near it. His direction of civil affairs was less sure and was certainly not exercised through the war cabinet, a body which seems to have acted only as an occasional court of appeal. Ministers and committees were left to do much what they thought best, with occasional interference or arbitration from Church-ill when things went wrong. None of the advances in social or

financial policy made during the war owed anything to Churchill
except a distant approval.

Churchill also claimed the supreme direction of foreign affairs. This
he attained partly by personal intimacy with Anthony Eden, who was
foreign secretary for most of the war, and partly by going his own
way, regardless of expert opinion in the Foreign Office. Churchill's
foreign policy was of his own devising, a mixture of impulse and
matured thought. His influencing of public opinion was also an odd
story. Official organizations, from the Ministry of Information to the
political parties, tried to take a defined line, and Churchill made
guerilla raids into publicity by means of radio addresses – addresses at
first enormously popular, later both less effective and out of tune with
what most people were thinking. Essentially Churchill, despite his
radio success, did not like political discussion except in the House of
Commons and, to a lesser extent, the newspapers. He believed that
ordinary people should get on with their work and rely on him to
guard their freedom, just as he believed that other ranks in the
services should be content with the position which the Tommies had
accepted during his own remote days in the army. If Churchill had
had his way, and he did to a considerable extent, the Second World
War would have been conducted in Great Britain by officers and
gentlemen, the sluice gates being opened only enough to admit trade
union officials also.

Churchill, though somewhat of a tyrant, imposed his will more by
discussion than by dictation. He never wearied of argument and
would even yield when faced with equal persistence. He has described
his method in an engaging phrase: 'All I wanted was compliance with
my wishes after reasonable discussion.' It was compliance he wanted
all the same, and those who opposed his ideas too persistently paid
the penalty. Thus Wavell and Auchinleck in turn forfeited the command in the Middle East for failing to provide an offensive when
Churchill needed one. Nor did he tolerate rivals near his political
throne. Halifax, the only possible alternative as prime minister among
the Conservatives, was early deported to Washington as ambassador,
and Stafford Cripps, a possible Labour alternative later on, was
similarly manoeuvred into obscurity. Churchill treated Eden as a
favourite son rather than as a competitor for power, and in this his
judgement was correct. The most successful ministers were former
civil servants or non-party experts, men accustomed to obey a master.

The one exception was Ernest Bevin, minister of labour, whom Churchill treated as a more or less independent power. Bevin had a strong enough personality to insist on this. As well, Churchill for once recognized that soft words were not enough to remove the distrust which his own past actions had caused. Though he never understood the working-class hostility towards him, he realized that it was there, and this made him dependent on Bevin to some extent. The treatment of labour was an outstanding success in the Second World War. Churchill's contribution was to leave the topic to Bevin.

With these limitations, Churchill held the supreme direction of British policy. The strategy of the war was his – at any rate so far as this strategy was determined from the British side. He also intruded into the detailed operations of war and, when told that Hitler constantly interfered with his generals, replied: 'I do the same.' Great Britain has never known any such civilian direction of war except perhaps in the case of the elder Pitt. This was a unique achievement among modern British statesmen. Churchill at once defined British war aims, or rather he laid down a single aim: the total defeat of Hitler and the undoing of all Germany's conquests. When he came to write his account of the war, he implied that this definition was hardly necessary and that the entire nation was united in pursuing total victory or, put the other way round, unconditional surrender by the Germans. It is unlikely that he played such a modest part. Despite Churchill's assertion that negotiations with Hitler were never discussed by the war cabinet, it is now known that Halifax raised the topic on 27 May. In fact Churchill was showing his usual generosity when he gave the impression that all his associates were as resolute as himself, and his cover for them perhaps appears less surprising if it be borne in mind that the weaker vessels were Conservatives, members of the party which Churchill led.

There are other indications that Churchill's extremism was not universally shared. Obscure approaches for peace were made towards Hitler in the summer of 1940, and the Foreign Office held out against repudiating the Munich settlement until 1942. In regard to Churchill himself, there can be no doubt. Compromise with Hitler could only have been made under some other leader. Churchill remarked: 'I have only one aim in life, the defeat of Hitler, and this makes things very simple for me.' The remark was not, of course, quite true. He wished to preserve the independence and greatness of the British

Empire so far as he could and even wished to preserve the existing social structure. But these wishes were firmly subordinated to his main aim. In this, Churchill probably interpreted aright the spirit of the British people. His popularity rested on many causes: his pre-war advocacy of resistance, his endearing ways, his rhetorical utterances. But it rested most of all on the universal belief that he was the certain guarantee against weakness or compromise and that he would shrink from no sacrifice for the sake of victory. There were those after the war who regretted this firmness and its consequences. Churchill was blamed where he had earlier been praised. The blame was misapplied. Churchill and the British people were at one. 'Victory at all costs' was the programme of all except a few leading politicians and, if the British people paid an excessive price for victory, they did it with their eyes open.

Churchill gave a new resolution to the British. He tried to give the same resolution to the French, as their armies crumbled before the German invaders. In this he was unsuccessful. He could not easily shake off the illusions about French strength which he had held before the war and tended to imagine that a few ringing phrases in counsel would restore French spirits. Like others, he was overwhelmed by events and could not weigh calmly the situation which would follow France's defeat. If he had had his way, British fighter squadrons would have been sent unavailingly to France, and victory in the Battle of Britain would have been jeopardized. Dowding, the head of Fighter Command, resisted this generous impulse – a resistance which Churchill did not forgive. The fighter squadrons did not go to France. Later attempts to invigorate the French, such as the offer of political union, were not of Churchill's doing.

On the other hand, Churchill exaggerated the eagerness of Frenchmen to resume the war against Hitler after the Franco-German armistice had been made. When de Gaulle came to London, Churchill saw in him the man around whom the French Empire and many Frenchmen at home would rally. His enthusiasm for de Gaulle led him into some wild ventures, of which the expedition to Dakar was the first. Churchill himself lamented later that he had to bear a cross – the Cross of Lorraine. Nevertheless his support for de Gaulle remained unshaken, despite many quarrels, and it followed inevitably from the similarity of their outlooks. De Gaulle, too, represented a cause of traditional greatness and loyalty, without much infusion of modern political ideas. By a curious irony, this cause ultimately triumphed in France, the defeated country, and was rejected in Great Britain, the victor.

Churchill fully accepted responsibility for the attack on the French fleet at Oran, in order to prevent its falling into German hands. The attack has sometimes been presented as a demonstration of British resolve, unfortunately at the expense of an old ally, to continue the war at all costs. The explanation is probably simpler: justified refusal to trust Hitler's word and further refusal, perhaps less justified, to admit that there could be any third course between resistance and surrender. Like most English people, Churchill never appreciated that collaboration with Hitler, however mistaken it turned out, could be advocated for genuinely patriotic reasons – as, after all, it had been in Great Britain until the outbreak of war. Churchill's judgement in such matters was both romantic and innocent. He regarded the British cause as the cause of freedom and national independence all over the world and therefore dismissed those who failed to support it as traitors. He supposed that this view was universally held and that in every country an indignant majority of eager patriots was held down by German agents. Churchill was easily led on from this to exaggerate greatly both the extent of resistance to the Germans and its effectiveness. However, in times of great peril it does no harm if men, even in the highest places, are buoyed up by false hopes.

The British mood in the summer of 1940 was strangely cheerful, and Churchill was cheerful with it. The defeat of the German Air Force, which is known as the Battle of Britain, owed little to Churchill except a generous admiration. He was inspired by this victory and used it to inspire others. For once, he did nothing wrong. Every speech was right. Every emphasis was right. He made people alert and active without making them fearful. Those summer months established Churchill's ultimate popularity. His position did not rest on a belief that he would always be right or that he possessed a superior wisdom. But he had spoken for the nation in a moment of emotional unity. Probably he could have exploited his position more if he had been less emotionally involved. A more calculating statesman would have deliberately engrossed personal power. Churchill tended to assume that the mood of national exaltation would last and that he would always be equally in tune with his fellow countrymen.

There was a more practical side to Churchill's activities in the course of 1940, and this set a clearer test for his statesmanship. Churchill, like the British people, was not content to survive. Even at the moment of greatest danger, he was thinking of ultimate victory. The first plans for victory were actually drawn on 27 May, the very day when the chances of German invasion were also seriously weighed. By the late summer the Germans controlled all the resources of Europe, either directly or indirectly. They had conquered or won over most of the Continent up to the Soviet frontier, and Soviet Russia was lavish in supplying them. The German Empire had far greater resources than Great Britain, even if the dominions were counted in, far greater manpower, and a more secure strategic position. Yet British policy never relapsed into a purely defensive attitude.

In a sense, this followed logically from the refusal to seek a compromise with Hitler. Since it was inconceivable that the war would last for ever, the only alternative to defeat was victory. Churchill himself never lost faith that this victory was not only desirable but possible, and he imposed this faith on the less confident. His faith was in part emotional or even mystical: a stubborn belief in the British Empire and its latent power. If victory did not wait on British arms, Churchill's lifework was meaningless. His faith had also rational grounds. He foresaw that the two neutral Powers, Soviet Russia and the United States, would ultimately be drawn into war against Hitler, as Great Britain had been, and he hoped to accelerate the process. Once more, he believed that something would happen because he wanted it to happen, and in this case his belief proved true.

Nevertheless, Churchill misjudged, to some extent, the factors working in Great Britain's favour. Fortified by his own American background and experience, he supposed that nearly all Americans were pro-British and that an Anglo-Saxon alliance was in the making. He never understood that even those Americans who wished to defeat Hitler were not equally anxious to save the British Empire. Again, he overrated the power of personal relations. Having easily developed an emotional attachment to President Roosevelt, he imagined that the president had a similar emotional attachment to him. This was a mistake. Though Roosevelt often used emotion, he was not swayed by it. He needed Great Britain for America's security. Otherwise he remained uninvolved.

Towards Soviet Russia, Churchill had no emotional commitments. He did not suppose that Soviet policy would be determined by anything except practical considerations. On the other hand, he had largely discarded the anti-Soviet prejudices which had earlier dominated his mind and which many Conservatives still held. He did not fear that Nazi Germany and Soviet Russia would develop a genuine cooperation simply because they were both totalitarian states. Such ideological considerations were outside his ken. Nor did he seriously fear at this time that Soviet Russia was anxious to promote international communism. If anything, he underrated Soviet strength, as most people, including the Soviet leaders, did at the time. Churchill expected that the United States would make the major contribution towards defeating Hitler and that Soviet Russia would provide at best a diversion.

These were refinements of the general assumption that Russia and America would be drawn into the war. There was, however, a further quality in Churchill's thought. He was not content to wait for the two neutral Powers. He wanted Great Britain to win on her own and sometimes believed that this could be done. Hence there were two Churchills in the period when Great Britain stood on her own, and these two Churchills continued even when she had great allies. One was the Churchill who worked for the Grand Alliance and held it together. The other Churchill directed a purely British strategy which had little relationship to the alliance.

British strategy for independent victory had two aims. The first was the bombing of Germany. Between the wars many experts had preached that bombing, unaided by land armies, could win future wars, and the RAF had been designed specifically for this purpose. As events proved, it was not well designed. It had neither the strength nor the equipment with which to achieve a decisive result. Nevertheless, the pursuit of a bombing victory went on all through the war, and Churchill did much to promote it. No doubt the most powerful motive was simply the lack of any alternative. If the British did not drop bombs on Germany, there was nothing they could do against her. But it was also a new version of the insular strategy in which Churchill had always essentially believed. British industrial power was to produce the bombers needed for victory, as in earlier times it had produced the Royal Navy. The army took second place. The mass army of the First World War would not be needed. The British Army would enter the Continent only to restore order when Germany had already collapsed.

Bombing strategy involved a moral judgement for which Churchill later was sometimes condemned. Originally bombing was to be directed solely against industrial targets and lines of communication. This precision proved impossible. Bombing became indiscriminate, at first by accident and then avowedly. The object was the destruction of German morale, in other words the killing of German civilians. The Germans themselves had a bad record in killing civilians and were not entitled to raise moral objections on their side. But it caused some disquiet in British circles which would have liked the war to be conducted in a high-minded way. Churchill himself was often uneasy, particularly as he did not share Bomber Command's wholehearted conviction of success. Rulers in other countries – not only Hitler, but also Stalin, Roosevelt, and later Truman – were ready to use methods equally destructive and equally barbarous. Churchill at least had the redeeming quality of disliking what he was compelled to do. Though he, too, waged war ruthlessly, he remained a humane man.

Churchill's heart was more deeply committed to the other aspect of British strategy. This was war in the Mediterranean. Like much else, it grew up partly by chance. The British and French navies had cooperated in the Mediterranean when France was still in the war. The larger part of the Royal Navy was at Alexandria; another force was at Gibraltar. Since the Germans had few capital ships, these forces were not needed at home. In previous wars, the British had kept the Mediterranean open for their shipping. During the First World War, they had continued to use the Suez Canal as their main route to India and the Far East. But when Italy entered the war and France fell out, the Mediterranean could no longer be used by British ships, and it remained closed until May 1943. British forces, however, remained in Egypt, ostensibly for a negative purpose: they barred Hitler's route to the oil of the Middle East. This was a precaution against an imaginary danger. Hitler's strategy, so far as he had one, was purely continental. If he ever contemplated Middle Eastern oil, he proposed to reach it by means of southern Russia and the Caucasus. His activities in the Mediterranean, such as assistance to Italy and the conquest of Greece, were defensive answers to British attacks, not preparations for an advance of his own.

Egypt as the starting point for a British offensive was indeed Churchill's idea. He was always anxious to renew the strategy which had failed at Gallipoli. With indomitable persistence, he pursued the dream that Turkey could be drawn into the war. Then the combined British and Turkish armies would sweep through the Balkans, picking up other allies on the way. Germany would be defeated from the rear or at least brought to an acceptable compromise. This was a strange fantasy. At one moment, Churchill was insisting that victory would be hard and prolonged even if Russia and America were in the war. At another, he was dreaming that it would be easy if only Turkey – a country without either modern resources or a modern army – became an ally. There is no explaining such a contradiction. Churchill remained himself even in his years of supreme responsibility. In one part of his nature, he was a clearsighted realist, facing the problems of modern war with precise calculation and long-term preparation. In the other part, he was still a gambler and an impulsive boy, forever hoping that some ingenious twist would work a miracle after all. Everyone else looked back to Gallipoli as a failure. Churchill remembered it as a short-cut to success.

The Turkish alliance was never achieved for any serious purpose, though Churchill pursued it throughout with unflagging persistence. Instead, the Mediterranean became the field of conflict with Italy. This had not been intended by either Churchill or Mussolini. Mussolini had entered the war only because he thought that it was already won, and he knew that Italy was not equipped for war on any large scale. Churchill had little sympathy with the idea that the war was a general crusade against fascism and would have tolerated Mussolini just as he tolerated Franco. He wrote later: 'Even when the issue of the war became certain Mussolini would have been welcomed by the Allies.' However, Mussolini was trapped on the German side, first in the hope of victory, later by fear of German might. The British had to fight Italy whether they wanted to or not, and they were in a position to do so. The naval war in the Mediterranean and the war in the desert provided victories which revived the spirit of the British people and helped to restore British prestige in the world. Churchill's own stock rose with each desert victory and sank with each defeat.

Thus Churchill's own inclination and the pressure of events combined to make North Africa the pivot of British strategy. Churchill needed victories for their own sake, in order to maintain his position at home. But he never relinquished his ultimate objective of a Balkan offensive. Even when the Mediterranean campaign extended from North Africa to Italy, the defeat of Italy was a secondary consideration in his mind. Italy was to be simply an alternative starting place for a Balkan advance. In the actual conduct of the campaign, Churchill displayed the mixture of wisdom and rashness which he had always shown. He 'prodded' the British commanders into premature offensives. He encouraged, though he did not alone promote, the rash expedition to Greece, which was supposed to enhance the British name and instead brought humiliating disaster. He counted unthinkingly on the ability of British sea power to hold Crete and shared responsibility for that disaster also.

There were larger prices to pay for Churchill's Mediterranean obsession. Preparations for a landing on the European continent had to take second place. This was not unwelcome to Churchill nor indeed to his military advisers. He steadily opposed a repetition of the large-scale land combats which had marked the First World War and remained confident that some other way could be found of bringing Germany to collapse. Perhaps bombing would succeed; perhaps a back door would be opened. If not, maybe economic difficulties or subversion in the occupied countries would produce the desired result. Europe was not the only field of operations to be sacrificed. The Far East had also to be neglected, despite the growing danger from Japan; and Churchill, who had extolled the glories of the British Raj, in fact took the decisions which brought down Great Britain's Far Eastern power. The decisions were no doubt imposed by events, but Churchill as ever threw himself wholeheartedly into what lay nearest at hand, particularly when it accorded with his own inclination. For the sake of North Africa, Churchill had to gamble that Japan would not enter the war.

This gamble could not be openly stated. Churchill never lost sight of American friendship as the overriding means of British salvation. Here he found the right combination. On the one hand he emphasized Great Britain's determination to go on with the war. On the other, he hinted that she could not go on, let alone win, without American aid. It was his aim to get British and American affairs, in his own phrase, 'somewhat mixed up'. Roosevelt had the same aim with a different context. He, too, wanted to keep Great Britain going, but not necessarily to maintain British greatness. The most important decision of Churchill's career, and indeed of modern British history, was made in the early days of 1941. By accepting lend-lease, the British gave up all attempt to maintain their economic independence and looked to

America for the resources which would enable them to continue the war. As Keynes said: 'We threw good housekeeping to the winds.' Churchill mistook calculation for generosity in American policy and supposed that the United States would restore Great Britain to her former position when the war was over. But once more he had little choice. The British people were ready to sacrifice the future for the sake of the present, and Churchill had to make the best of things.

Though Churchill secured lend-lease, he failed to draw the United States into the war. Roosevelt was ready to accept Churchill's claim that Great Britain could win on her own and perhaps believed it. Events provided a different ally. On 22 June 1941 Hitler invaded Soviet Russia. The same evening Churchill announced British support for Russia. This, too, was a great decision. It was a repudiation, at any rate until the war was over, of the old British dream that Germany and Russia could be somehow played off against each other. Again the decision was implicit in the line which Churchill had taken ever since the rise of Hitler and again it was imposed upon him in part by the will of the British people. It was a great decision all the same. Originally it meant no more than a readiness to keep Russia going until Great Britain and America were in a position to win the war. But it had to be maintained even when it meant that Soviet Russia would outstrip all European powers, including Great Britain herself.

Most military experts, both British and American, at first expected that Germany would defeat Soviet Russia within a relatively short time. Churchill, and Roosevelt too, were slightly more confident than their advisers – an indication that the two men shared a confident temperament and assumed that things would go well in the end. But for a long time neither weighed seriously the consequences of a Russian victory. It is significant that at the Atlantic meeting of August 1941 the subject of Soviet Russia was hardly mentioned. Probably Beaverbrook was the only leading man in either country who seriously believed that the Soviet card was the winning one to play. Churchill was still intent on drawing the United States into the war, and he tried to reassert British prestige in the Far East as a means of attracting American favour. His promise that, if Japan attacked the United States, a British declaration of war would follow within the hour, was intended to provoke a corresponding American promise in return, which it failed to do. The promise also assumed that there was a real threat behind it and that British power in the

Far East could actually help to deter Japan. Probably no British policy could have prevented a Japanese attack. But Churchill, intoxicated with high-sounding phrases, invited this attack on what was in fact a defenceless empire.

The Japanese attack on Pearl Harbor did what both Churchill and Hitler had failed to do: it brought the United States into the war. Churchill now had a double preoccupation. On the one hand, he had to enlist the main weight of American strength in the European theatre of war, though without jeopardizing the British Empire in the Far East. On the other, he had to ensure that this strength was directed towards the Mediterranean and not to north-west Europe. These two themes dominated Anglo-American relations for most of the war. Agreement was easily reached in regard to the first. Roosevelt and most of his generals accepted Germany as the main enemy, and even the American admirals who wished to concentrate on fighting Japan wished to conduct a more or less private war, unhampered by allies. Dispute over the second was more prolonged and was eventually decided, as such disputes often are, by logistics, not by argument. Though the Americans always favoured landing in north-west Europe, they lacked the forces with which to undertake it, and the British, who perhaps had the forces, did not believe that it was possible. Hence, by the summer of 1942, action in the Mediterranean was accepted by the Americans for want of anything better. Thus Churchill imposed his strategy on his potentially stronger ally. The war continued to be waged against Italy, not against Germany, and the most considerable success was the overthrow of Mussolini, an outcome which Churchill had never intended.

Against this, Churchill, the champion of the British Raj, was the man who in fact presided over its fall. Many men and many governments shared responsibility for the neglect of Singapore. Churchill completed what others had begun. The vital need at Singapore was for fighter aircraft, and this need could not be met because of the British obsession with heavy bombers. Churchill's individual contribution to the disaster at Singapore was the dispatch of two mighty warships, which were intended to deter the Japanese by a 'vague menace'. Lacking air cover, they were sunk by the Japanese within two days of the outbreak of war. Everything at Singapore from the sending of the two ships to the final capitulation reproduced Gallipoli in a defensive form. Words took the place of action. Rhetoric was substituted for reality. It is strange how Churchill, who at one moment appreciated the decisive importance of air power, at another imagined that the Japanese could be checked by a vague menace and the shadow of an imperial name.

In the earlier part of 1942, Allied strategy hardly existed, at Singapore or elsewhere, except as a series of improvised responses to grave dangers. The situation changed in the course of the year, as the three great Allies stabilized their position – the Americans in the Pacific, the British west of Alexandria, the Russians at Stalingrad. Thereafter the Allies not only began to prepare their own offensive plans, they also began to think, however vaguely, in terms of a coalition war. The battle of El Alamein was the last independent victory of British forces, and even it was won largely with American weapons. Churchill had now to show his capacity as a coalition statesman. Ever since May 1940, he had enjoyed supreme authority, despite occasional alarms. By 1943 he had two equals and was indeed hard-pressed to keep up with them.

No one, Churchill least of all, ever formally decided that Great Britain should continue to assert her position as a world power. This was taken for granted, much as continuing the war had been taken for granted in 1940. A more modest British statesman than Churchill might have been less determined about it and might have husbanded some British strength for the future. Great Britain, largely thanks to Churchill, kept in the front rank almost until the end of the war and exhausted her resources in doing so. The original decision to accept lend-lease was pressed to its logical conclusion. Great Britain abandoned the remnants of her export trade at America's behest and accumulated a vast debt in the form of sterling balances. Churchill's faith in American goodwill was inexhaustible. He assumed that somehow the United States would restore the British Empire to its former greatness, or maybe he thought that the empire would again become great of itself, once the Axis threat was removed. In a sense, there were no Anglo-American relations during the war. There was only Churchill's personal connection with Roosevelt.

Anglo-Soviet relations were more important. By 1943 it was clear that Soviet Russia would emerge from the war as a formidable power, and her future position in Europe became Churchill's preoccupation, second only to the defeat of Hitler. There is still some dispute on this subject, a dispute not clarified by Churchill's own writings later.

According to one version, Churchill was alarmed at the growth of Soviet power and tried to take precautions against it, if not in 1942 at least well before the end of the war. There are even those who suggest that Churchill would have liked to maintain a strong Germany as a barrier and balance against Russia. It is hard to sustain this view from contemporary records. Churchill never wavered from his determination that Nazi Germany must be utterly defeated. At the same time, he was concerned to strike some clear bargain with Soviet Russia before the war ended. This was his main, perhaps his only, disagreement with Roosevelt, who, in his usual evasive way, wanted to keep the situation open until the war ended.

Churchill's policy, brutally put, was partition. Assuming an American withdrawal from Europe, as Roosevelt's statements gave him every reason to do, he aimed at a division of Europe into British and Soviet spheres of influence. So far as we can tell, Stalin welcomed the idea and certainly applied it emphatically during the British intervention against the communists in Greece. Yet partition never came near to working out successfully. The underlying assumptions were too different. Churchill assumed that the countries of western Europe would produce peaceful democratic governments if they were allowed to do so. Stalin assumed that the countries of eastern Europe would produce governments hostile to Soviet Russia unless prevented from doing so. Both assumptions proved reasonably true. There was a curious exception. Yugoslavia, the one country where Soviet and British influence was supposed to be equal, was also the one country which produced a communist government thoroughly independent of Soviet Russia. Churchill's Second World War statesmanship has at least Tito to its credit.

Churchill had no European policy in any wider sense. His outlook was purely negative: the defeat of Germany. Then everything should be left to go back much as it was before. He had no faith that a new democratic spirit was being produced by the Resistance or that national antagonisms had been eroded by the experience of war. His ideas for a future Germany, such as the elimination of Prussia, had no more than an antiquarian interest. His scepticism was not unjustified, and no one did any better in planning the future. On the other hand, his old generosity also reasserted itself. Though he had made many fierce threats of vengeance against the Nazis during the war, he abandoned this attitude when Stalin and Roosevelt were still talking of killing 50,000 Germans. Churchill regarded the post-war trials of German leaders with extreme distaste and remarked to his military adviser: 'You and I must take care not to lose the next war' – the only fit comment on the Nuremberg proceedings.

With Churchill it was always one thing at a time. So long as Hitler had to be defeated, he thought virtually of nothing else. Once this defeat became certain, he was the first to talk of restoring Germany and even envisaged rearming the Germans against Russia before the war was actually over. Sounding the alarm had become a habit with him and, having risen by championing liberty against Hitler, he could not resist repeating the performance against Stalin. There was again, to borrow Churchill's phrase, an unnecessary war – this time cold and largely Churchill's doing. There may have been an element of more serious calculation in Churchill's new line. He never wavered from his desire to draw the United States fully into European affairs. This had to be done on an idealistic basis so long as Roosevelt was alive. After Roosevelt's death, idealism lost its force. Anti-Bolshevism and the Red Peril took its place, and Churchill turned this to Europe's advantage. Since he himself believed in this peril and even imagined that a Labour government would bring to Great Britain all the horrors of the Gestapo, the alarm came easily to him. Yet even this was not the end. In his last senile days as prime minister, Churchill once more announced the need for reconciliation with Soviet Russia and in particular emphasized that he was the man to accomplish it. Here was a last touch of the grandiose approach which Churchill had always shown to events. He lived for crisis. He profited from crisis. And when crisis did not exist, he strove to invent it.

Churchill was a rich character, exasperating in his earlier days, endearing and even admirable as the years went by. He incorporated the resolve of the British people at what was probably the last great moment in their history, and no Englishman who lived through 1940 can regard him dispassionately. In those days patriotism was enough, and Churchill provided it abundantly. Despite his many apparent aberrations, he never wavered in devotion to the British cause. All else, from isolation at one end of the scale to collective security at the other, were no more than means to this end. Palmerston, another great Englishman, once said: 'England has no eternal friends and no eternal enemies. Only her interests are eternal.' Churchill would have endorsed this with one exception, especially as he grew older. His devotion to the United States was almost as great as that to the British Empire, and he placed his faith for the future in the increasing unity of what he called the English-speaking peoples.

Fundamentally his outlook was sombre. He did not share the contemporary belief in universal improvement nor did he await the coming of some secular Heaven on Earth. He strove to ameliorate hardships without ever expecting that they could be finally removed. But he had also a combative cheerfulness which broke through the gloom, particularly when things were at their worst. He drew inspiration from disasters and inspired others also. In the direction of war, he was often rash and impetuous. A long catalogue of impatient blunders can be drawn against him. But the fact remains that he won the Second World War. Perhaps he paid an excessive price, but the British people agreed with Churchill that the price was worth paying.

As prime minister, Churchill often declared that he was the servant of the House of Commons, and his practice showed that this was true. What he served was the traditional institution, as embodied in his own writings and those of other romantically minded historians. Churchill did not serve the contemporary House of Commons and still less did he serve the British people. Rather he expected the people, like himself, to serve the traditional values of constitution and empire which had been handed down to them – or manufactured by historians. Churchill used words as weapons of power and was also enslaved by them. He took Macaulay's rhetoric and his own as reality and often sacrificed human beings for the sake of glittering phrases.

Behind the façade of a cheeky individualism, he was essentially conservative. He had great courage, an almost inexhaustible energy, and a generosity of spirit which could disarm all but the most implacable of opponents. He was fertile in expedients and remained unbowed by adversity. It is difficult to discern in him any element of creative statesmanship. He responded to events with infinite adaptability and persistent enthusiasm. But he had to be driven from without. Churchill had no vision for the future, only a tenacious defence of the past. The British people raised him up, and he failed them. The British ruling classes did their best to keep him down, and he preserved them. He is best described by words which were written about Bismarck in old age: 'He was no beginning, but an end, a grandiose final chord – a fulfiller, not a prophet.' Perhaps Churchill was the penalty people paid for reading history.

Lancashire

Alan Taylor always remained proud of his Lancashire Nonconformist back-ground. He was a very able writer about places, especially those he loved. This essay was first published in Vogue, *March 1960.*

Alan Taylor greatly admired the writing of Beatrix Potter and once wrote of The Tailor of Gloucester: *'I rank it with the masterpieces of Balzac.' When a memorial service was held for him in Magdalen College Chapel in April 1991, one of the readings chosen was from that volume.*

*　　*　　*

Since this piece was written great chunks have been hacked from Lancashire to satisfy some bureaucratic whim. I am prepared to renounce Merseyside. I shall never relinquish Lancashire North of the Sands.

Most English counties nowadays are merely administrative units, with little to show that you have passed from one to another. Not Lancashire. It is a real place, its character all its own, its people different from people anywhere else. You never have to ask yourself where you are. The talk of the people in the streets will tell you. The look of the buildings will tell you. They all say: this is Lancashire and could not be anywhere else in the world. Will you like Lancashire? It depends whether you like real life or chocolate-box beauty. Anyone who knows Lancashire finds himself at the start apologizing for it: apologizing for its weather, for the drab houses, for the dirt, for the general lack of smartness. Then he realizes that he is apologizing for life. Of course Lancashire has faults as well as virtues. You have to dig beneath the surface to discover how much greater the virtues are than the faults.

Lancashire people do not believe in showing off. You have a feeling that they were too busy in the past making money to care about appearances. I used to wonder, years ago, which was uglier – the buildings or the women. Now Lancashire, though still prosperous, is no more prosperous than anywhere else. Both women and buildings are better looking than they were – perhaps as a result. All the same, cotton, though no longer king, has set a mark on Lancashire which will take a hydrogen bomb to rub off. The mills were built for cotton, even though they have been gutted of their spindles, the sheds of their looms, and now make anything from children's toys to parts of motor cars. The long rows of houses have seen generations of cotton workers, roused by the call of the knocker-up, clattering off down the cobbled streets in their clogs. Cotton made Manchester and Liverpool great cities, though they depend on cotton no longer. Still more, cotton turned south-east Lancashire into the greatest urban agglomeration in the world, which it still is. Twenty or thirty years ago it was possible, if you were sufficiently wrongheaded, to travel for forty miles without getting away from tramlines, and Lancashire is still the ideal county for any motorist who likes being restricted to thirty miles an hour.

To get the flavour of real Lancashire, you must forget about the two cities and go to the cotton towns which push against the Pennines – Bury and Rochdale, Burnley, Nelson and Colne. Some of them have a long history. Bolton, for instance, was a parliamentary stronghold in the Civil War, and at Middleton there is a memorial window (probably the first of its kind) to the men of the district who fell at Flodden. But most of these were villages until the Industrial Revolution and the coming of the cotton mills. Each is dominated by a grandiose town hall, commissioned at the height of its Victorian prosperity. Down on the plain there are great Anglican churches in Victorian Gothic. The dissenters evidently took to the hills. Each mile up the valleys the Nonconformist chapels get bigger and bigger, until at the head they are the size of cathedrals – vast, classical temples where the hymns of the dwindled congregations now echo mournfully. Up here the rich Lancashire dialect is still unspoilt – ravishingly beautiful to those who can understand it. A woman is still *oo*, not *she*. A man takes his baggin for the midday break, and cows go to the shippon. Are Eccles cakes still made at Eccles? I doubt it. But there are shops which serve tripe and onions at all hours of the day. And throughout the county there is one supreme delicacy: Lancashire cheese, made in the Fylde and consumed by the inhabitants in such quantities that little makes its way to the south of England. No nonsense in Lancashire about 'cheese' (meaning New Zealand cheddar). Great Lancashire cheeses stand on the shelves, and the shopper chooses his favourite by scooping out mouthfuls with a sixpence.

Some of these cotton towns are dying with the closing of the mills.

Some have switched over to new industries and have saved their prosperity without losing their character. Anyone really interested in history, and not merely in the pretty side of it, should travel far to see them. A century ago they were the wonder of the world: the centre of British wealth and, supposedly, the future pattern for all mankind. When Karl Marx described capitalism and denounced it, he had Oldham and Rochdale in mind. Now history has passed them by, and they are just curious memorials of the past like the water mills which they displaced. It would be foolish to pretend that they will ever become places of pilgrimage even for the most romantically minded. They are gloomy, smoke-grimed, drab. But they are not ugly: their character is too strong for that, and their brick, even though stained, gives them a warmth which is lacking in the hard stone-built towns over the Pennines in Yorkshire. Lancashire certainly has its areas of unredeemed ugliness, the more obtrusive because they straddle across the main road to the north. Coal-mining can never have attractive results, and Wigan has long been a by-word. Unjustly. Wigan has a fine situation and green, spacious suburbs. You must go to the southern edge of the county to see some of the worst surroundings which civilized man has ever created for himself. St Helens produced Sir Thomas Beecham; Warrington once had a famous Nonconformist Academy. I can think of nothing to say in palliation of Widnes. But perhaps even its inhabitants think that they are citizens of no mean city.

Such are the ravages which the pursuit of wealth has made. Yet Lancashire is full of attractions also, its greatest being the people. In southern England local differences have almost vanished. In Lancashire there is still an unmistakable character. Northerners are supposed to be hard and dour. So they are in Yorkshire, or still more in Northumberland. People in Lancashire seem brisk and businesslike. But they are also sentimental and romantic. They have been softened by the damp climate and only become hard when they go south. Mrs Pankhurst was hard all right when she assaulted politicians and set fire to pillar-boxes, but what could be more romantic? And what more sentimental than to go campaigning for women's suffrage at all? I should like to claim Joan Littlewood as a typical Lancashire woman. Unfortunately she came from London, though on foot, and merely founded in Manchester the Theatre Union which she has now taken away again, and which has grown into the Theatre Workshop. Mrs

Gaskell, however, was the real thing: the most modern of Victorian novelists, and the only one who was improved by being a woman, instead of being handicapped by it. Her last gesture of romantic common-sense was to leave her family mansion as a maternity home for indigent members of the middle class.

Lancashire has not run much to great men. Until the eighteenth century it was a forgotten backwater, dominated by Tory squires. The Stanleys were the only great family. They have produced generations of public men, including a prime minister, and still provide the strongest element of genuine aristocracy in the county. Gladstone was born in Liverpool, but hardly belongs to Lancashire: he was Scotch by origin and spent most of his life at Hawarden. John Bright was unmistakably Lancashire: living all his life at Rochdale, where he played for the local cricket team, and preaching a creed of pacific radicalism which he believed to be peculiarly adapted to Lancashire's needs. His creed is supposed to have been rational and hard-headed, but he advocated it in romantic terms. I put him at the head of English orators, partly – but only partly – because I prefer his views to those of Burke or Macaulay. Throwing the net wider, one might recall that Sir Winston Churchill sat first for Oldham and then for North-West Manchester in the course of the long electoral wandering which terminated at Woodford. But there would be no end to a catalogue of those who have represented Lancashire constituencies at one time or another. It includes, for instance, Lord Beaverbrook, who sat for Ashton-under-Lyne before being precipitated into the House of Lords. Ranging further back, there is the once-famous radical, Orator Hunt, who won Preston at the height of the Reform Bill agitation. My great-grandfather was thrown out of work for voting for him and inadequately compensated with a medal.

Outside the world of politics the two universities have attracted men of great distinction. Rutherford is, I suppose, the most famous, though his feat of splitting the atom has brought us doubtful benefits. The universities give an added eminence to Liverpool and Manchester, but both have long been centres of civilization in their own right. Liverpool, which I know less, has the higher social tone; Manchester has perhaps more to be proud of in the Hallé Orchestra and the *Guardian*. The first is still the only permanent orchestra in England with a permanent conductor: the second [was once] the only national newspaper edited and produced outside London. Though Manchester naturally gets the greatest benefit from them, their influence radiates throughout Lancashire. The Hallé Orchestra visits many Lancashire towns. The *Guardian* produces a late edition, much superior to that sold in London, in time for most Lancashire breakfast-tables. It does not follow, of course, that Lancashire people are particularly musical, still less that they share the *Guardian's* political outlook.

They are lucky and do not always appreciate their luck. Life in Lancashire is often dirty and usually damp – though not, as it is generally supposed, excessively rainy. But there are more cultural amenities, independent of London, than in other parts of England.

Lancashire is a good place to live. It has also great attractions for the visitor, though it would be excessive to claim that a visit is compulsory for the lover of painting or architecture. The Walker Art Gallery in Liverpool is the only collection of paintings that reaches a national level – with no disrespect to the Pre-Raphaelites in Manchester. Manchester has, however, a very fine collection of drawings in the Whitworth Gallery, an incomparable collection of historic costumes, and all kinds of precious books in the John Rylands Library. The only buildings which indisputably merit three stars (*vaut le voyage*, as Michelin says of restaurants) are both in Liverpool. The Town Hall has the most palatial state-rooms in the country: roughly contemporary with the Pavilion at Brighton, but sober with civic pride where the Pavilion is frivolous and whimsical. The city fathers are less welcoming to sightseers than dukes and marquises, being less in need of money, and it is only possible to see the Town Hall by private invitation. Most people are unaware of its existence and confuse it with St George's Hall, which is also of the highest excellence. It has been described as the finest Greco-Roman building in existence. Certainly it is as fine a Renaissance building as any in Italy and finer in its position.

A good many places deserve two stars – worth going to see once you are in Lancashire. There are no ancient cathedrals – Manchester being a collegiate and parish church transformed into a cathedral a century ago. But there are some fine church-fittings – stalls and screens: in Manchester itself, at Lancaster, and, best of all, at Sefton near Liverpool. St Patrick's Chapel at Heysham is unique, perhaps deserving three stars: the only work of Celtic architecture in England. If you go on to the end of the peninsula, you reach Sunderland Point, the first place where cotton was landed in England and now a ghostly parable of the cotton industry itself. Grass grows on the wharves and on the walls of the eighteenth-century warehouses. Across the estuary Glasson Dock still flourishes. According to report, it has become the congregating place for the girls who work the road houses and transport cafés in big American cars. White slaves and the ghosts of slaves rub shoulders, and of course other people rub shoulders too. But this is hearsay, a legend which perhaps one should not disturb by putting it to the test.

Furness Abbey, near Barrow, is the only first-rate monastic remain; very rewarding for the historian and winning for others from its beautiful situation and its warm red sandstone. In southern Lancashire there are a number of half-timbered houses, some turned into local museums, some falling into ruin. Indeed, Lancashire has an unrivalled record, so far as England goes, for destroying its memorials of the past. Churches and great houses were pulled down ruthlessly in the nineteenth century to be replaced by something more pretentious. Now they are merely pulled down. Knowsley, of course, is a house on the grand scale, as interesting for its associations as for its architecture, and Wyatt produced one of his most accomplished works at Heaton Hall, now in a public park north of Manchester. I would put in a special word of praise for Leighton Hall near Carnforth. This has a Gothic sham-façade in front of a Georgian house. It is possible to walk between the house and the front – an unusual experience.

But Lancashire's greatest attraction from a tourist point of view is provided by nature. This surprises many people who think all Lancashire urban, like the south of England. On the contrary, Lancashire has the best of nearly everything: sea, lakes, rivers, mountains. The coast from Lytham to Fleetwood has a finer stretch of sand than the Lido, with the additional advantages of a tide and real waves. Set in the centre of it lies Blackpool, greatest of all seaside resorts. A lot of people go to Blackpool, but there is room for all and plenty to spare: miles of sand, miles of promenade. You can have a gay time at Blackpool, anywhere from the Pleasure Beach to the Tower Ballroom. You can also, with a little knowledge, doze undisturbed. Blackpool is the most innocent of resorts, or at any rate the least sinister. If anyone wrote *Blackpool Rock*, it would not be a murder story; it would be a sentimental, and inconclusive, romance. The sea is only one of many excellences. The river valleys, running up into the Pennines, are another: Ribble, Hodder, and Lune, each with its own quality.

Associated with them is that strange mountain road, the Trough of Bowland, a feature almost unknown to those outside the county. Last of all, Lancashire 'North of the Sands' takes in a special chunk of the Lake District: one mountain (Coniston Old Man), two lakes (Coniston and Esthwaite), and the remote valley of the Duddon. The countryside here is gentler than in the heart of the Lake District further north; it is soft, balmy, the vegetation as rich as Cornwall. Hawkshead is one of the least spoilt places in England: medieval church; sixteenth-century grammar school, attended by Wordsworth; eighteenth-century town hall, now given over to dances. The little shops and narrow streets will be recognized by every student of Beatrix Potter. I nearly left her out. She was certainly a Lancashire author of the first rank, and a characteristic one: sentimental, hard-headed at once. Most of the land round Hawkshead is now owned by the National Trust, thanks to the profits from Peter Rabbit and Jeremy Fisher. I suppose they were Lancastrians too. Who could ask for more than a county which has Manchester at one end of it and Hawkshead at the other?

Index